ENGLISH ROMANTIC POETS

English
Romantic Poets

MODERN ESSAYS IN CRITICISM

Edited by M. H. ABRAMS

Cornell University

A GALAXY BOOK

NEW YORK   OXFORD UNIVERSITY PRESS   1960

Printed in the United States of America

PREFACE

THIS BOOK brings together recent essays on the major English poets of the Romantic Age. Three of the essays are general; the others focus upon individual writers. With the exception of Professor Lovejoy's classic 'Discrimination of Romanticisms,' the emphasis is critical; those of the included writings which deal with literary history or with the life or ideas of a poet, bring these materials to bear on the interpretation and assessment of the poems. The essays represent the chief critical alignments now current, old and new, discursive and explicative, literal and archetypal, pro and con. A number of them were written in express opposition to each other, as part of the great debate about the Romantic achievement which has been the prime index to the shift in sensibility and standards during the generation just past. Each contribution, however, is a distinguished instance of its point of view.

The many scholars who have responded generously to my requests for counsel can testify to the pain it cost to omit essays that demand admission by every criterion except the availability of space. But nature, Imlac observed, 'sets her gifts on the right hand and on the left. . . . Of the blessings set before you, make your choice and be content.'

M. H. ABRAMS

Ithaca, New York
February, 1960

CONTENTS

The Romantic Period

Blake

Wordsworth

Coleridge

Byron

Shelley

Keats

ENGLISH ROMANTIC POETS

ARTHUR O. LOVEJOY

On the Discrimination of Romanticisms

I

We approach a centenary not, perhaps, wholly undeserving of notice on the part of this learned company. It was apparently in 1824 that those respected citizens of La-Ferté-sous-Jouarre, MM. Dupuis and Cotonet, began an enterprise which was to cause them, as is recorded, 'twelve years of suffering,' and to end in disillusionment—the enterprise of discovering what Romanticism is, by collecting definitions and characterizations of it given by eminent authorities. I conjecture, therefore, that one of the purposes of the Committee in inviting me to speak on this subject was perhaps to promote a Dupuis and Cotonet Centennial Exhibition, in which the later varieties of definitions of Romanticism, the fruit of a hundred years' industry on the part of literary critics and professors of modern literature, might be at least in part displayed. Certainly there is no lack of material; the contemporary collector of such articles, while paying tribute to the assiduity and the sufferings of those worthy pioneers of a century ago, will chiefly feel an envious sense of the relative simplicity of their task. He will find, also, that the apparent incongruity of the senses in which the term is employed has fairly kept pace with their increase in number; and that the singular potency which the subject has from the first possessed to excite controversy and breed divisions has in no degree diminished with the lapse of years.

For if some Dupuis of to-day were to gather, first, merely a few of the more recent accounts of the origin and age of Romanticism, he would learn from M. Lassere [1] and many others that Rousseau was the father of

---

From *Essays in the History of Ideas* (John Hopkins Press, 1948), pp. 228–53. Reprinted by permission of the publisher and author.

3

it; from Mr. Russell[2] and Mr. Santayana[3] that the honor of paternity might plausibly be claimed by Immanuel Kant; from M. Seillière that its grandparents were Fénelon and Madame Guyon;[4] from Professor Babbitt that its earliest well-identified forebear was Francis Bacon;[5] from Mr. Gosse that it originated in the bosom of the Reverend Joseph Warton;[6] from the late Professor Ker that it had 'its beginnings in the seventeenth-century' or a little earlier, in such books as 'the *Arcadia* or the *Grand Cyrus*';[7] from Mr. J. E. G. de Montmorency that it 'was born in the eleventh century, and sprang from that sense of aspiration which runs through the Anglo-French, or rather, the Anglo-Norman Renaissance';[8] from Professor Grierson that St. Paul's 'irruption into Greek religious thought and Greek prose' was an essential example of 'a romantic movement,' though the 'first great romantic' was Plato;[9] and from Mr. Charles Whibley that the Odyssey is romantic in its 'very texture and essence,' but that, with its rival, Romanticism was 'born in the Garden of Eden' and that 'the Serpent was the first romantic.'[10] The inquirer would, at the same time, find that many of these originators of Romanticism—including both the first and last mentioned, whom, indeed, some contemporaries are unable to distinguish—figure on other lists as initiators or representatives of tendencies of precisely the contrary sort.

These differing versions of the age and lineage of Romanticism are matched by a corresponding diversity in the descriptions offered by those of our time who have given special care to the observation of it. For Professor Ker Romanticism was 'the fairy way of writing,'[11] and for Mr. Gosse it is inconsistent with 'keeping to the facts';[12] but for Mr. F. Y. Eccles[13] (following M. Pellissier) 'the romantic system of ideas' is the direct source of 'the realistic error,' of the tendency to conceive of psychology as 'the dry notation of purely physiological phenomena' and consequently to reduce the novel and the drama to the description of 'the automaton-like gestures of *la bête humaine*.' To Professor Ker, again, 'romantic' implies 'reminiscence': 'the romantic schools have always depended more or less on the past.'[14] Similarly Mr. Geoffrey Scott finds 'its most typical form' to be 'the cult of the extinct.'[15] But Professor Schelling tells us that 'the classic temper studies the past, the romantic temper neglects it; . . . it leads us forward and creates new precedents';[16] while for some of the French 'Romantic' critics of the 1820s and 1830s, the slogan of the movement was *il faut être de son temps*.[17] Mr. Paul Elmer More defines Romanticism as 'the illusion of beholding the infinite within the stream of nature itself, instead of apart from that stream'— in short, as an apotheosis of the cosmic flux;[18] but a special student of

4

German Romanticism cites as typical Romantic utterances Friedrich Schlegel's 'alles Sichtbare hat nur die Wahrheit einer Allegorie,' and Goethe's 'alles Vergängliche ist nur ein Gleichnis'; [19] and for a recent German author the deepest thing in Romanticism is 'eine Religion die dieses Leben hasst . . . Romantik will die gerade Verbindung des Menschlichen mit dem Überirdischen.' [20] Among those for whom the word implies, *inter alia,* a social and political ideology and temper, one writer, typical of many, tells us that 'Romanticism spells anarchy in every domain . . . a systematic hostility to everyone invested with any particle of social authority—husband or *pater-familias,* policeman or magistrate, priest or Cabinet minister'; [21] but Professor Goetz Briefs finds 'the climax of political and economic thought within the Romantic movement' in the doctrine of Adam Müller, which sought to vindicate the sanctity of established social authority embodied in the family and the state; 'by an inescapable logic the Romanticist ideology was drawn into the camp of reaction.' [22] From M. Seillière's most celebrated work it appears that the Romantic mind tends to be affected with an inferiority-complex, 'une impression d'incomplètude, de solitude morale, et presque d'angoisse'; [23] from other passages of the same writer we learn that Romanticism is the 'imperialistic' mood, whether in individuals or nations—a too confident assertion of the will-to-power, arising from 'the mystic feeling that one's activities have the advantages of a celestial alliance.' [24] The function of the human mind which is to be regarded as peculiarly 'romantic' is for some 'the heart as opposed to the head,' [25] for others, 'the Imagination, as contrasted with Reason and the Sense of Fact' [26]—which I take to be ways of expressing a by no means synonymous pair of psychological antitheses. Typical manifestations of the spiritual essence of Romanticism have been variously conceived to be a passion for moonlight, for red waistcoats, for Gothic churches, for futurist paintings; [27] for talking exclusively about oneself, for hero-worship, for losing oneself in an ecstatic contemplation of nature.

The offspring with which Romanticism is credited are as strangely assorted as its attributes and its ancestors. It is by different historians—sometimes by the same historians—supposed to have begotten the French Revolution and the Oxford Movement; the Return to Rome and the Return to the State of Nature; the philosophy of Hegel, the philosophy of Schopenhauer, and the philosophy of Nietzsche—than which few other three philosophies more nearly exhaust the rich possibilities of philosophic disagreement; the revival of neo-Platonic mysticism in a Coleridge or an Alcott, the Emersonian transcendentalism, and scientific materialism; Wordsworth and Wilde; Newman and Huxley; the Waverley novels, the *Comédie Humaine,* and *Les Rougon-Macquart.* M. Seillière and Professor Babbitt have been especially active in tracing the progeny of Romanticism in the past century; the extraordinary number and still more extraordinary diversity of the descendants of it discovered by their researches are known to all here, and it therefore suffices to refer to their works for further examples.

All this is a mere hint, a suggestion by means of random samples, of the richness of the collection which might be brought together for our Centennial Exposition. The result is a confusion of terms, and of ideas, beside which that of a hundred years ago—mind-shaking though it was to the honest inquirers of La-Ferté-sous-Jouarre—seems pure lucidity. The word 'romantic' has come to mean so many things that, by itself, it means nothing. It has ceased to perform the function of a verbal sign. When a man is asked, as I have had the honor of being asked, to discuss Romanticism, it is impossible to know what ideas or tendencies he is to talk about, when they are supposed to have flourished, or in whom they are supposed to be chiefly exemplified. Perhaps there are some who think the rich ambiguity of the word not regrettable. In 1824, as Victor Hugo then testified, there were those who preferred to leave *à ce mot de romantique un certain vague fantastique et indéfinissable qui en redouble l'horreur,* and it may be that the taste is not extinct. But for one of the philosopher's trade, at least, the situation is embarrassing and exasperating; for philosophers, in spite of a popular belief to the contrary, are persons who suffer from a morbid solicitude to know what they are talking about.

Least of all does it seem possible, while the present uncertainty concerning the nature and *locus* of Romanticism prevails, to take sides in the controversy which still goes on so briskly with respect to its merits, the character of its general influence upon art and life. To do so would be too much like consenting to sit on a jury to try a criminal not yet identified, for a series of apparently incompatible crimes, before a bench of learned judges engaged in accusing one another of being accessories to whatever mischief has been done. It is to be observed, for example, that Messrs. Lasserre, Seillière, Babbitt and More (to mention no others) are engaged in arguing that something called Romanticism is the chief cause of the spiritual evils from which the nineteenth century and our own have suffered; but that they represent at least three different opinions as to what these evils are and how they are to be remedied. M. Lasserre, identifying Romanticism with the essential spirit of the French

Revolution, finds the chief cause of our woes in that movement's breach with the past, in its discarding of the ancient traditions of European civilization; and he consequently seeks the cure in a return to an older faith and an older political and social order, and in an abandonment of the optimistic fatalism generated by the idea of progress. M. Seillière, however, holds that 'the spirit of the Revolution in that in which it is rational, Stoic, Cartesian, classical . . . is justified, enduring, assured of making its way in the world more and more';[28] and that, consequently, the ill name of Romanticism should be applied to the revolutionary movement only where it has deviated from its true course, in 'the social mysticism, the communistic socialism of the present time.' He therefore intimates that the school of opinion which M. Lasserre ably represents is itself a variety of Romanticism.[29] But it is equally certain that M. Seillière's own philosophy is one of the varieties of Romanticism defined by Mr. Babbitt and Mr. More; while Mr. Babbitt, in turn, has been declared by more than one of the critics of his last brilliant book, and would necessarily be held by M. Seillière, to set forth therein an essentially Romantic philosophy. Thus Professor Herford says of it (justly or otherwise) that its 'temper is not that of a "positivist" of any school, but of a mystic,' and that 'it is as foreign to Homer and Sophocles, the exemplars of true classicism if any are, as it is to Aristotle.'[30]

What, then, can be done to clear up, or to diminish, this confusion of terminology and of thought which has for a century been the scandal of literary history and criticism, and is still, as it would not be difficult to show, copiously productive of historical errors and of dangerously undiscriminating diagnoses of the moral and aesthetic maladies of our age? The one really radical remedy—namely, that we should all cease talking about Romanticism—is, I fear, certain not to be adopted. It would probably be equally futile to attempt to prevail upon scholars and critics to restrict their use of the term to a single and reasonably well-defined sense. Such a proposal would only be the starting-point of a new controversy. Men, and especially philologists, will doubtless go on using words as they like, however much annoyance they cause philosophers by this unchartered freedom. There are, however, two possible historical inquiries which, if carried out more thoroughly and carefully than has yet been done, would, I think, do much to rectify the present muddle, and would at the same time promote a clearer understanding of the general movement of ideas, the logical and psychological relations between the chief episodes and transitions, in modern thought and taste. One of these measures would be somewhat analogous to the pro-

7

cedure of contemporary psychopathologists in the treatment of certain types of disorder. It has, we are told, been found that some mental disturbances can be cured or alleviated by making the patient explicitly aware of the genesis of his troublesome 'complex,' i. e., by enabling him to reconstruct those processes of association of ideas through which it was formed. Similarly in the present case, I think, it would be useful to trace the associative processes through which the word 'romantic' has attained its present amazing diversity, and consequent uncertainty, of connotation and denotation; in other words, to carry out an adequate semasiological study of the term. For one of the few things certain about Romanticism is that the name of it offers one of the most complicated, fascinating, and instructive of all problems in semantics. It is, in short, a part of the task of the historian of ideas, when he applies himself to the study of the thing or things called Romanticism, to render it, if possible, psychologically intelligible how such manifold and discrepant phenomena have all come to receive one name. Such an analysis would, I am convinced, show us a large mass of purely verbal confusions operative as actual factors in the movement of thought in the past century and a quarter; and it would, by making these confusions explicit, make it easier to avoid them.

But this inquiry would in practice, for the most part, be inseparable from a second, which is the remedy that I wish, on this occasion, especially to recommend. The first step in this second mode of treatment of the disorder is that we should learn to use the word 'Romanticism' in the plural. This, of course, is already the practice of the more cautious and observant literary historians, in so far as they recognize that the 'Romanticism' of one country may have little in common with that of another, and at all events ought to be defined in distinctive terms. But the discrimination of the Romanticisms which I have in mind is not solely or chiefly a division upon lines of nationality or language. What is needed is that any study of the subject should begin with a recognition of a *prima-facie* plurality of Romanticisms, of possibly quite distinct thought-complexes, a number of which may appear in one country. There is no hope of clear thinking on the part of the student of modern literature, if—as, alas! has been repeatedly done by eminent writers—he vaguely hypostatizes the term, and starts with the presumption that 'Romanticism' is the heaven-appointed designation of some single real entity, or type of entities, to be found in nature. He must set out from the simple and obvious fact that there are various historic episodes or movements to which different historians of our own or other periods have,

8

for one reason or another, given the name. There is a movement which began in Germany in the seventeen-nineties—the only one which has an indisputable title to be called Romanticism, since it invented the term for its own use. There is another movement which began pretty definitely in England in the seventeen-forties. There is a movement which began in France in 1801. There is another movement which began in France in the second decade of the century, is linked with the German movement, and took over the German name. There is the rich and incongruous collection of ideas to be found in Rousseau. There are numerous other things called Romanticism by various writers whom I cited at the outset. The fact that the same name has been given by different scholars to all of these episodes is no evidence, and scarcely even establishes a presumption, that they are identical in essentials. There may be some common denominator of them all; but if so, it has never yet been clearly exhibited, and its presence is not to be assumed *a priori*. In any case, each of these so-called Romanticisms was a highly complex and usually an exceedingly unstable intellectual compound; each, in other words, was made up of various unit-ideas linked together, for the most part, not by any indissoluble bonds of logical necessity, but by alogical associative processes, greatly facilitated and partly caused, in the case of the Romanticisms which grew up after the appellation 'Romantic' was invented, by the congenital and acquired ambiguities of the word. And when certain of these Romanticisms have in truth significant elements in common, they are not necessarily the same elements in any two cases. Romanticism A may have one characteristic presupposition or impulse, X, which it shares with Romanticism B, another characteristic, Y, which it shares with Romanticism C, to which X is wholly foreign. In the case, moreover, of those movements or schools to which the label was applied in their own time, the contents under the label sometimes changed radically and rapidly. At the end of a decade or two you had the same men and the same party appellation, but profoundly different ideas. As everyone knows, this is precisely what happened in the case of what is called French Romanticism. It may or may not be true that, as M. A. Viatte has sought to show,[31] at the beginning of this process of transformation some subtle leaven was already at work which made the final outcome inevitable; the fact remains that in most of its practically significant sympathies and affiliations of a literary, ethical, political, and religious sort, the French 'Romanticism' of the eighteen-thirties was the antithesis of that of the beginning of the century.

But the essential of the second remedy is that each of these Romanticisms—after they are first thus roughly discriminated with respect to their representatives or their dates—should be resolved, by a more thorough and discerning analysis than is yet customary, into its elements—into the several ideas and aesthetic susceptibilities of which it is composed. Only after these fundamental thought-factors or emotive strains in it are clearly discriminated and fairly exhaustively enumerated, shall we be in a position to judge of the degree of its affinity with other complexes to which the same name has been applied, to see precisely what tacit preconceptions or controlling motives or explicit contentions were common to any two or more of them, and wherein they manifested distinct and divergent tendencies.

II

Of the needfulness of such analytic comparison and discrimination of the Romanticisms let me attempt three illustrations.

1. In an interesting lecture before the British Academy a few years since, Mr. Edmund Gosse described Joseph Warton's youthful poem, *The Enthusiast*, written in 1740, as the first clear manifestation of 'the great romantic movement, such as it has enlarged and dwindled down to our day. . . . Here for the first time we find unwaveringly emphasized and repeated what was entirely new in literature, the essence of romantic hysteria. *The Enthusiast* is the earliest expression of complete revolt against the classical attitude which had been sovereign in all European literature for nearly a century. So completely is this expressed by Joseph Warton that it is extremely difficult to realize that he could not have come under the fascination of Rosseau, . . . who was not to write anything characteristic until ten years later.'[32] Let us, then, compare the ideas distinctive of this poem with the conception of *romantische Poesie* formulated by Friedrich Schlegel and his fellow-Romanticists in Germany after 1796. The two have plainly certain common elements. Both are forms of revolt against the neo-classical aesthetics; both are partly inspired by an ardent admiration for Shakespeare; both proclaim the creative artist's independence of 'rules.' It might at first appear, therefore, that these two Romanticisms, in spite of natural differences of phraseology, are identical in essence—are separate outcroppings of the same vein of metal, precious or base, according to your taste.

But a more careful scrutiny shows a contrast between them not less important—indeed, as it seems to me, more important—than their resemblance. The general theme of Joseph Warton's poem (of which, it will be remembered, the sub-title is 'The Lover of Nature') is one which had been a commonplace for many centuries: the superiority of 'nature' to 'art.' It is a theme which goes back to Rabelais's contrast of Physis and Antiphysie. It had been the inspiration of some of the most famous passages of Montaigne. It had been attacked by Shakespeare. Pope's *Essay on Man* had been full of it. The 'natural' in contrast with the artificial meant, first of all, that which is not man-made; and within man's life, it was supposed to consist in those expressions of human nature which are most spontaneous, unpremeditated, untouched by reflection or design, and free from the bondage of social convention. 'Ce n'est pas raison,' cried Montaigne, 'que l'art gagne le point d'honneur sur notre grande et puissante mère Nature. Nous avons tant rechargé la beauté et richesse de ses ouvrages par nos inventions, que nous l'avons tout à fait étouffée.' There follows the *locus classicus* of primitivism in modern literature, the famous passage on the superiority of wild fruits and savage men over those that have been 'bastardized' by art.[33]

Warton, then, presents this ancient theme in various aspects. He prefers to all the beauties of the gardens of Versailles

> Some pine-topt precipice
> Abrupt and shaggy.

He rhetorically inquires:

> Can Kent design like Nature?

He laments

> That luxury and pomp . . .
> Should proudly banish Nature's simple charms.

He inquires why 'mistaken man' should deem it nobler

> To dwell in palaces and high-roof'd halls
> Than in God's forests, architect supreme?

All this, if I may be permitted the expression, was old stuff. The principal thing that was original and significant in the poem was that Warton boldly applied the doctrine of the superiority of 'nature' over conscious art to the theory of poetry:

> What are the lays of artful Addison,
> Coldly correct, to Shakespeare's warblings wild?

11

That Nature herself was wild, untamed, was notorious, almost tautological; and it was Shakespeare's supposed 'wildness,' his non-conformity to the conventional rules, the spontaneous freedom of his imagination and his expression, that proved him Nature's true pupil.

Now this aesthetic inference had not, during the neo-classical period, ordinarily been drawn from the current assumption of the superiority of nature to art. The principle of 'following nature' had in aesthetics usually been taken in another, or in more than one other, of the several dozen senses of the sacred word.[34] Yet in other provinces of thought an analogous inference had long since and repeatedly been suggested. From the first the fashion of conceiving of 'nature' (in the sense in which it was antithetic to 'art') as norm had made for antinomianism, in some degree or other—for a depreciation of restraint, for the ideal of 'letting yourself go.' There seems to be an idea current that an antinomian temper was, at some time in the eighteenth century, introduced into aesthetic theory and artistic practise by some Romanticist, and that it thence speedily spread to moral feeling and social conduct.[35] The historic sequence is precisely the opposite. It was Montaigne again— not usually classified as a Romanticist—who wrote:

> J'ai pris bien simplement et crûment ce précepte ancien: 'que nous ne saurions faillir à suivre Nature' . . . Je n'ai pas corrigé, comme Socrate, par la force de la raison, mes complexions naturelles, je n'ai aucunement troublé, par art, mon inclination; je me laisse aller comme je suis venu; je ne combats rien.[36]

It was Pope who asked:

> Can that offend great Nature's God
> Which Nature's self inspires?

and who spoke of

> Wild Nature's vigor working at the root

as the source of the passions in which all the original and vital energies of men are contained.

Aside from a certain heightening of the emotional tone, then, the chief novelty of Warton's poem lay in its suggesting the application of these ideas to a field from which they had usually been curiously and inconsistently excluded, in its introduction of antinomianism, of a rather mild sort, into the conception of poetic excellence.[37] But this extension was obviously implicit from the outset in the logic of that protean 'naturalism' which had been the most characteristic and potent force in modern thought since the late Renaissance; it was bound to be made by somebody sooner or later. Nor was Warton's the first aesthetic application of the principle; it had already been applied to an art in the theory and practice of which eighteenth-century Englishmen were keenly interested—the art of landscape design. The first great revolt against the neo-classical aesthetics was not in literature at all, but in gardening; the second, I think, was in architectural taste; and all three were inspired by the same ideas.[38] Since, the 'artful Addison' had observed, 'artificial works receive a greater advantage from their resemblance of such as are natural,' and since Nature is distinguished by her 'rough, careless strokes,' the layer-out of gardens should aim at 'an artificial rudeness much more charming than that neatness and elegancy usually met with.'[39] This horticultural Romanticism had been preached likewise by Sir William Temple, Pope, Horace Walpole, Batty Langley, and others, and ostensibly exemplified in the work of Kent, Brown, and Bridgman. Warton in the poem in question describes Kent as at least doing his best to imitate in his gardens the wildness of Nature:

> He, by rules unfettered, boldly scorns
> Formality and method; round and square
> Disdaining, plans irregularly great.

It was no far cry from this to the rejection of the rules in the drama, to a revulsion against the strait-laced regularity and symmetry of the heroic couplet, to a general turning from convention, formality, method, artifice, in all the arts.

There had, however, from the first been a curious duality of meaning in the antithesis of 'nature' and 'art'—one of the most pregnant of the long succession of confusions of ideas which make up much of the history of human thought. While the 'natural' was, on the one hand, conceived as the wild and spontaneous and 'irregular,' it was also conceived as the simple, the naïve, the unsophisticated. No two words were more fixedly associated in the mind of the sixteenth, seventeenth, and early eighteenth centuries than 'Nature' and 'simple.' Consequently the idea of preferring nature to custom and to art usually carried with it the suggestion of a program of simplification, of reform by elimination; in other words, it implied primitivism. The 'natural' was a thing you reached by going back and by leaving out. And this association of ideas—already obvious in Montaigne, in Pope, and scores of other extollers of 'Nature'—is still conspicuous in Warton's poem. It was the 'bards of old' who were 'fair Nature's friends.' The poet envies

> The first of men, ere yet confined
> In smoky cities.

He yearns to dwell in some

> Isles of innocence from mortal view
> Deeply retired beneath a plantane's shade,
> Where Happiness and Quiet sit enthroned,
> With simple Indian swains.

For one term of the comparison, then, I limit myself, for brevity's sake, to this poem to which Mr. Gosse has assigned so important a place in literary history. There were, of course, even in the writings of the elder Warton, and still more in other phenomena frequently called 'Romantic,' between the 1740's and the 1790's, further elements which cannot be considered here. There is observable, for example, in what it has become the fashion to classify as the early phases of English Romanticism, the emergence of what may be called gothicism, and the curious fact of its partial and temporary fusion with naturalism. It is one of the interesting problems of the analytic history of ideas to see just how and why naturalism and gothicism became allied in the eighteenth century in England, though little, if at all, in France. But for the present purpose it suffices to take *The Enthusiast* as typical, in one especially important way, of a great deal of the so-called Romanticism before the seventeen-nineties—a Romanticism, namely, which, whatever further characteristics it may have had, was based upon naturalism (in the sense of the word which I have indicated) and was associated with primitivism of some mode or degree.

2. For in this fundamental point this earlier 'Romanticism' differed essentially from that of the German aesthetic theorists and poets who chose the term 'Romantic poetry' as the most suitable designation for their own literary ideals and program. The latter 'Romanticism' is in its very essence a denial of the older naturalistic presuppositions, which Warton's poem had manifested in a special and somewhat novel way. The German movement, as I have elsewhere shown, received its immediate and decisive impetus from Schiller's essay *On Naïve and Senti-*

mental Poetry; and what it derived from that confused work was the conviction that 'harmony with nature,' in any sense which implied an opposition to 'culture,' to 'art,' to reflection and self-conscious effort, was neither possible nor desirable for the modern man or the modern artist. The *Frühromantiker* learned from Schiller, and partly from Herder, the idea of an art which should look back no more to the primitive than to the classical—the notions of which, incidentally, Schiller had curiously fused—for its models and ideals; which should be the appropriate expression, not of a *natürliche* but of a *künstliche Bildung*; which, so far from desiring simplification, so far from aiming at the sort of harmony in art and life which is to be attained by the method of leaving out, should seek first fullness of content, should have for its program the adequate expression of the entire range of human experience and the entire reach of the human imagination. For man, the artificial, Friedrich Schlegel observed, *is* 'natural.' 'Die Abstraktion ist ein künstlicher Zustand. Dies ist kein Grund gegen sie, denn es ist dem Menschen gewiss natürlich, sich dann und wann auch in künstliche Zustände zu versetzen.' And again: 'Eine nur im Gegensatz der Kunst und Bildung natürliche Denkart soll es gar nicht geben.' To be unsophisticated, to revert to the mental state of 'simple Indian swains,' was the least of the ambitions of a German Romantic—though, since the unsophisticated is one type of human character, his art was not, at least in theory, indifferent even to that. The Shakespeare whom he admired was no gifted child of nature addicted to 'warblings wild.' Shakespeare, said A. W. Schlegel, is not 'eine blindes wildlaufendes Genie'; he had 'a system in his artistic practise and an astonishingly profound and deeply meditated one.' The same critic seems to be consciously attacking either Joseph Warton's or Gray's famous lines about Shakespeare when he writes: 'Those poets whom it is customary to represent as carefree nurslings of nature, without art and without schooling, if they produce works of genuine excellence, give evidence of exceptional cultivation (*Kultur*) of their mental powers, of practised art, of ripely pondered and just designs.' The greatness of Shakespeare, in the eyes of *these* Romantics, lay in his *Universalität*, his sophisticated insight into human nature and the many-sidedness of his portrayal of character; it was this, as Friedrich Schlegel said, that made him 'wie der Mittelpunkt der romantischen Kunst.' It may be added that another trait of the Romanticism found by Mr. Gosse in Joseph Warton, namely, the feeling that didactic poetry is not poetic, was also repudiated by early German Romanticism: 'How,' asked F. Schlegel again, 'can it be said that ethics (*die Moral*) belongs merely to philosophy, when the greatest part of poetry relates to the art of living and to the knowledge of human nature?'[40]

The difference, then, I suggest, is more significant, more pregnant, than the likeness between these two Romanticisms. Between the assertion of the superiority of 'nature' over conscious 'art' and that of the superiority of conscious art over mere 'nature'; between a way of thinking of which primitivism is of the essence and one of which the idea of perpetual self-transcendence is of the essence; between a fundamental preference for simplicity—even though a 'wild' simplicity—and a fundamental preference for diversity and complexity; between the sort of ingenuous naïveté characteristic of *The Enthusiast* and the sophisticated subtlety of the conception of romantic irony: between these the antithesis is one of the most radical that modern thought and taste have to show. I don't deny anyone's right to call both these things Romanticism, if he likes; but I cannot but observe that the fashion of giving both the same name has led to a good deal of unconscious falsification of the history of ideas. The elements of the one Romanticism tend to be read into the other; the nature and profundity of the oppositions between them tend to be overlooked; and the relative importance of the different changes of preconceptions in modern thought, and of susceptibilities in modern taste, tends to be wrongly estimated. I shall not attempt to cite here what seem to me examples of such historical errors; but the sum of them is, I think, far from negligible.

Between the 'Romanticism' which is but a special and belated manifestation of the naturalism that had flourished since the Renaissance (and before it) and the 'Romanticism' which began at the end of the eighteenth century in Germany (as well as that which appeared a little later in France) there is another difference not less significant. This is due to the identification of the meaning of 'Romantic' in the later movement with 'Christian'—and mainly with the medieval implications of that term. This was not the central idea in the original notion of 'Romantic poetry' as conceived by Friedrich Schlegel. Primarily, as I have elsewhere tried to show,[41] the adjective meant for him and the entire school 'das eigentümlich Moderne' in contrast with 'das eigentümlich Antike.' But it early occurred to him that the principal historic cause of the supposed radical differentiation of modern from classical art could lie only in the influence of Christianity. He wrote in 1796, before his own conversion to what he had already defined as the 'Romantic,' *i. e.,* modern, point of view:

So lächerlich und geschmacklos sich dieses Trachten nach dem
Reich Gottes in der christlichen Poesie offenbaren möchte; so wird es
dem Geschichtsforscher doch eine sehr merkwürdige Erscheinung, wenn
er gewahr wird, dass eben dieses Streben, das absolut Vollkommene und
Unendliche zu realisiren, eine unter dem unaufhörlichen Wechsel der
Zeiten und bei der grössten Verschiedenheit der Völker bleibende
Eigenschaft dessen ist, was man mit dem besten Rechte modern nennen
darf.[42]

When, after reading Schiller's essay, Schlegel himself became a
devotee of those aesthetic ideals which he had previously denounced, he
wrote (1797):

Nachdem die vollendete natürliche Bildung der Alten entschieden
gesunken, und ohne Rettung ausgeartet war, ward durch den Verlust
der endlichen Realität und die Zerrüttung vollendeter Form ein Streben
nach unendlicher Realität veranlasst, welches bald allgemeiner Ton des
Zeitalters wurde.[43]

'Romantic' art thus came to mean—for one thing—an art inspired by
or expressive of some idea or some ethical temper supposed to be essential in Christianity. 'Ursprung und Charakter der ganzen neuern Poesie
lässt sich so leicht aus dem Christentume ableiten, dass man die romantische eben so gut die christliche nennen könnte.'[44] said Richter in 1804,
repeating what had by that time become a commonplace. But the nature
of the essentially Christian, and therefore essentially Romantic, spirit
was variously conceived. Upon one characteristic of it there was, indeed,
rather general agreement among the German Romanticists: the habit of
mind introduced by Christianity was distinguished by a certain in-
satiability; it aimed at infinite objectives and was incapable of lasting
satisfaction with any goods actually reached. It became a favorite platitude to say that the Greeks and Romans set themselves limited ends to
attain, were able to attain them, and were thus capable of self-satisfac-
tion and finality; and that modern or 'romantic' art differed from this
most fundamentally, by reason of its Christian origin, in being, as
Schiller had said, a *Kunst des Unendlichen.* 'Absolute Abstraktion,
Vernichtung des Jetzigen, Apotheose der Zukunft, dieser eigentlich
bessern Welt!; dies ist der Kern des Geheisses des Christentums,' declared Novalis. In its application to artistic practice this 'apotheosis of
the future' meant the ideal of endless progress, of 'eine progressive
Universal-poesie' in the words of Fr. Schlegel's familiar definition; it implied the demand that art shall always go on bringing new provinces of

17

life within its domain and achieving ever fresh and original effects. But anything which was, or was supposed to be, especially characteristic of the Christian *Weltanschauung* tended to become a part of the current connotation of 'Romantic,' and also a part of the actual ideals of the school. Preoccupation with supersensible realities and a feeling of the illusoriness of ordinary existence was thus often held to be a distinctive trait of Romantic art, on the ground that Christianity is an otherworldly religion: 'in der christlichen Ansicht,' said A. W. Schlegel, 'die Anschauung des Unendlichen hat das Endliche vernichtet; das Leben ist zur Schattenwelt und zur Nacht geworden.'[45] Another recognized characteristic of Christianity, and therefore of the 'Romantic,' was ethical dualism, a conviction that there are in man's constitution two natures ceaselessly at war. The Greek ideal, in the elder Schlegel's words, was 'volkommene Eintracht und Ebenmass aller Kräfte, natürliche Harmonie. Die Neueren hingegen sind zum Bewusstsein der inneren Entzweiung gekommen, welche ein solches Ideal unmöglich macht.'[46] Directly related to this, it was perceived, was the 'inwardness' of Christianity, its preoccupation with 'the heart' as distinguished from the outward act, its tendency to introspection; and hence, as Mme de Stael and others observed, 'modern' or 'Romantic' art has discovered, and has for its peculiar province, the inexhaustible realm of the inner life of man:

> Les anciens avaient, pour ainsi dire, une âme corporelle, dont tous les mouvements étaient forts, directs, et conséquents; il n'en est pas de même du coeur humain développé par le christianisme: les modernes ont puisé dans le repentir chrétien l'habitude de se replier continuellement sur eux-mêmes. Mais, pour manifester cette existence tout intérieure, il faut qu'une grande variété dans les faits présente sous toutes les formes les nuances infinies de ce qui se passe dans l'âme.[47]

It is one of the many paradoxes of the history of the word, and of the controversies centering about it, that several eminent literary historians and critics of our time have conceived the moral essence of Romanticism as consisting in a kind of 'this-worldliness' and a negation of what one of them has termed 'the Christian and classical dualism.' Its most deplorable and dangerous error, in the judgment of these critics, is its deficient realization of the 'civil war in the cave' of man's soul, its belief in the 'natural goodness' of man. They thus define 'Romanticism' in terms precisely opposite to those in which it was often defined by the writers who first called their own ideals 'Romantic'; and this fashion, I cannot but think, has done a good deal to obscure the palpable and important historical fact that the one 'Romanticism' which (as I have said) has an indisputable title to the name was conceived by those writers as a re-discovery and revival, for better or worse, of characteristically Christian modes of thought and feeling, of a mystical and otherworldly type of religion, and a sense of the inner moral struggle as the distinctive fact in human experience—such as had been for a century alien to the dominant tendencies in 'polite' literature. The new movement was, al-most from the first, a revolt against what was conceived to be paganism in religion and ethics as definitely as against classicism in art. The earliest important formulation of its implications for religious philosophy was Schleiermacher's famous *Reden* (1799) addressed 'to the cultivated contemners of religion,' a work profoundly—sometimes, indeed, morbidly —dualistic in its ethical temper. Christianity, declares Schleiermacher, is *durch und durch polemisch*; it knows no truce in the warfare of the spiritual with the natural man, it finds no end in the task of inner self-discipline. And the *Reden,* it must be remembered, were (in the words of a German literary historian) 'greeted by the votaries of Romanticism as a gospel.'

Now it is not untrue to describe the ethical tendency of the 'Romanti-cism' which had its roots in naturalism—that is, in the assumption of the sole excellence of what in man is native, primitive, 'wild,' attainable without other struggle than that required for emancipation from social conventions and artificialities—as anti-dualistic and essentially non-moral. This aspect of it can be seen even in the poem of the 'blameless Warton,' when he describes the life of the state of nature for which he yearns. But as a consequence of the prevalent neglect to discriminate the Ro-manticisms, the very movement which was the beginning of a deliberate and vigorous insurrection against the naturalistic assumptions that had been potent, and usually dominant, in modern thought for more than three centuries, is actually treated as if it were a continuation of that tendency. Thesis and antithesis have, partly through accidents of language and partly through a lack of careful observation on the part of historians of literature, been called by the same name, and consequently have frequently been assumed to be the same thing. An ideal of ceaseless striving towards goals too vast or too exacting ever to be wholly attained has been confused with a nostalgia for the untroubled, because unas-piring, indolent, and unselfconscious life of the man of nature. Thus one of the widest and deepest-reaching lines of cleavage in modern thought has been more or less effectually concealed by a word.

3. This cleavage between naturalistic and anti-naturalistic 'Romanti-

cism' crosses national lines; and it manifestly cuts, so to say, directly through the person of one great writer commonly classed among the initiators of the Romantic movement in France. The author of the *Essai sur les révolutions* and of the earlier-written parts of *Atala* may perhaps properly be called a Romantic; the author of the later-written parts of the latter work and of the *Génie du Christianisme* may perhaps properly be called a Romantic; but it is obvious that the word has, in most important respects, not merely different but antithetic senses in these two applications of it to the same person. Chateaubriand before 1799 represented in some sort the culmination of the naturalistic and primitivistic Romanticism of which Mr. Gosse sees the beginning in Joseph Warton; he had not only felt intensely but had even gratified the yearning to live 'with simple Indian swains.' That the Chateaubriand of 1801 represents just as clearly a revolt against this entire tendency is sufficiently evident from the repudiation of primitivism in the first preface to *Atala*:

> Je ne suis point, comme M. Rousseau, un enthousiaste des sauvages; . . . je ne crois point que la *pure nature* soit la plus belle chose du monde. Je l'ai toujours trouvée fort laide partout où j'ai eu occasion de la voir . . . Avec ce mot de nature on a tout perdu.[48]

Thus the magic word upon which the whole scheme of ideas of the earlier writing had depended is now plainly characterized as the fruitful source of error and confusion that it was. And in his views about the drama the Chateaubriand of 1801 was opposed *both* to the movement represented by *The Enthusiast* and to the German Romanticism of his own time. Shakespeare was (though mainly, as we have seen, for differing reasons) the idol of both; but Chateaubriand in his *Essai sur la littérature anglaise*[49] writes of Shakespeare in the vein, and partly in the words, of Voltaire and Pope. In point of natural genius, he grants, the English dramatist was without a peer in his own age, and perhaps in any age: 'je ne sais si jamais homme a jeté des regards plus profonds sur la nature humaine.' But Shakespeare knew almost nothing of the requirements of the drama as an art:

> Il faut se persuader d'abord qu' écrire est un art; que cet art a nécessairement ses genres, et que chaque genre a ses règles. Et qu'on ne dise pas que les genres et les règles sont arbitraires; ils sont nés de la nature même; l'art a seulement séparé ce que la nature a confondu . . . On peut dire que Racine, dans toute l'excellence de son art, est plus naturel que Shakespeare.

Chateaubriand here, to be sure, still finds the standard of art in 'nature'; but it is 'nature' in the sense of the neo-classical critics, a sense in which it is not opposed, but equivalent, to an art that rigorously conforms to fixed rules. And the 'great literary paradox of the partisans of Shakespeare,' he observes, is that their arguments imply that 'there are *no* rules of the drama,' which is equivalent to asserting 'that an art is not an art.' Voltaire rightly felt that 'by banishing all rules and returning to *pure nature,* nothing was easier than to equal the *chefs-d'oeuvre* of the English stage'; and he was well advised in recanting his earlier too enthusiastic utterances about Shakespeare, since he saw that 'en relevant les beautés des barbares, il avait séduit des hommes qui, comme lui, ne sauraient séparer l'alliage de l'or.' Chateaubriand regrets that 'the *Cato* of Addison is no longer played' and that consequently 'on ne se délasse au théâtre anglais des monstruosités de Shakespeare que par les horreurs d'Otway.' 'Comment,' he exclaims, 'ne pas gémir de voir une nation éclairée, et qui compte parmi ses critiques les Pope et les Addison, de la voir s'extasier sur le portrait de l'apothicaire dans *Roméo et Juliette.* C'est le burlesque le plus hideux et le plus dégoûtant.' The entire passage might almost have been written with Warton's poem in mind, so completely and methodically does this later 'Romanticist' controvert the aesthetic principles and deride the enthusiasm of the English 'Romanticist' of 1740. It is worth noting, also, that Chateaubriand at this time thinks almost as ill of Gothic architecture as of Shakespeare and of *la pure nature:*

> Une beauté dans Shakespeare n'excuse pas ses innombrables défauts: un monument gothique peut plaire par son obscurité et la difformité même de ses proportions, mais personne ne songe á bâtir un palais sur son modèle.[50]

We have, then, observed and compared—very far from exhaustively, of course, yet in some of their most fundamental and determinative ideas—three 'Romanticisms.' In the first and second we have found certain common elements, but still more significant oppositions; in the second and third we have found certain other common elements, but likewise significant oppositions. But between the first and third the common elements are very scanty; such as there are, it could, I think, be shown, are not the same as those subsisting between either the first and second or the second and third; and in their ethical preconceptions and implications and the crucial articles of their literary creeds, the opposition between them is almost absolute.

All three of these historic episodes, it is true, are far more complex than I have time to show. I am attempting only to illustrate the nature of a certain procedure in the study of what is called Romanticism, to suggest its importance, and to present one or two specific results of the use of it. A complete analysis would qualify, without invalidating, these results, in several ways. It would (for one thing) bring out certain important connections between the revolt against the neo-classical aesthetics (common to two of the episodes mentioned) and other aspects of eighteenth-century thought. It would, again, exhibit fully certain *internal* oppositions in at least two of the Romanticisms considered. For example, in German Romanticism between 1797 and 1800 there grew up, and mainly from a single root, *both* an 'apotheosis of the future' and a tendency to retrospection—a retrospection directed, not, indeed, towards classical antiquity or towards the primitive, but towards the medieval. A belief in progress and a spirit of reaction were, paradoxically, joint offspring of the same idea, and were nurtured for a time in the same minds. But it is just these internal incongruities which make it most of all evident, as it seems to me, that any attempt at a *general* appraisal even of a single chronologically determinate Romanticism— still more, of 'Romanticism' as a whole—is a fatuity. When a Romanticism has been analyzed into the distinct 'strains' or ideas which compose it, the true philosophic affinities and the eventual practical influence in life and art of these several strains will usually be found to be exceedingly diverse and often conflicting. It will, no doubt, remain abstractly possible to raise the question whether the preponderant effect, moral or aesthetic, of one or another large movement which has been called by the name was good or bad. But that ambitious inquiry cannot even be legitimately begun until a prior task of analysis and detailed comparison—of the sort that I have attempted here to indicate—has been accomplished. And when this has been done, I doubt whether the larger question will seem to have much importance or meaning. What will then appear historically significant and philosophically instructive will be the way in which *each* of these distinguishable strains has worked itself out, what its elective affinities for other ideas, and its historic consequences, have shown themselves to be. The categories which it has become customary to use in distinguishing and classifying 'movements' in literature or philosophy and in describing the nature of the significant transitions which have taken place in taste and in opinion, are far too rough, crude, undiscriminating—and none of them so hopelessly so as the category 'Romantic.' It is not any large *complexes* of ideas, such as

22

that term has almost always been employed to designate, but rather certain simpler, diversely combinable, intellectual and emotional components of such complexes, that are the true elemental and dynamic factors in the history of thought and of art; and it is with the genesis, the vicissitudes, the manifold and often dramatic interactions of these, that it is the task of the historian of ideas in literature to become acquainted.

NOTES

1. *Le Romantisme français* (1919), 141 and *passim*.
2. *Jour. of Philosophy*, XIX (1922), 645.
3. *Egotism in German Philosophy*, 11–20, 54–64.
4. *Mme. Guyon et Fénelon précurseurs de Rousseau*, 1918.
5. 'Schiller and Romanticism,' *Mod. Lang. Notes*, XXXVII, 267 (1922), n. 28.
6. *Proc. Brit. Acad.*, 1915–16, 146–7.
7. *The Art of Poetry* (1923), 79–80.
8. *Contemporary Review*, April, 1919, p. 473.
9. *Classical and Romantic* (1923), 32, 31.
10. Editor's Introduction to *Essays in Romantic Literature* by George Wyndham, (1919), p. xxxiii.
11. *The Art of Poetry*, 79.
12. *Aspects and Impressions* (1922), 5.
13. *La Liquidation du Romantisme* (1919), 14 f.
14. *The Art of Poetry*, 50.
15. *The Architecture of Humanism* (1914), 39.
16. *P.M.L.A.*, XIII, 222.
17. Cf. George Boas in *Journal of Aesthetics*, I (1941), 52–65.
18. *The Drift of Romanticism* (1913), xiii, 247.
19. Marie Joachimi, *Die Weltanschauung der Romantik* (1905), 52.
20. Julius Bab, *Fortinbras, oder der Kampf des 19. Jahrhunderts mit dem Geiste der Romantik*.
21. G. Chatterton-Hill, *Contemporary Rev.* (1942), 720.
22. *Journal of the History of Ideas*, II (1941), 279 ff.
23. *Le mal romantique*, 1908, vii.
24. Cf. R. Gillouin, *Une nouvelle philosophie de l'histoire moderne et française*, 1921, 6 ff.; Seillière, *Le péril mystique*, etc., 2–6.
25. Wernaer, *Romanticism and the Romantic School in Germany*, p. 3.
26. Neilson, *Essentials of Poetry*, 1912, ch. III.
27. For the last mentioned, cf. Gosse in *Proc. Brit. Acad.*, 1915–16, 151.
28. *Le mal romantique*, xli.
29. 'Il y a même beaucoup de romantique dans la façon dont le combattent

certains traditionalistes imprudents, dont M. Lasserre parait avoir quelquefois écouté les suggestions dangereuses' *(loc. cit.)*.

30. *Essays and Studies by Members of the English Association,* VIII (1923).

31. *Le Catholicisme chez les Romantiques,* 1922.

32. 'Two Pioneers of Romanticism,' *Proc. Brit. Acad.,* 1915, pp. 146–8.

33. *Essais,* I, 31. There is a certain irony in the fact that the sort of naturalism here expressed by Montaigne was to be the basis of a Shakespeare-revival in the eighteenth century. For Shakespeare's own extreme antipathy to the passage is shown by the fact that he wrote two replies to it—a humorous one in *The Tempest,* a serious and profound one in *The Winter's Tale.*

34. This is not rhetorical exaggeration; more than sixty different senses or applications of the notion of 'nature' can be clearly distinguished.

35. So apparently Mr. Gosse: 'When the history of the [Romantic] school comes to be written, there will be a piquancy in tracing an antinomianism down from the blameless Warton to the hedonist essays of Oscar Wilde and the frenzied anarchism of the futurists' *(op. cit.,* 15.)

36. *Essais,* III. 12.

37. The title of the poem and some elements of its thought and feeling—especially its note of religious 'enthusiasm' for 'Nature' in the sense of the visible universe—are akin to, and probably derivative from, Shaftesbury's *Moralists.* But in Shaftesbury there is no opposition of 'nature' to 'art' and no antinomian strain, either ethical or aesthetic; 'decorum,' 'order,' 'balance,' and 'proportion' are among his favorite words.

38. Cf. my essay, 'The First Gothic Revival,' *etc.*

39 *Spectator,* No. 144.

40 Quotations in this paragraph from F. Schlegel are from *Athenaeum,* II, 1, p. 29; III, 1, p. 12; I, 2, p. 68; III, 1, p. 19. Those from A. W. Schlegel have already been cited by Marie Joachimi, *Weltanschauung der Romantik,* 179-183.

41. Cf. my essay on 'The Meaning of Romantic,' etc.

42. Review of Herder's *Humanitätsbriefe;* in Minor, *Fr. Schlegel, 1794–1802.*

43. Vorrede, *Die Griechen und Römer,* in Minor, *op. cit.,* I, 82.

44. Vorschule der Aesthetik, I, Programm V, § 23.

45. *Vorlesungen über dramatische Kunst und Literatur,* 1809–11, in *Werke,* 1846, V, 16. Cf. also Novalis's *Hymnen an die Nacht.*

46. *Op. cit.,* V, 17.

47. *De l'Allemagne,* Pt. II, chap. XI.

48. On the two strains in *Atala,* cf. Chinard, *L'Exotisme américain dans l'oeuvre de Chateaubriand,* 1918, ch. ix.

49. The section on Shakespeare was published in April, 1801 *(Mélanges politiques et littéraires,* 1854, pp. 390 ff.).

50. It is somewhat difficult to reconcile this with the eloquent passage on the Gothic church in the *Génie du Christianisme* (V, Ch. 8); yet even there, while ascribing to the Gothic style 'une beauté qui lui est particulière,' Chateaubriand also refers to its 'proportions barbares.'

W. K. WIMSATT

The Structure of Romantic Nature Imagery

STUDENTS of romantic nature poetry have had a great deal to tell us about the philosophic components of this poetry: the specific blend of deistic theology, Newtonian physics, and pantheistic naturalism which pervades the Wordsworthian landscape in the period of 'Tintern Abbey,' the theism which sounds in the 'Eolian Harp' of Coleridge, the conflict between French atheism and Platonic idealism which even in 'Prometheus Unbound' Shelley was not able to resolve. We have been instructed in some of the more purely scientific coloring of the poetry—the images derived from geology, astronomy, and magnetism, and the coruscant green mystery which the electricians contributed to such phenomena as Shelley's Spirit of Earth. We have considered also the 'sensibility' of romantic readers, distinct, according to one persuasive interpretation, from that of neoclassic readers. What was exciting to the age of Pope, 'Puffs, Powders, Patches, Bibles, Billet-doux' (even about these the age might be loath to admit its excitement), was not, we are told, what was so manifestly exciting to the age of Wordsworth. 'High mountains are a feeling, but the hum of cities torture.' Lastly, recent critical history has reinvited attention to the romantic theory of imagination, and especially to the version of that theory which Coleridge derived from the German metaphysicians, the view of poetic imagination as the *esemplastic* power which reshapes our primary awareness of the world into symbolic avenues to the theological.[1]

We have, in short, a *subject*—simply considered, the nature of birds and trees and streams— a *metaphysics* of an animating principle, a

From *The Verbal Icon* (University of Kentucky Press, 1954), pp. 103–16. Reprinted by permission of the publisher and author.

special *sensibility*, and a *theory* of poetic imagination—the value of the last a matter of debate. Romantic poetry itself has recently suffered some disfavor among advanced critics. One interesting question, however, seems still to want discussion; that is, whether romantic poetry (or more specifically romantic nature poetry) exhibits any imaginative *structure* which may be considered a special counterpart of the subject, the philosophy, the sensibility, and the theory—and hence perhaps an explanation of the last. Something like an answer to such a question is what I would sketch.

For the purpose of providing an antithetic point of departure, I quote here a part of one of the best known and most toughly reasonable of all metaphysical images:

> If they be two, they are two so
> As stiff twin compasses are two,
> Thy soul the fixed foot, makes no show
> To move, but doth, if th' other do.

It will be relevant if we remark that this similitude, rather farfetched as some might think, is yet unmistakable to interpretation because quite overtly stated, but again is not, by being stated, precisely defined or limited in its poetic value. The kind of similarity and the kind of disparity that ordinarily obtain between a drawing compass and a pair of parting lovers are things to be attentively considered in reading this image. And the disparity between living lovers and stiff metal is not least important to the tone of precision, restraint, and conviction which it is the triumph of the poem to convey. Though the similitude is cast in the form of statement, its mood is actually a kind of subimperative. In the next age the tension of such a severe disparity was relaxed, yet the overtness and crispness of statement remained, and a wit of its own sort.

> 'Tis with our judgments as our watches, none
> Go just alike, yet each believes his own.

We may take this as typical, I believe, of the metaphoric structure in which Pope achieves perfection and which survives a few years later in the couplets of Samuel Johnson or the more agile Churchill. The difference between our judgments and our watches, if noted at all, may be a pleasant epistemological joke for a person who questions the existence of a judgment which is taken out like a watch and consulted by another judgment.

But the 'sensibility,' as we know, had begun to shift even in the age of Pope. Examples of a new sensibility, and of a different structure, having something to do with Miltonic verse and a 'physico-theological nomenclature,' are to be found in Thomson's *Seasons*. Both a new sensibility and a new structure appear in the 'hamlets brown and dim-discovered spires' of Collins' early example of the full romantic dream. In several poets of the mid century, in the Wartons, in Grainger, or in Cunningham, one may feel, or rather see stated, a new sensibility, but at the same time one may lament an absence of poetic quality—that is, of a poetic structure adequate to embody or objectify the new feeling. It is as if these harbingers of another era had felt but had not felt strongly enough to work upon the objects of their feelings a pattern of meaning which would speak for itself—and which would hence endure as a poetic monument.

As a central exhibit I shall take two sonnets, that of William Lisle Bowles 'To the River Itchin' (1789)[2] and for contrast that of Coleridge 'To the River Otter' (1796)—written in confessed imitation of Bowles.[3] Coleridge owed his first poetic inspiration to Bowles (the 'father' of English romantic poetry) and continued to express unlimited admiration for him as late as 1796. That is, they shared the same sensibility—as for that matter did Wordsworth and Southey, who too were deeply impressed by the sonnets of Bowles. As a schoolboy Coleridge read eagerly in Bowles' second edition of 1789[4] (among other sonnets not much superior):

> Itchin, when I behold thy banks again,
> Thy crumbling margin, and thy silver breast,
> On which the self-same tints still seem to rest,
> Why feels my heart the shiv'ring sense of pain?
> Is it—that many a summer's day has past
> Since, in life's morn, I carol'd on thy side?
> Is it—that oft, since then, my heart has sigh'd,
> As Youth, and Hope's delusive gleams, flew fast?
> Is it—that those, who circled on thy shore,
> Companions of my youth, now meet no more?
> Whate'er the cause, upon thy banks I bend
> Sorrowing, yet feel such solace at my heart,
> As at the meeting of some long-lost friend,
> From whom, in happier hours, we wept to part.

Here is an emotive expression which once appealed to the sensibility of its author and of his more cultivated contemporaries, but which has with the lapse of time gone flat. The speaker was happy as a boy by the banks of the river. Age has brought disillusion and the dispersal of his friends. So a return to the river, in reminding him of the past, brings both sorrow and consolation. The facts are stated in four rhetorical questions and a concluding declaration. There is also something about how the river looks and how its looks might contribute to his feelings—in the metaphoric suggestion of the 'crumbling' margin and in the almost il-lusory tints on the surface of the stream which surprisingly have out-lasted the 'delusive gleams' of his own hopes. Yet the total impression is one of simple association (by contiguity in time) simply asserted—what might be described in the theory of Hume or Hartley or what Hazlitt talks about in his essay 'On the Love of the Country.' 'It is because natural objects have been associated with the sports of our childhood, . . . with our feelings in solitude . . . that we love them as we do ourselves.'

Coleridge himself in his 'Lines Written at Elbingerode in 1799' was to speak of a 'spot with which the heart associates Holy remembrances of child or friend.' His enthusiasm for Hartley in this period is well known. But later, in the *Biographia Literaria* and in the third of his essays on 'Genial Criticism,' he was to repudiate explicitly the Hartleyan and mechanistic way of shifting back burdens of meaning. And already, in 1796, Coleridge as poet was concerned with the more complex onto-logical grounds of association (the various levels of sameness, of corre-spondence and analogy), where mental activity transcends mere 'associa-tive response'—where it is in fact the unifying activity known both to later eighteenth century associationists and to romantic poets as 'imagi-nation.' The 'sweet and indissoluble union between the intellectual and the material world' of which Coleridge speaks in the introduction to his pamphlet anthology of sonnets in 1796 must be applied by us in one sense to the sonnets of Bowles, but in another to the best romantic poetry and even to Coleridge's imitation of Bowles. There is an important difference between the kinds of unity. In a letter to Sotheby of 1802 Coleridge was to say more emphatically: 'The poet's heart and intellect should be *combined*, intimately combined and unified with the great appearances of nature, and not merely held in solution and loose mixture with them.'[5] In the same paragraph he says of Bowles' later poetry: 'Bowles has indeed the *sensibility* of a poet, but he has not the *passion* of a great poet . . . he has no native passion because he is not a thinker.'

The sententious melancholy of Bowles' sonnets and the asserted con-nection between this mood and the appearances of nature are enough to explain the hold of the sonnets upon Coleridge. Doubtless the metaphoric coloring, faint but nonetheless real, which we have remarked in Bowles' descriptive details had also something to do with it. What is of great importance to note is that Coleridge's own sonnet 'To the River Otter' (while not a completely successful poem) shows a remarkable intensification of such color.

> Dear native Brook! wild Streamlet of the West!
> How many various-fated years have past,
> What happy and what mournful hours, since last
> I skimmed the smooth thin stone along thy breast,
> Numbering its light leaps! yet so deep imprest
> Sink the sweet scenes of childhood, that mine eyes
> I never shut amid the sunny ray,
> But straight with all their tints thy waters rise,
> Thy crossing plank, thy marge with willows grey,
> And bedded sand that veined with various dyes
> Gleamed through thy bright transparence! On my way,
> Visions of Childhood! oft have ye beguiled
> Lone manhood's cares, yet waking fondest sighs:
> Ah! that once more I were a careless Child!

Almost the same statement as that of Bowles' sonnet—the sweet scenes of childhood by the river have only to be remembered to bring both beguilement and melancholy. One notices immediately, however, that the speaker has kept his eye more closely on the object. There are more details. The picture is more vivid, a fact which according to one school of poetics would in itself make the sonnet superior. But a more analytic theory will find it worth remarking also that certain ideas, latent or involved in the description, have much to do with its vividness. As a child, careless and free, wild like the streamlet, the speaker amused himself with one of the most carefree motions of youth—skimming smooth thin stones which leapt lightly on the breast of the water. One might have thought such experiences would sink no deeper in the child's breast than the stones in the water—'yet so deep imprest'—the very antithesis (though it refers overtly only to the many hours which have intervened) defines imaginatively the depth of the impressions. When he closes his eyes, they *rise* again (the word *rise* may be taken as a trope which hints the whole unstated similitude); they rise like the tinted waters of the stream; they gleam up through the depths of memory—the 'various-fated years'—like the 'various dyes' which vein the sand of the river bed. In short, there is a rich ground of meaning in Coleridge's sonnet beyond what is overtly stated. The descriptive details of his sonnet gleam brightly because (consciously or unconsciously—it would be fruitless to inquire how deliberately he wrote these meanings into his lines) he has invested them with significance. Here is a special perception, 'invention' if one prefers, 'imagination,' or even 'wit.' It can be explored and tested by the wit of the reader. In this way it differs from the mere flat announcement of a Hartleian association, which is not open to challenge and hence not susceptible of confirmation. If this romantic wit differs from that of the metaphysicals, it differs for one thing in making less use of the central overt statement of similitude which is so important in all rhetoric stemming from Aristotle and the Renaissance. The metaphor in fact is scarcely noticed by the main statement of the poem.[6] Both tenor and vehicle, furthermore, are wrought in a parallel process out of the same material. The river landscape is both the occasion of reminiscence and the source of the metaphors by which reminiscence is described.[7] A poem of this structure is a signal instance of that kind of fallacy (or strategy) by which death in poetry occurs so often in winter or at night, and sweethearts meet in the spring countryside. The tenor of such a similitude is likely to be subjective—reminiscence or sorrow or beguilement—not an object distinct from the vehicle, as lovers or their souls are distinct from twin compasses. Hence the emphasis of Bowles, Coleridge, and all other romantics on spontaneous feelings and sincerity. Hence the recurrent themes of One Being and Eolian Influence and Wordsworth's 'ennobling interchange of action from within and from without.' In such a structure again the element of tension in disparity is not so important as for metaphysical wit. The interest derives not from our being aware of disparity where likeness is firmly insisted on, but in an opposite activity of discerning the design which is latent in the multiform sensuous picture.

Let us notice for a moment the 'crossing plank' of Coleridge's sonnet, a minor symbol in the poem, a sign of shadowy presences, the lads who had once been there. The technique of this symbol is the same as that which Keats was to employ in a far more brilliant romantic instance, the second stanza of his 'Ode to Autumn,' where the very seasonal spirit is conjured into reality out of such haunted spots—in which a gesture lingers—the half-reaped furrow, the oozing cider press, the brook where the gleaners have crossed with laden heads.[8] To return to our metaphysics—of an animate, plastic Nature, not transcending but immanent in and breathing through all things—and to discount for the moment such differences as may relate to Wordsworth's naturalism, Coleridge's theology, Shelley's Platonism, or Blake's visions: we may observe that the common feat of the romantic nature poets was to read meanings into the landscape. 'A puddle,' says Hazlitt, 'is filled with preternatural faces.' [9] The meaning might be such as we have seen in Coleridge's sonnet, but it might more characteristically be more profound, concerning the spirit or soul of things—'the one life within us and abroad.' And that meaning especially was summoned out of the very surface of nature itself. It was embodied imaginatively and without the explicit religious or philosophic statements which one will find in classical or Christian instances—for example in Pope's 'Essay on Man':

> Here then we rest: 'The Universal Cause
> Acts to one end, but acts by various laws,'

or in the teleological divines, More, Cudworth, Bentley, and others of the seventeenth and eighteenth centuries, or in Paley during the same era as the romantics. The romantic poets want to have it and not have it too—a spirit which the poet himself as superidealist creates by his own higher reason or esemplastic imagination. Here one may recall Ruskin's chapter of *Modern Painters* on the difference between the Greek gods of rivers and trees and the vaguer suffusions of the romantic vista—'the curious web of hesitating sentiment, pathetic fallacy, and wandering fancy, which form a great part of our modern view of nature.' Wordsworth's 'Prelude,' from the cliff that 'upreared its head' in the night above Ullswater to the 'blue chasm' that was the 'soul' of the moonlit cloudscape beneath his feet on Snowdon, is the archpoet's testament, both theory and demonstration of this way of reading nature. His 'Tintern Abbey' is another classic instance, a whole pantheistic poem woven of the landscape, where God is not once mentioned. After the 'soft inland murmur,' the 'one green hue,' the 'wreaths of smoke . . . as . . . Of vagrant dwellers in the houseless woods' (always something just out of sight or beyond definition), it is an easy leap to the 'still, sad music of humanity,' and

> a sense sublime
> Of something far more deeply interfused,
> Whose dwelling is the light of setting suns.

This poem, written as Wordsworth revisited the banks of a familiar stream, the 'Sylvan Wye,' is the full realization of a poem for which Coleridge and Bowles had drawn slight sketches. In Shelley's 'Hymn to Intellectual Beauty' the 'awful shadow' of the 'unseen Power' is substantiated of 'moonbeam' showers of light behind the 'piny mountain,' of 'mist o'er mountains driven.' On the Lake of Geneva in the summer of 1816 Byron, with Shelley the evangelist of Wordsworth at his side, spoke of 'a living fragrance from the shore,' a 'floating whisper on the hill.' We remark in each of these examples a dramatization of the spiritual through the use of the faint, the shifting, the least tangible and most mysterious parts of nature—a poetic counterpart of the several theories of spirit as subtile matter current in the eighteenth century, Newton's 'electric and elastic' active principle, Hartley's 'infinitesimal elementary body.' The application of this philosophy to poetry by way of direct statement had been made as early as 1735 in Henry Brooke's 'Universal Beauty,' where an 'elastick Flue of fluctuating Air' pervades the universe as 'animating Soul.' In the high romantic period the most scientific version to appear in poetry was the now well recognized imagery which Shelley drew from the electricians.

In such a view of spirituality the landscape itself is kept in focus as a literal object of attention. Without it Wordsworth and Byron in the examples just cited would not get a start. And one effect of such a use of natural imagery—an effect implicit in the very philosophy of a World Spirit—is a tendency in the landscape imagery to a curious split. If we have not only the landscape but the spirit which either informs or visits it, and if both of these must be rendered for the sensible imagination, a certain parceling of the landscape may be the result. The most curious illustrations which I know are in two of Blake's early quartet of poems to the seasons. Thus, 'To Spring':

> O THOU with dewy locks, who lookest down
> Thro' the clear windows of the morning, turn
> Thine angel eyes upon our western isle,
> Which in full choir hails thy approach, O Spring!
>
> The hills tell each other, and the list'ning
> Vallies hear; all our longing eyes are turned
> Up to thy bright pavillions; issue forth,
> And let thy holy feet visit our clime.
>
> Come o'er the eastern hills, and let our winds
> Kiss thy perfumed garments; let us taste
> Thy morn and evening breath; scatter thy pearls
> Upon our love-sick land that mourns for thee.

And 'To Summer':

O THOU, who passest thro' our vallies in
Thy strength, curb thy fierce steeds, allay the heat
That flames from their large nostrils! thou, O Summer,
Oft pitched'st here thy golden tent, and oft
Beneath our oaks hast slept, while we beheld
With joy thy ruddy limbs and flourishing hair.

Beneath our thickest shades we oft have heard
Thy voice, when noon upon his fervid car
Rode o'er the deep of heaven; beside our springs
Sit down, and in our mossy vallies, on
Some bank beside a river clear, throw thy
Silk draperies off, and rush into the stream.

Blake's starting point, it is true, is the opposite of Wordsworth's or Byron's, not the landscape but a spirit personified or allegorized. Nevertheless, this spirit as it approaches the 'western isle' takes on certain distinctly terrestrial hues. Spring, an oriental bridegroom, lives behind the 'clear windows of the morning' and is invited to issue from 'bright pavillions,' doubtless the sky at dawn. He has 'perfumed garments' which when kissed by the winds will smell much like the flowers and leaves of the season. At the same time, his *own* morn and evening breaths are most convincing in their likeness to morning and evening breezes. The pearls scattered by the hand of Spring are, we must suppose, no other than the flowers and buds which literally appear in the landscape at this season. They function as landscape details and simultaneously as properties of the bridegroom and—we note here a further complication—as properties of the land taken as lovesick maiden. We have in fact a double personification conjured from one nature, one landscape, in a wedding which approximates fusion. Even more curious is the case of King Summer, a divided tyrant and victim, who first appears as the source and spirit of heat, his steeds with flaming nostrils, his limbs ruddy, his tent golden, but who arrives in our valleys only to sleep in the shade of the oaks and be invited to rush into the river for a swim. These early romantic poems are examples of the Biblical, classical, and Renaissance tradition of allegory as it approaches the romantic condition of landscape naturalism—as Spring and Summer descend into the landscape and are fused with it. Shelley's Alastor is a spirit of this kind, making the 'wild his home,' a spectral 'Spirit of wind,' expiring 'Like some frail exhalation; which the dawn Robes in its golden beams.' Byron's Childe Harold desired that he himself might become a 'portion' of that around him, of the tempest and the night. 'Be thou,

33

Spirit fierce,' said Shelley to the West Wind, 'My spirit! Be thou me.'

An English student of the arts in the Jacobean era, Henry Peacham, wrote a book on painting in which he gave allegorical prescriptions for representing the months, quoted under the names of months by Dr. Johnson in his *Dictionary:*

> *April* is represented by a young man in green, with a garland of myrtle and hawthorn buds; in one hand primroses and violets, in the other the sign Taurus.

> *July* I would have drawn in a jacket of light yellow, eating cherries, with his face and bosom sunburnt.[10]

But that would have been the end of it. April would not have been painted into a puzzle picture where hawthorn buds and primroses were arranged to shadow forth the form of a person.[11] There were probably deep enough reasons why the latter nineteenth century went so far in the development of so trivial a thing as the actual landscape puzzle picture.

In his Preface of 1815 Wordsworth spoke of the *abstracting* and '*modifying* powers of the imagination.' He gave as example a passage from his own poem, 'Resolution and Independence,' where an old leech gatherer is likened to a stone which in turn is likened to a sea beast crawled forth to sun itself. The poems which we have just considered, those of Coleridge, Wordsworth, and Blake especially, with their blurring of literal and figurative, might also be taken, I believe, as excellent examples. In another of his best poems Wordsworth produced an image which shows so strange yet artistic a warping, or modification, of vehicle by tenor that, though not strictly a nature image, it may be quoted here with close relevance. In the ode 'Intimations of Immortality':

> Hence, in a season of calm weather,
> Though inland far we be,
> Our souls have sight of that immortal sea
> Which brought us hither;
> Can in a moment travel thither—
> And see the children sport upon the shore,
> And hear the mighty waters rolling evermore.

Or, as one might drably paraphrase, our souls in a calm mood look back to the infinity from which they came, as persons inland on clear days can look back to the sea by which they have voyaged to the land.

34

The tenor concerns souls and age and time. The vehicle concerns travelers and space. The question for the analyst of structure is: Why are the children found on the seashore? In what way do they add to the solemnity or mystery of the sea? Or do they at all? The answer is that they are not strictly parts of the traveler-space vehicle, but of the soul-age-time tenor, attracted over, from tenor to vehicle. The travelers looking back in both space and time see themselves as children on the shore, as if just born like Venus from the foam. This is a sleight of words, an imposition of image upon image, by the *modifying* power of imagination.

Poetic structure is always a fusion of ideas with material, a statement in which the solidity of symbol and the sensory verbal qualities are somehow not washed out by the abstraction. For this effect the iconic or directly imitative powers of language are important—and of these the well known onomatopoeia or imitation of sound is only one, and one of the simplest. The 'stiff twin compasses' of Donne have a kind of iconicity in the very stiffness and odd emphasis of the metrical situation. Neoclassic iconicity is on the whole of a highly ordered, formal, or intellectual sort, that of the 'figures of speech' such as antithesis, isocolon, homoeoteleuton, or chiasmus. But romantic nature poetry tends to achieve iconicity by a more direct sensory imitation of something headlong and impassioned, less ordered, nearer perhaps to the subrational. Thus: in Shelley's 'Ode to the West Wind' the shifts in imagery of the second stanza, the pell-mell raggedness and confusion of loose clouds, decaying leaves, angels and Maenads with hair uplifted, the dirge, the dome, the vapors, and the enjambment from tercet to tercet combine to give an impression beyond statement of the very wildness, the breath and power which is the vehicle of the poem's radical metaphor. If we think of a scale of structures having at one end logic, the completely reasoned and abstracted, and at the other some form of madness or surrealism, matter or impression unformed and undisciplined (the imitation of disorder by the idiom of disorder), we may see metaphysical and neoclassical poetry as near the extreme of logic (though by no means reduced to that status) and romantic poetry as a step toward the directness of sensory presentation (though by no means sunk into subrationality). As a structure which favors implication rather than overt statement, the romantic is far closer than the metaphysical to symbolist poetry and the varieties of postsymbolist most in vogue today. Both types of structure, the metaphysical and the romantic, are valid. Each has gorgeously enriched the history of English poetry.

NOTES

1. This paragraph alludes especially to Joseph Warren Beach, *The Concept of Nature in Nineteenth-Century English Poetry* (New York, 1936), chaps. II–VIII; Newton P. Stallknecht, *Strange Seas of Thought* (Durham, 1945), chaps. II–III; Carl H. Grabo, *A Newton among Poets* (Chapel Hill, 1930), chaps. VI–VII, and *Prometheus Unbound: An Interpretation* (Chapel Hill, 1935), 142-43, 151; Frederick A. Pottle, *The Idiom of Poetry* (Ithaca, 1941), chap I. For a survey of recent writing on the English romantic theory of imagination, see Thomas M. Raysor (ed.), *The English Romantic Poets, A Review of Research* (New York, 1950).

2. The sonnet 'To the River Lodon' (1777) by Bowles' Oxford senior, Thomas Warton, shows sensibility with even less structural support.

3. Coleridge's sonnet first appears in its entirety and as a separate poem in the pamphlet collection which he published privately in 1796; the sonnet reappears in the 1797 *Poems* of Coleridge under the half-title 'Sonnets attempted in the manner of the Rev. W. L. Bowles.'

4. 'I made, within less than a year and a half, more than forty transcriptions, as the best presents I could offer.' *Biographia Literaria*, chap. I.

5. Coleridge has in mind such loose resemblances as need to be stated 'in the shape of formal similes.' *Letters* (Boston, 1895), I, 404. Cp. Bowles, *Sonnets* (2d ed., Bath, 1789), Sonnet V, 'To the River Wenbeck,' 'I listen to the wind, And think I hear meek sorrow's plaint'; Sonnet VI, 'To the River Tweed,' 'The murmurs of thy wand'ring wave below Seem to his ear the pity of a friend.'

6. See the more overt connections in the poem 'Recollection' *(Watchman,* no. V, April 2, 1796) from which lines 2–11 of this sonnet were taken. 'Where blameless Pleasures dimpled Quiet's cheek, As water-lilies *ripple* thy slow stream!' 'Ah! fair tho' faint those forms of memory seem, Like Heaven's bright bow on thy smooth evening stream.'

7. 'It is among the chief excellencies of Bowles that his imagery appears almost always prompted by surrounding scenery.' Coleridge to Southey, December 17, 1794 *(Letters,* I, 115).

8. Compare the 'wooden bridge' in Arnold's Keatsian 'Scholar Gipsy.'

9. 'On Mr. Wordsworth's *Excursion.*'

10. With these prescriptions compare the allegorical panels of seasons and months in Spencer's *Cantos of Mutabilitie,* VII, xxviii ff.

11. Perhaps too sweeping. See, for instance, Alfred H. Barr, Jr. (ed.), *Fantastic Art, Dada, Surrealism* (New York, 1947), 83, 'Head-Landscape' in the tradition of Arcimboldo.

M. H. ABRAMS

The Correspondent Breeze:
A Romantic Metaphor

WRITING in 1834, Henry Taylor noted that Wordsworth's attacks on eighteenth-century diction had succeeded in making poetry, in some particulars, more plain spoken. But Taylor also remarked that in effect a new poetic diction had covertly replaced the old. If Romantic poets no longer refer to the nightingale by the Greek name, Philomel, some of them refer to it by the Persian name, Bulbul; Taylor cites one reader who said 'he had learnt, for the first time, from Lord Byron's poetry, that two bulls make a nightingale.' Worse still are the stock terms scattered through poetry 'with a sort of feeling senselessness,' such as 'wild,' 'bright,' 'lonely,' and 'dream,' and especially the variant forms of the word 'breathing'; 'to breathe,' Taylor says, has become 'a verb poetical which [means] anything but respiration.'[1]

To this shrewd observation I would add that 'breathing' is only one aspect of a more general component in Romantic poetry. This is air-in-motion, whether it occurs as breeze or breath, wind or respiration—whether the air is compelled into motion by natural forces or by the action of the human lungs. That the poetry of Coleridge, Wordsworth, Shelley, Byron should be so thoroughly ventilated is itself noteworthy; but the surprising thing is how often, in the major poems, the wind is not only a property of the landscape, but also a vehicle for radical changes in the poet's mind. The rising wind, usually linked with the outer transition from winter to spring, is correlated with a complex subjective process: the return to a sense of community after isolation,

From *The Kenyon Review*, XIX (1957), pp. 113-30. Revised version copyright © 1960 by M. H. Abrams.

the renewal of life and emotional vigor after apathy and a deathlike torpor, and an outburst of creative power following a period of imaginative sterility.

Coleridge's *Dejection: An Ode,* written in 1802, provides the earliest inclusive instance of this symbolic equation. The poetic meditation is set in April, which turns out, as in Eliot's *Waste Land,* to be the cruelest month because, in breeding life out of the dead land, it painfully revives emotional life in the observer, mixing memory and desire. And as the poem opens, a desultory breeze makes itself audible on a wind-harp— an instrument whose eerie modulations sound through most of the writings with which we are concerned.

James Bowyer, Coleridge's schoolmaster and pre-Wordsworthian reformer of poetic diction, had vigorously proscribed the traditional lyre as an emblem for poetizing. 'Harp? Harp? Lyre? Pen and ink, boy, you mean!' [2] But by the process already noted—we might call it Taylor's principle—the lyre of Apollo was often replaced in Romantic poetry by the Aeolian lyre, whose music is evoked not by art, human or divine, but by a force of nature. Poetic man, in a statement by Shelley which had close parallels in Coleridge and Wordsworth, is an instrument subject to impressions 'like the alterations of an ever-changing wind over an Aeolian lyre, which move it by their motion to ever-changing melody.' [3] The wind-harp has become a persistent Romantic analogue of the poetic mind, the figurative mediator between outer motion and inner emotion. It is possible to speculate that, without this plaything of the eighteenth century, the Romantic poets would have lacked a conceptual model for the way the mind and imagination respond to the wind, so that some of their most characteristic passages might have been, in a literal sense, inconceivable.

In Coleridge's *Dejection* the moaning wind-harp foretells a storm which the lyric speaker in his lethargy awaits in the hope that, as in the past, it may send 'my soul abroad' and release the

> stifled, drowsy, unimpassioned grief,
> Which finds no natural outlet, no relief . . . .

The speaker reviews the afflictions that have made him take refuge in 'abstruse research,' and have destroyed his inner joy and any possibility of emotional commerce with the outer scene. Worst of all is the attendant paralysis of his poetic power, the 'shaping spirit of Imagination.' But even as the speaker inventories the conditions of his death in life, the outer wind mounts to a storm of driving rain and compels the wind-harp into loud and violent music. In implicit parallel with the wind-harp, the poet also responds to the storm with mounting vitality—what he calls 'the passion and the life, whose fountains are within,' once more break out—until, in a lull of the wind, the poem rounds on itself and ends where it began, with a calm both of nature and of mind. But the poet has moved from the calm of apathy to one of peace after passion. By the agency of the wind storm it describes, the poem turns out to contradict its own premises: the poet's spirit awakens to violent life even as he laments his inner death, achieves release in the despair at being cut off from all outlet, and demonstrates the power of imagination in the process of memorializing its failure.

That the poem was grounded in experience is evident from Coleridge's many letters testifying to his delight in wind and storms, which he watched 'with a total feeling worshipping the power and "eternal Link" of Energy,' and through which he had walked, 'stricken . . . with barreness' in a 'deeper dejection than I am willing to remember,' seeking the inspiration for completing *Christabel*.[4] In one passage, written some nine months after he had completed *Dejection*, we find a symbolic wind again involving the revival of feeling and imagination, and leading to the sense of the one life within us and abroad:

> In simple earnest, I never find myself alone within the embracement of rocks and hills, a traveller up an alpine road, but my spirit courses, drives, and eddies, like a Leaf in Autumn: a wild activity, of thoughts, imagination, feelings, and impulses of motion, rises up from within me— a sort of *bottom-wind*, that blows to no point of the compass, and comes from I know not whence, but agitates the whole of me. . . . Life seems to me then a universal spirit, that neither has, nor can have, an opposite. . . . where is there *room* for death?[5]

Similarly with Coleridge's friend, Wordsworth: 'Winter winds,' Dorothy wrote, 'are his delight—his mind I think is often more fertile in this season than any other.'[6] Of this phenomenon Wordsworth himself gave remarkable testimony in the autobiographical *Prelude*. From the beginning of this work, in fact, the recurrent wind serves unobtrusively as a leitmotif, representing the chief theme of continuity and interchange between outer motions and the interior life and powers, and providing the poem with a principle of organization beyond chronology.

Earlier poets had launched their epics by invoking for inspiration a

Muse, Apollo, or the Holy Spirit. Wordsworth's opening lines, which have an identical function, are:

> Oh there is blessing in this gentle breeze
> That blows from the green fields and from the clouds
> And from the sky . . . .

Released at last from the city and the oppressive weight of the past, the poet says 'I breathe again'; but so, we find, is nature breathing, in a passage where the wind becomes both the stimulus and outer correspondent to a spring-like revival of the spirit after a wintry season, and also to a revival of poetic inspiration which Wordsworth, going beyond Coleridge, equates with the inspiration of the Prophets when touched by the Holy Spirit. There is even a glancing metaphoric parallel between the resulting poetic creation and the prototypal creation by divine utterance—For 'Nature's self,' as Wordsworth said later, 'is the breath of God' (*Prelude*, 1805 ed., V, 222.)

> For I, methought, while the sweet breath of Heaven
> Was blowing on my body, felt within
> A corresponding mild creative breeze,
> A vital breeze which travell'd gently on
> O'er things which it had made, and is become
> A tempest, a redundant energy
> Vexing its own creation. 'Tis a power
> That does not come unrecogniz'd, a storm
> Which, breaking up a long-continued frost
> Brings with it vernal promises . . .
> The holy life of music and of verse . . . .
>
> To the open fields I told
> A prophecy: poetic numbers came
> Spontaneously, and cloth'd in priestly robe
> My spirit, thus singled out, as it might seem,
> For holy services. . . .

And a bit farther on comes the remaining element of the Romantic complex, the analogy between poetic mind and Aeolian harp:

> It was a splendid evening; and my soul
> Did once again make trial of the strength
> Restored to her afresh; nor did she want
> Eolian visitations; but the harp
> Was soon defrauded. . . .   (1805 ed., I, 1-105)

Later Wordsworth parallels Milton's reinvocations of his divine guides by recalling the 'animating breeze' which had made a 'glad preamble to this Verse,' and now, made visible by the tossing boughs of his favorite grove, once again

> Spreads through me a commotion like its own,
> Something that fits me for the Poet's task.   (VII, 1-56)

Wordsworth's account of his mental breakdown in *The Prelude* runs broadly parallel to the autobiographical passages in Coleridge's *Dejection*. And at the nadir of his apathy, when he felt 'utter loss of hope itself, And things to hope for,' Wordsworth signalized his recovery by addressing again the correspondent breeze:

> Not with these began
> Our Song, and not with these our Song must end:
> Ye motions of delight, that through the fields
> Stir gently, breezes and soft airs that breathe
> The breath of Paradise, and find your way
> To the recesses of the soul!   (XI, 7-12)

'Spring returns, I saw the Spring return'; and even the influence of Dorothy is apprehended as a revivifying spring breeze—

> Thy breath,
> Dear Sister, was a kind of gentler spring
> That went before my steps. (XII, 23-4; XIII, 244-6)

Time and again Wordsworth's most arcane statements similarly involve, as he put it in *The Excursion* (IV, 600), 'the breeze of nature stirring in his soul.'[7] In the *Intimations Ode*, 'The winds come to me from the fields of sleep'; and in *The Prelude*, the poet listens to sounds that

> make their dim abode in distant winds.
> Thence did I drink the visionary power;

or asserts that

> visionary power
> Attends the motions of the viewless winds,
> Embodied in the mystery of words.

The shell of the Arab, in Wordsworth's dream, which utters 'A loud prophetic blast of harmony,'

> Had voices more than all the winds, with power
> To exhilarate the spirit. . . . (1850 ed., II, 310-11;
> V, 595-7; 92-108)

Of the two 'spots of time'—the indelible memories by which his imagination, having, like Coleridge's, been 'impaired,' was 'nourished and invisible repaired'—one incorporated a woman with 'her garments vexed and tossed By the strong wind,' and the other 'the wind and sleety rain' evoking 'the bleak music of that old stone wall.' The result is that to this very time, whether in winter storm and rain or when the summer trees rock

> In a strong wind, some working of the spirit,
> Some inward agitations thence are brought. . . .
> (1850 ed., XII, 208-332)

Wordsworth read his completed masterpiece to Coleridge in 1807, five years after the writing of *Dejection*, and when Coleridge's spirits were at their lowest ebb. In his memorial on that occasion 'To William Wordsworth,' Coleridge duly noted that Wordsworth had described the quickening effect within his mind of the springtime wind: of 'vital breathings secret as the soul of vernal growth.' Then, as he listened to those passages in which Wordsworth expressed his love and hope for Coleridge himself, suddenly the poet's solemn voice seized upon his friend as though it were itself a great wind which, like the literal storm in *Dejection*, fanned his torpid spirit, 'whose hope had seem'd to die,' into a momentary and painful rebirth. The episode is one of the most moving in literature.

> The storm
> Scatter'd and whirl'd me, till my thoughts became
> A bodily tumult. . . . .
> Ah! as I listened with a heart forlorn,
> The pulses of my being beat anew:
> And even as Life returns upon the drowned,
> Life's joy rekindling roused a throng of pains—
> Keen pangs of Love, awakening as a babe
> Turbulent, with an outcry in the heart. . . .[8]

It is easy to multiply similar quotations, from these and other Romantic writers. Childe Harold, for example, found his spirit participating in the violence of an Alpine tempest, and drew a parallel with the violent explosion of his mind in poetry (Canto III, xcii–vii). And while De Quincey, a child of six, stood secretly and alone by the deathbed of a beloved sister, 'a solemn wind began to blow'; as his 'ear caught this vast Aeolian intonation' and his eye turned from 'the golden fulness of life' outdoors in the midsummer noon to settle 'upon the frost which overspread my sister's face, instantly a trance fell upon me. . . . I, in spirit, rose as if on billows. . . .' [9]

One poet, the most visionary and vatic of all these, demands special attention. Shelley's best known poem is addressed directly to the wind, in the form of a sustained invocation and petition. In the opening stanzas the Wild West Wind is at once destroyer and preserver because in the autumn it tears down the dead leaves and the seeds, but only so that in a later season another west wind—'thine azure sister of the spring'— may blow the clarion of resurrection, revive the seeds, and call out the buds to feed, like flocks of sheep, on the moving air, the wind itself. In the last stanza Shelley, like Coleridge in *Dejection*, cries out to the wind, in the autumn of his spirit, to blow through him as through a wind-harp— 'Make me thy lyre, even as the forest is'—and to drive the withered leaves of his dead thoughts over the universe 'to quicken a new birth.' And in the coda, to the blast of the wind sounding this time the apocalyptic trumpet of the general destruction and resurrection, the immense analogy is consummated between the effect of the wind on the unawakened earth, the singer's inspiration to poetry and prophecy, and the springtime of the human spirit everywhere.

> Be thou, Spirit fierce,
> My spirit! Be thou me, impetuous one! . . .
> Be through my lips to unawakened earth
> The trumpet of a prophecy! O, Wind,
> If Winter comes, can Spring be far behind?

Elsewhere the wind served Shelley repeatedly as a stimulus and symbol of inspiration, in his prose essays as well as his verse. *Alastor* opens with an invocation to the 'Mother of this unfathomable world!'

> Serenely now
> And moveless, as a long-forgotten lyre. . .
> I wait thy breath, Great Parent, that my strain
> May modulate with murmurs of the air. . . .[10]

Shelley's use of the wind in *Adonais* is of particular interest. This poem follows the classic elegiac pattern—consonant also with the evolution of earlier Romantic poems of dejection—from despair to consolation; although Shelley's consolation involves a death wish:

> Die,
> If thou wouldst be with that which thou dost seek! . . .
> Why linger, why turn back, why shrink, my Heart?

The conclusion, however, is astonishing. Most of these poems begin with a literal wind which transforms itself into the metaphorical wind of inspiration. Shelley reverses the sequence. At the end of *Adonais* the inspiration he had evoked 'in song' (that is, in his *Ode to the West Wind*) actually descends upon him; and what he feels is a tangible breath which rises to the violence of a literal storm of wind:

> The breath whose might I have invoked in song
> Descends on me; my spirit's bark is driven,
> Far from the shore, far from the trembling throng
> Whose sails were never to the tempest given;
> The massy earth and spherèd skies are riven!
> I am borne darkly, fearfully, afar . . . .[11]

II

Taken singly the symbolic equations between breeze, breath, and soul, respiration and inspiration, the reanimation of nature and of the spirit, are not peculiarly Romantic, nor in any way recent. All are older than recorded history; they are inherent in the constitution of ancient languages, are widely current in myth and folklore, and make up some of the great commonplaces of our religious tradition.

When Shelley, for example, made the West Wind the breath of autumn's being and a spirit, which became his breath and his spirit and blew, through him, the trumpet prophesying a universal resurrection, he may seem radically innovative. But from a philological point of view Shelley was reactionary; he merely revived and exploited the ancient undivided meanings of these words. For the Latin *spiritus* signified wind and breath, as well as soul. So did the Latin *anima*, and the Greek *pneuma*, the Hebrew *ruach*, the Sanskrit *atman*, as well as the equivalent words in Arabic, Japanese, and many other languages, some of them totally unrelated. In myth and religion, moreover, wind and breath often play an essential part in the creation both of the universe and of man.

44

In the beginning the spirit, or breath, or wind (*ruach*) of God moved upon the face of the waters; and after forming man, God 'breathed into his nostrils the breath of life; and man became a living soul.' Even in the Old Testament breath and wind were given the added power of renewing life after death, as in Ezekiel 37:9: 'Prophesy, son of man, and say to the wind . . . "Come from the four winds, O breath, and breathe upon these slain, that they may live." ' Similarly Jesus said (John 3:7–8): 'Marvel not that I said unto thee, Ye must be born again. The wind bloweth where it listeth . . . so is every one that is born of the Spirit.' But God's breath in the Bible could also be a destroying storm (as in I Kings 19:11; Ezekiel 13:13), symbolizing the explosion of God's wrath as well as the gift of life or grace. In parallel fashion the Wind Gods of Greek and Roman myth were regarded as destructive, requiring propitiation; but they also—especially the West Wind, 'Zephyrus,' or 'Favonius'—were held to possess an animating or impregnating power, a fact noted by medieval encyclopedists, and by Chaucer:

> Whan Zephyrus eek with his swete breeth
> Inspired hath in every holt and heeth
> The tendre croppes. . . .

Shelley thus had ample precedent, pagan and Christian, for his West Wind, both breath and spirit, destroyer as well as preserver, which is equally the revitalizing Zephyrus of the Romans and the trumpet blast of the Book of Revelation, announcing the simultaneous destruction of the present world and a new life in a world recreated. The additional connection between wind and inspiration is, of course, implicit in the latter term, for 'to inspire' once meant 'to blow or breathe into,' and when a man received the divine 'afflatus' he received, literally, the breath or wind of a god or muse. According to classical belief, this supernatural breath stimulated the visionary utterances of religious oracles and prophetic poets. Eliphaz the Temanite, in the Book of Job (4:13–16), expressed a similar view: 'In thoughts from the visions of the night . . . a spirit [or breeze: *ruach*] passed before my face. . . . There was silence, and I heard a voice.' And on the day of Pentecost, in the Acts of the New Testament (2:1–4), 'suddenly there came a sound from heaven as of a rushing mighty wind. . . . And they were all filled with the Holy Ghost, and began to speak with other tongues, as the Spirit gave them utterance.'

One other historical item is pertinent. The Stoic concept of the World Soul—of the Pneuma, or Spiritus Sacer, or Anima Mundi—originally involved, in the literal sense of these names, the concept of a kind of breath, a divine gas, which infuses the material world and constitutes also the individual human psyche. The poet Lucan said that Apollo founded the Delphic oracle at a huge chasm where 'the earth breathed forth divine truth, and . . . gave out a wind that spoke'; and he suggested that the Pythian priestess stationed there is inspired by inhaling the very breath of the World Soul.[12] It is noteworthy that the familiar Romantic Soul of Nature, or Spirit of the Universe, sometimes retained its primitive airy essence, homogeneous with the soul of man, as well as its power of quasi-literal inspiration. In *The Eolian Harp* Coleridge speculated that all animated nature may be but organic wind harps, diversely framed, through which sweeps 'one intellectual breeze, At once the Soul of each, and God of all.' Wordsworth in *The Prelude* invoked the 'Wisdom,' 'Spirit,' and 'Soul' of the Universe,

> That givest to forms and images a breath
> And everlasting motion,

and also the 'Soul of things,' that in its love renews

> Those naked feelings, which, when thou woulds't form
> A living thing, thou sendest like a breeze
> Into its infant being![13]

Shelley called upon the West Wind, the 'breath of Autumn's being,' to blow through him: 'Be thou, spirit fierce, My spirit!' The Soul of the worlds, Emerson later declared in 'The Over-Soul,' 'can inspire whom it will, and behold! their speech shall by lyrical and sweet, and universal as the rising of the wind.'

III

In the Biblical commentaries of the Church Fathers it was commonly recognized that the moving air, the breath of the Lord, the Holy Spirit, the life and spiritual rebirth of man, and the inspiration of the Prophets in the Old and New Testaments were connected, if not literally, then allegorically, or by a system of correspondence, or by some other exegetical relation. Before the end of the fourth century, Saint Augustine had imported the spiritual breeze into the context of autobiography that is common to all the Romantic writings I have cited. In the central passage of his *Confessions* (VIII, xi–xii), Augustine described his tortured state as he hesitated at the brink of conversion, 'soul-sick . . . and tormented,' as he said, 'hesitating to die to death and live to life.' Then one day he retired into the garden next his lodging, and 'when a deep consideration had from the secret bottom of my soul drawn together and heaped up all my misery in my heart, there arose a mighty wind, bringing a mighty shower of tears'; with the result that 'by a light as it were of serenity infused into my heart, all the darkness of doubt vanished away.'

Even the typical procedure in Romantic wind-poems of beginning with the description of a natural scene and then moving to inner correspondences had precedents in prose and verse. During the Middle Ages the mode of self-inquisition and spiritual inventory, of which Augustine's *Confessions* became a prime exemplar, led to the identification of a standard condition of apathy and spiritual torpor called 'acedia,' or 'aridity,' or 'interior desolation,' closely related, according to Cassian, to another state of the soul called 'dejection' (*tristitia*).[14] The descriptions of this interior condition and of its relief were sometimes couched in natural and seasonal metaphors: winter, drought, and desert, as against spring, the coming of rain, and the burgeoning plant or garden. Coleridge echoed the technical language of theology when, in a letter of March 25, 1801 which was a prose rehearsal for *Dejection*, he described his 'intellectual *exsiccation*,' a state in which 'the Poet is dead in me,' his imagination 'lies, like a Cold Snuff on the circular Rim of a Brass Candle-stick,' and he remains 'squat and square on the earth amid the hurricane.'[15]

In the later Renaissance the alternation of aridity and freshness, in which spiritual and imaginative death and rebirth are equated with aspects of the natural scene, became a frequent topic in the meditations of the religious poets. An instance in George Herbert is the pair of poems called *Employment*, which inspired Coleridge's *Work Without Hope*; another is *The Flower*, also a favorite of Coleridge, in which we find a complex interplay between the death-in-life and revival of the soul, of the poetic faculty, and of a perennial plant.

> How fresh, O Lord, how sweet and clean
> Are thy returns! Ev'n as the flowers in spring,
>   To which, besides their own demean,
> The late-past frosts tributes of pleasure bring. . . .
>
>   And now in age I bud again,
> After so many deaths I live and write;
>   I once more smell the dew and rain,

And relish versing. O my only light,
        It cannot be
        That I am he
    On whom thy tempests fell all night.

Henry Vaughan at times approximates still more closely the familiar
Romantic pattern of inner depression and revival, paralleled to changes
in the landscape in diverse weathers and seasons. And the role of the
wind is made explicit in poems such as *The Storm* and *Mount of Olives*
(2), but above all in *Regeneration*. 'One day,' he says in that poem, 'I
stole abroad.' 'It was high spring. . . . Yet was it frost within.' After
traversing a spiritual landscape and toiling up a purgatorial mountain,
he entered a flowery grove reminiscent of several earlier pleasances, all
of them wind-blown: Dante's Earthly Paradise, the garden which had
been the setting of Augustine's conversion, and that favorite medieval
symbol, the *hortus conclusus,* the closed garden, of the Song of Songs: [16]

    Here musing long, I heard
        A rushing wind
    Which still increased, but whence it stirred
        Nowhere I could not find. . . .

    But while I list'ning sought
        My mind to ease
    By knowing where 'twas, or where not,
        It whispered: Where I please.

    Lord, then said I, on me one breath,
    And let me die before my death!

    The Romantic wind, then, is remote in kind from the pleasingly
horrific storm dear to eighteenth-century connoisseurs of the natural
sublime; and the confessional lyrics of dejection and recovery in which
this wind plays its part are not (as common report would have it) in the
tradition of the eighteenth-century poems of melancholy and spleen.
These lyrics are rather secularized versions of an older devotional poetry,
employed in the examination of the soul's condition as it approaches
and retreats from God. Secularized—yet the religious element remains
as at least a formal parallel, or a verbal or rhetorical echo. Coleridge's
finest odes, including *Dejection* and *To William Wordsworth,* use theological language and end in the cadence of a prayer. Wordsworth's poetic
meditations commonly involve a presence whose dwelling is the light of

setting suns. And even the pagan Shelley's *Ode to the West Wind* is a formal orison addressed to the Spirit and Breath of Autumn's Being.

IV

And now the question: What are we to make of the phenomenon of the correspondent breeze in Romantic poetry? These days the answer seems obvious enough, and it may have occasioned surprise that I have so long resisted calling the wind an 'archetypal image.' I should not hesitate to use so convenient a term, if it were merely a neutral way of identifying a persistent material symbol for a psychological condition. In the context of present critical theory, however, the term 'archetypal' commits the user to implications which are equally unnecessary and undesirable. For example, in order to explain the origin and currency of the correspondent wind it would seem adequate to point to the inescapable conditions of the human endowment and of its physical milieu. That breath and wind are both instances of air in motion, and that breathing is a sign of life and its cessation of death, are matters evident to casual observation, as are the alternations of inhalation and exhalation, despair and elation, imaginative energy and torpor, birth and death, in the constant environmental rhythms of calm and storm, drought and rain, winter and spring. If a connection between a universal inner experience and an omnipresent outer analogue has been made once, it will be made again, and may readily become a commonplace of oral and written tradition; there is no rational need to assume, as Jung does, that after leaving its mark on the nervous system the image goes underground, to emerge sporadically from the racial unconscious. But of course if we neutralize the archetype by eliminating dark allusions to 'primordial images,' or 'the racial memory,' or 'timeless depths,' archetypal criticism is drained of the mystique or pathos which is an important condition of its present vogue.

For literary criticism, moreover, the ultimate criterion is not whether a doctrine is a justifiable psychological hypothesis, but what it does when put to work interpreting a text. And from this point of view standard archetypal criticism can be charged with blurring, if it does not destroy, the properties of the literary products it undertakes to explicate. A mode of reading that persists in looking through the literal, particular, and artful qualities of a poem in order to discover a more important ulterior pattern of primitive, general, and unintended mean-

49

ings eliminates its individuality, and threatens to nullify even its status as a work of art. For the result of such reading is to collapse the rich diversity of individual works into one, or into a very limited number, of archetypal patterns, which any one poem shares not only with other poems, but with such unartful phenomena as myth, dreams, and the fantasies of psychosis.

Maud Bodkin's influential book, *Archetypal Patterns in Poetry*, intelligent and extremely suggestive though it is, provides a radical illustration of this process. Miss Bodkin begins her study by considering the significance of the wind in Coleridge's *Ancient Mariner*, and of the contrast between the becalmed ship and, after the blessing of the water snakes, the storm which drives the ship into violent motion. In the Romantic poems I have discussed, the rising wind was explicitly paralleled to a change in the inner state of the lyric speaker. *The Ancient Mariner*, on the other hand, is explicitly a narrative about the actions and sufferings of an unfortunate sailor; yet Miss Bodkin has no hesitation in reading the change from calm to storm as a symbolic projection—by the author—of the mental states that Jung calls 'progression and regression.' This psychic sequence constitutes the 'Rebirth archetype,' which is also manifested by the vegetation god of ritual and myth, is echoed in the resurrection of Christ, reappears in dreams, and in literature constitutes the basic pattern, among other works, of *Oedipus, Hamlet*, the Book of Jonah, the *Aeneid*, the *Divine Comedy, Paradise Lost, Kubla Khan*, and *Women in Love*. Once unleashed, indeed, the archetype proves insatiable, and goes on to assimilate even subhuman phenomena: Miss Bodkin (page 75) detects the characteristic pattern of the Night Journey and Rebirth in the behavior of Wolfgang Köhler's experimental apes, who passed through a period of baffled bewilderment before the flash of insight which enabled them to reach their banana.

These are astonishing equations, but the logical procedure by which they were achieved is simple enough. It consists in treating loose analogy as though it were identity. This strategy, to be sure, has a singular virtue; it cannot fail. Only leave out enough of the qualities that make a poem, or any complex experience, distinctive, and it can be reduced to an abstract pattern—almost any abstract pattern, including, if that is our inclination, the pattern of the vegetational cycle of death and rebirth. But by what a prodigious abstraction of everything that matters is a literary ballad, *The Ancient Mariner*, shown to be identical in ultimate significance with tragedies, epics, novels, and lyrics, together with the basic formulae of myth and religion!

A procedure which ingeniously contrives to reduce all—or at least a great many—serious poems to variations upon a timeless theme is not much to the purpose of the literary critic, whose chief concern is with the particularity of a work; nor is it more useful to the literary historian, despite his greater interest in establishing literary types and the general qualities of a literary period. For example, we know that the use of the wind in Romantic poetry had ample precedent in myth, religion, and the poetry of religious meditation. Yet the correspondent breeze, like the guilt-haunted wanderer and the Promethean or Satanic figure of the heroic rebel, can justly be identified as a distinctively Romantic image, or icon. For one thing, there is no precedent for the way in which the symbolic wind was called upon by poet after poet, in poem after poem, all within the first few decades of the nineteenth century. For another, the fact that they explored the literary possibilities of myth and primitive thinking, and played secular variations on ancient devotional patterns, is itself characteristic of the Romantic poets. But above all, these writers exploited attributes of the wind which rendered it peculiarly apt for the philosophical, political, and aesthetic preoccupations of the age.

Thus Wordsworth's are, specifically, 'viewless winds,' which are 'unseen though not inaudible,' [17] and Shelley's wind is an 'unseen presence.' When Blake denounced 'Single vision and Newton's sleep,' and Coleridge warned repeatedly against 'the despotism of the eye,' and Wordsworth, recalling his joy 'before the winds, And roaring waters, and in lights and shades,' decried the 'bodily eye 'as 'the most despotic of our senses,' all attributed to an obsession with what is materially visible the diverse shortcomings of the eighteenth century, from its sensationist philosophy to its theory and practice of the arts.[18] The wind, as an invisible power known only by its effects, had an even greater part to play than water, light, and clouds in the Romantic revolt against the world-view of the Enlightenment. In addition, the moving air lent itself pre-eminently to the aim of tying man back into the environment from which, Wordsworth and Coleridge felt, he had been divorced by post-Cartesian dualism and mechanism. For not only are nature's breezes the analogue of human respiration; they are themselves inhaled into the body and assimilated to its substance—the 'breezes and soft airs,' as Wordsworth said, 'find [their] way To the recesses of the soul,' and so fuse materially, as well as metaphorically, the 'soul' of man with the 'spirit' of nature. Lastly, the Romantic wind is typically a wild wind and a free one—Shelley's 'thou uncontrollable'—which, even when gentle, holds the threat of destructive violence. Wordsworth's 'gentle breeze,' greeted as messenger and friend by a captive 'coming from a house Of bondage, from yon City's walls set free,' soon, like the breeze in Coleridge's *Dejection,* mounts to 'a tempest. . . . Vexing its own creation.' These traits made the windstorm, as it had been earlier, a ready counterpart for the prophetic furor of the inspired poet. But they also rendered it a most eligible model for Romantic activism, as well as an emblem of the free Romantic spirit; and in an era obsessed with the fact and idea of revolution, they sanctioned a parallel, manifest in Shelley, with a purifying revolutionary violence which destroys in order to preserve.[19]

The Romantic ideal, it should be added, is that of a controlled violence, of a self-ordering impetus of passion, which Coleridge described in *To Matilda Betham,* and once again by analogy to the wind:

> Poetic feelings, like the stretching boughs
> Of mighty oaks, pay homage to the gales,
> Toss in the strong winds, drive before the gust,
> Themselves one giddy storm of fluttering leaves;
> Yet, all the while self-limited, remain
> Equally near the fixed and solid trunk
> Of Truth and Nature in the howling storm,
> As in the calm that stills the aspen grove.

This sovereign order in rage is, I think, characteristic of the longer Romantic lyric at its best. The tide of the systematic derogation of that achievement seems to be receding, but it may still be worth registering the judgment that the Romantic lyric at its best is equal to the greatest.

NOTES

1. 'Essay on the Poetical Works of Mr. Wordsworth,' *The Works of Sir Henry Taylor* (London, 1878), V, 1–4.
2. Coleridge, *Biographia Literaria,* ed. John Shawcross (Oxford, 1907), I, 5.
3. *A Defence of Poetry, Shelley's Literary and Philosophical Criticism,* ed. John Shawcross (London, 1909), p. 121.
4. Letters of 18 Oct. and 1 Nov. 1800, *Collected Letters,* ed. E. L. Griggs (Oxford, 1956), I, 638, 643. Genius, Coleridge wrote in his Notebook in 1806, may 'lie hid as beneath embers, till some sudden and awakening Gust

of regenerating Grace. . .rekindles and reveals it anew.' (Cited by George Whalley, *Coleridge and Sara Hutchinson*, London, 1955, p. 128).

5. 14 Jan. 1803, *Collected Letters*, II, 916. On October 20 of that year Coleridge wrote in his Notebook: 'Storm all night—the wind scourging and lashing the rain. . . I, half-dozing, list'ning to the same, not without solicitations of the poetic Feeling. . . .' (*The Notebooks of S. T. Coleridge*, ed. Kathleen Coburn, New York, 1957, I, Entry 1577).

6. 29 Nov. 1805, *The Early Letters of Wm. and Dorothy Wordsworth*, ed. E. de Selincourt (Oxford, 1935), I, 547.

7. In his 'Prospectus' for *The Recluse*, Wordsworth wrote (*Poetical Works*, ed. E. de Selincourt and Helen Darlinshire, Oxford, 1949, V, 3):

> To these emotions, whencesoe'er they come,
> Whether from breath of outward circumstance,
> Or from the soul—an impulse to herself—
> I would give utterance in numerous verse.

8. I have inserted a passage from MS W into the standard version from *Sybelline Leaves*; see *The Complete Poetical Works of Samuel Taylor Coleridge*, ed. E. H. Coleridge (Oxford, 1912), I, 403–407.

9. *Autobiographic Sketches*, Chap. I: 'The Affliction of Childhood.'

10. *Alastor*, 41–6. In *A Defence of Poetry*, 'the mind in creation is as a fading coal, which some invisible influence, like an inconstant wind, wakens to transitory brightness.'

11. Cf. Dante's *Paradiso* II, 7ff.:

> L'acqua ch'io prendo già mai non si corse;
> Minerva spira, e conducemi Apollo.

Shelley's passage has a weak counterpart in the conclusion to Tennyson's *Locksley Hall*, where the abrupt turn from despair to hope, accompanied by the welling of 'ancient founts of inspiration,' materializes in a sudden outer storm:

> Let it fall on Locksley Hall, with rain or hail, or fire or snow;
> For the mighty wind arises, roaring seaward, and I go.

Valery's *Cimetière Marin* concludes with a similar turn:

> Le vent se lève. Il faut tenter de vivre.

12. *The Civil War*, V. 82–101. In a draft of *Epipsychidion* Shelley described 'a Power' in mortal hearts,

> A Pythian exhalation, which inspires
> Love, only love—a wind which o'er the wires
> Of the soul's giant harp. . .

(*The Complete Poetical Works*, ed. Thomas Hutchinson, London, 1934, p. 429).

13. 1805 ed., I, 428–31; and MS fragment in de Selincourt, *The Prelude* (Oxford, 1950), p. 508.

14. Cassian, *The Institutes of the Coenobia*, Books IX and X. And see Sister Mary Madeleva, *Pearl: A Study in Spiritual Dryness* (New York, 1925).

15. *Collected Letters*, II, 713–14; cf. I, 470–1 (12 Mar. 1799), describing his imagination as 'flat and powerless,' and his inner state 'as if the *organs* of Life had been dried up; as if only simple BEING remained, blind and stagnant!'

16. For the winds in these gardens see Dante's *Purgatorio*, XXVIII, 7–21,

103–114; Augustine, *Confessions*, cited above; Song of Solomon 4: 12–16.

17. See above, and *The Prelude*, ed. de Selincourt, p. 3n.

18. Blake, letter to Thomas Butts, 22 Nov. 1802; Coleridge, *Biographia Literaria*, I, 74, and *Coleridge on Logic and Learning*, ed. Alice Snyder (New Haven, 1929), p. 126; Wordsworth, *The Prelude* (1850 ed.), XII, 93–131.

19. See also Northrop Frye's comment on Blake's 'the wind of Beulah that unroots the rocks and hills' as an analogue both of inspiration and destruction, in 'Notes for a Commentary on Milton,' *The Divine Vision*, ed. Vivian de S. Pinto (London, 1957), p. 125.

NORTHROP FRYE

Blake After Two Centuries

THE VALUE of centenaries and similar observances is that they call attention, not simply to great men, but to what we do with our great men. The anniversary punctuates, so to speak, the scholarly and critical absorption of its subject into society. From this point of view, a centenary date might well be more impressive for those interested in William Blake than his birth on November 28, 1757. The year 1857 would bring us to a transitional point in the life of Alexander Gilchrist, who had recently got a life of Etty off his hands, married, moved to Chelsea to be near his idol Carlyle, was busy winding up some family business, and was preparing to start in earnest on *The Life of William Blake, Pictor Ignotus*. This last was no empty phrase. Scattered notices of Blake had appeared in collections of artists' biographies, but nothing like a full volume had been devoted to Blake in the thirty years since his death. Blake was fortunate in his first posthumous group of admirers. Gilchrist was a remarkable person, his wife Anne equally so, and Rossetti and Swinburne, if not exactly emancipated spirits, were at least sufficiently free of the more lethal Victorian virtues to admire Blake without undue inhibitions. They make an instructive contrast to the Ruskin who cut up one of the two coloured copies of *Jerusalem*, the anonymous worthy who apparently destroyed the great 'Vision of the Last Judgement,' and the member of the Linnell family who erased the genitalia from the drawings on the *Four Zoas* manuscript.

Gilchrist died in 1861 with his masterpiece unfinished: Anne Gilchrist brought it out in 1863 in two volumes. The first volume was Gilchrist's

From the *University of Toronto Quarterly*, XXVII (Oct. 1957), pp. 10–21.
Reprinted by permission of the publisher and author.

55

biography: no better biography has been written since, for all our advance in understanding. The main part of the second volume was Rossetti's edition of the lyrics, where Blake, however expurgated and improved in his metres, still did achieve something like a representative showing as a poet. Swinburne's critical essay appeared in 1868, and soon afterwards there began, a slow trickle at first, then a flood still in full spate, of critical studies, biographies, editions, illustrated editions, collections of paintings and engravings, handbooks, catalogues, appreciations, research articles, chapters in other books, and specialized studies pouring out of the presses of at least twenty countries. Max Beerbohm's Enoch Soames sold his soul to the devil in exchange for a glance at the future British Museum catalogue of critical work on him, only to discover that posterity took the same view of him that his contemporaries had done. Such irony is not for Blake, who in his lifetime was something of an Enoch Soames too, but an Enoch Soames who was right.

Much more than a Cinderella success story is involved here. In her little British Council bibliography, Miss Kathleen Raine remarks on the spontaneous personal affection shown in the public response to the recent discovery of a large and rather confused allegorical picture by Blake in a house in Devon. A new Michelangelo would have been more important, but it would not have aroused that specific reaction of affectionate pride. Blake's deep love of England is clearly not an unrequited love, nor is the sense that he is one of us confined to Englishmen. People get attracted to him through feeling that he is for them a personal discovery and something of a private possession. I constantly hear of doctors, housewives, clergymen, teachers, manual workers, shopkeepers, who are, in the most frequent phrase used, 'frightfully keen on Blake,' who have bought every book on him they could afford, and kept him around like an amiable household god. I have taught Blake to Jesuits and I have taught him to Communist organizers; I have taught him to deans of women and I have taught him to ferocious young poets of unpredictable rhythms and unprintable (or at least privately printed) diction. His admirers have nothing in common except the feeling that Blake says something to them that no one else can say: that whatever their standards and values may be, Blake has the charity to include them, not as part of a general principle of benevolence, which Blake himself would have despised, but uniquely as individuals.

Undergraduates, too, have fewer barriers against Blake than against most poets: besides the absence of unfamiliar conventions or a special poetic language, he lacks the two qualities that undergraduates are most afraid of, sentimentality and irony. Again, some poets travel better than others, and just as Byron and Poe in the nineteenth century proved to be more readily exportable than Wordsworth or Hawthorne, so in the twentieth century Blake seems the easiest of all our poets to export to India or Japan. He can hardly ever lack admirers among the fellow countrymen of Rouault and of Gérard de Nerval, or of Hölderlin and of Novalis. Within ninety years after the first critical study of him was published, Blake appears to be headed for what at one time seemed his least likely fate: a genuine, permanent, and international popularity.

This popularity has been achieved in spite of Blake's reputation for being difficult and esoteric, someone not to be understood without pre-liminary study of a dozen occult systems of thought and several thou-sand pages of commentary. I have written one of the thickest of the com-mentaries myself, and I certainly meant all I said, but I quite realize how often the popular estimate of Blake is sounder in perspective than the scholarly one. Scholars will assert that the famous 'Jerusalem' hymn is crypto-Anglo-Israelitism or what not; but when it was sung in front of Transport House at the Labour victory of 1945 the singers showed that they understood it far better than such scholars did. Scholars will assert that the question in *The Tyger,* 'Did he who made the lamb make thee?' is to be answered with a confident yes or no: yes if Blake is be-lieved to be a pantheist, no if he is believed to be a Gnostic. Most of those who love the poem are content to leave it a question, and they are right. 'You say,' wrote Blake to the Rev. Dr. Trusler, author of *The Way to be Rich and Respectable,* 'that I want somebody to Elucidate my Ideas. But you ought to know that What is Grand is necessarily obscure to Weak men. That which can be made Explicit to the Idiot is not worth my care.' Having thus brought his correspondent into focus, he goes on: 'But I am happy to find a Great Majority of Fellow Mortals who can Elucidate My Visions, & Particularly they have been Elucidated by Children, who have taken a greater delight in contemplating my Pictures than I even hoped.' Children have always found Blake easier than the Truslers have done.

II

Clearly, if Blake can be popular we need a new definition of popu-larity. Several very different things are included under the term popular, and the simple conception 'What the public wants' will not do. Best-seller popularity depends more on news value than on any aesthetic qualities, whether good or bad. But there is another sense in which the term popular may be used, as referring to the art which affords a key to imaginative experience for the untrained. The centre of gravity of popular fiction in this sense is the folk tale, and in American culture, for instance, it would be represented by *Huckleberry Finn, Rip van Winkle*, some tales of Poe, of Uncle Remus, and the various cycles of native humour like the Western tall tale. Much that is popular even in this context is still rubbish, and some of it may be quite unpopular in the best-seller meaning of the word. The popular in the second sense is the contemporary primitive, and it tends to become primitive with the passing of time. Such primitive and popular elements recur in great art, even very difficult and complex art. One thinks of Shakespeare's late romances, with their archaic nature myths and their improbable co-incidences turning up 'like an old tale.' One thinks more particularly of the Bible, which is one long folk tale from beginning to end, and the most primitive and popular book in the world.

The two senses of popular seem to be, up to a point, connected with the distinction of content and form. 'What the public wants,' as the first word suggests, relates primarily to content: certain conventional choices of subject—domestic, sentimental, heroic, sexually provocative—come into vogue by turns. Certain story types, on the other hand, which remain fairly constant from ancient myth to contemporary comic strip, are isolated in the art which is popular in the second sense. Like the corresponding primitive and popular forms in the plastic arts, they are abstract and stylized, and have a curiously archaic look about them whenever they appear. The generic term for such story types is myth, because myths are stories about divine beings which are abstract and stylized stories in the sense that they are unaffected by canons of realism or probability.

Blake's only fictions are in his Prophetic Books, and although they are certainly mythical enough, there are other aspects of popular literature in its formal sense more obviously relevant to him. The conceptual element in poetry is also a part of its content, and conceptual thinking in poetry is more or less assimilated to another kind of thinking which organizes the poetic structure. The unit of this formally poetic thinking is the metaphor, and the metaphor is inherently illogical, an identification of two or more things which could never be identified except by a lunatic, a lover, or a poet—one may perhaps add an extremely primitive

58

savage. We are educated in conceptual thinking, and so usually find poetry which comes to terms with it easier to read, like Wordsworth's. Poetry which is popular in the sense of having a vogue is popular by reason of having such a conceptual content: it talks about the Deity in the eighteenth century, or Duty in the nineteenth, or it speaks to the eternal bourgeois in the heart of man, like Kipling's *If*, Longfellow's *Psalm of Life*, or Burns's *A Man's a Man for a' that*. Poetry which concentrates on metaphor to the point of appearing to exclude conceptual thought altogether, like surrealist poetry, impresses most readers as wilfully crazy, or, if they are compelled to take it seriously, as incredibly difficult and esoteric.

Yet greater experience with literature soon shows that it is metaphor which is direct and primitive, and conceptual thought which is sophisticated. Hence there is a body of verse that can be called popular in the sense of providing the direct, primitive, metaphorical key to poetic experience for educated and uneducated alike. Most good teaching anthologies are largely composed of such verse, and in such anthologies the lyrics of Blake leap into the foreground with a vividness that almost exaggerates Blake's relative importance as a poet:

> O Rose, thou art sick!
> The invisible worm
> That flies in the night,
> In the howling storm,
>
> Has found out thy bed
> Of crimson joy,
> And his dark secret love
> Does thy life destroy.

I say exaggerates, because there are many fine poets who do not have this specific kind of directness. One may always meet a poem with a set of questions designed to avoid its impact: what does it mean; why is it considered a good poem; is it morally beneficial; does it say profound things about life, and so forth. But such a poem as *The Sick Rose* has a peculiar power of brushing them aside, of speaking with the unanswerable authority of poetry itself. Blake's lyrics, with many of those of Herrick, Burns, and Donne, the sonnets of Shakespeare, Wordsworth's Lucy poems, and a few of the great ballads, are popular poetry in the sense that they are a practically foolproof introduction to poetic experience.

Metaphor, then, is a formal principle of poetry, and myth of fiction.

We begin to see how Blake hangs together: his prophecies are so intensely mythical because his lyrics are so intensely metaphorical. At present his prophecies seem to have little to do with popular literature in any sense of the word, but opinion will have changed on this point long before the tercentenary rolls around. It will then be generally understood that just as Blake's lyrics are among the best possible introductions to poetic experience, so his prophecies are among the best possible introductions to the grammar and structure of literary mythology. His practice again is consistent with his theory, which lays an almost exclusive emphasis on the imagination or forming power. However, there comes a point at which our distinction of form and content breaks down, and we have to raise the question of what kind of content formal art has.

'The Nature of my Work is Visionary or Imaginative,' said Blake: 'it is an Endeavour to Restore what the Ancients call'd the Golden Age.' By vision he meant the view of the world, not as it might be, still less as it ordinarily appears, but as it really is when it is seen by human consciousness at its greatest height and intensity. It is the artist's business to attain this heightened or transfigured view of things, and show us what kind of world is actually in front of us, with all its glowing splendours and horrifying evils. It is only the direct, metaphorical, and mythical perceptions, which work without compromise with unimaginative notions of reality, that can clearly render the forms of such a world. Such psychological experiments as those recorded in Mr. Aldous Huxley's *The Doors of Perception* (the title of which comes from Blake, although taking mescalin is not precisely what Blake meant by 'cleansing' the doors of perception) seem to show that the formal principles of this heightened vision are constantly latent in the mind, which perhaps explains the communicability of such visions. For Blake, however, the Bible provides the key to the relation between the two worlds. The ordinary world is 'fallen,' the manifestation of man's own sin and ignorance; the true world is the apocalypse presented at the end of the Bible and the paradise presented at the beginning of it: the true city and garden that is man's home, and which all existing cities and gardens struggle to make manifest in the lower world.

The apocalypse of the Bible is a world in which all human forms are identified, as Blake says at the end of his *Jerusalem*. That is, all forms are identified as human. Cities and gardens, sun moon and stars, rivers and stones, trees and human bodies—all are equally alive, equally parts of the same infinite body which is at once the body of God and of risen man. In this world 'Each Identity is Eternal,' for 'In Eternity one Thing never Changes into another Thing.' It is a world of forms like Plato's except that in Blake these forms are images of pure being seen by a spiritual body, not ideas of pure essence seen by a soul, a conception which would rule out the artist as a revealer of reality. To Blake this vision of apocalypse and resurrection was the grammar of poetry and painting alike, and it was also the source of the formal principles of art. He lived in a way that brought him into the most constant contact with this world, for we notice that isolation, solitude, and a certain amount of mental stress or disturbance have a tendency to light up this vision in the mind. When Christopher Smart is shut into a madhouse with no company except his cat Jeffrey, the cat leaps into the same apocalyptic limelight as Blake's tiger:

> For he keeps the Lord's watch in the night against the adversary.
> For he counteracts the powers of darkness by his electrical skin and
>   glaring eyes. . .
> For he is of the tribe of Tiger.
> For the Cherub Cat is a term of the Angel Tiger . . .
> For by stroaking of him I have found out electricity.
> For I perceived God's light about him both wax and fire.
> For the electrical fire is the spiritual substance, which God sends from
>   heaven to sustain the bodies both of man and beast.

Similarly when John Clare is confined to an asylum and is in the depths of schizophrenia, the luminous fragility of Blake's *Book of Thel,* along with the glowing lights and gemmed trees of Mr. Huxley's adventures in heaven and hell, appear in his vision:

> The birds sing on the clouds in that eternal land,
> Jewels and siller are they a', and gouden is the sand.
> The sun is one vast world of fire that burneth a' to-day,
> And nights wi' hells of darkness for ever keeps away.
> And dearly I love the queen o' that bright land,
> The lily flowers o' woman that meeteth no decay.

Blake's attitude to art makes no psychological distinctions among the arts, and the same imagination that the poet uses appears in Blake's theory of painting as 'outline,' which again is an intense concentration on the formal principles of the art. The abstract school of painting today assumes that the formal principles of painting are quasi-geometrical, but Blake, with the faded white ghosts of eighteenth-century classicism in front of him, warned sharply against the preference of 'mathematic

61

form' to 'living form.' Blake despised everything that was amorphous
or vague in art: the imagination for him could express itself only as
rigorous and exactly ordered form. But by living form he meant a
vitalized classicism, where the outline is held in the tight grip of imaginative intensity, a classicism that would have more in common with Van
Gogh than with Flaxman or David. Blake's painting, though strongly
formalized, is not abstract in tendency, but what one might call hieroglyphic in tendency. It presents the same world that his poetry presents;
yet (except in lapses) it is not literary painting. The tense stylized
figures of the Byzantines with their staring eyes and weightless bodies;
mediaeval primitives with their glittering gold haloes and childlike sense
of primary colour; Eastern 'mandalas' that communicate the sense of
powerful spiritual discipline in repose; the calligraphic distortions of
Klee: these all belong in different ways to the hieroglyphic tradition in
painting, and are allied to the vision that Blake evolved from his study
of Renaissance prints.

III

The conception of formally popular art which underlies the present
argument is still an unexplored subject in criticism, and many aspects
of it can be only suggested here. It has been neglected partly because the
original proponents of it, notably Herder, confused it by mixing it up
with a pseudo-historical myth of the Golden Age family. Formally
popular art was supposed to have been derived from a 'folk' whose art
was rural and spontaneous and communal and unspecialized and a
number of other things that no art can be. When we remove this notion
of a 'folk,' we are left with a third conception of popular art as the art
which is central to a specific cultural tradition. There is no question here
of looking for *the* centre or isolating an imaginary essence of a tradition,
but only of seeing what some of its prevailing and recurrent rhythms
have been. The sources of a cultural tradition are, of course, its religious
and social context as well as its own earlier products. In English culture
we notice at once a strong and constant affinity with art which is popular
in the formal sense, in striking contrast to, say, French culture, which
has much more the character of something deliberately imposed.

One characteristic of the English tradition has obviously been affected
by Protestantism. This is the tendency to anchor the apocalyptic vision
in a direct individual experience, as the product, not of sacramental

discipline, but of imaginative experiment. The experience may be as forced as *Grace Abounding* or as relaxed as Keats's speculations about a vale of soul-making, but it tends to be autonomous, to make the experience its own authority. The 1611 Bible is not a 'monument of English prose,' but the exact opposite of what a monument is: it is a translation with a unique power of making the Bible a personal possession of its reader, and to this its enormous popularity as well as its importance in English culture is due. It has also fostered, of course, the kind of Biblical culture that has made *The Pilgrim's Progress* one of the most popular books in the language, that has given *Paradise Lost* its central place in English literature, and that has instigated some very inadequate performances of Handel's *Messiah* (a work with a unique power of catching this quality of direct vision in music) in Midland towns. Such Biblical culture, absorbed as part of a poet's own imaginative experience, was inspiring visions of revelation and resurrection at least as early as the *Pearl* poet, and had lost nothing of its intensity when Dylan Thomas was shattering the sedate trumpet of the BBC with the same tones:

> Though they be mad and dead as nails,
> Heads of the characters hammer through daisies;
> Break in the sun till the sun breaks down,
> And death shall have no dominion.

Blake, who was brought up on the Bible and on Milton, is unusually close to this simple and naïve Biblism even for an English poet. The occult and esoteric elements in his thought have been grossly exaggerated by critics who, as Johnson said of Hume, have not read the New Testament with attention. What is so obviously true of most of his paintings is true also of his poetry: it is the work of a man whose Bible was his textbook. The prophecies recreate the Bible in English symbolism, just as the 1611 translation recreates it in the English language, and, no less than *Paradise Lost* or *The Pilgrim's Progress,* they record a direct search for the New Jerusalem which exists here and now in England's green and pleasant land.

A second characteristic of the English tradition is of social origin, and is derived from an apparently permanent English tendency to political resistance. This tendency has taken different forms in different ages—Roundhead, Whig, radical, liberal, socialist—but is so constant that it may be actually a kind of anarchism, or what in a play of Bernard Shaw's is called an obstinate refusal to be governed at all. From Milton's defence of the liberty of prophesying to Mill's defence of the right to be eccentric, it is pervaded by a sense that the final cause of society is the free individual. This sense distinguishes it sharply from such revolutionary traditions as those of America or Russia, where a fundamental social pattern is established *a priori* by the revolution, and other patterns are rejected as un-American or counter-revolutionary.

In Blake's political outlook one finds a radicalism of a common English type, which includes a strong individual protest against all institutional radicalism. Blake was brought up in the centre of English social resistance, the city of London, in the period of Wilkes and the Gordon riots. His sympathy first with the American and then with the French revolution placed him as far to the left as he could go and still continue to function as an artist. Yet his denunciation of what he called the 'Deism' of the French revolutionaries, and of the ideology of Voltaire and Rousseau, is nearly as strong as Burke's. At the same time his poems point directly towards the English society of his time: even his most complex prophecies have far more in common with Dickens than they have with Plotinus. And though he said 'Houses of Commons & Houses of Lords appear to me to be fools; they seem to me to be something Else besides Human Life,' this expresses, not a withdrawal from society, but a sense of the inadequacy of everything that falls short of the apocalyptic vision itself. Blake's is the same impossible vision that caused Milton to break with four kinds of revolt in England, and which still earlier had inspired the dream of John Ball, a dream based, like *Areopagitica* and *The Marriage of Heaven and Hell*, on a sense of ironic contrast between the fallen and unfallen worlds:

> When Adam delved and Eve span,
> Who was then the gentleman?

In breaking with all forms of social organization, however, Blake is merely following the logic of art itself, whose myths and visions are at once the cause and the clarified form of social developments. Every society is the embodiment of a myth, and as the artist is the shaper of myth, there is a sense in which he holds in his hand the thunderbolts that destroy one society and create another. Another busy and versatile English radical, William Morris, not a mythopœic poet himself but a mere collector of myths, nevertheless portrayed those myths in *The Earthly Paradise* as a group of old men who had outgrown the desire to be made kings or gods. In this cycle they are ineffectual exiles, but in Morris's later work they return as revolutionary dreams, though of a kind that, again, rejects all existing types of revolutionary organization.

The possibility is raised in passing that formally popular art has a perennially subversive quality about it, whereas art that has a vogue popularity remains subservient to society. We note that Russian Communism denounced 'formalism' as the essence of the bourgeois in art, and turned to vogue popularity instead, a vogue artificially sustained by political control, as part of its general policy of perverting revolutionary values. This tendency follows the example set by Tolstoy, who, though a greater artist than Morris, was also more confused about the nature of popular art.

Blake formed his creative habits in the age immediately preceding Romanticism: still, his characteristics are romantic in the expanded sense of giving a primary place to imagination and individual feeling. Like the Romantics, Blake thought of the 'Augustan' period from 1660 to 1760 as an interruption of the normal native tradition. This sense of belonging to and restoring the native tradition helps to distinguish Romanticism in England from Romanticism on the Continent, especially in France. It also enabled the English Romantic writers—in their fertile periods at any rate—to lean less heavily on religious and political conservatism in their search for a tradition.

The great achievement of English Romanticism was its grasp of the principle of creative autonomy, its declaration of artistic independence. The thing that is new in Wordsworth's *Prelude*, in Coleridge's criticism, in Keats's letters, is the sense, not that the poet is superior or inferior to others, but simply that he has an authority, as distinct from a social function, of his own. He does not need to claim any extraneous authority, and still less need he take refuge in any withdrawal from society. The creative process is an end in itself, not to be judged by its power to illustrate something else, however true or good. Some Romantics, especially Coleridge, wobble on this point, but Blake, like Keats and Shelley, is firm, and consistent when he says, 'I will not Reason & Compare: my business is to Create.' The difficulties revealed by such poems as Shelley's *Triumph of Life* or Keats's *Fall of Hyperion* are concerned with the content of the poetic vision, not with any doubts about the validity of that vision as a mean between subjective dream and objective action. 'The poet and the dreamer are distinct,' says Keats's Moneta, and Rousseau in Shelley's poem is typically the bastard poet whose work spilled over into action instead of remaining creative.

Hence the English Romantic tradition has close affinities with the individualism of the Protestant and the radical traditions. In all three the tendency is to take the individual as the primary field or area of

65

operations instead of the interests of society, a tendency which is not necessarily egocentric, any more than its opposite is necessarily altruistic. English Romanticism is greatly aided in its feeling of being central to the tradition of English literature by the example of Shakespeare, who was in proportion to his abilities the most unpretentious poet who ever lived, a poet of whom one can predicate nothing except that he wrote plays, and stuck to his own business as a poet. He is the great poetic example of an inductive and practical approach to experience in English culture which is another aspect of its individualism.

I have no thought of trying to prefer one kind of English culture to another, and I regard all value-judgments that inhibit one's sympathies with anything outside a given tradition as dismally uncritical. I say only that this combination of Protestant, radical, and Romantic qualities is frequent enough in English culture to account for the popularity, in every sense, of the products of it described above. There have been no lack of Catholic, Tory, and Classical elements too, but the tradition dealt with here has been popular enough to give these latter elements something of the quality of a consciously intellectual reaction. During the twenties of the present century, after the shock of the First World War, this intellectual reaction gathered strength. Its most articulate supporters were cultural evangelists who came from places like Missouri and Idaho, and who had a clear sense of the shape of the true English tradition, from its beginnings in Provence and mediaeval Italy to its later developments in France. Mr. Eliot's version of this tradition was finally announced as Classical, royalist, and Anglo-Catholic, implying that whatever was Protestant, radical, and Romantic would have to go into the intellectual doghouse.

Many others who did not have the specific motivations of Mr. Eliot or of Mr. Pound joined in the chorus of denigration of Miltonic, Romantic, liberal, and allied values. Critics still know too little of the real principles of criticism to have any defence against such fashions, when well organized; hence although the fashion itself is on its way out, the prejudices set up by it still remain. Blake must of course be seen in the context of the tradition he belonged to, unless he is to be unnaturally isolated from it, and when the fashionable judgments on his tradition consist so largely of pseudo-critical hokum, one's understanding of Blake inevitably suffers. We come back again to the reason for anniversaries. There may be others in the English tradition as great as Blake, but there can hardly be many as urgently great, looming over the dither of our situation with a more inescapable clarity, full of answers to

66

questions that we have hardly learned how to formulate. Whatever other qualities Blake may have had or lacked, he certainly had courage and simplicity. Whatever other qualities our own age may have or lack, it is certainly an age of fearfulness and complexity. And every age learns most from those who most directly confront it.

ROBERT F. GLECKNER

Point of View and Context in Blake's Songs

> A flower was offered to me;
> Such a flower as May never bore.
> But I said I've a Pretty Rose-tree,
> And I passed the sweet flower o'er.
>
> Then I went to my Pretty Rose-tree:
> To tend her by day and by night.
> But my Rose turnd away with jealousy:
> And her thorns were my only delight.

JOSEPH WICKSTEED, the only critic to devote an entire book to Blake's songs, said this about Blake's poem, *My Pretty Rose Tree*: it 'shows how virtue itself is rewarded only by suspicion and unkindness.' And Thomas Wright, Blake's early biographer, commented on the poem as follows: ' "My Pretty Rose Tree," Blake's nearest approach to humour, may be paraphrased thus: "I was much taken with a charming flower (girl), but I said to myself, No, it won't do. Besides, I have an equally pretty wife at home. Then, too, what would the world say? On the whole it would be policy to behave myself." But his wife takes umbrage all the same. The thorns of her jealousy, however, instead of wounding him give him pleasure, for they excuse his inclination for the flower. Moral: See what comes of being good!'

On the contrary, the moral is that such off-the-mark commentary is

From *Bulletin of The New York Public Library*, LXI (1957), pp. 531–6. Reprinted by permission of the publisher and author. This material also appears in slightly different form in *The Piper and the Bard* by Robert F. Gleckner (1959), Wayne State University Press.

what comes of ignoring the context of Blake's songs (that is, whether the poem is a song of innocence or song of experience) and the point of view from which a given poem is written. *My Pretty Rose Tree* is not about virtue perversely rewarded, nor does it have to do with 'policy' or morality in the ordinary sense of those words. Virtue by itself meant nothing to Blake unless clarified by context: in the state of innocence it is *The Divine Image*; in experience it is perverted to *A Divine Image* and *The Human Abstract*. Real virtue Blake defined in *The Marriage of Heaven and Hell*: 'No virtue can exist without breaking these ten commandments. Jesus was all virtue, and acted from impulse, not from rules.' In *My Pretty Rose Tree* the speaker acts from rules when he refuses the offer of the sweet flower. For, as Blake wrote elsewhere,

> He who binds to himself a joy
> Does the winged life destroy;
> But he who kisses the joy as it flies
> Lives in eternity's sun rise.

The speaker in *My Pretty Rose Tree* not only has let the moment go, but also has bound to himself a joy. Furthermore, since this is a *Song of Experience*, about the state of experience, the flower offered the speaker is the opportunity for a joy, a love, an ascent to a higher innocence. We recall that it was not just *any* flower, but a superb one, 'such a flower as May never bore.' Still, the offer is refused—because the speaker already has a rose-tree. Now, conventionally, this is admirable fidelity; for Blake, however, it is enslavement by what he called the marriage ring. The speaker thus passes up the chance of a spiritual joy (sweet flower) to return to the limited joy of an earthly relationship (pretty rose-tree). He is sorely tempted—but his desire has fallen subject to an extrasensual force symbolized by the existence of, and his relationship to, the rose-tree.

The result, of course, is the speaker's retreat from desire to the only substitute for desire in Urizen's world of experience, duty:

> Then I went to my Pretty Rose-tree
> To tend her by day and by night.

The last two lines of the poem are the crushing commentary on the whole affair. Virtuous in terms of conventional morality, the speaker is rewarded with disdain and jealousy, ironically the same reaction which would have been forthcoming had the speaker taken the offered flower. It is Blake's trenchant way of showing the 'rules' to be inane.

How easily, then, in reading Blake's *Songs of Innocence and of Experience* we can ignore Blake's own individual method. Basically that method is simple, its roots lying in his concept of states and their symbols. Like many other artists Blake employed a central group of related symbols to form a dominant symbolic pattern; his are the child, the father, and Christ, representing the states of innocence, experience, and a higher innocence. These *major* symbols provide the context for all the 'minor,' contributory symbols in the songs; and my purpose here is to suggest a method of approach that is applicable to all of them—and thus to all the songs.

Each of Blake's two song series (or states or major symbols) comprises a number of smaller units (or states or symbols), so that the relationship of each unit to the series as a whole might be stated as a kind of progression: from the states of innocence and experience to the *Songs of Innocence* and *Songs of Experience,* to each individual song within the series, to the symbols within each song, to the words that give the symbols their existence. Conceivably ignorance of or indifference to one word prohibits the imaginative perception and understanding of the whole structure. As Blake wrote in the preface to *Jerusalem,* 'Every word and every letter is studied and put into its fit place; the terrific numbers are reserved for the terrific parts, the mild and gentle for the mild and gentle parts, and the prosaic for inferior parts; all are necessary to each other.'

For the serious reader of Blake's songs, then, a constant awareness of the context or state in which a poem appears is indispensable; and since each state is made up of many poems, the other poems in that state must be consulted to grasp the full significance of any one poem. Each song out of its context means a great deal less than Blake expected of his total invention, and occasionally it may be taken to mean something quite different from what he intended. Blake created a system of which innocence and experience are vital parts; to deny to the *Songs of Innocence,* then, the very background and basic symbology which it helps to make up is as wrong as reading *The Rape of the Lock* without reference to the epic tradition. Without the system, Blake is the simplest of lyric poets and every child may joy to hear the songs. Yet with very little study the child of innocence can be seen to be radically different from the child of experience, and the mother of innocence scarcely recognizable in experience. The states are separate, the two contrary states of the human soul, and the songs were written not merely for our enjoyment, or even for our edification, but for our salvation.

Closely related to the necessity of reading each song in terms of its state is the vital importance of point of view. Often it is unobtrusive, but many times upon a correct determination of speaker and perspective depends a faithful interpretation of the poem. Blake himself suggests this by his organization of the songs into series, *Innocence* introduced and sung by the piper, *Experience* by the Bard. Superficially there seems to be little to distinguish one from the other since the piper clearly exhibits imaginative vision and the Bard 'Present, Past, & Future sees.' Yet for each, the past, present, and future are different: for the piper the past can only be the primal unity, for the present is innocence and the immediate future is experience; for the Bard the past is innocence, the present experience, the future a higher innocence. It is natural, then, that the piper's point of view is prevailingly happy; he is conscious of the child's essential divinity and assured of his present protection. But into that joyous context the elements of experience constantly insinuate themselves so that the note of sorrow is never completely absent from the piper's pipe. In experience, on the other hand, the Bard's voice is solemn and more deeply resonant, for the high-pitched joy of innocence is now only a memory. Within this gloom, though, lies the ember which can leap into flame at any moment to light the way to the higher innocence. Yet despite this difference in direction of their vision, both singers are imaginative, are what Blake called the poetic or prophetic character. And though one singer uses 'mild and gentle numbers' and the other more 'terrific' tones, both see the imaginative (and symbolic) significance of all the activity in the songs. The inexplicit, Blake said, 'rouzes the faculties to act.' The reader of Blake, then, must rouse his faculties to consider this imaginative point of view always no matter who is speaking or seeing or acting in a poem.

Both singers are of course William Blake. And since he, or they, sing all the songs, whether they are identifiable or not with a character in a poem contributes most importantly to the total meaning of the poem. To take an extreme example, in *The Little Vagabond* of *Songs of Experience* there are four points of view: that of the mother, who is now out of her element and can no longer protect her child as she did in *Songs of Innocence*; that of the parson, who is a part of the major symbol of experience, father-priest-king; that of the vagabond himself, a child of experience, not the carefree, irresponsible. thoughtless child of innocence; and that of the Bard, through whose vision each of the other points of view can be studied and evaluated. Without an awareness of this complexity in *The Little Vagabond* the poem dissipates into sentimental drivel. Another good example is *Holy Thursday* of *Songs of Innocence*:

> 'Twas on a Holy Thursday, their innocent faces clean,
> The children walking two and two, in red and blue and green,
> Grey-headed beadles walk'd before, with wands as white as snow,
> Till into the high dome of Paul's they like Thames' waters flow.
>
> O what a multitude they seem'd, these flowers of London town!
> Seated in companies they sit with radiance all their own.
> The hum of multitudes was there, but multitudes of lambs,
> Thousands of little boys and girls raising their innocent hands.
>
> Now like a mighty wind they raise to heaven the voice of song,
> Or like harmonious thunderings the seats of Heavens among.
> Beneath them sit the aged men, wise guardians of the poor;
> Then cherish pity, lest you drive an angel from your door.

From a conventional point of view it is thoughtful and kind of the 'wise guardians of the poor' to run charity schools and to take the children occasionally to St. Paul's to give thanks for all their so-called blessings. But from the piper's point of view (and Blake's of course) the children clearly are disciplined, regimented, marched in formation to church in the uniforms of their respective schools—mainly to advertise the charitable souls of their supposed guardians. The point here (seen only through the piper's vision) is that in the state of innocence there is, or ought to be, no discipline, no regimentation, no marching, no uniforms, and no guardians—merely free, uninhibited, irresponsible, thoughtless play on the echoing green. Accordingly the children in *Holy Thursday* assert and preserve their essential innocence, not by going to church, but by freely and spontaneously, 'like a mighty wind,' raising to 'heaven the voice of song.' This simple act raises them to a level far above their supposed benefactors, who are without vision, without innocence, without love: 'Beneath them sit the aged men, wise guardians of the poor.' The irony is severe, but lost upon us unless we are aware of context and point of view.

As a final example consider the *Introduction* of *Songs of Experience*:

> Hear the voice of the Bard!
> Who Present, Past, and Future, sees;

Whose ears have heard
The Holy Word
That walk'd among the ancient trees,

Calling the lapsèd Soul,
And weeping in the evening dew;
That might control
The starry pole,
And fallen, fallen light renew!

'O Earth, O Earth, return!
'Arise from out the dewy grass;
'Night is worn,
'And the morn
'Rises from the slumberous mass.

'Turn away no more;
'Why wilt thou turn away?
'The starry floor,
'The wat'ry shore,
'Is giv'n thee till the break of day.'

The main difficulty here seems to be Blake's chaotic punctuation and the ambiguity it causes. Stanzas 1, 3, and 4 seem to be an invitation to Earth to arise from the evil darkness and reassume the light of its pre-lapsarian state. Such an orthodox Christian reading, however, is possible only if we forget (1) that this is a *Song of Experience*, and (2) that the singer of these songs is Bard, not God or a priest. In similar fashion, while ignoring the context or the point of view, one might quickly point out the obvious reference in stanza 1 to Genesis iii and forget that the speaker in that chapter is the old Testament God, Jehovah, the cruel law-giver and vengeful tyrant who became in Blake's cosmos the father-priest-king image. And finally, the Holy word in Genesis walked in the garden not in the 'evening dew' but in the 'cool of day,' not to weep and forgive but to cast out and curse his children, to bind them to the soil, and to place woman in a position of virtual servitude to man. In view of this, if the second stanza is read as a clause modifying 'Holy Word,' it is either hopelessly contradictory or devastatingly ironic.

Blake himself hints at the correct reading immediately by means of the ambiguity of the first stanza. There are actually two voices in the poem, the Bard's ('Hear the voice of the Bard'), and the Holy-Word's ('Calling the lapsed Soul'); and the second stanza, *because* of its apparently chaotic punctuation, must be read as modifying both voices. The last two stanzas are the words of *both* voices, perfectly in context when the dual purpose of the poem is recognized. Only in this way can the poem be seen for what it is, an introduction to the state and the songs of experience, in which the Holy Word of Jehovah is hypocritical, selfish, and jealous, thinking and acting in terms of the physical phenomena of day and night and the earthly morality of rewards and punishments. The Bard, mortal but prophetically imaginative, thinks and acts by eternal time and according to eternal values.

But how does one discover the all-important point of view in Blake's songs? One way is to observe the reactions of various characters to the same symbolic act, object, or character, for both the characters and the symbols ultimately resolve themselves into aspects of the major symbol governing that particular poem. Thus the mother of *Songs of Innocence* is symbolic in that her protection of the child contributes to the over-all picture of the child as major symbol of the state of innocence. In addition, many of Blake's symbols are recurrent, so that once a symbol's basic significance is revealed in a kind of archetypal context, each successive context adds association to association within the song series. When the beadle's wand appears in the first stanza of *Holy Thursday* of *Innocence,* for example, its immediate connotation is authority. But since a *beadle* wields the symbol, it is also religious authority, the organized church, institutionalized religion. It also represents an act of restraint which forces the children to act according to rule rather than impulse. The Wand is 'white as snow' to suggest the frigidity of man-made moral purity as opposed to the warmth of young, energetic, exuberant innocence. And finally, it suggests the worldly, non-innocent concept of duty (and its corollary, harm), the duty of worship which clashes with all of Blake's ideas of freedom and spontaneity. But all of this, it will be said, strongly suggests the world of experience, and *Holy Thursday is a Song of Innocence*; the over-all point of view is the piper's. The point to be made here is simply this. If we do not read the poem as a *Song of Innocence,* about the *state* of innocence and its major symbol, the joyous child, we *can* read it as a rather pleasant picture of nicely dressed charity children being led to church by a gentle beadle to sing hymns; or as a terrible view of unfortunate, exploited charity children under the thumbs of their elders. And we would *not* see that despite outward appearance the children *are* innocent, essentially free and happy, as they spontaneously sing their songs. Without an awareness of context the symbols do not work as Blake intended them to, and the song becomes a fairly inconsequential bit of sentimental social comment.

Considering, then, the care Blake took with point of view, recurring symbols, and symbolic action, we can see that gradually many of Blake's characters merge. The final products of these mergers are what I have called the major symbols. Kindred points of view tend to unite the holders of these points of view; characters who are associated continually with the same or similar symbols tend to melt into one another; and a similar pattern of action reveals a fundamental affinity among the actors. In these ways the significance and value of any one character in any one song are intensified and expanded beyond the immediate context. The physical identity may shift, but the symbolic value remains constant—or better, is constantly enriched. When the beadle's wand in *Holy Thursday* is recognized as part of the basic sceptre motif, the beadle's identity, while being retained as representative of church law, merges with that of Tiriel, say, and the father—and ultimately with the 'selfish father of men' in *Earth's Answer*, the pebble in *The Clod and the Pebble*, the 'cold and usurous hand' of *Holy Thursday*, God in *The Chimney Sweeper*, the mother, parson, and 'Dame Lurch' in *The Little Vagabond*, 'Cruelty,' 'Humility,' and the 'Human Brain' in *The Human Abstract*, and Tirzah in *To Tirzah*. Within the identity are inherent all the other identities which combine to make up the major symbol of the context. The priests of *The Garden of Love* may bind with briars love and desire, but they do so because they are selfish, fatherly, cold and usurous, worldly, cruel, humble, hypocritical, and so forth.

One serious question remains: how does one distinguish among all these characters, or are they all precisely alike and hence redundant? Professor Mark Schorer answers the question this way—I know of none better: 'The point is,' he says, 'that the individuality of these creations lies not in their rich diversity but in the outline that separates them from their backgrounds.' That is, each individual identity in its specific context is at once a part of the whole context and the whole of which it is a part. Both the priest of *The Garden of Love* and the flower in *My Pretty Rose Tree* are self-sufficient for some understanding of these two poems. Blake simply asked his reader to do more than merely understand: that he said, is a 'corporeal' function. He wanted them to imagine as he imagined, to see as he saw, even to recreate as he created. Only then does his method make sense, only then can one see the minor symbols as parts of a major symbol, only then can the individual song take its rightful place as a *Song of Innocence* or *Song of Experience*.

75

HAROLD BLOOM

Dialectic In The Marriage of Heaven and Hell

THE *Marriage of Heaven and Hell* assaults what Blake termed a 'cloven fiction' between empirical and a priori procedure in argument. In content, the *Marriage* compounds ethical and theological 'contraries'; in form it mocks the categorical techniques that seek to make the contraries appear as 'negations.' The unity of the *Marriage* is in itself dialectical, and cannot be grasped except by the mind in motion, moving between the Blakean contraries of discursive irony and mythical visualization.

Apocalypse is dialectical in the *Marriage,* as much so as in Shelley's *Prometheus* or the poems by Yeats written out of *A Vision,* or in Blake's own 'Night the Ninth' of *The Four Zoas.* The great difficulty of dialectical apocalypse is that it has got to present itself as prophetic irony, in which the abyss between aspiration and institution is *both* anticipated and denounced. The specific difficulty in reading *The Marriage of Heaven and Hell* is to mark the limits of its irony: where does Blake speak straight? In Blake, rhetoric subsumes dialectic, and usurps its place of privilege. But the process of usurpation is not clear, though this is no flaw in Blake as poet and polemicist. *The Marriage of Heaven and Hell* is a miniature 'anatomy,' in Northrop Frye's recently formulated sense of the term, and reserves to itself the anatomy's peculiar right to mingle satire with vision, furious laughter with the tonal complexity involved in any projection of the four or more last things.

I suggest that we need to distinguish between the *Marriage* as in itself dialectical and the dialectic it attempts to present. The same distinction, rigorously set forth, would clear away much of Yeats's deliber-

---

From *PMLA*, LXXIII (Dec. 1958), pp. 501–4. Reprinted by permission of the publisher and author.

ate perverseness in *A Vision,* and might help in the comprehension of the epics of Blake. The *schemata* of those epics, though dialectical, are yet systematic; the local life in them maddeningly (but gratefully) defies the system. The *schemata,* as Frye in particular has extracted them, present *the* dialectics, early and late, of Blake; the texture, of *Jerusalem* especially, is so dialectical as to put *the* dialectics in doubt. Not that Blake mocks himself; only that he mocks the Corporeal Understanding (including his own) and refuses unto death to cease setting traps for it. There is, in consequence, a true way of reading Blake, put forward by Blake himself, a first-class critic of his own works. But this is a true way which, as Kafka once remarked of true ways in general, is like a rope stretched several inches above the ground, put there not to be walked upon but to be tripped over.

I shall attempt to reduce the *Marriage* to Blake's own overt dialectic in what follows, but because it is not primarily a discursive work I make this attempt in a spirit of tentativeness, respecting its innate trickery.

The poem that opens the *Marriage* as 'argument' has not been much admired, nor much understood. Rintrah, the angry man in Blake's pantheon, rears and shakes his fires in the burdened air; clouds, hungry with menace, swag on the deep. The poem is a prelude, establishing the tone of prophetic fury which is to run beneath the *Marriage;* the indignation of Rintrah presages the turning over of a cycle.

The poem itself has the cyclic irony of *The Mental Traveller.* The 'just man' or 'Devil' now rages in the wilds as outcast, having been driven out of 'perilous paths' by the 'villain' or 'Angel.' This reversal is simple enough, if it is true reversal, which it is not. The initial complication is provided by the sixth to ninth lines of the poem:

> Roses are planted where thorns grow,
> And on the barren heath
> Sing the honey bees.

Grow, not *grew; sing,* not *sang.* We are already involved in the contraries. Cliff is opposed to river, tomb to spring, bleached bones to the red clay of Adam (literal Hebrew meaning). The turning of this cycle converts the meek just man into the prophetic rager, the easeful villain into the serpent sneaking along in mild humility. The triple repetition of 'perilous path' compounds the complication. First the just man keeps the perilous path as he moves towards death. But '*then* the perilous path was planted . . ./ *Till* the villain left the path of ease,/To walk in perilous paths.'

77

We grasp the point by embracing both contraries, not by reconciling them. There is progression here, but only in the ironic sense of cycle. The path, the way of generation that can only lead to death, is always being planted, the just man is always being driven out; the villain is always usurping the path of life-in-death. When the just man returns from being a voice in the wilderness, he drives the villain back into the nonexistence of 'paths of ease.' But 'just man' and 'villain' are very nearly broken down as categories here; the equivocal 'Devil' and 'Angel' begin to loom as the *Marriage*'s contraries. The advent of the villain upon the perilous path marks the beginning of a new 'heaven,' a 'mild humility' of angelic restraint. So Blake leaves his argument and plunges into his satiric nuptial song:

> As a new heaven is begun and it is now thirty-three years since its advent, the Eternal Hell revives.

Swedenborg, writing in his *True Christian Religion*, had placed the Last Judgment in the spiritual world in 1757, the year of Blake's birth. In 1758 Swedenborg published *his* vision of judgment, *Heaven and Hell*. Now, writing in 1790, at the Christological age of thirty-three, Blake celebrates in himself the reviving of the Eternal Hell, the voice of desire and rebellion crying aloud in desert places against the institution of a new divine restraint, albeit that of the visionary Swedenborg, himself a Devil rolled round by cycle into Angelic category.

Before the *Marriage* moves into diabolical gear, Blake states the law of his dialectic:

> Without Contraries is no progression. Attraction and Repulsion, Reason and Energy, Love and Hate, are necessary to Human existence.

The key here is *Human*, which is both descriptive and honorific. This is a dialectic without transcendence, in which heaven and hell are to be married but without becoming altogether one flesh or one family. By the 'marriage' of contraries Blake means only that we are to cease valuing one contrary above the other in any way. Echoes of Isaiah xxxiv and xxxv crowd through the *Marriage*, and a specific reference to those chapters is given here by Blake. Reading Isaiah in its infernal sense, as he read *Paradise Lost*, Blake can acknowledge its apocalypse as his own. As the imaginative hell revives, the heaven of restraint comes down.

And all the host of heaven shall be dissolved, and the heavens shall be rolled together as a scroll: and all their host shall fall down.

(Isaiah xxxiv. 4)

The Promethean release that has come to Blake with his full maturity is related to the titanic fury of French revolution and English unrest that is directly contemporary with the *Marriage*.[1] The Revolution is the active springing from Energy, called Evil by the 'religious,' who assign it to Hell. Frye has stated the central idea of the *Marriage* as being the analogy of this unrest to the Biblical time of troubles that precedes the end of the world.[2] The *Marriage* thus enters the category not of 'How long O Lord?' prophecy but of the 'turn now' injunction based on Hillel's famous question, 'If not now, when?' So that its dialectic must cease to be purely descriptive and cyclic, which is to say, must cease to be merely dialectic. Apocalypse does not argue, and hardly needs to convince. The verse of the Negro spiritual carries in a kernel the authoritative message of apocalypse, taking place between the sardonic warning and the dreaded effect: 'You will shout when it hits you, yes indeed.'

Therefore, the contraries, when next stated in the famous 'Voice of the Devil' passage, have ceased strictly to be contraries. Blake's lower or earthly paradise, Beulah Land, is a state of being or place where contraries are equally true, but the *Marriage* is written out of the state of Generation, our world in its everyday aspect, where progression is necessary. Christian dualism is therefore a negation, hindrance, not action, and is cast out beyond the balance of contraries. Blake does not build truth by dialectic, being neither a rational mystic like Plato nor a mystic rationalist like Hegel. Nothing eternal abides behind forms for Blake; he seeks reality in appearances, though he rejects appearance as it is perceived by the lowest-common-denominator kind of observer. Between the cloven fiction of St. Paul's mind-body split and the emotionalism of the celebrator of a state of nature exists the complex apocalyptic humanism of the *Marriage*, denying metaphysics, accepting the hard given of this world, but only insofar as this appearance is altogether human.

Here it has been too easy to mistake Blake—for Nietzsche, for D. H. Lawrence, for Yeats, for whatever heroic vitalist you happen most to admire. The *Marriage* preaches the risen body breaking bounds, exploding upwards into psychic abundance. But here Blake is as earnest as Lawrence, and will not tolerate the vision of recurrence, as Nietzsche and Yeats do. The altogether human escapes cycle, evades irony, cannot be categorized discursively. But Blake is unlike Lawrence, even where they touch. The Angel teaches light without heat, the vitalist—or Devil—heat without light; Blake wants both, hence the marriage of contraries. The paradise of Milton needs the heat of hell; the earth of Lawrence needs the light of Eden, the rational fire of intellect and creation. Rhetoric now carries the *Marriage* through its implicit irony; Blake speaks straight for once before subjecting *Paradise Lost* to the play of dialectic:

> Energy is the only life, and is from the Body; and Reason is the bound or outward circumference of Energy.
> Energy is Eternal Delight.

This does not mean that Reason, the bound, is Eternal Torment; it does mean that Reason's story would hold that unbounded Energy *is* such torment. Hence the *Marriage's* curious double account of fall and negative creation, whether of hell or heaven:

> For this history has been adopted by both parties.
> It indeed appear'd to Reason as if Desire was cast out; but the Devil's account is, that the Messiah fell, and formed a heaven of what he stole from the Abyss.

In crude terms, the problem is where the stuff of life comes from; where does Reason, divinity of the 'Angels,' obtain the substance that it binds and orders, the energy that it restrains? By stealing it from the *Urgrund* of the abyss, is Blake's diabolic answer. We are almost in the scheme of *The Four Zoas:* the Messiah *fell*, stole the stuff of creativity, and formed 'heaven.' One contrary is here as true as another: this history has been adopted by both parties. One party, come again to dominance among us, now condemns Blake as a persuasive misreader of *Paradise Lost.* When, in another turn of the critical wheel, we go back to reading *Paradise Lost* in its infernal or poetic sense, as Blake, Shelley, and a host of nineteenth-century poets and scholars did, we will have to condemn a generation of critical dogmatists for not having understood the place of dialectic in literary analysis.

The 'Memorable Fancies,' brilliant exercises in satire and humanism, form the bulk of the *Marriage*, and tend to evade Blake's own dialectic, being, as they are, assaults, furious and funny, on Angelic culpability. The dialectic of the *Marriage* receives its definitive statement once more in the work, in the opposition of the Prolific and the Devouring. If one grasps that complex passage, one is fortified to move frontally against the most formidable and properly most famous section of the *Marriage*, the 'Proverbs of Hell,' where dialectic and rhetoric come together combatively in what could be judged the most brilliant aphorisms written in English, seventy gnomic reflections and admonitions on the theme of diabolic wisdom.

The Titanic myth, the story of 'the Antediluvians who are our Energies,' is always present in Blake, though frequently concealed in some contrapuntal fiction. In the *Marriage* the myth is overt and 'Messiah *or* Satan' is identified with these Giant Forms. The *or* establishes again the marriage of contraries. The Giant Forms, huge Ids, or Orcs, to use Blake's vocabulary, are bound down by the cunning of weak and tame minds:

> Thus one portion of being is the Prolific, the other the Devouring: to the Devourer it seems as if the producer was in his chains; but it is not so, he only takes portions of existence and fancies that the whole.
> But the Prolific would cease to be Prolific unless the Devourer, as a sea, received the excess of his delights.

This terrifying vision of the economy of existence is mitigated by its irony, and yet moves into mystery in its final statement. Reason and the senses do not bound our energies; Eternal Delight, the primal Exuberance that is Beauty, exists beyond the bounds. Blake is not predicating an unconscious mind, for that would be only a widening of the circumference of the bound. The Freudian hypothesis of the unconscious would have represented for Blake what it does to the phenomenologists—a premature cessation of mental activity, a refusal to analyze all of the given. But Blake more than anticipates Husserl here; he gives a definitive statement of the phenomenology of existence, the ceaseless dialectic of daily appearance. Yeats, in *A Vision*, proudly asserted his refusal to be logical, lest he be trapped by his own dialectic. He had never believed with Hegel, he wrote, that the spring vegetables were refuted because they were over. In this he was caught up in Blake's spirit, in the vision of existential contraries. The Angel or Devourer takes all the negative force of Blake's rhetoric, but dialectically he is a necessity. The Prolific will not be confined, but it needs constraint, it thirsts for battle. The Devourer is a sea, a moat imprisoning the creator, who would otherwise be choked in the excess of his own delight. Without the hard given (a wall is as good a symbol as a moat) we do not engage in the mutable struggle. This war cry passes into the most defiant sentences in the *Marriage*:

> Some will say: 'Is not God alone the Prolific?' I answer: 'God only Acts and Is, in existing beings or Men.'
>
> These two classes of men are always upon earth, and they should be enemies: whoever tries to reconcile them seeks to destroy existence.
>
> Religion is an endeavour to reconcile the two.

The nontheism of Blake is never more clearly stated than here, and yet is still being misread by many. If God only acts *and is* in Men, then *God* has become an unnecessary hypothesis, having no abstract being beyond our powers of visualization and confrontation. To destroy enmity between Prolific and Devourer would destroy existence, such destruction being religion's attempt to inflict upon us the greatest poverty of not living in a physical world. Blake's dialectical stance, with its apotheosis of the physical and its rejection of the merely natural, is most frequently misunderstood at just this point. Against the supernaturalist, Blake asserts the reality of the body as being all of the soul that the five senses can perceive. Against the naturalist, he asserts the unreality of the merely given body as against the imaginative body, rising through an increase in sensual fulfillment into a realization of its unfallen potential.

Religion seeks to end the warfare of contraries because it claims to know a reality *beyond* existence; Blake wants the warfare to continue because he seeks a reality *within* existence. Milton's heaven knows no strife, and therefore no progression, and is to Blake—hell.

We can see Blake's interplay between dialectic and espousing one pole of the dialectic most vividly in the 'Proverbs of Hell,' where the revelation of the laws of process and a fierce antinomianism are frequently interleaved:

> The road of excess leads to the palace of wisdom. (3)
>
> Prudence is a rich, ugly old maid courted by Incapacity. (4)
>
> He who desires but acts not, breeds pestilence. (5)
>
> If the fool were to persist in his folly he would become wise. (18)
>
> The Tygers of wrath are wiser than the horses of instruction. (44)
>
> You never know what is enough unless you know what is more than enough. (46)
>
> Exuberance is Beauty. (64)
>
> Sooner murder an infant in its cradle than nurse unacted desires. (67)
>
> Where man is not, nature is barren. (68)

Each of these proverbs depends for its true meaning on a dialectic definition of desire and act, though rhetorically the meaning is overtly antinomian. Desire is positive; it leads to an action which is not the hindrance of another. Act is positive and is virtue; Blake, commenting on Lavater, defines its contrary as 'accident':

> Accident is the omission of act in self & the hindering of act in another; This is Vice, but all Act is Virtue. To hinder another is not an act; it is the contrary; it is a restraint on action both in ourselves & in the person hinder'd, for he who hinders another omits his own duty at the same time.[3]

The road of excess has therefore nothing to do with sadism or self-destruction, but is the way to that all, less than which cannot satisfy us. Incapacity, which courts Prudence, is a mode of hindrance. Desire which does not lead to action is also 'accident,' vice, and is self-destructive. The fool persisting in his folly at least acts; ceasing, he is merely foolish, and falls into self-negation. Instruction may draw you on, but wrath will take you sooner into wisdom, for wrath embodies desire. The boundary of desire you learn only by moving beyond, and the furious energy of this liberation is definitive of beauty. To *nurse* an unacted desire *is* to murder an infant in its cradle; overt murder is at least more positive. Last, take man and his struggle of contraries out of nature, and you are left with the barren, with the same dull round over again, the merely cyclic movement, if such it can be termed, of negations.

The last plate of the *Marriage* has upon it the figure of King Nebuchadnezzar eating grass like an ox, in a hideous emblem of the return to a state of nature. Nebuchadnezzar haunted Blake; Blake meant him to haunt us. When you forget the contrary of vision, when waking you reject the lessons of the night, then you suffer the negation: you feed like beasts upon the grass.

NOTES

1. David V. Erdman, *Blake, Prophet Against Empire* (Princeton, 1954), pp. 160–166.
2. *Fearful Symmetry* (Princeton, 1947), p. 194.
3. *Poetry and Prose of William Blake*, ed. Geoffrey Keynes (London, 1948), p. 735.

BASIL WILLEY

On Wordsworth and the Locke Tradition

I

THE manner in which the triumph of the mechanical philosophy affected poetry can be illustrated, I think, by comparing a representative serious poem of the earlier eighteenth century, Pope's *Essay on Man*, with *Paradise Lost* as representing the previous century. It has been pointed out that there is no Satan in Pope's poem. From one standpoint this fact merely exemplifies Pope's optimistic 'philosophy.' With the characteristic desire of his time to explain, and to explain favourably, Pope unquestioningly makes his poem a theodicy, a vindication of an order of things in which evil appears, but only appears, to exist. To 'explain' evil is almost necessarily to explain it away. But taking a more general view, one is struck by the absence, in Pope's poem, of any sort of mythological machinery. In giving pointed expression to the real beliefs of his time, Pope instinctively adopts an explanatory method. It would have been unthinkable in Pope's time that a serious poet should have used any such machinery, or even an allegorical convention, for such a purpose. Mythologies, including the Christian, were now felt to be exploded; what may have been 'true' in them is that part which can be conceptually or intellectually stated. Milton, as we have seen, although himself a considerable rationaliser, could still employ the concrete symbols of the faith without feeling that he was deliberately utilising what was fictitious. God and Satan were real beings to him, as well as 'principles.' But though Pope and his contemporaries were debarred by their intellectual climate from using any great system of commonly-accepted

From *The Seventeenth Century Background*, 1950 (Columbia University Press; Chatto & Windus, Ltd., London), pp. 296–309. Reprinted by permission of the publishers.

symbols, as Dante and Milton could, they could still employ mythological material for other purposes, as Pope did in the *Rape of the Lock,* for example. They could use it consciously, for technical convenience and for purposes of 'delight.' It is in this manner that the mythologies of the ancient world are generally used by eighteenth century poets. These poets employ their personifications and their other mythological apparatus in full awareness that they are 'fiction.' They are 'fictions' of proved evocative power and of long association with poetic experience, and they can thus still be made use of to assist in producing poetry out of the dead-matter of modernity. But fictions they are still felt to be, and they cannot therefore be used with full conviction. Their employment involves the deliberate exploitation of obsolete modes of feeling, a conscious disregard of contemporary truth-standards. It was, one may suppose, his sense of this situation which made Johnson dislike *Lycidas* and Gray's *Odes.*

As a consequence of these developments it was inevitable that when a major poet again appeared he should be 'left alone, seeking the visible world.' No existing mythology could express the 'real,' as the 'real' was now felt to be. A final effort had been made, by Erasmus Darwin, to enlist poetry under the banner of science by describing the Loves of the Plants with all the apparatus of 'poetical machinery,' but of this unholy alliance it would be hard to say whether it was more degrading to science or to poetry. The new poet must therefore either make poetry out of the direct dealings of his mind and heart with the visible universe, or he must fabricate a genuine new mythology of his own (not necessarily rejecting all old material in so doing). Keats and Shelley often follow the second of these methods; Wordsworth typically follows the first.

Wordsworth's relation to the 'scientific' tradition is not quite simple. In a sense he is in violent reaction against it, and yet it conditioned much of his poetic experience. What he owed to it was his instinctive repudiation of any concrete mythology. His poetry was 'scientific' in that his interest lay in the free relations between the mind of man and the universe to which, he believes, it is 'so exquisitely fitted.' According to him, we 'build up the being that we are' by 'deeply drinking-in the soul of things.' That is, there must be no abstractions, no symbols, no myths, to stand between the mind and its true object. In so far as it was the abstract world-picture (the world as 'machine') of the seventeenth century natural philosophers which had exploded the mythologies, Wordsworth may be said to have owed to them (as well as to his own temperament) his root-assumption that truth could only be achieved by 'making verse deal boldly with substantial things.' Wordsworth was the kind of poet who could only have appeared at the end of the eighteenth century, when mythologies were exploded, and a belief in the visible universe as the body of which God was the soul alone remained. In this sense his beliefs can be viewed as data furnished to him by a tradition; in this sense he, as well as Dante, may be said to have employed his sensibility within a framework of received beliefs. But his debt to tradition, unlike Dante's, was a negative one; he owed to it his *deprivation* of mythology, his aloneness with the universe. His more positive beliefs, those by which he appears in reaction against the scientific tradition, were built up by him out of his own poetic experiences, and it is this which makes him representative of the modern situation—the situation in which beliefs are made out of poetry rather than poetry out of beliefs. To animise the 'real' world, the 'universe of death' that the 'mechanical' system of philosophy had produced, but to do so without either using an exploded mythology or fabricating a new one, this was the special task and mission of Wordsworth. Wordsworth's conviction that the human mind was capable of this task was the most important of his 'positive' beliefs, and this belief he owed chiefly to his own experiences. It is this which distinguishes his 'deism' from that of, for instance, Thomson's *Seasons,* to which it bears an obvious superficial resemblance. For Thomson, as for Pope, mythologies were almost as 'unreal' as for Wordsworth, but their positive belief, their Deism (in so far as they genuinely held it), was 'intellectually' held, and it consequently appears in poetry mainly as rhetoric. The poetry exists to decorate, to render agreeable, a set of abstract notions; and these abstractions have been taken over, as truth, from the natural philosophers—from Descartes, Newton, Locke, or Leibnitz. Wordsworth's beliefs, on the other hand, were largely the formulation of his own dealings with 'substantial things'; they were held intellectually only because they had first been 'proved upon the pulses.' That the result of his 'dealings' was not a *Divine Comedy* or a *Paradise Lost* was due, we may say, to the scientific movement and the sensationalist philosophy of Locke and Hartley; that the result was not an *Essay on Man*, a *Seasons*, or a *Botanic Garden* was due to himself. For it was the 'visible world,' no abstract machine, that Wordsworth sought; and he felt that mechanical materialism had substituted a 'universe of death for that which moves with light and life instinct, actual, divine, and true.'[1] The belief that Wordsworth constructed out of his experiences was a belief in the capacity of the mind to co-operate with this 'active universe,' to contribute something of its own to it in perceiving it, and not, as sensationalism taught, merely to receive, passively, impressions from without. It was this belief, or the experiences upon which the belief was based, which encouraged him to hope that poetry might be delivered from the fetters of the mechanical tradition without being allowed to fall into disrepute as 'unreal' or 'fanciful.'

Of this belief, as intellectually formulated, there are many explicit statements in Wordsworth's poetry, especially in the *Prelude*, as well as in his prose. There is, for example, the passage on the child (the 'inmate of this active universe'):

> 'For feeling has to him imparted power
> That through the growing faculties of sense
> Doth like an agent of the one great Mind
> Create, creator and receiver both,
> Working but in alliance with the works
> Which it beholds.' [2]

In a later passage of the same Book he distinguishes the true creative power from arbitrary fancy:

> 'A plastic power
> Abode with me, a forming hand, at times
> Rebellious, acting in a devious mood,
> A local spirit of his own, at war
> With general tendency, but, for the most,
> Subservient strictly to external things
> With which it communed.' [3]

The classic 'locus' is in the Preface to the *Excursion,* where in deliberately Miltonic language he has been claiming more than epic dignity for his own subject-matter: [4]

> ' Paradise, and groves
> Elysian, Fortunate Fields—*why should they be*
> *A history only of departed things,*
> *Or a mere fiction of what never was?*
> *For the discerning intellect of Man,*
> *When wedded to this goodly universe*
> *In love and holy passion, shall find these*
> *A simple produce of the common day.*
> —I, long before the blissful hour arrives,

Would chant in lonely peace the spousal verse
Of this great consummation:—and, *by words*
Which speak of nothing more than what we are,
Would I arouse the sensual from their sleep
Of Death, and win the vacant and the vain
To noble raptures; while my voice proclaims
How exquisitely the individual Mind
                    to the external World
Is fitted, and how exquisitely too—
Theme this but little heard of among men—
The external World is fitted to the Mind;
And the Creation (by no lower name
Can it be called) *which they with blended might
Accomplish.'*

The famous 'Fancy-Imagination' distinction of Wordsworth and Coleridge, and their followers, may best be understood as arising from the existence in them of the particular 'belief-state' I have tried to indicate. The fact-world of modern scientific consciousness was the primary datum. In this 'inanimate cold world' 'objects, *as* objects, are essentially fixed and dead.' [5] But just as a 'known and familiar landscape' may be transmuted by moonlight or 'accidents of light and shade,' [6] so, owing to the bond between nature and the soul of man, this dead world may be brought to life by the modifying colours of the 'imagination.' Of the *imagination,* for this is the faculty which works the required magic without producing what is now felt to be 'fictitious.' Where there is consciousness of fiction, it is the *fancy* that has been at work. The test of the 'imaginative,' as distinct from the 'imaginary,' is that external objects shall have been coloured by the poet's own mood, or made the symbol of it; that the plastic power shall have been exercised, but kept 'subservient strictly to external things.' Modifications *so* wrought, values *so* ascribed to the fact-world, have a reality-status which is unassailable, because they are psychological in origin; they spring, that is, from states of mind, of which the 'reality' cannot be questioned.

Wordsworth's belief in the possibility of this creation which the mind and the universe may 'with blended might accomplish' was, I have suggested, largely built up out of his own poetic experience. One need only consider a number of passages in which Wordsworth has commemorated those of his experiences which he felt to be most significant, to see that they are generally occasions on which he had (for the most part unconsciously at the time) exerted the 'visionary,' the 'plastic' power upon

some external object. In the celebrated 'spots of time' passage at the
end of Book XII of the *Prelude*,[7] he says explicitly that of all the recollections which hold for him a 'renovating virtue,' he values most those
which record moments of the greatest self-activity, those which 'give
knowledge to what point, and how, the mind is lord and master, outward
sense the obedient servant of her will'; recollections, that is, which
show the mind 'not prostrate, overborne, as if the mind herself were
nothing, a mere pensioner on outward forms—' (as in sensationalist
philosophy), but in its native dignity, creating significance in alliance
with external things. It is unfortunately true that Wordsworth frequently
discusses his experiences, and states the results which his intellect has
extracted from them, instead of communicating them to us. The modern
reader demands the experience, and cares little or nothing what metaphysical or psychological principle they are supposed to exemplify.
This criticism is perhaps applicable to the passage in Book XII to which
I have referred, for Wordsworth there avows his inability to communicate the 'visionary dreariness' which then invested the moor, the lonely
pool, and the woman with the pitcher, although the knowledge that
his imagination had been strong enough to impart the visionary quality
to the scene was his reason for valuing the recollection. But he has given
enough examples of his sensibility in action for us to see that its workings
were independent of, and antecedent to, the formulation of the belief.
When (to take a few illustrations at random):

> ' a gentle shock of mild surprise
> Has carried far into his heart the voice
> Of mountain torrent'; [8]

when he saw the Leech-Gatherer pace

> 'About the weary moors continually,
> Wandering about alone and silently'; [9]

when the Highland woman's greeting seemed

> 'a sound
> Of something without place or bound'; [10]

when

> 'the high spear-grass on that wall
> By mist and silent rain-drops silvered o'er,
> As once I passed, into my heart conveyed
> So still an image of tranquillity,

> So calm and still, and looked so beautiful
> Among the uneasy thoughts which filled my mind,'[11]

these experiences, and many another that could be collected from his best poetry, depended upon no special beliefs (and of course no beliefs are needed by the reader in order to share them to the full). It was out of the repetition of these imaginative moments that the belief arose; the belief itself was the intellectual formulation of what they seemed to mean. It must be recognised, nevertheless, that the formulation, once made (no doubt with Coleridge's assistance), gave added importance to the recollected 'moments,' the 'spots of time,' and that Wordsworth would probably not have conducted his *recherche du temps perdu* with such eagerness and such conviction if he had not so formulated it.

II

Wordsworth's poetic activity, then, was largely conditioned by the 'reality-standards' of his time, which left him alone with the visible universe. But his 'creative sensibility' had taught him that he was not alone with an 'inanimate cold world,' but with an 'active universe,' a universe capable of being moulded and modified by the 'plastic power' which abode within himself. As long as he could be a poet, this belief in the bond between man and nature was valid. Poetry becomes, with Wordsworth, the record of moments of 'ennobling interchange of action from within and from without';[12] it takes on, in fine, a *psychological* aspect. 'There is scarcely one of my poems,' Wordsworth wrote to Lady Beaumont, 'which does not aim to direct the attention to some moral sentiment, or to some general principle, or law of thought, or of our intellectual constitution.'[13]

I have emphasised this 'aloneness' of Wordsworth with the universe, because I think it marks his position in the history of 'poetry and beliefs,' and because it seems to determine the quality of much of his work. Centuries of intellectual development had now brought matters to this, that if poetry were still to be made, it must be made by the sheer unaided power of the individual poet. And what was it that he must make? A record of successes; of successful imaginative dealings with the world of eye and ear. And what was to be the criterion of success? That plastic power shall have been exerted upon the 'vulgar forms of every day,' but in such a way that there shall be no departure from 'nature's living images.' The midnight storm may grow darker in presence of the poet's' eye, the visionary dreariness, the consecration, may be spread over sea or land, but the transforming power must work 'subservient strictly to external things'; there must be intensification without distortion. Fact and value were to be combined in this 'fine balance of truth in observing, with the imaginative faculty in modifying, the object observed.' But what sort of 'truth' may be claimed for the creation which world and mind 'with blended might accomplish'?—for, that poetry is 'the most philosophic of all writing,' that 'its object is truth,' is Wordsworth's profound conviction.[14] I suppose the answer would be, 'psychological' truth; that is to say, the poetry is faithfully expressive of certain states of consciousness. Of the two elements of which these states are composed, fact and value, Wordsworth is equally sure of both. He is sure of the fact, because he knows no man has observed it more intently; he is sure of the value, because this was intuitively apprehended in himself, it came from within. He is no less sure of the truth of the resulting creation, because it had been experienced as a modification of his own consciousness. But it was only as long as his mind was dealing thus nakedly with observed fact that Wordsworth could feel this conviction of truthfulness. Any translation of his experience into myth, personification or fable, though not necessarily always culpable, is inevitably a lapse towards a lower level of truth, a fall, in fact, from imagination to fancy. Poetry exists to transform, to make this much-loved earth more lovely; and in former times men could express their sense of fact, without misgiving, in mythologies. But since the coming of the enlightened age this was becoming almost impossible. The efforts of eighteenth century poets to vitalise the dead matter of the Cartesian universe by using the symbols of an outworn mythology had ended in fiasco, and the abandonment of the symbols, at any rate for a time, became a necessity.

But this abandonment threw upon Wordsworth, as it throws still more emphatically upon the contemporary poet, an enormous burden, no less, in fact, than 'the weight of all this unintelligible world.' He must be continually giving proofs of strength in order to maintain his belief that the load *could* be lightened. To keep the vast encompassing world from becoming 'cold and inanimate' by transferring to it a 'human and intellectual life' from the poet's own spirit; to 'dissolve, diffuse, and dissipate in order to re-create'; to 'idealize, and to unify,' to 'shoot one's being through earth, air and sea'—what a stupendous task for the unaided spirit of man! Is it to be wondered at that Wordsworth, after bearing the heavy and the weary weight, Atlas-like, for many years, should at last, like Atlas, have turned into a mountain of stone? Youth, and Coleridge, and Dorothy, and the moonlight of Alfoxden—these could and did lighten the burden for him for a while. But there are many signs that after this his material began to resist him more and more stubbornly. Was there not something in the very nature of the poetic task he had set himself which made this inevitable? 'To spread the tone, the atmosphere, and with it the depth and height of the ideal world around forms, incidents and situations, of which, for the common view, custom had bedimmed all the lustre, had dried up the sparkle and the dew-drops' [15]— this is probably the special prerogative of youth. In youth the imagination poured the modifying colours prodigally over all things, and only when its vitality began to sink did the man discover how much virtue had been going out of him. With the realisation that 'objects *as* objects, are essentially fixed and dead,' comes the disturbing sense that 'in our life alone does nature live.' That Wordsworth had reached this point at about the age of thirty-five is fairly clear from the passage in Book XII of the *Prelude*, where, echoing Coleridge, he declares

> 'That from thyself it comes, that thou must give,
> Else never canst receive.' [16]

The whole context from which these words are taken shows also how habitually, by this time, Wordsworth had come to find in *memory* his chief reservoir of strength. Certain memories are the 'hiding-places of man's power'; memories, that is, of former successful exertions of imaginative strength. In the *Prelude* pre-eminently, though elsewhere as well, Wordsworth, now fighting a losing battle with *das Gemeine*, supported his strength for a while by drawing upon the past. But he was living upon capital, and when that was spent, what was to remain?

III

Poetry, as we have since learnt, has other tasks than that of imparting psychological values to the visible world. Had Wordsworth turned his attention towards these, his genius might not have atrophied so soon. It remains to indicate briefly, in conclusion, what gave Wordsworth his initial direction towards 'Nature' as the inevitable raw material for his creative sensibility. Here we meet, I think, with two other groups of beliefs current in his age, which may be said to have conditioned his poetic experience: postulates ('doctrines-felt-as-facts') without which his poetry would not have been what it actually is. The first was the product of the deistic tradition of the seventeenth and eighteenth centuries, to which I have already alluded in passing. Ever since the Renaissance the Creation had been steadily gaining in prestige as the 'art of God,' the universal divine Scripture which 'lies expans'd unto the eyes of all.'[17] The emotion of the 'numinous,' formerly associated with super-nature, had become attached to Nature itself; and by the end of the eighteenth century the divinity, the sacredness of nature was, to those affected by this tradition, almost a first datum of consciousness. Wordsworth, then, did not have to construct this belief wholly out of his experience; much of it was given to him.

Much the same is true of the second of these fundamental beliefs, the belief in the grandeur and dignity of man, and the holiness of the heart's affections. This, too, was the product of forces originating (for our purposes) in the Renaissance; it had arisen out of the ruins of the theological view of man. As the 'Fall' receded further and further into the region of fable, man was increasingly regarded as a creature not only made in, but retaining, God's image; and Wordsworth could acknowledge, without misgiving, 'a grandeur in the beatings of the heart,' and speak in good faith of 'man and his noble nature.' In Wordsworth's lifetime this humanism had taken a colouring from Rousseau, and the special nobility of man was therefore only to be looked for 'in huts where poor men lie.' The 'higher' grades of society, in which the culture of the Renaissance had been exclusively fostered, were now

> 'A light, a cruel, and vain world, cut off
> From the natural inlets of just sentiment,
> From lowly sympathy, and chastening truth.'[18]

The blend of these two closely-related beliefs resulted, with Wordsworth, in his typical celebration of figures like the Leech-Gatherer, Michael, or 'Nature's Lady': beings whose humanity is ennobled by close association with 'mute insensate things.' Wordsworth is indebted to the traditions I have mentioned for his preconception that humanity is in closest touch with 'reality,' as well as in its healthiest, most wisely tranquil, state when it is most intimately blended with the cosmic processes.

Many and great changes have taken place since Wordsworth's time, changes which have involved the evaporation of most of his characteristic beliefs, both inherited and self-wrought. Few now have any faith in 'nature,' or in 'man,' or in the bond between man and nature. Most readers seem to find it harder to yield 'imaginative assent' to these doc-trines than to others more remote from our present habits of mind. The poetic tradition founded by Wordsworth is probably now dead and superseded. Yet as he is the first, so he remains the type, of the 'modern' poets who, 'left alone' with a vaster material than his, must bear as best they can, unaided by any universally-held mythology, the 'weight of all this unintelligible world.'

NOTES

1. *Prelude,* xiv. 160.
2. *Prelude,* ii. 254.
3. *Ibid.,* 362.
4. The italics are mine.
5. Coleridge, *Biog. Lit.,* ch. xiii. (vol i. p. 202 in Shawcross).
6. Phrases from the opening of ch. xiv. of *Biog. Lit.*
7. Lines 208–286.
8. *Prelude,* v. 382.
9. *Resolution and Independence,* stanza xix.
10. *Stepping Westward,* verse 2.
11. *Excursion,* i. 943.
12. *Prelude,* xiii. 375.
13. In *Wordsworth's Literary Criticism,* ed. Nowell C. Smith (London, 1925), p. 51.
14. *Lyrical Ballads,* Pref., p. 25 in *Wordsworth's Lit. Crit.*
15. Coleridge, *Biog. Lit.,* ch. v. vol. i, p. 59. The other quoted phrases on this and the former page are also Coleridge's.
16. xii. 276.
17. Sir T. Browne, *Rel. Med.,* i. sect. xvi.
18. *Prelude,* ix, 349.

CARLOS BAKER

Sensation and Vision in Wordsworth

FOR all those moderns to whom poetry matters, the continual re-examination of the poetry of the past is just as vital an obligation as the encouragement of good new poetry now. If we believe, as we are justified in doing, that there are literary giants on our earth today, it is well to remember that there were also giants in the earth in times past. And William Wordsworth, as John Crowe Ransom has recently reminded us, is one of the giants of English poetry.

Giantism, of course, has its embarrassments—for giants. When Captain Lemuel Gulliver visited the land of the Brobdingnagians, he discovered that the minor physical imperfections of his hulking hosts became unhappily visible. If Wordsworth is indeed a giant, the fact may help to explain why some of his faults are glaringly evident to those of us whose stature is lower than his own. That he shows imperfections, not even his hardiest admirers deny. As early as 1800, the poet warned prospective readers that they might 'frequently have to struggle with feelings of strangeness and awkwardness' as they read the second edition of *Lyrical Ballads*. 'They will look round for poetry and will be induced to inquire by what species of courtesy these attempts can be permitted to assume that title.' In certain respects, readers have felt, looked, and inquired as Wordsworth predicted, not only in 1800, but ever since.

Among the earliest of these were his peers. Coleridge idolized him, even leaned upon him at times as a sturdy moral monolith, yet devoted some thousands of words in the *Biographia Literaria* to the errors of

From the Introduction to William Wordsworth's *The Prelude*, with a selection from *The Shorter Poems, The Sonnets, The Recluse,* and *The Excursion.* Introduction copyright 1948, 1954, by Carlos Baker. New York: Rinehart Editions, 1954. Reprinted by permission.

style, tone, and syntax into which he thought Wordsworth had been led by overabsorption in an indefensible theory of poetry. It seems to be a fact that Coleridge set the sights for what has been a continuing, though sporadic, critical barrage. Coleridge's list of the ineptitudes in Wordsworth has not been improved upon, nor has it been appreciably added to: inconstancy of style producing inadvertent bathos; occasional mental bombast; linguistic incongruities; a certain oversolemn matter-of-factness suggesting an underdeveloped sense of humor; and an eddying rather than a progression of thought, suggesting the muddy backwashes of a river rather than the clear, swift-running current of the main stream. Such errors of commission are scattered up and down the collected works like Brobdingnagian blemishes.

A few others have been observed. Byron found him dull, overmild, and flat, like a sauce into which the cook had forgotten to shake pepper. The bumptious young lord of *English Bards and Scotch Reviewers* called Wordsworth a 'dull disciple' of Robert Southey's, and a 'mild apostate' from the neoclassical rules. Homespun narratives like those of Martha Ray, the unwed mother of 'The Thorn,' or Betty Foy, 'the idiot mother of the idiot boy,' struck Byron (as they have since struck others) as 'Christmas stories tortured into rhyme'; it was hardly to be expected, by anyone but Wordsworth, that they should 'contain the essence of the true sublime.' Keats approached the problem of sublimity from another angle. Having taken Shakespeare as his model for the poet's self-immolation in poetry, Keats was discomfited by the ever-recurrent 'I' in Wordsworth; he spoke, not unkindly, of 'the Wordsworthian, or egotistical sublime,' and wondered, half-aloud, whether Wordsworth's grandeur was not in some respects contaminated and rendered obtrusive by the poet's sonorous ego. Shelley's latent satirical impulse was aroused by similar considerations. In his travesty, 'Peter Bell the Third,' he wrote of Wordsworth that

> He had a mind which was somehow
> At once circumference and centre
> Of all he might or feel or know;
> Nothing went ever out, although
> Something did ever enter.
> He had as much imagination
> As a pint-pot; he never could
> Fancy another situation,
> From which to dart his contemplation,
> Than that wherein he stood.

Yet that same group could not help admiring Wordsworth; as practicing poets they had the calipers to measure his stature. Coleridge in
his conversation poems and Byron in *Childe Harold's Pilgrimage* paid
him the compliment of imitation. Keats's letters are often punctuated
with periods of praise for the master. And Shelley, whose *Alastor* sometimes reads as if Wordsworth had been guiding the pen, continues the
'Peter Bell' poem with this astute comment:

> Yet his was individual mind,
> And new-created all he saw
> In a new manner, and refined
> Those new creations, and combined
> Them, by a master-spirit's law.
> Thus, though unimaginative,
> An apprehension clear, intense,
> Of his mind's work, had made alive
> The things it wrought on; I believe
> Wakening a sort of thought in sense.

Parody, however, is always more fun than balanced criticism. Whenever the giant nods, the caricaturists and parodists can be counted on to
tiptoe out of the oven like mischievous small Jacks-of-the-Beanstalk, and
to take up their stations behind his chair. Admirers of 'We Are Seven'
can never quite forget Max Beerbohm's acidulous portrait of a whey-
faced old gentleman pontifically expostulating with the little wench in
the sunbonnet on the fact that seven less two leaves five. Laurence
Housman, himself a skilled parodist, was probably reflecting the Beerbohm influence when he refused to reprint the poem in a recent Wordsworth anthology because, he said, it annoyed him from end to end.
Almost anyone with a stiletto, an inkstand of vitriol, and a groatsworth
of wit can wreak wonderful havoc among the more solemn poems.
Witness J. K. Stephen's manipulation of Wordsworth's sonnet entitled
'Thoughts of a Briton on the Subjugation of Switzerland':

> Two voices are there; one is of the deep;
> It learns the storm-cloud's thunderous melody,
> Now roars, now murmurs with the changing sea,
> Now bird-like pipes, now closes soft in sleep;
> And one is of an old half-witted sheep
> Which bleats articulate monotony,
> And indicates that two and one are three,
> And grass is green, lakes damp, and mountains steep;
> And Wordsworth, both are thine; at certain times,

Forth from the heart of thy melodious rhymes,
The form and pressure of high thoughts will burst;
At other times—Good Lord! I'd rather be
Quite unacquainted with the ABC
Than write such hopeless rubbish as thy worst.

The man the parodists call Wordswords or Worstworst is occasionally (but not often) capable of being dull, homely, flat, earth-bound, egotistical, humorless, obscure, and entangled in prosaism. At worst, his 'incidents and agents from common life' seem merely trite, his ultra-simplified language merely silly—as if, say, we were being asked to genuflect before Mother Goose as the patron saint of the English Lake District. But his worst is infinitely less frequent than the parodists would have us think.

The Victorians were wise enough to see what must be done about it: they stressed the need of editing Wordsworth, cracking off the common clay that disguised and obscured the durable gems. When Arnold made his own selection of the poems in 1879, he said unequivocally that 'the poetical performance of Wordsworth is, after that of Shakespeare and Milton ... undoubtedly the most considerable in our language from the Elizabethan age to the present time.' The impression made by one of his fine poems was, however, 'too often dulled and spoiled by a very inferior piece coming after it.' Wordsworth had permitted 'a great deal of poetical baggage' to encumber the collected works. What Arnold called baggage, Walter Pater thought of as débris. Few artists work quite cleanly, said Pater. They do not always cast off all débris and leave us only 'what the heat of their imagination has wholly fused and transformed' into diamond-hard crystalline form. The critic, the editor, the anthologist must assume the obligation of carting off the débris, chucking out the baggage (Wordsworth at worst) in order to reveal what was there all the time—strong, clear, firm, deep, and lasting—Wordsworth at his best. For behind the shale in the valley, beyond the common lower hills, like Skiddaw in the Lake District or Snowdon in Wales, looms the old giant, a commanding presence.

II

If we ask what the particular virtue is which gives backbone to Wordsworth's giantism, Pater provides us with an excellent starting point. To expunge the worst and to concentrate on the best is, says he, to 'trace the action of his unique incommunicable faculty, that strange, mystical sense of a life in natural things, and of man's life as a part of nature, drawing strength and color and character from local influences, from the hills and streams, and from natural sights and sounds. . . . That is the virtue, the active principle in Wordsworth's poetry.' An example would be those parts of 'Michael' where this sense of the beneficial interaction of man and nature is projected—not the fable itself, not the story of Luke's going bad in the Big City, not even the memorable image of a father-son relationship in the unfinished sheepfold, but rather the portrait of old Michael himself, formed and strengthened by his mountainous environment and his enduring and durable will. *Levavi oculos meos in montes* runs the psalm; and this is part of Wordsworth's testament. Another instance, milder and less rugged, is the Lucy poem which begins, 'Three years she grew'—

> The stars of midnight shall be dear
> To her; and she shall lean her ear
> In many a secret place
> Where rivulets dance their wayward round,
> And beauty born of murmuring sound
> Shall pass into her face.

Housman rightly believes that the last two lines could not have been written by any of the other major English poets: they are emphatically Wordsworth's. They display the essential quality and character of his poetical mind at its best. Wordsworth himself knew that this was so. As early as 1800 he set himself to oppose the widespread and degrading 'thirst after outrageous stimulation' which resulted from the atmosphere of war and genocide, 'the increasing accumulation of men in cities,' the sensationalism of newspapers, and the deluge of cheap fiction. 'Reflecting,' he said, 'upon the magnitude of the general evil, I should be oppressed with no dishonorable melancholy, had I not a deep impression of certain inherent and indestructible qualities of the human mind, and likewise of certain powers in the great and permanent objects that act upon it, which are equally inherent and indestructible.' Out of this deep impression, long brooded over, arises the inherent and indestructible *virtue of* Wordsworth's poetry.

His dimensions are heightened also by his being (what Coleridge called him) a philosophical poet. Reading the neohumanist critics, one would gather that Wordsworth was some sort of blend of the hard-shelled naturalist Lucretius and the soft-shelled naturalist Rousseau.

This view is false. It will never do to overstress the naturalistic element in his thought as over against the humanistic and theistic components. All three conspire to fructify in his belief in the motherhood of nature, the brotherhood of man, the fatherhood of God, and—it may be seriously added, the neighborhood of pain. If Wordsworth can write like a nature-mystic, a pantheist, or a pan-psychist, he can never be said to have forgotten the human figures in the foreground or the supreme Intelligence in the background. The Wordsworthian equivalent of the Miltonic 'great argument' comes clear in the eloquent opening of his unfinished masterwork, *The Recluse*. Turning aside from the ancient epic theme of arms and the man, he chose to tell instead

> Of Truth, of Grandeur, Beauty, Love, and Hope,
> And melancholy Fear subdued by Faith;
> Of blessed consolations in distress;
> Of moral strength, and intellectual Power;
> Of joy in widest commonalty spread;
> Of the individual Mind that keeps her own
> Inviolate retirement, subject there
> To Conscience only, and the law supreme
> Of that Intelligence which governs all—
> I sing:—'Fit audience let me find though few!'

The individual mind of man, subject to the inner checks of conscience and of consciousness of the laws of God ('that Intelligence which governs all'), is surely a problem vast enough to preoccupy any poet. 'Not Chaos,' he wrote, still thinking of Milton, not

> The darkest pit of lowest Erebus,
> Nor aught of blinder vacancy, scooped out
> By help of dreams—can breed such fear and awe
> As fall upon us often when we look
> Into our Minds, into the Mind of Man—
> My haunt, and the main region of my song. . . .

If it was necessary for him to see 'ill sights of madding passions mutually inflamed'; if in country and town alike he

> Must hear Humanity in fields and groves
> Pipe solitary anguish; or must hang
> Brooding above the fierce confederate storm
> Of sorrow, barricadoed evermore
> Within the walls of cities . . .

he had found means to encompass the sound of wailing into a symphony whose overtones were not ultimately tragic. One means was through the timely 'utterance of numerous verse.' Another, and anterior, means was to fix his contemplation upon the inherent and indestructible powers visible alike in nature and human nature. From that vantage point, it was possible to understand that moral evil ('what man has made of man') cannot finally cancel out the universal good. Under 'nature's holy plan,' by observing the myriad ways in which the mind is 'fitted' to the external world, as well as the world to the mind, one could discover a sufficient justification of God's ways to men. 'Nature is made to conspire with spirit to emancipate us.' This was Emerson's cogent summary of the point Wordsworth made in a thousand ways throughout the course of his poetical career. Followed through all its ramifications, it is the point which permits us to claim for him the title of philosophical poet.

Emerson, the prophet of democratic vistas, helps to make us aware of yet another source of Wordsworth's strength and stature. It is that, like another giant named Antaeus, he believes that the poet must keep his feet on the ground, deriving substance and sustenance from his mother, the earth. The politics of Antaeus are unknown, but no one can read Wordsworth for very long without the conviction that at the deeper levels his democracy never wavers. In passages like those relating to Beaupuy in the ninth book of *The Prelude*, his political views come to the surface; later on, as we know, these views were subject to some adjustment in the direction of conservatism. Yet the readjustment does not affect the basic tenet of his democratic faith; few modern poets have embodied in their work, whether by statement or by implication, so firm a sense of the dignity or worth of the common individual man.

Whoever would read the famous preface of 1800 afresh and without preliminary prejudice can scarcely do better than to see it as a declaration of the need for democracy in poetry. Essentially the defence of a theory of poetry, it has long been a battleground for critics because of Wordsworth's espousal of a special doctrine of poetic diction. There is more to it than that. The preface makes a whole series of distinctions and connections whose importance to esthetic theory are not so much modern as timeless. He distinguishes true elevation of style from the false methods employed by certain eighteenth-century poetasters, noting especially the frozen artifice of perception and expression and the 'curious elaboration' which beset that cult. In a searching passage he distinguishes the task of the poet from that of the scientist. He indicates the triple necessity of thought, feeling, and good sense in all good poetry.

He compares the language of poetry to that of prose. He tries to show the relationship between poetry and the primary psychological laws of human nature, including the pleasure-pain principle as enunciated by Jeremy Bentham. His outline of the creative process is astute and valuable; like Coleridge he is a good psychologist because he is able to contemplate objectively the operations of his own mind. He is also enough of a proponent of the 'low' and the 'common' to insist throughout his essay on the remarriage of poetry to *things;* for to him democracy is not an abstraction but a way of life empirically learned.

It is, however, in his conception of the poet and of poetry itself that his democratic leanings are most apparent. This is not to say that he treats the subject exhaustively, but only to suggest from what quarter his winds of doctrine blow. The poet, he insists, is 'a man speaking to men,' not differing from them in kind but only in degree. Here is no vessel for the divine afflatus, set apart from his kind in lordly magnificence. Here is no frenzied enthusiast, no hierophant writing better than he knows, but rather one man, among men, speaking quietly to his fellows of what most moves his heart and what is most central to his deeper thoughts on the inter-relations of man, nature, and transcendental or immanent supernature. The poet's sensibility is livelier, of course. He is uncommonly imaginative, has more enthusiasm, tenderness, and knowledge than the common man. He is more articulate, and has a deeper capacity for delight in all he sees and knows. But he is only the uncommon common man, risen naturally from the ranks of the natural *aristoi,* coming of no diviner race than those to whom he speaks and writes.

Or take, on the same grounds, the question of what poetry is. It is, says Wordsworth, 'the image of man and nature.' It is also 'the most philosophic' (that is, wisdom-loving, and the wisdom loved is that of the people) of all writing. 'Its object is truth, not individual and local, but general and operative; not standing upon external testimony, but carried alive into the heart by passion.' It is truth which 'is its own testimony' because, having been proclaimed, it will immediately be recognized by other men as pertinent to the human situation in which they find themselves. It is thus a direct revelation of reality, or of the poet's considered version of the actual. Therefore Wordsworth is able to say that 'in spite of difference of soil and climate, of language and manners, of laws and customs; in spite of things silently gone out of mind, and things violently destroyed; the poet binds together by passion and knowledge the vast empire of human society, as it is spread over the whole earth, and over all time.' To do so, poetry must keep the reader 'in the company of flesh and blood.' It is not involved with the tears of angels, but with 'natural and human tears.' No celestial ichor distinguishes its language from that of prose: 'the same human blood circulates through the veins of them both.' The poetry of earth is never dead; but we may be best assured of this, thinks Wordsworth, if we assert the ultimate democracy of poetic language: the words of a man speaking to men in the tongue all men know because they are men.

The revolution Wordsworth led was not primarily a back-to-nature movement. It was rather a movement which called for a fresh and mutually fructifying reunion of reality and ideality. His special individual *virtue* as a poet comes from his preoccupation with the indestructibles in nature and in mind. His method is to combine the instruments and insights of the poet with the ideals of the philosopher whose bias is strongly humanistic. His continuing belief in the dignity and dependability of the common man brings his work into spiritual alignment with those democratic revolutions which in his time, both in Europe and America, were coming to the fore after the long years of the *ancien régime*.

III

Finally, there is the artist. As befits a giant, his most persistent theme is growth. Because, in a special sense, the child is father to the man, he becomes absorbed in the growth of children. The youngster may be Wordsworth himself passing through the three stages up the stairway towards maturity, as in 'Tintern Abbey.' It may be the child whose 'progress' is detailed in the Great Ode. Gradually losing what Hazlitt called 'the feeling of immortality in youth,' he finds, somewhat reluctantly, that he must settle for 'the faith which looks through death' rather than at it, and the 'philosophic mind' of the Christian stoic who has kept watch over man's mortality and learned, in the end, what it takes to be a man. It may be his beloved sister Dorothy, or Coleridge, or the child called Lucy, or the small son of his friend Basil Montagu who appears charmingly in the 'Anecdote for Fathers.' The theme of such early lyrics as 'Expostulation and Reply,' 'The Tables Turned,' 'Lines Written in Early Spring,' and 'To My Sister' is once again growth. He wishes to show how the mind develops through sense experience and reflection—John Locke's two great 'fountains' of empirical knowledge.

Or we may learn through the sudden leap of intuition, the unlooked-for epiphany by which one 'impulse' (the word is a favorite of Locke's) from a springtime woodland *may* (Wordsworth does not say it necessarily *will*) teach the man of sensibility more about how men's minds work than a reading of all the sages. An overstatement used for shock value? Clearly it is. Yet what is an epiphany but a visionary overstatement which one hopes time will prove to have been approximately right? A perceptive and reflective observer of nature and its laws is provided with all sorts of emblems, analogies, and implications by the simple expedient of taking a walk and keeping his eyes open. Wordsworth, the perambulatory poet, well knew that the growth of our minds is controlled both by what we perceive and by 'what we half-create.' If we have imagination, together with a considered body of knowledge and conviction, we can 'build up greatest things from least suggestions'— like the emblem writers of the Renaissance, or the Fathers of the medieval Church, or like any first-rate poet.

The subtitle of *The Prelude,* Wordsworth's most intricate exploration of the subject, is 'Growth of a Poet's Mind.' He undertook it partly as a practice poem, a way of learning to handle blank verse, but mainly as an exercise in understanding on the Socratic principle, 'Know thyself.' What were the formative forces which had been brought to bear upon that 'stripling of the hills,' that northern villager with whom, of all people, Wordsworth was most closely acquainted? His childhood luckily had been spent in Nature's lap. A nurse both stern and kindly, she had planted seeds of sympathy and understanding in that growing mind. 'Fair seedtime had my soul,' says Wordsworth. Its growth had been 'fostered alike by beauty and by fear.' The milder discipline of beauty informs such lines as those on the river Derwent, winding among its 'grassy holms' with ceaseless calm music like a lullaby. The discipline of fear is embodied in the trap-robbing and boat-stealing episodes. The boy, troubled in conscience, seemed to hear low breathings coming after him in the woods. From a thwart of the stolen rowboat, he watched horror-struck the huge looming of the black peak from beyond the sheltering grove by the lakeside—something like the incarnation of a Mosaic commandment, which it was not, except as his conscience made it seem so. He is aware, of course, that Nature has no moral ideas. Natural scenes like the grassy Derwent riverbank or the monster shape of the night-shrouded mountain played a 'needful part' in the development of his mind simply by having been there on occasions afterwards recognized as crucial. What gave them significance was the condition of mind with which they entered into permanent association.

There is a kind of 'wise passiveness' (Keats called it 'diligent indolence') in which Nature is a veritable treasure house of suggestion. Natural scenes, taken in their intricate totality, often awakened in Wordsworth what he called 'the visionary power.' Once he tells how he stood, for shelter from an approaching storm, under a brow of rock, listening all awake and aware to 'the ghostly language of the ancient earth.'

> Thence did I drink the visionary power;
> And deem not profitless those fleeting moods
> Of shadowy exultation: not for this
> That they are kindred to our purer mind
> And intellectual life; but that the soul,
> Remembering how she felt, but what she felt
> Remembering not, retains an obscure sense
> Of possible sublimity, whereto
> With growing faculties she doth aspire,
> With faculties still growing, feeling still
> That whatsoever point they gain, they yet
> Have something to pursue.

He records dozens of these natural scenes, not for themselves but for what his mind could learn through the stimuli they offered. This one provided a long vista or distant prospect up the way he knew he must go. Often, at such times, he seems to catch with his mind's eye 'gleams like the flashing of a shield.' The gleam is nearly always Merlin-like, magical, anticipating a period of epiphany when apprehensions hitherto disparate will suddenly coalesce to form another level of understanding. From there he can go on.

Since the structure of *The Prelude* is pyramidal, with a broad base in sense impressions and a capstone of semimystical insight into the ultimate unity of God's mighty plan, it is no accident, it is rather a triumph of the artistic intellect, that it should close with the Mount Snowdon episode. Once again the natural scene plays an emblematic part in what is essentially a religious intuition. Coming suddenly from the fog on the lower flanks of the mountain into bright clear moonlight; looking down on the cloud surface through which the backs of lesser peaks show like whales at sea; hearing, as from an abyss, the roar of mighty waters, the combined voices of innumerable streams, the poet has gained a symbol of such complexity as to be relatively inexhaustible to meditation. When he comes to recollect the scene's emotional impact in the tranquillity of a later time, he recognizes it, not for what it was, but for what, after rumination, it had become *for him:* a Gestalt pattern standing for the human mind at its highest stage of development, a mind sustained

> By recognitions of transcendent power,
> In sense conducting to ideal form.

Such minds are no longer the prisoners of sense impressions. Instead, the 'quickening impulse' provided by sense stimuli prepares such minds all the better 'to hold fit converse with the spiritual world' and to discover, as was never possible before, the true meanings of liberty and love. No wonder that Coleridge, having heard this poem read aloud, rose up at the end to find himself 'in prayer.'

Another way of watching the operation of the growth principle in Wordsworth is to see how and how often he uses it as an organizational device in the shorter poems. It may be called the double-exposure technique. Because he is interested in the stages of growth, he often juxtaposes two widely separated periods of time in such a way that we are made dramatically conscious of the degree of growth that has taken place between Stage One and Stage Two. It resembles the effect that might be produced by our seeing a double exposure on photographic film, where the same person appears in the same setting, except that ten years have elapsed between exposures.

The device is not uniquely Wordsworth's, though he has given to it his own special stamp and hallmark, as one of his ways of seeing. Shakespeare, for instance, uses the technique for dramatic effect in the two balcony scenes of *Romeo and Juliet.* The first of these is an almost perfect embodiment of romantic young love, untested in the alembic of mature experience, surrounded by danger, overstrewn with moonlight, punctuated with extravagant vows, compliments, and conceits. Between this and the second and far quieter balcony scene a process of accelerated maturation has set in. Mercutio and Tybalt have been killed, Romeo has been banished, a forced marriage for Juliet is in the offing, the lovers have made their secret matrimony and spent their wedding night together. The effect of the second balcony scene is then to remind us of the first, and to underscore dramatically how far adverse circumstances and their own responses to them have matured the youthful lovers in the meantime.

Something very like this is constantly happening in the poetry of Wordsworth. We have the picture which has long been held in memory; over against it is laid the picture of things as they are in the historical 'now.' Between the two exposures, subtle changes have always taken place. These may involve a simple translation of the protagonist from the conditions of the country to those of the city as in the early lyric, 'The Reverie of Poor Susan.' Here the song of the caged thrush at the corner of Wood Street in a poor part of London is the auditory image which, for a brief instant, opens the shutter in the camera obscura of Susan's mind. The film of memory still holds the impress of the rural scene, the 'green pastures' where she happily spent the season of her childhood. Momentarily, and ironically, the drab present and the green past are juxtaposed. Then the vision fades and once more the prison house of the city closes round her.

The technique which gives 'The Reverie' whatever distinction it possesses is used far more subtly in many of the better lyrics. In 'Tintern Abbey,' for example, the light in the eyes of his sister seems to reflect for Wordsworth the very set of mind with which, five years before, he had exulted over the beauties of this quiet rural panorama beside the river Wye. 'I behold in thee what I was once.' As he overlooks the scene once more, with the mental landscape of the past still in his purview, he is made doubly aware of a sense of loss (the past will not return) and a sense of compensation greater than the loss (the new maturity and insight which the advancing years have brought). Again, however, it is the collocation of two separate 'spots of time' which dramatizes for him (and for us) the degree and kind of his growth in the intervening period. Again it is the technique of double exposure, this odd co-presence in the mind of the then and the now, which gives dramatic life to his reflective lyric.

The great ode, 'Intimations of Immortality,' abounds, of course, in a complexity of metaphorical activity that differentiates it markedly from 'Tintern Abbey.' Yet its broad strategy of deployment strikingly resembles that of the earlier poem. For its vitality once more depends upon a dialectical interplay between ideas of innocence and ideas of experience. Here is the picture of the true innocent, trailing his clouds of glory, clothed with the sun. Yet here beside it is also the voice of experience, neither harsh nor grating, though deeply informed with the knowledge of the possibilities of good and evil. The two voices make a sort of antiphonal chant which runs throughout this wonderful poem, accounting, perhaps, for the incantational quality it has for the ear when read aloud. The visual aspects, however, are more important than the auditory. Through the mind's eye we are made to see the two states of being in the sharpest contrast, but with the one overlying though not obscuring the other, as in a palimpsest. Thereby the interior drama of the poem—a parable, essentially, of experience and innocence—is made to transpire; and with what effect only the reader of the poem can truly know.

The same principle is at work in 'The Two April Mornings,' 'She was a phantom of delight,' and the 'Ode to Duty.' It gives special dramatic impact to a number of the best sonnets, including such triumphs as 'Composed upon Westminster Bridge' and that moving sonnet of bereavement which begins, ironically, with the phrase, 'Surprised by joy.' A very clear manifestation appears in the 'Elegiac Stanzas Suggested by a Picture of Peele Castle.' Here one finds, still, the two pictures. One is in memory: a calm summer Wordsworth spent long ago by the seaside in the vicinity of the castle. The second is an actual canvas painted by the poet's friend and sometime patron, Sir George Beaumont. It shows the same castle in a season of storm and stress, ruggedly fronting the fierce onslaughts of waves and wind. Between these two moralized landscapes stretches the poem. The first eight stanzas set up the poet's dream of human life through the sunsmitten image of the castle 'sleeping in a glassy sea.' Recantation comes in the last seven stanzas with a farewell to the youthful dream and a willing acceptance of the actual as the passage of time has discovered it to be.

The examination of these poems leads at last to an explanation of the elegiac tone which overlies or penetrates so much of the work of this lyricist of human growth. Regret, a certain kind of lamentation, does battle with joy, a certain kind of paean for the blessings of this life, and the joy tends, on the whole, to win out. The regret is for things lost: a vision of immortality in youth, an absolute sense of nature's ultimate beneficence, an unchartered freedom, or (it may be) a daughter, or the 'phantom of delight' one's wife was when first she gleamed upon the sight. At the same time Wordsworth accepts, not only without demur or sentimental self-pity but also with positive joy, those substitutes which life makes for the early raptures. These may be a faith that looks through death, a sense of the value of the 'pageantry of fear' in natural scenes, a responsible pleasure in following the dictates of duty, a beautiful child to be admired though not owned, and (with all that means) a woman in place of a phantom loveliness that could never be real.

Maturity for Wordsworth is not, of course, a state in which peace or happiness are guaranteed. A number of the shorter poems—'Resolution and Independence' is a good example—offer 'frequent sights of what is to be borne' by all men, everywhere, at some time or other. Ills of the spirit, like those of the body, must be endured and if possible overcome. The road the mature man travels may have its detours through the seasons of hell, unreasoning despairs, despondencies that will not be denied. This is mainly what *The Excursion* is about: an eloquent 'morality' in the form of quasi-dramatic dialogue. The heart of its meaning is in the titles of Books III and IV—'Despondency' and 'Despondency Corrected.' Wordsworth knows what human life is, and what is required of us if we are to learn how to live in it. He is gigantic in the final sense that he is a moral realist.

Too much has probably been made of the alleged shrinkage of power in Wordsworth, as if, after forty, his stature had suddenly declined to that of a dwarf. We read of how his genius decays, of how 'tragically' he is carried off the stage on the double shield of religious orthodoxy and political conservatism. This is a 'despondency' about Wordsworth that needs to be corrected, and a number of modern critics have undertaken the task of correction. 'Some think,' wrote the poet, 'I have lost that poetic ardour and fire 'tis said I once had—the fact is perhaps I have: but instead of that I hope I shall substitute a more thoughtful and quiet power.' The poet speaking here is not Wordsworth; the sentences come from a letter by John Keats. Yet it is a clear statement of what happened to Wordsworth. His powers ripened gradually, reached a peak in his middle and late thirties, and thereafter very gradually declined. In that development and decline, as in so many other respects, the giant Wordsworth is one of us: the epitome of the normal man.

CHARLES WILLIAMS

———

Wordsworth

FROM Milton,' said Landor, 'one must descend, whichever road one takes.' Even to find Shakespeare or find Wordsworth, though then in order to reascend; and of Shakespeare and Wordsworth it is true also. There are other poets of almost equal height, but they are only peaks compared with those three great ranges. There are other ranges, but they are not so high and they are made up of many poets.

To ascend Wordsworth is to ascend a mountain around which there clings a perpetual mist. Often that mist disappears or is blown apart, and then landscapes open below us, landscapes comparable to those we see from Milton or Shakespeare, landscapes of the mind of men. And then the mist gathers again and we are for awhile lost in it. It is this uncertainty gathering over the certainty, this intermission of sight, which is unique in Wordsworth among the three greatest poets. He possesses a power as great in its opening maturity as Milton's, yet that maturity never itself matures; the greatness of his poetry suffers no diminution even when compared with that other sublime sound; yet it moves to no final state of resolution. At its greatest his poetry is as far beyond the capacity of the human voice to utter as either Milton's or Shakespeare's. 'She should have died hereafter' cannot be spoken; it means more than our voice can carry: so does

> Jehovah, who in one night when he passed
> From Egypt, marching.

———

From *The English Poetic Mind* (Clarendon Press, Oxford, 1932), pp. 153–71. Reprinted by permission of the publisher.

Our tongues cannot echo that divine exodus; we feel it as the soldiers felt the music when the god left the palaces of Alexandria. So with the finest things of Wordsworth—

> In beauty exalted as it is itself
> In quality and fabric more divine.

> Mighty poets in their misery dead.

> Diversity of strength
> Attends us, if but once we have been strong.

> And O ye Fountains, Meadows, Hills, and Groves,
> Forebode not any severing of our Loves;
> I only have relinquished one delight
> To live beneath your more habitual sway.

The solemn sincerity of such lines is beyond the compass of our voices. The manner in which Shakespeare, Milton, and Wordsworth respectively defeat us would form the subject for another inquiry. Roughly, it may be suggested that Shakespeare does it by a unison of many implied if not expressed (but usually expressed) intellectual as well as emotional intensities; Milton does it by arousing a sense of the awful spiritual importance of a particular intensity; Wordsworth by arousing a sense of the unity of individual life with universal life. The shell of his verse 'murmurs of the ocean whence it came'; something more than us, more than Wordsworth, more than the poetry of Wordsworth, seems to open up and expand in the sound, as afterwards it withdraws and closes itself in the more expected, but still noble, verse to which it returns. Those central successes in all poets dispose themselves through the rest of the verse, which approaches or recedes from them, and is affected by them. But Wordsworth's style is more dangerous than Milton's. Milton's includes everything in its godlike capacity; if we protest and rebel, we are hurled headlong from that ethereal sky. But Wordsworth's is natural and has the dangers of nature. It is diffused; we do not escape from it—or from nature—so easily as we think. A page even of the worst part of the *Excursion* has often something attractive about it. The details Wordsworth inserts are there because they were there or would be there in nature, and Wordsworth is reluctant to leave anything out. But we are more easily tired.

At its greatest, this is his poetry. But there is, not merely the rest of it but, the depressing rest of it. Of course, he wrote badly sometimes;

that is nothing. Shakespeare did it so often that we have—some of us—almost had to rob him of most of his work. Milton did it sometimes; a personal confession may admit that a few lines at the end of *Samson* (of all places in poetry!) appear almost funny:

> His lot unfortunate in nuptial choice,
> From whence captivity and loss of eyes.

Even the 'tame villatic fowl,' just previously? I do not myself find the explanation of angelic digestion funny, and the use of artillery seems just an intellectual mistake, like the temporal begetting of the Son. But however this may be, even Milton occasionally lost hold. These poetic failures do not count. We can excuse, we can even enjoy, such a break as

> 'Impute it not to impatience, if,' exclaimed
> The Wanderer, 'I infer that he was healed
> By perseverance in the course prescribed.'

It should never be imputed to our impatience that we over-zealously protested against such things; nor against 'Spade! with which Wilkinson hath tilled his land,' or 'then cheered by short refreshment, sallied forth.' But what generations of readers have protested against is the appearance of something in Wordsworth which sounds like poetry and is not poetry, of something neither richly good nor richly bad; in two words, of dull verbiage.

> And shall the venerable halls ye fill
> Refuse to echo the sublime decree?

Who cares? 'Life,' Wordsworth had told us, 'is energy of love'; what we need is the corresponding poetic energy.

That he wrote so much when that energy was lacking suggests that he did not recognize his want of it. On the other hand, he never completed the philosophical poem which he purposed, which the *Prelude* was to have preluded, of which the *Excursion* was to have been the second part, and the *Recluse* an extract from the first. The *Excursion* itself is a poem from which poetic energy can be sensibly understood to depart. There are great and noble things in it, as there were scattered through all Wordsworth's later life; and it has a right to demand—what it is not always allowed—that it should be a poem of its own kind and not of ours. But when we have done our best, it remains true that though the *Excursion* has nobler poetry in it than *Don Juan* has, yet *Don Juan* is a better poem and more homogeneous poetry than the *Excursion*. It would be a saint, a 'holy fool' of poetry, who would consent to keep the *Excursion* and lose *Don Juan*. And his sanctity and his folly would be equal.

This mass of unsuccessful stuff, this slow change in the *Excursion*, this abandonment of the great poem which Wordsworth had intended—to what cause are they due? to what cause in his poetry, not in his personal life (with which this essay is not concerned)? The answer is that his poetry could not sufficiently trust itself.[1]

Wordsworth had one poetic habit in common with Milton—the habit of introducing solitary figures. But there is a difference between them: Milton's are active, Wordsworth's are passive. Milton's are in revolt; Wordsworth's are in—what are they in? They are not in revolt; they are not entirely in acceptance, at least they are not in willing and exalted acceptance. They express—or some of them do—a trust in God. But this is secondary, even where it occurs, and it does not always occur. They communicate a strange sensation of semi-mystical fear; they rise before us in that verse, as shapes partly of terror, partly of sympathy, wholly of mystery. Examples are the soldier at the end of Book IV of the *Prelude*; the beggar in Book VII (ll. 635–49); the girl in Book XII (ll. 248–61); 'the single sheep, and the one blasted tree' also in Book XII (ll. 292–302, 317–23); the Leech-Gatherer; Margaret (in the *Affliction of Margaret*—though here the solitary figure speaks); the old Cumberland Beggar; the Solitary Reaper. These are the most striking among many solitudes; there are many others of less apparent significance—Lucy Gray is one—whose ghost

> sings a solitary song
> That whistles in the wind;

Margaret in the First Book of the *Excursion*, and other figures scattered through that poem; the Shepherd at the end of *Michael*; Leonard in the *Brothers*; the Forsaken Indian Woman; Ruth—all these, and more, sing their own solitary songs or preserve their solitary silences. And around them is that third circle which is only by accident solitary—the flowers and birds whom Wordsworth names singly, the Skylark, the Daisy, the Lesser Celandine, the Swan on still Saint Mary's lake, the Linnet, the Butterfly. Add the solitude of Lucy and the recurrent solitude of Wordsworth himself, and the groups will be sufficiently presented. Now among these there are, of course, many human solitaries, many who have been made lonely by their own actions or those of others, and this the poems tell us, arousing in us a sense of our own capacity for solitude and endurance. It is such things as those that make part of Wordsworth's greatness, confirming his instinctive claim to be part of our philosophic mind. Michael by the sheepfold, and Leonard and the Indian Woman, and Wordsworth, are all presentations of humanity. But that first group are not in fact presentations of humanity at all; they are something vaster and stranger.

Of the London beggar Wordsworth says that his own 'mind turned round as with the might of waters,'

> And on the shape of that unmoving man,
> His steadfast face and sightless eyes, I gazed
> As if admonished from another world.

Of the soldier—or just before—he says, speaking of Solitude, that by night

> the soul of that great Power is met,
> Sometimes embodied on a public road,

and it is only after 'subduing my heart's specious cowardice' that he dares speak to that appearance

> —Companionless
> No dog attending, by no staff sustained,
> He stood
> his form
> Kept the same awful steadiness—at his feet
> His shadow lay, and moved not.

These are unnerving apparitions—at least, they almost unnerved Wordsworth; they came to him like the incarnations of the otherness he had in childhood known more vaguely in the 'low breathings,' or the peak which called up

> huge and mighty forms that do not live
> Like living men.

And greater than beggar or soldier is the Leech-Gatherer. Wordsworth gave that poem a second title—'Resolution and Independence.' It is very proper that we should read it as, apparently, he meant us to; it is proper that we should realize what a great and moving poem it is. But it is permissible also that we should derive from it all that it contains; and one of the things it does contain is a sense that the Leech-Gatherer is the impersonated thought of some other state of being, which the acceptance of the noble doctrine it teaches leaves in itself unexplored.

He seems 'the oldest man . . . that ever wore grey hairs'; he was like 'a huge stone . . . on the bald top of an eminence,' that seems 'a thing endowed with sense'; again he was like a

> sea-beast, that on a shelf
> Of rock or sand reposeth, there to sun itself.

He is 'motionless as a cloud that heareth not the loud winds.' He speaks 'in solemn order'—'a lofty utterance.'

> His voice to me was like a stream
> Scarce heard; nor word from word could I divide.
> And the whole body of the man did seem
> Like one whom I had met with in a dream.

His shape, his speech, 'the lonely place,' all trouble Wordsworth.

> In my mind's eye I seemed to see him pace
> About the weary moors continually,
> Wandering about alone and silently.

Confronted with this great experience Wordsworth might have done one of two things—in doing the very thing he did do. He asked him, out of the midst of his own bother about his future income—and God, He knows how real and urgent that bother can be; we shall never understand the poets if we pretend that money is not of high importance—he asked him, 'How is it that you live, and what is it you do?' And—as if 'sent To give me human strength'—the Leech-Gatherer told him, and Wordsworth listened and admired and believed and went away comforted. Nevertheless, that question might have been asked with another meaning—with the desire for some knowledge similar to that which caused Jacob to wrestle with the Angel: 'What is thy *name*?' It might have been asked not for strength and comfort, but for discovery and increase of poetic wisdom.

What *is* this apparition—this stone—this sea-beast—this cloud—this dream-like body—this undivided stream of lofty utterance? What is it in itself? Never mind what it means to our lives, what moral or message it has for us, or let that be secondary; 'what is thy *name*?' He belongs to that strange world from which the woman came, who bore a pitcher on her head and walked leaning against the wind, and the beggar who wore a label that seemed

> to typify the utmost we can know
> Both of ourselves and of the universe;

and the soldier who was an embodiment of the power of Solitude; and the Highland Reaper who sang 'the melancholy song,' 'the plaintive numbers,' of which Wordsworth knew that they might be 'of old unhappy far-off things.'

Lear on the heath, Satan on Niphates—if these had not been forced by the poets to speak, and speaking, to explain their being, would not they too have seemed to belong to that terrifying world?

In effect they do. Wordsworth drew from figures looming as Lear and Satan loomed, as Othello, and the Ghost of Caesar, and Samson in Gaza, a high and lofty doctrine. But it was a doctrine: his poetry ceased to inquire into them; perhaps therefore inevitably his poetry ceased. For it was a doctrine that concerned itself more with the way men should live than with poetry itself.

But so did Milton? *Nego*; at least not before his poetry had done all it could with Satan. Milton trusted poetry absolutely—Satan is the proof— and he was justified. Shakespeare trusted poetry absolutely—Lear and Macbeth are the proofs—and he was justified. But Wordsworth did not, could not, quite do that; therefore his poetry left his philosophy to get on as best it could, and his philosophy could not get on. The great philosophical poem was never written.

I do not suggest that either Milton or Shakespeare put it like that to themselves. But it is clear that both of them did wholly what they had to do, and left the rest to the Muse. It was, after all, *Milton* who dared the sublime defiance of 'Evil, be thou my good'; he himself must have trusted poetry profoundly before he could believe that his poem would get over that. He did not refuse it because his intelligence told him that it might prove harmful or shocking or wrong, just as he did not do it because it was harmful or shocking or wrong. It was Satan. Now there is a sense in which Wordsworth was compelled to avoid his own Solitaries. It is a sense so rare that, though he did it, Wordsworth remains our third greatest poet. But it is a sense so definite that he came near to thinking that good intentions would write poetry for him. It is a sense so unimportant that what he did is still 'felt in the blood and felt along the heart.' But it is a sense so important that what he did is thought to be good for the young and is consistently misapprehended and disliked by the young.[2]

And yet Wordsworth was a very great poet; if he had not been we should not even have known that he missed the final wrestling. It is not to any slackness on his part that we dare attribute this last—this very last—lack. It is to be attributed, little though they knew it, to Pitt and all those who declared war on the Revolution. Or so his poetry states, and what his poetry dared not or did not state must be left to students of his individual life.

The crisis of Troilus and the crisis of Satan is related to the crisis which fell on Wordsworth: at least as he discovers and expresses it in the *Prelude*. There is not only the account itself—'pity and shame,' 'change and subversion,' a shock 'to my moral nature,' 'a revolution, at this one time,' 'a stride Into another region,' 'from that pleasant station torn And tossed about in whirlwind,' 'a conflict of sensations without name.' These are the direct phrases—I do not see how they could be stronger. But there is more—he exulted when Englishmen were defeated, killed, and put to flight. And there follows the picture of Wordsworth, who loved the village and its people, and its people in the church at common prayer, himself sitting in the church, 'like an uninvited guest,' silent, feeding 'on the day of vengeance yet to come.' The last line has to be fully felt before the depth of this part of Wordsworth's poetry can be realized. If any one had asked him what England had done to 'soil our mothers' he might have answered, exactly in Troilus' words, 'nothing at all, unless that this were she.'

But *Troilus* was written half-way through Shakespeare's poetic life; so was *Paradise Lost* in Milton's. It was the poetic immaturity of Wordsworth's *Evening Walk* and *Descriptive Sketches* which suffered subversion. In 1792 Wordsworth all but became a leader of the Girondins; in 1793 he received this shock; in 1795–6 he wrote the *Borderers;* in 1797–8 he wrote the *Lyrical Ballads,* the *Recluse, Peter Bell*; in 1799 he began the *Prelude,* and ended it in 1805. It covered the second half of his great ten years; somewhere about the 1803–6 period he wrote also the *Ode on the Intimations of Immortality*, and in 1805–6 the *Happy Warrior.* The important point is that his personal experiences preceded nearly all his poetry; his poetry followed his personal experiences. No wonder he talked about emotion recollected in tranquillity! And how unwise of us to apply the phrase to any one but Wordsworth.

For from these dates it is clear that when that crisis of destiny fell on

Wordsworth he could not attempt to explore it in high poetry, because he did not, till afterwards, reach high poetry.

It is of course just possible, in the abstract, that he might, in that state of outraged being, have destroyed all the unpublished poetry he had up to then written. It is just possible that as Othello struck at Desdemona, so Wordsworth struck at what was dearest to him. Poetry was not guilty as Othello supposed Desdemona to be. But if the universe had played him false, he might, for a few moments, have loved and hated what the universe and England had given him, and in that insanity destroyed it. 'Evil, be thou my good.' It is not likely, but it would be possible with any poet, and it is barely possible with Wordsworth. But it is likely that there would have been some trace of it in Dorothy's journals or elsewhere, and it may fairly safely be assumed that he did not. Besides, there is *Guilt and Sorrow*—but he might have left *that*.

His poetry therefore reflected his life up to then; his concern with Nature, and with man, his consciousness of that dreadful separation of the thing inseparate, and the means by which he was healed. But his healing, his recovery, was on the hither side of that divided universe, not on the yonder. His poetic genius therefore remained on the hither side. It knew there was another; it knew there was some greater resolution of the strife in man's heart. But it never had the strength to go there.

The abdication of the pure poetic authority in his verse in favour of some other authority is because it was by some other authority than the purely poetic that he was revived. 'Imagination and Taste,' is the title of the last two books of the *Prelude*, 'how impaired and restored.' They were restored; they were no more than restored—except for the operative faculty of discovering themselves in poetry. The comparison of certain lines in the *Prelude* with the discussion between the Trojan princes in *Troilus* is too marked to be neglected. 'What is aught but as 'tis valued?' What is value?

> What the rule and whence
> The sanction ?

Hector had broken off the discussion, by Shakespeare's choice, either designedly or accidentally, long before that point had been reached. The end of the argument there is not decision, but Hector. The farther search was carried on not by the working of intellect but by the writing of poetry. It is true that Wordsworth's great subject was not men acting

118

and suffering; these serve only as illustrations. His subject was the mind of man in relation to men, to the universe, and to God. He was—or would have been—a philosophical and not a dramatic poet. But poetry is all one; its glory equal, its majesty co-eternal. It uses doctrines; it does not obey them. It discovers ways through chaos; it does not follow them. It sits brooding on the vast abyss; it does not wait till the abyss has been delimited—even by Nature and Dorothy.

It could not do this at that time for Wordsworth, and for that single reason—he was a poet and he was not writing poetry. His soul relied on other authorities. His poetry, therefore, when it came to be, did not sufficiently distinguish between its own authority and that of other traditions. Towards the end of the *Excursion,* Wordsworth really does seem to think that to mention 'the voice of wisdom whispering Scripture texts' or Baptism was enough; he thought those things themselves had authority in themselves. So they may have, but not in poetry. If poetry is to refer to 'Scripture texts' it must make of them a poetic experience; if poetry is to thrill us with Baptism, it must make Baptism part of its own mythology. Wordsworth assumed that merely to mention seduction would make us disapprove of it; but in poetry this is not so, we must be urged by the poetic force. Poetry has to do all its own work; in return it has all its own authority.

Yet for ten years, and at intervals thereafter, how close to that central subject his poetry lay! how near it seems to be to holding in itself the great awareness of the divided consciousness, and presenting some new resolution of it! It has its doctrine for us, and it has more—it has the continual approach of something greater. There is in it the knowledge of something it cannot quite discover. 'We feel that we are greater than we know,' 'Thoughts that lie . . . too deep for tears,' 'we will teach them how,' 'high instincts,' the label on the beggar, the 'brightness' of the Happy Warrior. There are strange and solitary forms appearing, on lonely roads, on moors, in cities; and somehow—as in certain antique legends—the poet never asks quite the right question. Wordsworth took part with Coleridge in the *Lyrical Ballads,* and it is not always noticed that the actual themes of their verse are sometimes close. The Ancient Mariner is kindred to those other apparitions; only *they* could not speak of themselves, but must be challenged. The verse which Coleridge added to the *Ancient Mariner*—and blamed himself for adding—is a Wordsworthian verse translated into Coleridgian. 'He prayeth best who loveth best. . . .' But Coleridge was right; it ought not to be there.

The *Ancient Mariner* is a tale of a similar crisis—of accident, doom, death, and life-in-death—but it flies between Wordsworth and Shakespeare. It has no reference either to man's enduring mind as Wordsworth has, nor to the hiding-places of the new power as Shakespeare has. It is faerie, and therefore the Mariner is compelled to tell the unrelated story. Had it been human, his embodied power would have had to wait to be challenged. Could that figure which was like a sea-beast sunning itself have held Wordsworth as the Mariner held the Wedding Guest . . . but alas, it was not to be.

Nevertheless, what came to be was a great thing. From the *Borderers* to the *Excursion* there is communicated a sense of the human spirit that does everything but what only Shakespeare did. The earliest long poem after the recovery was the *Borderers*. The *Borderers* is precisely an attempt to present a similar crisis to that through which Wordsworth passed—

> There was a plot,
> A hideous plot against the soul of man.
>
> A man by pain and thought compelled to live,
> Yet loathing life.
>
> Suffering is permanent, obscure, and dark,
> And shares the nature of infinity.
>
> The mind of man, upturned,
> Is in all natures a strange spectacle,
> In some a hideous one.

But there is no suggestion of a resolution. Then there came the many noble poems 'on man, on nature, and on human life,' in which the authority of poetry is everywhere present. Among them are the solitaries who are significant of other things, but also those who awake our own knowledge of mighty endurance.

> The gods approve
> The depth and not the tumult of the soul;

the depth of the soul is shown here in the repose which had been restored to Wordsworth, and which he now searched out. Everywhere it is that to which his genius returns, with counsel, with wisdom, with exalted hope. He explores that state of being, even if he leaves others undetermined. The noblest expression of it—outside the *Prelude*—is the

Intimations of Immortality. It is a platitude to say that it is not about immortality; it is about his own poetry. It is that which 'hath kept watch o'er man's mortality,' which feels the 'fallings from us, vanishings,' which in certain rare encounters trembles 'like a guilty thing surprised.' It is this which, after the 'hour Of splendour in the grass, of glory in the flower' has disappeared, is to find 'strength in what remains behind.' But strength in what remains behind is not the strength of Imogen, of Perdita, of Pericles, or of Ariel, nor the knowledge of the Chorus in *Samson*.

In the *Excursion* Wordsworth made an effort—a final effort—to gather everything in. He succeeded in manufacturing four eidola of himself: the Wanderer, who is Wordsworth's idea of the incarnation of his own poetic mind; the Solitary, who is Wordsworth's idea of himself gone wrong; the Vicar, who is Wordsworth's idea of himself ordained, and the narrator, who is just Wordsworth. After the first book or two it is almost impossible to be greatly interested. Yet even there poetry breaks out—of the same kind and concern—

> poor humanity's afflicted will
> Struggling in vain with ruthless destiny.
>
> The intellectual power, through words and things,
> Went sounding on, a dim and perilous way.

It is the very description of poetry making itself; it is a description of Shakespeare and Milton. It is a way, nevertheless, which Wordsworth's genius did not wholly take: it paused almost at the exact point at which he used the lines. For it was humanity's afflicted will struggling *in vain* of which his poetry was most intensely aware. He shaped the image of man repulsed by destiny, and made it into an everlasting nobility. The *Happy Warrior* is a single poem's vision of something else; but it is the *Ode to Duty*, the end of the *Immortality* Ode, the *Elegiac Stanzas*, and other poems of the kind, including parts of the *Prelude* and the *Excursion*, which do the work. This unique presentation we owe to Wordsworth and to Wordsworth alone. The depressing, the uninteresting, verse is a necessary accident of that achievement; we may not read it, but we ought to realize that it is a condition of what we have and do read, and no more to be regarded in itself than the plot of *Cymbeline* is to be solemnly discussed apart from Imogen and the Dirge. That Wordsworth wrote it is due to the same cause that shaped the particular burden of his great poetry—the fact that he, whose subject was his own experience, did not write poetry while he was undergoing that experience. He could not explore his own crisis by meeting it in poetry. He had to deal with his crisis as it had been resolved by other aids, and those aids and their result his poetry never fully assumed. But if we could be allowed to attribute will and intention to the English Muse, it might seem that she deliberately refrained from visiting her son until his central experience was ended, in order that we might have for our delight that great song of solemn endurance and hope. It is a music which might have accompanied Adam and Eve as they passed from Eden at the close of *Paradise Lost*.

NOTES

1. To say that Wordsworth did not trust it is hardly sufficient. A man cannot write poetry by willing it. Besides which, we have no right to dogmatize about Wordsworth's personal mind. And besides which again, the very fact that he wrote so much suggests that he meant to trust, and thought he was trusting, in it. It was his genius that misled him, not he who miscompelled his genius. But of course that misleading was partly due to mortal things. I prefer myself to think that his genius was right in the account which it gave of the whole matter itself. For these reasons I have not discussed Annette.

2. There are no doubt exceptions. But any one who has spoken of Wordsworth to the young will know how dull they suppose him to be. Well, of course, as long as we send them to him to discover moral impulses—and at that probably our own—in vernal woods, what can we expect? Bliss is it in *that* dawn to be alive?

LIONEL TRILLING

The Immortality Ode

I

CRITICISM, we know, must always be concerned with the poem itself. But a poem does not always exist only in itself: sometimes it has a very lively existence in its false or partial appearances. These simulacra of the actual poem must be taken into account by criticism; and sometimes, in its effort to come at the poem as it really is, criticism does well to allow the simulacra to dictate at least its opening moves. In speaking about Wordsworth's 'Ode: Intimations of Immortality from Recollections of Early Childhood,' I should like to begin by considering an interpretation of the poem which is commonly made. According to this interpretation—I choose for its brevity Dean Sperry's statement of a view which is held by many other admirable critics—the Ode is 'Wordsworth's conscious farewell to his art, a dirge sung over his departing powers.'

How did this interpretation—erroneous, as I believe—come into being? The Ode may indeed be quoted to substantiate it, but I do not think it has been drawn directly from the poem itself. To be sure, the Ode is not wholly perspicuous. Wordsworth himself seems to have thought it difficult, for in the Fenwick notes he speaks of the need for competence and attention in the reader. The difficulty does not lie in the diction, which is simple, or even in the syntax, which is sometimes obscure, but rather in certain contradictory statements which the poem makes, and in the ambiguity of some of its crucial words. Yet the erroneous interpretation I am dealing with does not arise from any intrinsic difficulty

---

of the poem itself but rather from certain extraneous and unexpressed assumptions which some of its readers make about the nature of the mind.

Nowadays it is not difficult for us to understand that such tacit assumptions about the mental processes are likely to lie hidden beneath what we say about poetry. Usually, despite our general awareness of their existence, it requires great effort to bring these assumptions explicitly into consciousness. But in speaking of Wordsworth one of the commonest of our unexpressed ideas comes so close to the surface of our thought that it needs only to be grasped and named. I refer to the belief that poetry is made by means of a particular poetic faculty, a faculty which may be isolated and defined.

It is this belief, based wholly upon assumption, which underlies all the speculations of the critics who attempt to provide us with explanations of Wordsworth's poetic decline by attributing it to one or another of the events of his life. In effect any such explanation is a way of *defining* Wordsworth's poetic faculty: what the biographical critics are telling us is that Wordsworth wrote great poetry by means of a faculty which depended upon his relations with Annette Vallon, or by means of a faculty which operated only so long as he admired the French Revolution, or by means of a faculty which flourished by virtue of a particular pitch of youthful sense-perception or by virtue of a certain attitude toward Jeffrey's criticism or by virtue of a certain relation with Coleridge.

Now no one can reasonably object to the idea of mental determination in general, and I certainly do not intend to make out that poetry is an unconditioned activity. Still, this particular notion of mental determination which implies that Wordsworth's genius failed when it was deprived of some single emotional circumstance is so much too simple and so much too mechanical that I think we must inevitably reject it. Certainly that we know of poetry does not allow us to refer the making of it to any single faculty. Nothing less than the whole mind, the whole man, will suffice for its origin. And such was Wordsworth's own view of the matter.

There is another unsubstantiated assumption at work in the common biographical interpretation of the Ode. This is the belief that a natural and inevitable warfare exists between the poetic faculty and the faculty by which we conceive or comprehend general ideas. Wordsworth himself did not believe in this antagonism—indeed, he held an almost contrary view—but Coleridge thought that philosophy had encroached upon and destroyed his own powers, and the critics who speculate on Wordsworth's artistic fate seem to prefer Coleridge's psychology to Wordsworth's own. Observing in the Ode a contrast drawn between something called 'the visionary gleam' and something called 'the philosophic mind,' they leap to the conclusion that the Ode is Wordsworth's conscious farewell to his art, a dirge sung over departing powers.

I am so far from agreeing with this conclusion that I believe the Ode is not only not a dirge sung over departing powers but actually a dedication to new powers. Wordsworth did not, to be sure, realize his hopes for these new powers, but that is quite another matter.

II

As with many poems, it is hard to understand any part of the Ode until we first understand the whole of it. I will therefore say at once what I think the poem is chiefly about. It is a poem about growing; some say it is a poem about growing old, but I believe it is about growing up. It is incidentally a poem about optics and then, inevitably, about epistemology; it is concerned with ways of seeing and then with ways of knowing. Ultimately it is concerned with ways of acting, for, as usual with Wordsworth, knowledge implies liberty and power. In only a limited sense is the Ode a poem about immortality.

Both formally and in the history of its composition the poem is divided into two main parts. The first part, consisting of four stanzas, states an optical phenomenon and asks a question about it. The second part, consisting of seven stanzas, answers that question and is itself divided into two parts, of which the first is despairing, the second hopeful. Some time separates the composition of the question from that of the answer; the evidence most recently adduced by Professor de Selincourt seems to indicate that the interval was two years.

The question which the first part asks is this:

> Whither is fled the visionary gleam?
> Where is it now, the glory and the dream?

All the first part leads to this question, but although it moves in only one direction it takes its way through more than one mood. There are at least three moods before the climax of the question is reached.

The first stanza makes a relatively simple statement. 'There was a time' when all common things seemed clothed in 'celestial light,' when they had 'the glory and the freshness of a dream.' In a poem ostensibly about immortality we ought perhaps to pause over the word 'celestial,' but the present elaborate title was not given to the poem until much later, and conceivably at the time of the writing of the first part the idea of immortality was not in Wordsworth's mind at all. Celestial light probably means only something different from ordinary, earthly, scientific light; it is a light of the mind, shining even in darkness—'by night or day'—and it is perhaps similar to the light which is praised in the invocation to the third book of *Paradise Lost*.

The second stanza goes on to develop this first mood, speaking of the ordinary, physical kind of vision and suggesting further the meaning of 'celestial.' We must remark that in this stanza Wordsworth is so far from observing a diminution of his physical senses that he explicitly affirms their strength. He is at pains to tell us how vividly he sees the rainbow, the rose, the moon, the stars, the water and the sunshine. I emphasize this because some of those who find the Ode a dirge over the poetic power maintain that the poetic power failed with the failure of Wordsworth's senses. It is true that Wordsworth, who lived to be eighty, was said in middle life to look much older than his years. Still, thirty-two, his age at the time of writing the first part of the Ode, is an extravagantly early age for a dramatic failure of the senses. We might observe here, as others have observed elsewhere, that Wordsworth never did have the special and perhaps modern sensibility of his sister or of Coleridge, who were so aware of exquisite particularities. His finest passages are moral, emotional, subjective; whatever visual intensity they have comes from his response to the object, not from his close observation of it.

And in the second stanza Wordsworth not only confirms his senses but he also confirms his ability to perceive beauty. He tells us how he responds to the loveliness of the rose and of the stars reflected in the water. He can deal, in the way of Fancy, with the delight of the moon when there are no competing stars in the sky. He can see in Nature certain moral propensities. He speaks of the sunshine as a 'glorious birth.' But here he pauses to draw distinctions from that fascinating word 'glory': despite his perception of the sunshine as a glorious birth, he knows 'That there hath past away a glory from the earth.'

Now, with the third stanza, the poem begins to complicate itself. It is *while* Wordsworth is aware of the 'optical' change in himself, the loss of the 'glory,' that there comes to him 'a thought of grief.' I emphasize the word 'while' to suggest that we must understand that for some time he had been conscious of the 'optical' change *without* feeling grief. The grief, then, would seem to be coincidental with but not necessarily caused by the change. And the grief is not of long duration, for we learn that

> A timely utterance gave that thought relief,
> And I again am strong.

It would be not only interesting but also useful to know what that 'timely utterance' was, and I shall hazard a guess; but first I should like to follow the development of the Ode a little further, pausing only to remark that the reference to the timely utterance seems to imply that, although the grief is not of long duration, still we are not dealing with the internal experiences of a moment, or of a morning's walk, but of a time sufficient to allow for development and change of mood; that is, the dramatic time of the poem is not exactly equivalent to the emotional time.

Stanza IV goes on to tell us that the poet, after gaining relief from the timely utterance, whatever that was, felt himself quite in harmony with the joy of Nature in spring. The tone of this stanza is ecstatic, and in a way that some readers find strained and unpleasant and even of doubtful sincerity. Twice there is a halting repetition of words to express a kind of painful intensity of response: 'I feel—I feel it all,' and 'I hear, I hear, with joy I hear!' Wordsworth sees, hears, feels—and with that 'joy' which both he and Coleridge felt to be so necessary to the poet. But despite the response, despite the joy, the ecstasy changes to sadness in a wonderful modulation which quite justifies the antecedent shrillness of affirmation:

> —But there's a Tree, of many, one,
> A single Field which I have looked upon,
> Both of them speak of something that is gone:
> The Pansy at my feet
> Doth the same tale repeat.

And what they utter is the terrible question:

> Whither is fled the visionary gleam?
> Where is it now, the glory and the dream?

III

Now, the interpretation which makes the Ode a dirge over departing powers and a conscious farewell to art takes it for granted that the visionary gleam, the glory, and the dream, are Wordsworth's names for the power by which he made poetry. This interpretation gives to the Ode a place in Wordsworth's life exactly analogous to the place that 'Dejection: An Ode' has in Coleridge's life. It is well known how intimately the two poems are connected; the circumstances of their composition makes them symbiotic. Coleridge in his poem most certainly does say that his poetic powers are gone or going; he is very explicit, and the language he uses is very close to Wordsworth's own. He tells us that upon 'the inanimate cold world' there must issue from the soul 'a light, a glory, a fair luminous cloud,' and that this glory *is* Joy, which he himself no longer possesses. But Coleridge's poem, although it responds to the first part of Wordsworth's, is not a recapitulation of it. On the contrary, Coleridge is precisely contrasting his situation with Wordsworth's. As Professor de Selincourt says in his comments on the first version of 'Dejection,' this contrast 'was the root idea' of Coleridge's ode.[1] In April of 1802 Wordsworth was a month away from his marriage to Mary Hutchison, on the point of establishing his life in a felicity and order which became his genius, while Coleridge was at the nadir of despair over his own unhappy marriage and his hopeless love for Sara, the sister of Wordsworth's fiancée. And the difference between the situations of the two friends stands in Coleridge's mind for the difference in the states of health of their respective poetic powers.

Coleridge explicitly ascribes the decay of his poetic power to his unhappiness, which worked him harm in two ways—by forcing him to escape from the life of emotion to find refuge in intellectual abstraction and by destroying the Joy which, issuing as 'a light, a glory, a fair luminous cloud,' so irradiated the world as to make it a fit object of the shaping power of imagination. But Wordsworth tells us something quite different about himself. He tells us that he has strength, that he has Joy, but still he has not the glory. In short, we have no reason to assume that, when he asks the question at the end of the fourth stanza, he means, 'Where has my creative power gone?' Wordsworth tells us how he made poetry; he says he made it out of the experience of his senses as worked upon by his contemplative intellect, but he nowhere tells us that he made poetry out of visionary gleams, out of glories, or out of dreams.

To be sure, he writes very often about gleams. The word 'gleam' is a favorite one with him, and a glance at the Lane Cooper concordance will confirm our impression that Wordsworth, whenever he has a moment of insight or happiness, talks about it in the language of light. His great poems are about moments of enlightenment, in which the metaphoric and the literal meaning of the word are at one—he uses 'glory' in the abstract modern sense, but always with an awareness of the old concrete iconographic sense of a visible nimbus.[2] But this momentary and special light is the subject matter of his poetry, not the power of making it. The moments are moments of understanding, but Wordsworth does not say that they make writing poetry any easier. Indeed, in lines 59–131 of the first book of *The Prelude* he expressly says that the moments of clarity are by no means always matched by poetic creativity.

As for dreams and poetry, there is some doubt about the meaning that Wordsworth gave to the word 'dream' used as a metaphor. In 'Expostulation and Reply' he seems to say that dreaming—'dream my time away'—is a good thing, but he is ironically using his interlocutor's depreciatory word, and he really does not mean 'dream' at all. In the Peele Castle verses, which have so close a connection with the Immortality Ode, he speaks of the 'poet's dream' and makes it synonymous with 'gleam,' with 'the light that never was, on sea or land,' and with the 'consecration.' But the beauty of the famous lines often makes us forget to connect them with what follows, for Wordsworth says that gleam, light, consecration, and dream would have made an 'illusion ' or, in the 1807 version, a 'delusion.' Professor Beatty reminds us that in the 1820 version Wordsworth destroyed the beauty of the lines in order to make his intention quite clear. He wrote:

> and add a gleam
> Of lustre known to neither sea nor land,
> But borrowed from the youthful Poet's Dream.

That is, according to the terms of Wordsworth's conception of the three ages of man, the youthful Poet was, as he had a right to be, in the service of Fancy and therefore saw the sea as calm. But Wordsworth himself can now no longer see in the way of Fancy; he has, he says, 'submitted to a new control.' This seems to be at once a loss and a gain. The loss:

'A power is gone, which nothing can restore.' The gain: 'A deep distress hath humanized my Soul'; this is gain because happiness without 'humanization' 'is to be pitied, for 'tis surely blind'; to be 'housed in a dream' is to be 'at distance from the kind' (i.e., mankind). In the 'Letter to Mathetes' he speaks of the Fancy as 'dreaming'; and the Fancy is, we know, a lower form of intellect in Wordsworth's hierarchy, and peculiar to youth.

But although, as we see, Wordsworth uses the word 'dream' to mean illusion, we must remember that he thought illusions might be very useful. They often led him to proper attitudes and allowed him to deal successfully with reality. In *The Prelude* he tells how his reading of fiction made him able to look at the disfigured face of the drowned man without too much horror; how a kind of superstitious conviction of his own powers was useful to him; how, indeed, many of the most critical moments of his boyhood education were moments of significant illusion; and in *The Excursion* he is quite explicit about the salutary effects of superstition. But he was interested in dreams not for their own sake but for the sake of reality. Dreams may *perhaps* be associated with poetry, but reality *certainly* is; and reality for Wordsworth comes fullest with Imagination, the faculty of maturity. The loss of the 'dream' may be painful, but it does not necessarily mean the end of poetry.

IV

And now for a moment I should like to turn back to the 'timely utterance,' because I think an understanding of it will help get rid of the idea that Wordsworth was saying farewell to poetry. Professor Garrod believes that this 'utterance' was 'My heart leaps up when I behold,' which was written the day before the Ode was begun. Certainly this poem is most intimately related to the Ode—its theme, the legacy left by the child to the man, is a dominant theme of the Ode, and Wordsworth used its last lines as the Ode's epigraph. But I should like to suggest that the 'utterance' was something else. In line 43 Wordsworth says, 'Oh evil day! if I were sullen,' and the word 'sullen' leaps out at us as a striking and carefully chosen word. Now there is one poem in which Wordsworth says that he was sullen; it is 'Resolution and Independence.'

We know that Wordsworth was working on the first part of the Ode on the 27th of March, the day after the composition of the rainbow poem. On the 17th of June he added a little to the Ode, but what he added we do not know. Between these two dates Wordsworth and Dorothy had paid their visit to Coleridge, who was sojourning at Keswick; during this visit Coleridge, on April 4, had written 'Dejection: an Ode,' very probably after he had read what was already in existence of the Immortality Ode. Coleridge's mental state was very bad—still, not so bad as to keep him from writing a great poem—and the Wordsworths were much distressed. A month later, on May 3, Wordsworth began to compose 'The Leech-Gatherer,' later known as 'Resolution and Independence.' It is this poem that is, I think, the timely utterance.[3]

'Resolution and Independence' is a poem about the fate of poets. It is also a poem about sullenness, in the sense that the people in the Fifth Circle are said by Dante to be sullen: ' "Sullen were we in the sweet air, that is gladdened by the sun, carrying lazy smoke within our hearts; now lie sullen here in the black mire!" This hymn they gurgle in their throats, for they cannot speak it in full words'[4]—that is, they cannot now have relief by timely utterance, as they would not on earth. And 'sullenness' I take to be the creation of difficulties where none exist, the working of a self-injuring imagination such as a modern mental physician would be quick to recognize as a neurotic symptom. Wordsworth's poem is about a sudden unmotivated anxiety after a mood of great exaltation. He speaks of this reversal of feeling as something experienced by himself before and known to all. In this mood he is the prey of 'fears and fancies,' of 'dim sadness' and 'blind thoughts.' These feelings have reference to two imagined catastrophes. One of them— natural enough in a man under the stress of approaching marriage, for Wordsworth was to be married in October—is economic destitution. He reproaches himself for his past indifference to the means of getting a living and thinks of what may follow from this carefree life: 'solitude, pain of heart, distress, and poverty.' His black thoughts are led to the fate of poets 'in their misery dead,' among them Chatterton and Burns. The second specific fear is of mental distress:

> We Poets in our youth begin in gladness;
> But thereof come in the end despondency and madness.

Coleridge, we must suppose, was in his thoughts after the depressing Keswick meeting, but he is of course thinking chiefly of himself. It will be remembered how the poem ends, how with some difficulty of utterance the poet brings himself to speak with an incredibly old leech-gatherer, and, taking heart from the man's resolution and independence, becomes again 'strong.'

This great poem is not to be given a crucial meaning in Wordsworth's life. It makes use of a mood to which everyone, certainly every creative person, is now and again a victim. It seems to me more likely that it, rather than the rainbow poem, is the timely utterance of which the Ode speaks because in it, and not in the rainbow poem, a sullen feeling occurs and is relieved. But whether or not it is actually the timely utterance, it is an autobiographical and deeply felt poem written at the time the Ode was being written and seeming to have an emotional connection with the first part of the Ode. (The meeting with the old man had taken place two years earlier and it is of some significance that it should have come to mind as the subject of a poem at just this time.) It is a very precise and hard-headed account of a mood of great fear and it deals in a very explicit way with the dangers that beset the poetic life. But although Wordsworth urges himself on to think of all the bad things that can possibly happen to a poet, and mentions solitude, pain of heart, distress and poverty, cold, pain and labor, all fleshly ills, and then even madness, he never says that a poet stands in danger of losing his talent. It seems reasonable to suppose that if Wordsworth were actually saying farewell to his talent in the Ode, there would be some hint of an endangered or vanishing talent in 'Resolution and Independence.' But there is none; at the end of the poem Wordsworth is resolute in poetry.

Must we not, then, look with considerable skepticism at such interpretations of the Ode as suppose without question that the 'gleam,' the 'glory,' and the 'dream' constitute the power of making poetry?—especially when we remember that at a time still three years distant Wordsworth in *The Prelude* will speak of himself as becoming a *creative* soul' (book XII, line 207; the italics are Wordsworth's own) despite the fact that, as he says (book XII, line 281), he 'sees by glimpses now.'

V

The second half of the Ode is divided into two large movements, each of which gives an answer to the question with which the first part ends. The two answers seem to contradict each other. The first issues in despair, the second in hope; the first uses a language strikingly supernatural, the second is entirely naturalistic. The two parts even differ in the statement of fact, for the first says that the gleam is gone, whereas the second says that it is not gone, but only transmuted. It is necessary to understand this contradiction, but it is not necessary to resolve it, for from the circuit between its two poles comes much of the power of the poem.

The first of the two answers (stanzas v–viii) tells us where the visionary gleam has gone by telling us where it came from. It is a remnant of a pre-existence in which we enjoyed a way of seeing and knowing now almost wholly gone from us. We come into the world, not with minds that are merely *tabulae rasae,* but with a kind of attendant light, the vestige of an existence otherwise obliterated from our memories. In infancy and childhood the recollection is relatively strong, but it fades as we move forward into earthly life. Maturity, with its habits and its cares and its increase of distance from our celestial origin, wears away the light of recollection. Nothing could be more poignantly sad than the conclusion of this part with the heavy sonority of its last line as Wordsworth addresses the child in whom the glory still lives:

> Full soon thy Soul shall have her earthly freight,
> And custom lie upon thee with a weight,
> Heavy as frost, and deep almost as life!

Between this movement of despair and the following movement of hope there is no clear connection save that of contradiction. But between the question itself and the movement of hope there is an explicit verbal link, for the question is: 'Whither has *fled* the visionary gleam?' and the movement of hope answers that 'nature yet remembers/What was so *fugitive.*'

The second movement of the second part of the Ode tells us again what has happened to the visionary gleam: it has not wholly fled, for it is remembered. This possession of childhood has been passed on as a legacy to the child's heir, the adult man; for the mind, as the rainbow epigraph also says, is one and continuous, and what was so intense a light in childhood becomes 'the fountain-light of all our day' and a 'master-light of all our seeing,' that is, of our adult day and our mature seeing. The child's recollection of his heavenly home exists in the recollection of the adult.

But what exactly is this fountain-light, this master-light? I am sure that when we understand what it is we shall see that the glory that Wordsworth means is very different from Coleridge's glory, which is

Joy. Wordsworth says that what he holds in memory as the guiding heritage of childhood is exactly not the Joy of childhood. It is not 'delight,' not 'liberty,' not even 'hope'—not for these, he says, 'I raise/The song of thanks and praise.' For what then does he raise the song? For this particular experience of childhood:

> . . . those obstinate questionings
> Of sense and outward things,
> Fallings from us, vanishings;
> Blank misgivings of a Creature
> Moving about in worlds not realised.

He mentions other reasons for gratitude, but here for the moment I should like to halt the enumeration.

We are told, then, that light and glory consist, at least in part, of 'questionings,' 'fallings from us,' 'vanishings,' and 'blank misgivings' in a world not yet *made real*, for surely Wordsworth uses the word 'realised' in its most literal sense. In his note on the poem he has this to say of the experience he refers to:

> . . . I was often unable to think of external things as having external existence, and I communed with all that I saw as something not apart from, but inherent in, my own material nature. Many times while going to school have I grasped at a wall or tree to recall myself from this abyss of idealism to the reality. At this time I was afraid of such processes.

He remarks that the experience is not peculiar to himself, which is of course true, and he says that it was connected in his thoughts with a potency of spirit which made him believe that he could never die.

The precise and naturalistic way in which Wordsworth talks of this experience of his childhood must cast doubt on Professor Garrod's statement that Wordsworth believed quite literally in the notion of pre-existence, with which the 'vanishings' experience is connected. Wordsworth is very careful to delimit the extent of his belief; he says that it is 'too shadowy a notion to be recommended to faith' as an evidence of immortality. He says that he is using the idea to illuminate another idea—using it, as he says, 'for my purpose' and 'as a poet.' It has as much validity for him as any 'popular' religious idea might have, that is to say, a kind of suggestive validity. We may regard pre-existence as being for Wordsworth a very serious conceit, vested with relative belief, intended to give a high value to the natural experience of the 'vanishings.' [5]

The naturalistic tone of Wordsworth's note suggests that we shall be doing no violence to the experience of the 'vanishings' if we consider it scientifically. In a well-known essay, 'Stages in the Development of the Sense of Reality,' the distinguished psychoanalyst Ferenczi speaks of the child's reluctance to distinguish between himself and the world and of the slow growth of objectivity which differentiates the self from external things. And Freud himself, dealing with the 'oceanic' sensation of 'being at one with the universe,' which a literary friend had supposed to be the source of all religious emotions, conjectures that it is a vestige of the infant's state of feeling before he has learned to distinguish between the stimuli of his own sensations and those of the world outside. In *Civilization and Its Discontents* he writes:

> Originally the ego includes everything, later it detaches from itself the outside world. The ego-feeling we are aware of now is thus only a shrunken vestige of a more extensive feeling—a feeling which embraced the universe and expressed an inseparable connection of the ego with the external world. If we may suppose that this primary ego-feeling has been preserved in the minds of many people—to a greater or lesser extent—it would co-exist like a sort of counterpart with the narrower and more sharply outlined ego-feeling of maturity, and the ideational content belonging to it would be precisely the notion of limitless extension and oneness with the universe—the same feeling as that described by my friend as 'oceanic.'

This has its clear relation to Wordsworth's 'worlds not realised.' Wordsworth, like Freud, was preoccupied by the idea of reality, and, again like Freud, he knew that the child's way of apprehension was but a stage which, in the course of nature, would give way to another. If we understand that Wordsworth is speaking of a period common to the development of everyone, we are helped to see that we cannot identify the vision of that period with his peculiar poetic power.

But in addition to the experience of the 'vanishings' there is another experience for which Wordsworth is grateful to his childhood and which, I believe, goes with the 'vanishings' to make up the 'master-light,' the 'fountain-light.' I am not referring to the

> High instincts before which our mortal Nature
> Did tremble like a guilty Thing surprised,

but rather to what Wordsworth calls 'those first affections.'

I am inclined to think that with this phrase Wordsworth refers to a later stage in the child's development which, like the earlier stage in which the external world is included within the ego, leaves vestiges in the developing mind. This is the period described in a well-known passage in Book II of *The Prelude*, in which the child learns about the world in his mother's arms:

> Blest the infant Babe,
> (For with my best conjecture I would trace
> Our Being's earthly progress), blest the Babe,
> Nursed in his Mother's arms, who sinks to sleep,
> Rocked on his Mother's breast; who with his soul
> Drinks in the feelings of his Mother's eye!
> For him, in one dear Presence, there exists
> A virtue which irradiates and exalts
> Objects through widest intercourse of sense.
> No outcast he, bewildered and depressed:
> Along his infant veins are interfused
> The gravitation and the filial bond
> Of nature that connect him with the world.
> Is there a flower, to which he points with hand
> Too weak to gather it, already love
> Drawn from love's purest earthly fount for him
> Hath beautified that flower; already shades
> Of pity cast from inward tenderness
> Do fall around him upon aught that bears
> Unsightly marks of violence or harm.
> Emphatically such a Being lives,
> Frail creature as he is, helpless as frail,
> An inmate of this active universe:
> For feeling has to him imparted power
> That through the growing faculties of sense,
> Doth like an agent of the one great Mind
> Create, creator and receiver both,
> Working but in alliance with the works
> Which it beholds.—Such, verily, is the first
> Poetic [6] spirit of our human life,
> By uniform control of after years,
> In most, abated or suppressed; in some,
> Through every change of growth and of decay
> Pre-eminent till death.

The child, this passage says, does not perceive things merely as objects; he first sees them, because maternal love is a condition of his perception, as objects-and-judgments, as valued objects. He does not learn about a flower, but about the pretty-flower, the flower that-I-want-and-that-mother-will-get-for-me; he does not learn about the bird and a broken wing but about the poor-bird-whose-wing-was-broken. The safety, warmth, and good feeling of his mother's conscious benevolence is a circumstance of his first learning. He sees, in short, with 'glory'; not only is he himself not in 'utter nakedness' as the Ode puts it, but the objects he sees are not in utter nakedness. The passage from *The Prelude* says in naturalistic language what stanza v of the Ode expresses by a theistical metaphor. Both the *Prelude* passage and the Ode distinguish a state of exile from a state of security and comfort, of at-homeness; there is (as the *Prelude* passage puts it) a 'filial bond,' or (as in stanza x of the Ode) a 'primal sympathy,' which keeps man from being an 'outcast . . . bewildered and depressed.'

The Ode and *The Prelude* differ about the source of this primal sympathy or filial bond. The Ode makes heavenly pre-existence the source, *The Prelude* finds the source in maternal affection. But the psychologists tell us that notions of heavenly pre-existence figure commonly as representations of physical prenatality—the womb is the environment which is perfectly adapted to its inmate and compared to it all other conditions of life may well seem like 'exile' to the (very literal) 'outcast.'[7] Even the security of the mother's arms, although it is an effort to re-create for the child the old environment, is but a diminished comfort. And if we think of the experience of which Wordsworth is speaking, the 'vanishings,' as the child's recollection of a condition in which it was very nearly true that he and his environment were one, it will not seem surprising that Wordsworth should compound the two experiences and figure them in the single metaphor of the glorious heavenly pre-existence.[8]

I have tried to be as naturalistic as possible in speaking of Wordsworth's childhood experiences and the more-or-less Platonic notion they suggested to him. I believe that naturalism is in order here, for what we must now see is that Wordsworth is talking about something common to us all, the development of the sense of reality. To have once had the visionary gleam of the perfect union of the self and the universe is essential to and definitive of our human nature, and it is in that sense connected with the making of poetry. But the visionary gleam is not in itself the poetry-making power, and its diminution is right and inevitable.

That there should be ambivalence in Wordsworth's response to this diminution is quite natural, and the two answers, that of stanzas v–viii and that of stanzas IX–XI, comprise both the resistance to and the acceptance of growth. Inevitably we resist change and turn back with passionate nostalgia to the stage we are leaving. Still, we fulfill ourselves by choosing what is painful and difficult and necessary, and we develop by moving toward death. In short, organic development is a hard paradox which Wordsworth is stating in the discrepant answers of the second part of the Ode. And it seems to me that those critics who made the Ode refer to some particular and unique experience of Wordsworth's and who make it relate only to poetical powers have forgotten their own lives and in consequence conceive the Ode to be a lesser thing than it really is, for it is not about poetry, it is about life. And having made this error, they are inevitably led to misinterpret the meaning of the 'philosophic mind' and also to deny that Wordsworth's ambivalence is sincere. No doubt it would not be a sincere ambivalence if Wordsworth were really saying farewell to poetry, it would merely be an attempt at self-consolation. But he is not saying farewell to poetry, he is saying farewell to Eden, and his ambivalence is much what Adam's was, and Milton's, and for the same reasons.[9]

To speak naturalistically of the quasi-mystical experiences of his childhood does not in the least bring into question the value which Wordsworth attached to them, for, despite its dominating theistical metaphor, the Ode is largely naturalistic in its intention. We can begin to see what that intention is by understanding the force of the word 'imperial' in stanza VI. This stanza is the second of the four stanzas in which Wordsworth states and develops the theme of the reminiscence of the light of heaven and its gradual evanescence through the maturing years. In stanza V we are told that the infant inhabits it; the Boy beholds it, seeing it 'in his joy'; the Youth is still attended by it; 'the Man perceives it die away,/And fade into the light of common day.' Stanza VI speaks briefly of the efforts made by earthly life to bring about the natural and inevitable amnesia:

> Earth fills her lap with pleasures of her own;
> Yearnings she hath in her own natural kind,
> And even with something of a Mother's mind,
>   And no unworthy aim,
>   The homely Nurse doth all she can
> To make her Foster-child, her Inmate Man,
>   Forget the glories he hath known,
> And that imperial palace whence he came.

'Imperial' suggests grandeur, dignity, and splendor, everything that stands in opposition to what, in *The Excursion,* Wordsworth was to call 'littleness.' And 'littleness' is the result of having wrong notions about the nature of man and his connection with the universe; its outcome is 'deadness.' The melancholy and despair of the Solitary in *The Excursion* are the signs of the deadness which resulted from his having conceived of man as something less than imperial. Wordsworth's idea of splendid power is his protest against all views of the mind that would limit and debase it. By conceiving, as he does, an intimate connection between mind and universe, by seeing the universe fitted to the mind and the mind to the universe, he bestows upon man a dignity which cannot be derived from looking at him in the actualities of common life, from seeing him engaged in business, in morality and politics.

Yet here we must credit Wordsworth with the double vision. Man must be conceived of as 'imperial,' but he must also be seen as he actually is in the field of life. The earth is not an environment in which the celestial or imperial qualities can easily exist. Wordsworth, who spoke of the notion of imperial pre-existence as being adumbrated by Adam's fall, uses the words 'earth' and 'earthly' in the common quasi-religious sense to refer to the things of this world. He does not make Earth synonymous with Nature, for although Man may be the true child of Nature, he is the 'Foster-child' of Earth. But it is to be observed that the foster mother is a kindly one, that her disposition is at least quasi-maternal, that her aims are at least not unworthy; she is, in short, the foster mother who figures so often in the legend of the Hero, whose real and unknown parents are noble or divine.[10]

Wordsworth, in short, is looking at man in a double way, seeing man both in his ideal nature and in his earthly activity. The two views do not so much contradict as supplement each other. If in stanzas v–viii Wordsworth tells us that we live by decrease, in stanzas ix–xi he tells us of the everlasting connection of the diminished person with his own ideal personality. The child hands on to the hampered adult the imperial nature, the 'primal sympathy / Which having been must ever be,' the mind fitted to the universe, the universe to the mind. The sympathy is not so pure and intense in maturity as in childhood, but only because another relation grows up beside the relation of man to Nature—the relation of man to his fellows in the moral world of difficulty and pain. Given Wordsworth's epistemology the new relation is bound to change the very aspect of Nature itself: the clouds will take a sober coloring from an eye that hath kept watch o'er man's mortality, but a sober color is a color still.

There is sorrow in the Ode, the inevitable sorrow of giving up an old habit of vision for a new one. In shifting the center of his interest from Nature to man in the field of morality Wordsworth is fulfilling his own conception of the three ages of man which Professor Beatty has expounded so well. The shift in interest he called the coming of 'the philosophic mind,' but the word 'philosophic' does not have here either of two of its meanings in common usage—it does not mean abstract and it does not mean apathetic. Wordsworth is not saying, and it is sentimental and unimaginative of us to say, that he has become less a feeling man and less a poet. He is only saying that he has become less a youth. Indeed, the Ode is so little a farewell to art, so little a dirge sung over departing powers, that it is actually the very opposite—it is a welcome of new powers and a dedication to a new poetic subject. For if sensitivity and responsiveness be among the poetic powers, what else is Wordsworth saying at the end of the poem except that he has a greater sensitivity and responsiveness than ever before? The 'philosophic mind' has not decreased but, on the contrary, increased the power to feel.

> The clouds that gather round the setting sun
> Do take a sober colouring from an eye
> That hath kept watch o'er man's mortality;
> Another race hath been and other palms are won.
> Thanks to the human heart by which we live,
> Thanks to its tenderness, its joys, and fears,
> To me the meanest flower that blows can give
> Thoughts that do often lie too deep for tears.

The meanest flower is significant now not only because, like the small celandine, it speaks of age, suffering, and death, but because to a man who is aware of man's mortality the world becomes significant and precious. The knowledge of man's mortality—this must be carefully noted in a poem presumably about immortality—now replaces the 'glory' as the agency which makes things significant and precious. We are back again at optics, which we have never really left, and the Ode in a very honest fashion has come full circle.

The new poetic powers of sensitivity and responsiveness are new not so much in degree as in kind; they would therefore seem to require a new poetic subject matter for their exercise. And the very definition of the new powers seems to imply what the new subject matter must be—thoughts that lie too deep for tears are ideally the thoughts which are brought to mind by tragedy. It would be an extravagant but not an absurd reading of the Ode that found it to be Wordsworth's farewell to the characteristic mode of his poetry, the mode that Keats called the 'egotistical sublime' and a dedication to the mode of tragedy. But the tragic mode could not be Wordsworth's. He did not have the 'negative capability' which Keats believed to be the source of Shakespeare's power, the gift of being able to be 'content with half-knowledge,' to give up the 'irritable reaching after fact and reason,' to remain 'in uncertainties, mysteries, doubts.' In this he was at one with all the poets of the Romantic Movement and after—negative capability was impossible for them to come by and tragedy was not for them. But although Wordsworth did not realize the new kind of art which seems implied by his sense of new powers, yet his bold declaration that he had acquired a new way of feeling makes it impossible for us to go on saying that the Ode was his 'conscious farewell to his art, a dirge sung over his departing powers.'

Still, was there not, after the composition of the Ode, a great falling off in his genius which we are drawn to connect with the crucial changes the Ode records? That there was a falling off is certain, although we must observe that it was not so sharp as is commonly held and also that it did not occur immediately or even soon after the composition of the first four stanzas with their statement that the visionary gleam had gone; on the contrary, some of the most striking of Wordsworth's verse was written at this time. It must be remembered too that another statement of the loss of the visionary gleam, that made in 'Tintern Abbey,' had been followed by all the superb production of the 'great decade'—an objection which is sometimes dealt with by saying that Wordsworth wrote his best work from his near memories of the gleam, and that, as he grew older and moved farther from it, his recollection dimmed and thus he lost his power: it is an explanation which suggests that mechanical and simple notions of the mind and of the poetic process are all too tempting to those who speculate on Wordsworth's decline. Given the fact of the great power, the desire to explain its relative deterioration will no doubt always be irresistible. But we must be aware, in any attempt to make this explanation, that an account of why Wordsworth ceased to write great poetry must at the same time be an account of how he once did write great poetry. And this latter account, in our present state of knowledge, we cannot begin to furnish.

NOTES

1. *Wordsworthian and Other Studies,* Oxford, 1947.

2. We recall that in *The Varieties of Religious Experience* William James speaks of the 'hallucinatory or pseudo-hallucinatory luminous phenomena, *photisms,* to use the term of the psychologists,' the 'floods of light and glory,' which characterize so many moments of revelation. James mentions one person who, experiencing the light, was uncertain of its externality.

3. I follow Professor Garrod in assuming that the 'utterance' was a poem, but of course it may have been a letter or a spoken word. And if indeed the 'utterance' does refer to 'Resolution and Independence,' it may not refer to the poem itself—as Jacques Barzun has suggested to me, it may refer to what the Leech-gatherer in the poem says to the poet, for certainly it is what the old man 'utters' that gives the poet 'relief.'

4. The Carlyle-Wicksteed translation. Dante's word is *'tristi';* in 'Resolution and Independence' Wordsworth speaks of 'dim sadness.' I mention Dante's sinners simply to elucidate the emotion that Wordsworth speaks of, not to suggest an influence.

5. In his *Studies in the Poetry of Henry Vaughan,* a Cambridge University dissertation, Andrew Chiappe makes a similar judgment of the quality and degree of belief in the idea of pre-existence in the poetry of Vaughan and Traherne.

6. The use here of the word 'poetic' is either metaphorical and general, or it is entirely literal, that is, it refers to the root-meaning of the word, which is 'to make'—Wordsworth has in mind the creative nature of right human perception and not merely poetry.

7. 'Before born babe bliss had. Within womb won he worship. Whatever in that one case done commodiously done was.'—James Joyce, *Ulysses.* The myth of Eden is also interpreted as figuring either childhood or the womb—see below Wordsworth's statement of the connection of the notion of pre-existence with Adam's fall.

8. Readers of Ferenczi's remarkable study, *Thalassa,* a discussion, admittedly speculative but wonderfully fascinating, of unconscious racial memories of the ocean as the ultimate source of life, will not be able to resist giving an added meaning to Wordsworth's lines about the 'immortal sea/Which brought us hither' and of the unborn children who 'Sport upon the shore.' The recollection of Samuel Butler's delightful fantasy of the Unborn and his theory of unconscious memory will also serve to enrich our reading of the Ode by suggesting the continuing force of the Platonic myth.

9. Milton provides a possible gloss to several difficult points in the poem. In stanza viii, the Child is addressed as 'thou Eye among the blind,' and to the Eye are applied the epithets 'deaf and silent'; Coleridge objected to these epithets as irrational, but his objection may be met by citing the brilliant precedent of 'blind mouths' of 'Lycidas.' Again, Coleridge's question of the

propriety of making a master *brood* over a slave is in part answered by the sonnet 'On His Being Arrived at the Age of Twenty-three,' in which Milton expresses his security in his development as it shall take place in his 'great Task-master's eye.' Between this sonnet and the Ode there are other significant correspondences of thought and of phrase, as there also are in the sonnet 'On His Blindness.'

10. Carlyle makes elaborate play with this idea in his account of Teufelsdröckh. The fantasy that their parents are really foster parents is a common one with children, and it is to be associated with the various forms of the belief that the world is not real.

Coleridge's Conversation Poems

A YOUNG poet whom I love has just left my house and driven away in the soft darkness of a spring night, to the remote cottage in the Delaware valley where he meditates a not thankless Muse. Before he came I was in despair, sitting bewildered with my heaps of notes on Coleridge spread before me, having much to say, but not knowing how to begin. Now it should be easier, for one fire kindleth another, and our talk was of friendship and poetry. Samuel Taylor Coleridge, to those who know him well, exists in three modes, as Philosopher, Poet, Friend. If the truth were told, we should all be obliged to admit that the Philosopher escapes us. We hear his voice and enter the room where he is speaking, only to see his retreating figure down some dim corridor. 'Aids to Reflection,' 'Table Talk,' and other echoes of his speech yield merely a confused murmur, baffling, and the more exasperating because the tones are in themselves melodious. It was an unprofitable heritage that Coleridge left to his disciple, Joseph Henry Green, and to his daughter Sara and her husband, the task of arranging and publishing his philosophical writings and the records of his innumerable monologues. In Green's case the labor lasted twenty-eight years. The sum of all this toil is neither a rounded system nor a clear view of anything in particular. They tried earnestly to catch the vanishing metaphysician, but in vain.

It is the opinion of many that Coleridge as Poet is almost equally an evanescent shadow; and though the many are in this quite mistaken, they have some excuse for thinking thus, because his fulfilment falls far

---

From *Spirit of Delight*, copyright 1928 by Henry Holt and Co., Inc., copyright 1956 by George McLean Harper, pp. 3–27. Reprinted by permission of the publisher.

short of his promise. But they fail to appreciate how very great, after all, the fulfilment is. The causes of this injustice to Coleridge the Poet are the splendor of the three poems of his which everybody knows and admires, and also the habit of regarding him as a mere satellite of Wordsworth, or at least as Wordsworth's weaker brother. Those who are so dazzled by 'The Rime of the Ancient Mariner,' 'Kubla Khan,' and 'Christabel,' that all the rest of Coleridge's poetry seems to them color-less, are invited to reopen his book, but first to read J. Dykes Campbell's Life of him or the collection of his wonderful letters edited by the late Ernest Hartley Coleridge, his grandson; and I wish to direct the atten-tion of those from whom he is obscured by the greater glory of Words-worth to a group of poems which can be compared only to the 'Lines composed a few miles above Tintern Abbey.'

These are his Poems of Friendship. They cannot be even vaguely understood unless the reader knows what persons Coleridge has in mind. They are, for the most part, poems in which reference is made with fine particularity to certain places. They were composed as the expression of feelings which were occasioned by quite definite events. Between the lines, when we know their meaning, we catch glimpses of those delightful people who formed the golden inner circle of his friends in the days of his young manhood: Charles Lamb, his oldest and dearest, Mary Lamb, practical Tom Poole, William and Dorothy Words-worth in their days of clearest vision and warmest enthusiasm, and in the later pieces Mrs. Wordsworth and Sarah Hutchinson her young sister. They may all be termed, as Coleridge himself names one or two of them, Conversation Poems, for even when they are soliloquies the sociable man who wrote them could not even think without supposing a listener. They require and reward considerable knowledge of his life and especially the life of his heart.

This is not so certainly the case with his three famous Mystery Poems, in which the spellbound reader sees visions and hears music which float in from a magic realm and float out again into unfathomable space. Their perfection is not of this world nor founded on history or circum-stance. No knowledge of their origin or mechanism can increase their beauty or enrich their charm. To attempt to account for them, to write footnotes about them, if it were hoped thereby to make them more powerful in their effect upon the imagination, would be ridiculous and pedantic, however fruitful of knowledge and interest the exercise might be.

While the Philosopher has wandered away into a vague limbo of unfinished projects and the Poet of 'Christabel' and its companion stars can only gaze in mute wonder upon the constellation he fixed in the heavens, the Poet of the Friendly Pieces lingers among us and can be questioned. We owe it to him and to ourselves to appreciate them. It is unfair to his genius that he should be represented in most anthologies of English verse only by the Mystery Poems, and that those who read the Poems of Friendship should so generally be ignorant of their meaning. It is unfair to ourselves that we should refuse the companionship of the most open-hearted of men, a generous spirit, willing to reveal to us the riches of his mind, a man whom all can understand and no one can help loving. There is not so much kindness, humor, wisdom, and frankness offered to most of us in the ordinary intercourse of life that we can afford to decline the outstretched hand of Coleridge.

Poetry draws mankind together, breaks down barriers, relieves loneliness, shows us ourselves in others and others in ourselves. It is the friendly art. It ignores time and space. National, racial, and secular differences fall at its touch, which is the touch of kinship, and when we feel this we laugh shamefacedly at our pretensions, timidities, and reserves. Everything in antiquity is antiquated except its art and especially its poetry. That is scarcely less fresh than when it fell first from living lips. The religion of the ancients is to us superstition, their science childishness, but their poetry is as valid and vital as our own. We appropriate it, and it unites us with our fathers.

> 'One precious, tender-hearted scroll
> Of pure Simonides'

shines through the mist more brightly than the Nicomachean Ethics or the Constitution of Athens. What is most enduring in the Old Testament is the humanity revealed here and there in veins of poetry, not only as psalms and prophecies but gleaming out from the historical books. It is the nature of all great poetry to open and bring together the hearts of men. And few poets have so generously given themselves out to us as Coleridge. The gift is rare and wonderful because he was a very good man, even more than because of his marvellous mind. When I say he was good, I mean that he was loving. However many other kinds of goodness there may be, this is the indispensable element. Some one has been trying to persuade me that artists should abandon themselves wholly to art. If this means that they should dissociate themselves from their fellow men who have the misfortune to be mere ordinary mortals, or should neglect the duties and forgo the pleasures that other people perform and enjoy, it is a heresy at which the Muse of Literary History shrugs her shoulders.

The Poems of Friendship make yet another claim on our attention: they are among the supreme examples of a peculiar kind of poetry. Others not unlike them, though not surpassing them, are Ovid's 'Cum subit illius tristissima noctis imago,' and several of the Canti of Leopardi. Some passages in Cowper's 'Task' resemble them in tone. Poignancy of feeling, intimacy of address, and ease of expression are even more perfectly blended in Coleridge's poems than in any of these.

The compositions which I denominate Poems of Friendship or Conversation Poems are 'The Eolian Harp,' 'Reflections on having left a Place of Retirement,' 'This Lime-Tree Bower my Prison,' 'Frost at Midnight,' 'Fears in Solitude,' 'The Nightingale,' 'Dejection,' and 'To William Wordsworth' (sometimes printed 'To a Gentleman'). The list is not complete; there are shorter pieces which might be added; but these are the most substantial and, I think, the best. The qualities common to all the eight are qualities of style no less than of subject. Wordsworth is clearly more entitled than Coleridge to be considered the leader in creating and also in expounding a new kind of poetry, though a careless examination of their early works might lead one to think that they came forward simultaneously and independent of each other as reformers. Until he met Wordsworth, which was probably in 1795, Coleridge wrote in the manner which had been fashionable since the death of Milton, employing without hesitation all those poetic licences which constituted what he later termed 'Gaudyverse,' in contempt. Wordsworth, on the other hand, though employing the same devices in his first published poems, 'An Evening Walk' and 'Descriptive Sketches,' showed, here and there even in those juvenile compositions, a naturalness which foretold the revolt accomplished in 'Guilt and Sorrow,' dating from 1794. If one reads Coleridge's early poems in chronological order, one will perceive that Gaudyverse persists till about the middle of 1795, and then quickly yields to the natural style which Wordsworth was practising.

'The Eolian Harp,' composed on Aug. 20, 1795, in the short period when Coleridge was happy in his approaching marriage, sounds many a note of the *dolce stil nuovo*, and is moreover in substance his first important and at the same time characteristic poem. The influence of Wordsworth, whose early works he had read, is to be seen in small details, such as a bold and faithful reference to the scents 'snatched from yon beanfield.' The natural happiness of Coleridge, which was to break forth from him in spite of sorrow through all his darkened later years, flows like a sunlit river in this poem. In two magnificent passages he anticipates by nearly three years the grand climax of the 'Lines composed a few miles above Tintern Abbey,' singing:

> 'O! the one Life within us and abroad,
> Which meets all motion and becomes its soul,
> A light in sound, a sound-like power in light,
> Rhythm in all thought, and joyance everywhere—
>
> .   .   .
>
> And what if all of animated nature
> Be but organic Harps diversely framed,
> That tremble into thought, as o'er them sweeps,
> Plastic and vast, one intellectual breeze,
> At once the Soul of each, and God of all.'

Here is the Philosopher at his best, but he steps down from the intellectual throne at the bidding of love; and out of consideration for Sarah's religious scruples, and in obedience to his own deep humility, apologizes for

> 'These shapings of the unregenerate mind.'

It is to be noted also that the blank verse is more fluent and easy than Milton's, or any that had been written since Milton, moving with a gentle yet sufficiently strong rhythm, and almost free from the suggestion of the heroic couplet, a suggestion which is *felt* in nearly all 18th-century unrhymed verse, as of something recently lost and not quite forgotten. The cadences are long and beautiful, binding line to line and sentence to sentence in a way that the constant use of couplets and stanzas had made rare since Milton's time.

A few weeks later Coleridge wrote 'Reflections on having left a Place of Retirement.' The poem begins with a quiet description of the surrounding scene and, after a superb flight of imagination, brings the mind back to the starting-point, a pleasing device which we may call the 'return.' The imagination, in the second poem, seeks not, as in the first, a metaphysical, but an ethical height. The poet is tormented in the midst of his happiness by the thought of those who live in wretchedness or who die in the war, and asks himself:

> 'Was it right
> While my unnumbered brethren toiled and bled,

> That I should dream away the entrusted hours
> On rose-leaf beds, pampering the coward heart
> With feelings all too delicate for use?'

The problem is not stated in abstract, but in concrete terms. In fact, the only abstract passages in the Conversation Poems are the two quoted above, from 'The Eolian Harp'; and in general it is noticeable that Coleridge, whose talk was misty and whose prose writings are often like a cloud, luminous but impossible to see through, is one of the simplest and most familiar of poets. He, the subtlest metaphysician in England, was, as a poet, content to express elementary and universal feelings in the plainest terms.

On July 2, 1797, Coleridge, with Dorothy Wordsworth sitting beside him, drove from Racedown in Dorset to Nether Stowey in Somerset, and for about two weeks the small cottage behind Tom Poole's hospitable mansion sheltered William and Dorothy and perhaps Basil Montague's little boy, whom they were educating, besides Coleridge and Mrs. Coleridge and Hartley the baby and Nanny their maid. To fill up the measure, Charles Lamb joined them on the 7th and stayed a week. Coleridge, writing to Southey, says:

> 'The second day after Wordsworth came to me, dear Sara accident-
> ally emptied a skillet of boiling milk on my foot, which confined
> me during the whole time of C. Lamb's stay, and still prevents me from all
> walks longer than a furlong. While Wordsworth, his sister, and Charles
> Lamb were out one evening, sitting in the arbour of T. Poole's garden,
> which communicates with mine, I composed these lines, with which I
> am pleased.'

He encloses the poem 'This Lime-Tree Bower my Prison,' in which he refers tenderly to his guests as 'my Sister and my Friends.' It begins:

> 'Well, they are gone, and here I must remain,
> This lime-tree bower my prison! I have lost
> Beauties and feelings such as would have been
> Most sweet to my remembrance even when age
> Had dimmed mine eyes to blindness!'

In imagination he follows them as they 'wander in gladness along the hill-top edge,' and thinks with special satisfaction of the pleasure granted to his gentle-hearted Charles, who had been long 'in the great City pent,' an expression which he uses again in 'Frost at Midnight' and which Wordsworth later adopted, both of them echoing a line of Milton. The idea of storing up happy memories for some wintry season of the heart, an idea expanded by Wordsworth in 'Tintern Abbey,' and again in 'I wandered lonely as a Cloud,' occurs in the lines quoted above; and Wordsworth's famous brave remark,

> 'Nature never did betray
> The heart that loved her,'

is also anticipated in this poem when Coleridge declares,

> 'Henceforth I shall know
> That Nature ne'er deserts the wise and pure,'

the wise and pure, we may be certain, being in their eyes those who love Nature. In this third Conversation Poem Coleridge has risen above the level attained in the former two; Gaudyverse is gone entirely, and unaffected simplicity, the perfection of tranquil ease, reigns without a rival. No better example, even in Wordsworth's own verse, could be found to illustrate the theory set forth three years later in the Preface to 'Lyrical Ballads.' The beauty and truth of the poem and the picture it gives of Coleridge's yearning heart of love do not depend upon the fact that it was an illustrious trio whom he followed in imagination as they roved 'upon smooth Quantock's airy ridge'; it is a clear boon to us that they happened to be no less than Charles Lamb and Dorothy and William Wordsworth. The significant thing is Coleridge's unselfish delight in the joys of others. Happiness of this kind is an inexhaustible treasure to which all have access.

'Frost at Midnight,' composed in February, 1798, also dates from that most blessed time, when he was living in concord with his wife, under the wide-branching protection of strong Thomas Poole, with William and Dorothy near and poetry pouring unto him from the heaven's height. It is the musing of a father beside the cradle of his child, and the passage is well known in which he foretells that Hartley shall

> 'wander like a breeze
> By lakes and sandy shores, beneath the crags
> Of ancient mountain.'

The chief beauty of the poem, however, is in its 'return,' which is the best example of the peculiar kind of blank verse Coleridge had evolved, as natural-seeming as prose, but as exquisitely artistic as the most complicated sonnet:

'Therefore all seasons shall be sweet to thee,
Whether the summer clothe the general earth
With greenness, or the redbreast sit and sing
Betwixt the tufts of snow on the bare branch
Of mossy apple-tree, while the nigh thatch
Smokes in the sun-thaw; whether the eave-drops fall
Heard only in the trances of the blast,
Or if the secret ministry of frost
Shall hang them up in silent icicles,
Quietly shining to the quiet Moon.'

'Fears in Solitude,' written in April 1798, 'during the alarm of an invasion,' is the longest of the Conversation Poems. It begins characteristically in a low key, with a quiet description of the poet's surroundings. He is reposing, happy and tranquil, in a green dell, above which sings a skylark in the clouds. Then quite suddenly his conscience cries out, when he thinks, as in 'Reflections on having left a Place of Retirement,' of the dangers and sufferings of others. From self-tormenting he passes into an indictment of his countrymen for going lightly to war and for having 'borne to distant tribes' slavery, suffering, and vice. In words of terrible sincerity he charges society and his age with hardness and frivolity. 'We have loved,' he cries, 'to swell the war-whoop, passionate for war.' To read of war has become 'the best amusement for our morning meal.' We have turned the forms of holy religion into blasphemy, until

'the owlet Atheism,
Sailing on obscene wings athwart the noon,
Drops his blue-fringèd lids, and holds them close,
And hooting at the glorious sun in Heaven,
Cries out "Where is it?"'

Down to the 129th line the strain of passionate pacificism continues. It is the confession of a tender-hearted, conscience-stricken man, to whom has been revealed a region above partisan and national views. We feel that if the passage had been declaimed to an army before battle, the men would have broken ranks in horror of their own designs. Quite unexpectedly, however, the tone changes at this point, and he bursts into a tirade against the French, calling upon Englishmen to stand forth and 'repel an impious foe.' The violence of the transition is disconcerting. But anon, with a thrust in each direction, at the over-sanguine English friends of the Revolution and at its unreasonable foes, he sings a glorious pæan to 'dear Britain,' his 'native Isle.' Then comes a sweet 'return': he bids farewell to the soft and silent spot where he has been reclining; he thinks with joy of his beloved Stowey and his friend Poole and the lowly cottage where his babe and his babe's mother dwell in peace. It was like Coleridge to see both sides of the problem raised by the war, by all war, and to express both with equal poignancy. Extreme as are the limits to which his imagination carries him, his eloquence is vitiated by no sentimentalism or self-delusion. The dilemma is fairly stated; the distress is genuine. Were it not for the exquisite frame in which the fears and questionings are set, were it not for the sweet opening and the refreshing 'return,' the pain excited by this poem would outweigh our pleasure in the aptness of its figures and the melody of its verse. But the frame saves the picture, as the profound psychological truth of the picture justifies the beauty of the frame. Coleridge was unaware how successful he had been, for in a note in one of his manuscript copies of this superb work of art he says: 'The above is perhaps not Poetry, but rather a sort of middle thing between Poetry and Oratory, *sermoni propriora*. Some parts are, I am conscious, too tame even for animated prose.' These words must have been dictated by humility rather than by critical judgment. He would have made no such deduction had Wordsworth or Lamb written the verses.

In the same productive month, April 1798, he wrote 'The Nightingale,' which he himself terms a Conversation Poem, though it is neither more nor less conversational than the others of this kind. It was printed five months later in 'Lyrical Ballads.' Hazlitt, in his account of a visit he made that spring to Nether Stowey, tells of a walk he took with William and Dorothy and Coleridge: 'Returning that same evening, I got into a metaphysical argument with Wordsworth, while Coleridge was explaining the different notes of the nightingale to his sister, in which we neither of us succeeded in making ourselves perfectly clear and intelligible.' In Dorothy's Alfoxden journal are brief mentions of many a walk by moon or star light with 'dear Col.' The friendship had ripened fast. 'My Friend, and thou, our Sister' are addressed in the poem, and we may be sure the nightingales themselves sang nothing half so sweet to Dorothy's ears as the liquid lines of the music-master. Many little incidents of their walks would crowd her memory in later years as she read them. The 'castle huge' mentioned in the poem is a romantic exaggeration for Alfoxden house, and she is the 'gentle maid' who dwelt hard by. 'Thus Coleridge dreamed of me,' might she sigh in her old age, when he had passed into the eternity of his fame and she was lingering by shallower streams of life, *assise auprès du feu, devisant et filant.*

Thus far we have seen Coleridge in his day of strength. If he has written of sorrow, it has been sorrow for suffering mankind; if he has written of sin, it has been the sin of his country. He has been too manly to invent reasons for self-pity. But he is wretched without the companionship of loving friends. In Germany, when separated from the Wordsworths, he sends a wistful call across the frozen wastes of the Lüneburg Heath:

> 'William, my head and my heart, dear William and dear
>   Dorothea!
> You have all in each other; but I am lonely and want you!'

And when he ran away from them in Scotland, perhaps to escape their anxious care of his health, he was soon in distress and crying out:

> 'To be beloved is all I need,
> And whom I love I love indeed.'

Prior to his return from Germany, in the summer of 1799, he had not become a slave to opium, though the habit of taking it had been formed. In the next three years the vice grew fixed, his will decayed, he produced less, and fell into depths of remorse. From Dorothy's Grasmere journal it appears unlikely that she or her brother understood the reason for the change which they undoubtedly perceived in him. Love blinded them to the cause, while making them quick to see and lament the effects. She kept a journal for her own eyes alone, and one feels like an intruder when one reads it in print, and sees in it sure signs that she loved with romantic tenderness the visitor who came from time to time over the hills from Keswick, and whose letters she placed in her bosom for safe-keeping, and whose sufferings, as she detected them in his altered countenance, made her weep. The situation was not rendered less delicate by the fact that he was unhappy with his wife; and Dorothy's extraordinary power of self-abnegation must have been strained almost unendurably when she found that the woman for whom Coleridge felt most affection was Sarah Hutchinson. There was something innocent and childlike in all his sympathies and likings and lovings. He never permanently alienated a friend; he never quite broke the tie between himself and his wife; he could, it seems, love without selfishness and be loved without jealousy. Ernest Hartley Coleridge once told me that he was quite sure the 'Asra' of Coleridge's poems was Sarah Hutchinson, and that the poet loved her. Mr. Gordon Wordsworth has told me the same thing. 'Sara' in the poems before 1799 refers, of course, to Mrs. Coleridge; after that date to Miss Hutchinson. She was his amanuensis and close companion when he lived, as he did for months at a time, with the Wordsworths at Grasmere. Their hospitality knew no bounds where he was concerned, and their patience with him as he bent more and more under the power of narcotics and stimulants was almost inexhaustible.

In the winter of 1801–1802, the two causes of Coleridge's unhappiness, opium and domestic discord, worked havoc with him and brought him to despair. The wings of poesy were broken, as he realized full well. Meanwhile Wordsworth was in high poetic activity, healthy, forward-looking, and happy. On April 4, 1802, when William and Dorothy were on a visit to Keswick, and could judge for themselves of his misery, he composed, in part at least, the poem 'Dejection,' which is a confession of his own failure, and one of the saddest of all human utterances. But it is a glorious thing, too, for as the stricken runner sinks in the race he lifts up his head and cheers the friend who strides onward, and this generosity is itself a triumph. On Oct. 4, Wordsworth's wedding day and the seventh anniversary of Coleridge's marriage, the poem was printed in the 'Morning Post.' It is an ode in form only; in contents it is a conversation. It is not an address to Dejection, but to William Wordsworth. As printed in the newspaper, it purports to be directed to some one named Edmund; in Coleridge's editions of his collected works this name is changed to Lady; but in the three extant early manuscripts the word is sometimes William and sometimes Wordsworth. In this sublime and heartrending poem Coleridge gives expression to an experience of double consciousness. His sense-perceptions are vivid and in part agreeable; his inner state is faint, blurred, and unhappy. He sees, but cannot feel. The power of feeling has been paralysed by chemically induced excitements of his brain. The seeing power, less dependent upon bodily health, stands aloof, individual, critical, and very mournful. By 'seeing' he means perceiving and judging; by 'feeling' he means that which impels to action. He suffers, but the pain is dull, and he wishes it were keen, for so he should awake from lethargy and recover unity at least. But nothing from outside can restore him. The sources of the soul's life are within. Even from the depth of his humiliation and self-loathing he ventures to rebuke his friend for thinking it can be otherwise; William, with his belief in the divinity of Nature, his confidence that all knowledge comes from sensation, his semi-atheism, as Coleridge had called this philosophy:

> 'O William! we receive but what we give,
> And in our life alone does Nature live.'

Coleridge never faltered in his conviction that spirit was independent of matter. His unhappy experience deepened his faith in the existence of God, and of his own soul as something detachable from his 'body that did him grievous wrong.' Yet he had once been a disciple of David Hartley and had, it seems, made a convert of Wordsworth, whose persistence in a semi-materialistic philosophy now alarmed him. In every other respect he venerates him and humbles himself before him. Wordsworth, pure in heart, that is to say, still a child of Nature, and free, has not lost his birthright of joy, which is the life-breath of poetry. But Oh! groans Coleridge, I have lost my gift of song, for each affliction

> 'Suspends what Nature gave me at my birth,
> My shaping spirit of Imagination.'

His own race prematurely ended, he passes the torch to the survivor:

> 'Dear William, friend devoutest of my choice,
> Thus mayst thou ever, evermore rejoice.'

Another awful day of remorse and humiliating comparison was approaching. In April, 1804, Coleridge left England for Sicily and Malta, where he sank very low in what had now become an incurable disease, though he subsequently at various times made heroic stands against it, through religious hope, the marvellous energy of an originally strong and joyous nature, and the devotion of one friend after another. While he was distant from his staunch supporters, Poole and Wordsworth, his creative powers, through the exercise of which he might have preserved some degree of self-respect, more nearly failed than at any period of his life. He came back to England in August, 1806, so ashamed that for months he avoided his family and his friends. After many anxious efforts the Wordsworths and good Sarah Hutchinson captured him and kept him with them for several days at an inn in Kendal. Following their advice, he agreed upon a more definite separation from Mrs. Coleridge, to which she, however, would not consent. They had him now within reach, and in January, 1807, he visited them at a farmhouse, on Sir George Beaumont's estate, in which they had been living for several months. Here, one long winter night, Wordsworth began reading to him from the manuscript of 'The Prelude,' that poem dedicated to him, in which the Growth of a Poet's Mind is narrated. What subject could have been more interesting or more painful to him? On the night when Wordsworth's deep voice ceased declaiming the firm pentameters, his brother poet, roused from lethargy, composed in response his lines 'To William Wordsworth.' Lingering in his ear was the graceful tribute which recalled the glory of his youth, so few years past and yet so completely gone:

> 'Thou in bewitching words, with happy heart,
> Didst chaunt the vision of that Ancient Man,
> The bright-eyed Mariner, and rueful woes
> Didst utter of the Lady Christabel.'

Coleridge's reply, touching for the gratitude, reverence, and humbleness which it expresses, is remarkable too for the lightning flashes in which it shows us the course of Wordsworth's life and of his own, and summarizes 'The Prelude.' There is even, in the phrase about a tranquil sea 'swelling to the moon,' a reminiscence of a remark made by Dorothy one night years before as they walked by the Bristol Channel. How her heart must have jumped when she recognized this touch! The childlike candor of a beautiful spirit shines in the following lines, in which unconquered goodness and imperishable art unite:

> 'Ah! as I listened with a heart forlorn
> The pulses of my being beat anew:
> And even as Life returns upon the drowned,
> Life's joys rekindling roused a throng of pains—
> Keen pangs of Love, awakening as a babe,
> Turbulent, with an outcry in the heart;
> And fears self-willed, that shunned the eye of Hope;
> And Hope that scarce would know itself from Fear;
> Sense of past Youth, and Manhood come in vain,
> And Genius given, and Knowledge won in vain.'

In the divine economy and equilibrium of the world all things have their uses and every disturbed balance is restored. Genius is *not* given in vain, goodness is never wasted, love comes at last into its own. The misfortunes, nay, even the faults of Coleridge, which were so grievous to him, can be seen now as a purifying discipline. I do not wish to preach a sermon in defence of weakness; but in all justice, not to say charity, let us ask ourselves whether the frailty of this great and essentially good man did not enhance his virtues and make him more lovable. He had no pride except in the achievements of his friends. He distrusted himself, and his dependence on the love and regard of his friends gave them the joy that women feel in caring for helpless babes. He lost at times the sense of his own personality, and found communion with others, with Nature, and with the Divine Spirit. He hated himself for his sins, and was innocent of envy, presumption, self-deception, pretence. He sank in his own opinion, and humility became his crown of glory. His power of feeling failed from excessive use, and he took keen pleasure in the happiness of others. He suffered burning remorse for wasted gifts and opportunities, but never whined about the futility of life. He trifled with his own sensations, but was no sentimentalist. He wandered, athirst and weak, in sandy places, but saw on the horizon a 'shady city of palm trees,' and pointed the way thither.

G. W. KNIGHT

Coleridge's Divine Comedy

I SHALL concentrate on *Christabel, The Ancient Mariner,* and *Kubla Khan.* Within a narrow range these show an intensity comparable with that of Dante and Shakespeare. As with those, strong human feeling mixes with stern awareness of evil, without artistic confusions. Coleridge's main negation tends to a subjective sin-fear: his use of *fear* is, indeed, the secret of his uncanny power, this being the most forceful medium for riveting poetic attention.

Christabel is one nightmare; so, pretty nearly, is *The Ancient Mariner;* and *Kubla Khan* at one point strikes terror. Coleridge is expert in nightmarish, yet fascinating, experience. The human imagination can curl to rest, as in a warm bed, among horrors that would strike pallor in actual life, perhaps recognizing some unknown release, or kinship: as in Wordsworth, who, however, never shows the nervous *tension* of Coleridge. These three poems, moreover, may be grouped as a little *Divina Commedia* exploring in turn Hell, Purgatory, and Paradise.

Christabel is akin to *Macbeth.* There is darkness (though moon-lit), the owl, the restless mastiff. There is sleep and silence broken by fearsome sounds. The mastiff's howl is touched with deathly horror: 'some say she sees my lady's shroud.' Opposed to the nightmarish are images of religious grace. This first part is strangely feminine: the mastiff is a 'bitch,' the heroine set between Geraldine and the spirit of her own mother as forces of evil and grace respectively. 'Mary Mother' and 'Jesu Maria' find a natural home in the phraseology. Some sort of sexual desecration, some expressly physical horror, is revealed by Geraldine's undressing. She insinuates herself into Christabel's religious, mother-

---

From *The Starlit Dome* (Methuen and Co., London, 1941), pp. 83-97. Reprinted by permission of the publisher.

watched, world; she is mortally afraid of the mother-spirit and addresses her invisible presence with extreme dramatic intensity. As so often a seemingly sexual evil is contrasted with a parental good, yet Geraldine gets her opportunity through Christabel's charity, and when she lies with her is imaged as a mother with a child. Some hideous replacing of a supreme good is being shadowed, with an expression of utter surprise, especially in the conclusion to Part I, that so pure a girl can have contact with so obscene an horror. It is something Christabel cannot confess: she is powerless to tell her father. She is under a spell. The evil is nerve-freezing yet fascinating. There is vivid use of light in the tongue of flame shooting from the dying brands, and before that Geraldine's first appearance in the moonlight is glitteringly pictured. Stealth, silence, and sleep are broken by sudden, fearful, sound. In Part II we get perhaps the most intense and nightmarish use of the recurring serpent-image in our literature: both in Bracy's dream of Christabel as a 'sweet bird' (the usual opposite) with a 'bright green snake' coiled round it and Christabel's tranced hissing later, mesmerized by 'shrunken' serpent eyes. The poem expresses fear of some nameless obscenity. Christabel, we gather, has a lover, but he is of slight importance in the poem as we have it, though there is reason to suppose the conflict between him and Geraldine was to have been made dramatically explicit.

Christabel helps our understanding of *The Ancient Mariner*, which describes the irruption into the natural human festivity of a wedding party of the Mariner's story of sin, loneliness, and purgatorial redemption. These somewhat Wordsworthian elements are set against the 'merry din,' the 'loud bassoon.' The wedding guest is agonizedly torn from human, and especially sexual, normality and conviviality.

The story starts with a voyage into 'the land of ice and of fearful sounds.' There is snow and fog. From this the Albatross saves them: it is as 'a Christian soul.' Its snowy whiteness would naturally grip Coleridge: he is fascinated by whiteness. The bird seems to suggest some redeeming Christ-like force in creation that guides humanity from primitive and fearful origins. Anyway, the central crime is the slaying of it and by their wavering thoughts the crew 'make themselves accomplices'; and the dead bird is finally hung round the Mariner's neck 'instead of the cross' as a sign of guilt. Indeed, the slaying of the Albatross in the Mariner's story may correspond to the death of Christ in racial history. It is, moreover, an act of unmotivated and wanton, semi-sadistic, destruction, explicitly called 'hellish.' As a result the ship is calmed in a tropic sea. Parching heat replaces icy cold. The 'land of ice and snow' may be allowed to suggest primeval racial sufferings or primitive layers in the psychology of man; and yet also, perhaps, something more distant still, realms of ultimate and mysterious being beyond nature as we know it, and of a supreme, if inhuman, purity and beauty. The central crime corresponds to the fall, a thwarting of some guiding purpose by murderous self-will, or to loss of innocence in the maturing personality, and the consequent suffering under heat to man's present mental state. In poetic language you may say that whereas water parallels 'instinct' (with here a further reach in 'ice and snow' suggesting original mysteries of the distant and primeval), flames, fire, and light hold a more intellectual suggestion: they are instinct becoming self-conscious, leading to many agonies and high aspirations. The bird was a nature-force, eating human food, we are told, for the first time: it is that in nature which helps man beyond nature, an aspect of the divine purpose. Having slain it, man is plunged in burning agony. The thirst-impressions recall Eliot's *Waste Land,* which describes a very similar experience. The new mode is knowledge of evil, symbolized in the 'rotting' ocean, the 'slimy things' that crawl on it, the 'death-fires' and 'witches oils' burning by night. It is a lurid, colourful, yet ghastly death-impregnated scene, drawn to express aversion from physical life in dissolution or any reptilian manifestation; and, by suggestion, the sexual as seen from the mentalized consciousness of an alien, salty, and reptilian force. It is a deathly paralysis corresponding, it may be, to a sense of sexually starved existence in the modern world: certainly 'water, water everywhere, nor any drop to drink' fits such a reading.

Next comes the death-ship. 'Nightmare Life-in-Death' wins the Mariner's soul. This conception relates to deathly tonings in literature generally, the *Hamlet* experience, and the metaphorical 'death' of Wordsworth's *Immortality Ode.* It is, significantly, a feminine harlot-like figure, and is neatly put beside Death itself. She 'begins her work' on the Mariner. The other sailors all die: observe how he is to endure *knowledge* of death, with guilt. He is 'alone on a wide wide sea' in the dark night of the soul; so lonely—compare Wordsworth's solitaries—that God Himself seemed absent. The universe is one of 'beautiful' men dead and 'slimy things' alive, as in Shelley's *Alastor.* The 'rotting sea' is now directly associated with the 'rotting dead,' while he remains eternally cursed by the dead men's 'eyes.' At the extremity of despair and therefore self-less feeling, his eyes are suddenly aware of the beauty of the 'water-snakes' as he watches their rich colours and fiery tracks: 'O happy living things.' The exquisite prose accompaniment runs: 'By the light of the moon he beholdeth God's creatures of the great calm.' A fertilizing 'spring of love' gushes from his 'heart' and he blesses them *unaware*—the crucial word is repeated—with unpremeditated recognition and instinctive charity. Immediately the Albatross slips from him and sinks like lead into the sea. An utterly organic and unforced forgiveness of God conditions God's forgiveness of man.

The exact psychological or other conceptual equivalents of poetic symbolism cannot be settled. If they could, there would be no occasion for such symbols, and my use of the term 'sexual' might seem rash to anyone unaware of the general relation of snakes and water to sexual instincts in poetry, as in *Antony and Cleopatra* and Eliot's use of water and sea-life. Christabel's enforced and unhappy silence whilst under Geraldine's serpent spell may be directly related to the water-snakes of *The Ancient Mariner*. She, like the becalmed ship, is helpless; perhaps, in her story too, until a certain frontier, involving spontaneous, but not willed, recognition, is reached. Just as she cannot speak, that is, confess, so the Mariner, when, as it were, saved, spends the rest of his life confessing.

The immediate results of conversion are (i) gentle sleep after feverish and delirious horror, and (ii) refreshing rain after parching heat. These are imaginative equivalents and may be said to touch the concept of *agapé* as opposed to *eros*, and are here logically related to Christian symbols. A sense of purity and freedom replaces horror and sin. Energy is at once released: the wind blows and the dead rise and work, their bodies being used by a 'troop of spirits blest,' who next make music, clustering into a circle, with suggestion of Dante's paradisal lives. Now the ship starts to move like Eliot's similar ships in *The Waste Land* and *Ash Wednesday*; yet no wind, but rather the 'lonesome spirit from the South-pole,' is causing the motion, and demanding vengeance still. Why? and who is he? Coleridge's prose definition scarcely helps. He works 'nine fathom' deep—in man or creation, at once instinct and accuser, and not quite stilled by conversion. At last he is placated by the Mariner's penance. Next *'angelic* power' drives on the ship. There is more trouble from the dead men's eyes and another release. As the ship draws near home, each body has a burning seraph upright above it. These seraphic forms that twice seem conditioned by dead bodies, yet not, as individuals, precisely the 'souls' of the men concerned, must, I think, be vaguely identified with the concept of human immortality, the extra dimension of their upright stature over the bodies being pictorially cogent.

At home there is the 'kirk,' the woodland 'hermit,' and safety. After such fiery experience the normality of the hermit's life, its homely and earthy quality, is emphasized. We meet his 'cushion' of 'moss' and 'oak-stump' and his daily prayers. He is a figure of unstriving peace such as Wordsworth sought, associated with earth and solid fact after nightmare and transcendent vision. Extreme sensual and spiritual adventure has brought only agony. Therefore:

> O sweeter than the marriage-feast,
> 'Tis sweeter far to me,
> To walk together to the kirk
> With a goodly company.

It is an embracing of *agapé* with a definitely lower place, if not a rejection, accorded to *eros*; a welcoming of earth and refreshing rain ('the gentle rain from heaven' is an *agapé*-phrase in Shakespeare) with a rejection of the sun in its drawing, tormenting, heat. I doubt if there is any relieving synthesis implicit in the 'youths and maidens' that go to church at the end of the poem with the Wordsworthian 'old men and babes': the balance is scarcely in favour of youthful assertion. The final lesson is a total acceptance of God and his universe through humility, with general love to man and beast. But the specifically sexual is left unplaced: the wedding-guest is sadder and wiser henceforth, and presumably avoids all festive gatherings from now on; though forgiveness of *reptilian* manifestation remains basic.

This is Coleridge's *Purgatorio,* as *Christabel* is a fragmentary attempt at a little *Inferno*. Whether we can call the central criminal act 'sexual' is arguable: it certainly resembles that in Wordsworth's *Hart-leap Well,* but the Mariner's compulsion to tell his tale suggests rather Eliot's Sweeney and his grim account. One might notice that the imaginative tonings in *Lucrece* and *Macbeth* are identical, and that 'sadism' may be only a conscious recognition of a deeper relation than has yet been plumbed: motiveless cruelty is, moreover, a general and most valuable poetic theme, as in Heathcliff's ill-treatment of a dog. Such thoughts help to integrate into the whole the mystery of an unmotivated action which, with the South-pole spirit itself, is left rationally undefined, as Shakespeare leaves the motives of Macbeth and Iago and the pain of Hamlet rationally undefined. The new life comes from acceptance of the watery and the reptilian, at which the sea no longer appears to be 'rotting,' that is, dead, though all these drop out of the picture afterwards. The crime, together with rejection of the unrefreshing 'rotting sea' and its creatures, brings parched agony, but acceptance of those brings the other, heavenly and refreshing, water of rain. Also acceptance precedes repentance, not vice versa. A spontaneous, unsought, upspring of love alone conditions the down-flow of grace.

The poem is lively and colourful, as A. C. Bradley has well emphasized. The movement and appearance of sun and moon are described in stanza after stanza; and stars too. The sun peeps in and out as though uncertain whether or not to give its blessing on the strange scene. The poem glitters: the Mariner holds the Wedding Guest with a 'glittering eye,' which, if remembered with his 'skinny hand,' preserves a neat balance. The light is somewhat ghastly: as in the strange sheen of it on ice or tropic calm, and the witches' oils burning 'green and blue and white.' Green light is a favourite in Coleridge (cp. in *Dejection* 'that green light that lingers in the west'). The snakes move in 'tracks of shining white,' making 'elfish' illumination. Their colours are 'blue, glossy-green and velvet black' and by night their every motion pencils 'a flash of golden fire.' The ghost-ship comes barred across the blood-red sun. The 'charmed water' is said to burn 'a still and awful red.' There is a very subtle interplay of light and colour. The Life-in-Death figure is a garish whore with red lips, yellow hair, white leprosy skin; the evil creatures are colourful; the supernatural seraphs brilliant. The whole is dominated by a fearful intensity summed in the image, rather dark for this poem, of a night-walker aware of a demon following his steps. But the play of light and colour helps to give the somewhat stringy stanza succession and thinly narrative, undramatic sequence of events a certain intangible poetic mass. I doubt if the rhyme-links, the metrical rhythms, even the phrase-life, so to speak, would be considered fine poetry without this and, what is equally important, the substance of idea and meaning we have been analysing.

The strangeness and ghastly yet fascinating lights of the experience must guide our judgement of the solution. The experience is of fearful fascination; a feverish horror that is half a positive delight, mental pre-eminently; and the return is a return to earth, the hermits' cell and mossy stone, a return to reality and sanity. Whatever our views of the implied doctrine there is no artistic confusion or lack of honesty. The balancing of symbols, as in the contrast of bird-life and the reptilian, is subtle as Dante's (the *Purgatorio* has a very similarly reiterated observation of the sun in varied position and mood) and Shakespeare's, though without the massive scheme of the one or the sympathetic range of the other. It is a little poem greatly conceived. The supernatural figures dicing for the Mariner's soul suggest, inexactly, the balancing of the Eumenides against Apollo in respect of Orestes in Aeschylus; while the 'lonesome spirit' from the South Pole in its office of accuser performs exactly the function of those Eumenides, furies of guilt and accusation. It is replaced eventually by swift angelic power, as in Eliot's *Family Reunion* the furies of *Sweeney Agonistes* turn into angels.

Poetry of any worth is a rounded solidity which drops shadows only on the flat surfaces of philosophical statement. Concretely it bodies forth symbols of which our ghostly concepts of 'life,' 'death,' 'time,' 'eternity,' 'immortality' are only very pallid analogies. They are none the less necessary, if we are to enchain our normal thinking to the creations of great literature, and I next translate the domed symbolism of *Kubla Khan* into such shadow-terms corresponding to the original in somewhat the same way as the science of Christian theology corresponds, or should correspond, to the New Testament.

The pleasure-dome dominates. But its setting is carefully described and very important. There is a 'sacred' river that runs into 'caverns measureless to man' and a 'sunless sea.' That is, the river runs into an infinity of death. The marked-out area through which it flows is, however, one of teeming nature: gardens, rills, 'incense-bearing' trees, ancient forests. This is not unlike Dante's earthly paradise. The river is 'sacred.' Clearly a sacred river which runs through nature towards death will in some sense correspond to life. I take the river to be, as so often in Wordsworth (whose *Immortality Ode* is also throughout suggested), a symbol of life.

Born on a *height*, it descends from a 'deep romantic chasm,' a place 'savage,' 'holy,' and 'enchanted,' associated with both a 'waning moon' and a 'woman wailing for her demon lover.' The river's origin blends romantic, sacred, and satanic suggestions. Whatever our views on sex it would be idle to suppose them anything but a tangle of inconsistencies. Moreover, the idea of original sin, the 'old serpent,' and its relation to sex is not only Biblical but occurs in myth and poetry ancient and modern. We have not yet compassed the straightforward sanity on this vital issue which D. H. Lawrence said would, if attained, make both nasty sex stories and romantic idealisms alike unnecessary: a certain obscene and savage sex-desecration seems to have fixed itself as a disease in the human mind. That is why we find the virgin-symbol, in both paganism and Christianity, sublimated; especially the virgin mother.

Sex is overlaid with both high romantic and low satanic conceptions, complexities, fears, taboos, and worship of all sorts, but the necessity and goodness of pure creativeness no one questions. Our lines here hint a mystery, not altogether unlike Wordsworth's dark grandeurs, blending satanism with sanctity and romance with savagery. They express that mystic glamour of sex that conditions human creation and something of its pagan evil magic; and touch the enigma of the creator-god beyond good and evil, responsible for eagle and boa-constrictor alike.

Whatever our minds make of them, sex-forces have their way. Nature goes on cheerily blasting families and uniting true lovers in matrimonial bonds of 'perdurable toughness,' with an equal efficiency working through rake and curate alike, and not caring for details so long as her work be done. Goethe's poetry well presents this seething, torrential, over-mastering creative energy. Look now at our next lines: at the 'ceaseless turmoil,' the earth-mother breathing in 'fast thick pants,' the fountain 'forced' out with 'half intermitted burst,' the fragments rebounding like hail, the 'chaffy grain beneath the flail,' the 'dancing rocks.' What riotous impression of agony, tumult, and power: the dynamic enginery of birth and creation.

Then off the river goes 'meandering in a mazy motion': observe the rhythm of this line. The maze is, of course, a well-known figure suggesting uncertain and blind progress and is sometimes expressly used for the spiritual complexities of human life; and the general symbolism of mazes and caves throughout my present study might be compared with my brother's inspection of such symbolisms in the ancient world (*Cumaean Gates*, by W. F. Jackson Knight). After five miles of mazy progress the river reaches the 'caverns measureless to man,' that is, infinity, nothingness; and sinks, with first more tumult (i.e. death-agony), to a 'lifeless ocean,' that is to eternal nothingness, death, the sea into which Timon's story closes. This tumult is aptly associated with war: the principle of those conflicting and destructive forces that drive man to his end. The 'ancestral voices' suggest that dark compulsion that binds the race to its habitual conflicts and is related by some psychologists to unconscious ancestor-worship, to parental and pre-parental authority. We find an interesting analogy in Byron's *Sardanapalus*.

So in picture-language we have a symbolical pattern not unlike Addison's *Vision of Mirza*, though less stiffly allegorical. As for Kubla Khan himself, if we bring him within our scheme, he becomes God: or at least one of those 'huge and mighty forms,' or other similar intuitions of gigantic mountainous power, in Wordsworth. Or we can, provisionally

—not finally, as I shall show—leave him out, saying that the poet's genius, starting to describe an oriental monarch's architectural exploits, finds itself automatically creating a symbolic and universal panorama of existence. This is a usual process, since the poet continually starts with an ordinary tale but universalizes as he proceeds: compare the two levels of meaning in *The Tempest*, where Prospero performs a somewhat similarly superhuman role to Kubla Khan here; or Yeats's emperor in *Byzantium*.

In *The Christian Renaissance* I wrote at length on the concept of immortality as it emerges from interpretation of poetry. I concluded that, though we must normally think in temporal terms and imagine immortality as a state after death, yet poetry, in moments of high optimistic vision, reveals something more closely entwined than that with the natural order. It expresses rather a new and more concrete perception of life here and now, unveiling a new *dimension* of existence. Thus immortality becomes not a prolongation of the time-sequence, but rather that whole sequence from birth to death lifted up vertically to generate a super-temporal area, or solidity. I used such a scheme to explain parts of the New Testament, Shakespeare, Goethe, and other poets: especially here I would point to my interpretation of Wordsworth's *Immortality Ode*. But I did not use *Kubla Khan*, my scheme being evolved from inspection of other poets.

I come now to the latter movement of our poem, whose form is not unlike an expansion of the Petrarchan Sonnet. This is the sestet. Observe that the metre changes: a lilting happy motion, a shimmering dance motion, replaces heavy resonance and reverberation. Our minds are tuned to a new apprehension, something at once assured, happy, and musical. A higher state of consciousness is suggested: and see what it shows us.

The dome's *shadow* falls half-way along the river, which is, we remember, the birth-death time-stream. This shadow—a Wordsworthian impression—is cast by a higher, more dimensional reality such as I have deduced from other poets to be the pictured quality of immortality. It is directly associated with the 'mingled measure' of the sounds coming from the two extremes. In Wordsworth, and elsewhere, immortality may by associated closely with birth, though that is by way of a provisional and preliminary approach to the greater truth; while in our own thinking it is found most often to function in terms of a life after death. But both are finally unsatisfying; birth and death are both mysteries that time-thinking distorts, and personal life beyond their limits a somewhat tenuous concept. The true immortality is extra-dimensional to all this: it is the *pleasure-dome itself,* arching solid and firm above creation's mazy progress and the 'mingled' sounds of its conflicts, just as in Wordsworth the child's immortality is said to 'brood' over it 'like the day': that is, arching, expansive, immovable.

The 'mingled-measure' suggests the blend and marriage of fundamental oppositions: life and death, or creation and destruction. These 'mingle' under the shadow of the greater harmony, the crowning dome-circle. Observe that it is a paradoxical thing, a 'miracle of rare device'; 'sunny,' but with 'caves of ice,' which points the resolution of antinomies in the new dimension, especially those of light and heat, for Eros-fires of the mind; and ice, for the coldness of inorganic ·nature, ultimate being, and death, the ice-caves being perhaps related to our earlier caverns, only more optimistically toned; light instead of gloomy, just as 'sunny' suggests no torturing heat. The 'caves of ice' may also hint cool cavernous depths in the unconscious mind (a usual Wordsworthian cave-association) blending with a *lighted* intelligence: whereby at last coldness becomes kind. These, ice and sun-fire, are the two elemental antitheses of *The Ancient Mariner,* and their mingling may lead us farther. We are at what might be called a marriage-point in life's progress half-way between birth and death: and even birth and death are themselves here mingled or married. We may imagine a sexual union between life, the masculine, and death, the feminine. Then our 'romantic chasm' and 'cedarn cover,' the savage and enchanted yet holy place with its 'half intermitted burst' may be, in spite of our former reading, vaguely related to the functioning of a man's creative organs and their physical setting and, too, to all principles of manly and adventurous action; while the caverns that engulf the sacred river will be correspondingly feminine with a dark passivity and infinite peace. The pleasure-dome we may fancy as the pleasure of a sexual union in which birth and death are the great contesting partners, with human existence as the life-stream, the blood-stream, of a mighty coition. The poet glimpses that for which no direct words exist: the sparkling dome of some vast intelligence enjoying that union of opposites which to man appears conflict unceasing and mazed wandering pain between mystery and mystery.

I would leave a space after 'caves of ice.' I am not now so sure about the sonnet form: those six lines are central. So next we have our third and final movement, starting with the Abyssinian damsel seen in a vision playing music. The aptness of a girl-image here is obvious. In

Shakespeare and Milton music suggests that consciousness which blends rational antinomies, and so our poet equates the once-experienced mystic and girl-born music with his dome. Could he revive in himself that music he would build the spiritual dome 'in air'; that is, I think, in words, in poetry. Or, maybe, he would become himself the domed consciousness of a cold, happy, brilliance, an ice-flashing, sun-smitten, wisdom. The analogy between music and some form of architecture is not solitary: it receives a fine expression in Browning's *Abt Vogler*, a valuable commentary on *Kubla Khan*. The analogy is natural enough for either music or poetry: we talk of architectonics in criticizing poetry or a novel, for the very reason that literary or musical art bears to rational thought the relation of a solid, or at least an area, to a line. Tennyson's *Palace of Art* is a direct analogy, and Wordsworth compares his life's work to a 'Gothic Church.'

The poem's movement now grows ecstatic and swift. There is a hint of a new speed in the drawn-out rhythm of 'To such a deep delight 'twould win me. . . .' Now the three rhymed lines gather up the poet's message together with his consciousness of its supreme meaning with a breathless expectancy toward crescendo. Next follows a fall to a ritualistic solemnity, a Nunc Dimittis, phrased in long vowels and stately measured motion, imaged in the 'circle' and the eyes dropped in 'holy dread' before the prophet who has seen and re-created 'Paradise': not the earthly, but the heavenly paradise; the 'stately' permanence above motion, the pleasure-dome enclosing and transcending human agony and frustration. To tune our understanding we might go to such a passage as Wordsworth's:

> incumbencies more awful, visitings
> Of the Upholder of the tranquil soul,
> That tolerates the indignities of Time,
> And, from the centre of Eternity
> All finite motions overruling, lives
> In glory immutable. (*The Prelude*, III. 116)

Which transmits a similar recognition.

Kubla Khan is a comprehensive creation, including and transcending not only the dualisms of *The Ancient Mariner* ('sun,' 'ice,' and sexual suggestions recurring with changed significance) but also the more naturalistic, Wordsworthian, grandeurs. Though outwardly concentrating on an architectural synthesis, there is the other, mountainous, elevation suggested in Mount Abora; and indeed the dome itself is a kind of mountain with 'caves,' the transcendent and the natural being blended, as so often in Wordsworth. It must be related to other similar statements of an ultimate intuition where the circular or architectural supervenes on the natural: in particular to the mystic dome of Yeats's *Byzantium*. The blend here of a circular symbolism with a human figure (the Abyssinian maid) and images of human conflict may be compared both to Dante's final vision and an important passage in Shelley's *Prometheus*. *Kubla Khan* is classed usually with *Christabel* and *The Ancient Mariner,* both profound poems with universal implications. The one presents a nightmare vision related to some obscene but nameless sex-horror; the other symbolizes a clear pilgrim's progress (we may remember Coleridge's admiration of Bunyan's work) through sin to redemption. It would be strange if *Kubla Khan,* incorporating together the dark satanism and the water-purgatory of those, did not, like its sister poems, hold a comparable, or greater, profundity, its images clearly belonging to the same order of poetic reasoning. Its very names are so lettered as to suggest first and last things: Xanadu, Kubla Khan, Alph, Abyssinian, Abora. 'A' is emphatic; Xanadu, which starts the poem, is enclosed in letters that might well be called eschatological; while Kubla Khan himself sits alphabetically central with his alliterating 'k's. Wordsworth's line 'of first, and last, and midst, and without end,' occurring in a mountain-passage (*The Prelude,* VI. 640) of somewhat similar scope, may be compared. The poem's supposed method of composition is well known. How it comes to form so compact and satisfying a unit raises questions outside the scheme of my study. The poem, anyway, needs no defence. It has a barbaric and oriental magnificence that asserts itself with a happy power and authenticity too often absent from visionary poems set within the Christian tradition.

The Ancient Mariner

THE OPENING of the Prefatory Note to 'The Wanderings of Cain' describes how that curious prose fragment came into being, and it ends by saying that the whole scheme for the collaboration with Wordsworth in a poem about Cain 'broke up in a laugh: and the Ancient Mariner was written instead.' This is only one among a number of partial records left by Coleridge himself, or by the Wordsworths, of the origin of the 'Mariner.' These different records piece together into a quite intelligible and consistent account, too familiar to repeat.[1] But 'The Wanderings of Cain' has a special place in that account because it shows how the subject of terrible guilt, suffering, expiation and wandering was already in Coleridge's mind before the various hints which were to form the outline of the Mariner's story came together. Cain's 'countenance told in a strange and terrible language of agonies that had been, and were, and were still to continue to be.' These agonies were related to a landscape in tune with them:

> The scene around was desolate; as far as the eye could reach it was desolate: the bare rocks faced each other, and left a long and wide interval of thin white sand.[2]

It is even verbally but a few steps to 'the wide, wide sea.'

In another draft fragment of the Cain poem[3] a rather obscure and evasive sentence says that God inflicted punishment on Cain 'because

---

From *Coleridge: The Clark Lectures 1951–52* (Rupert Hart-Davis, London, 1953), pp. 84–113. Reprinted by permission of the publisher.

he neglected to make a proper use of his senses, etc.' Later in this draft come alligators and tigers in close conjunction, just as they occurred together in a speech of the Wandering Jew in Lewis's *The Monk*, which Coleridge reviewed in *The Critical Review* for February 1797.[4] The Mariner bears traces of both these two traditional figures, Cain and the Wandering Jew.[5]

Not only once, but twice, Coleridge and Wordsworth began to collaborate in an exceedingly light-hearted way in works which dealt with crime, guilt, expiation and wandering. If we are broadly able to trust Coleridge's account, 'The Wanderings of Cain' was begun as a composition-race: and there is no reason at all to doubt that 'The Ancient Mariner' was begun by them jointly to raise £5 to pay the expenses of a walking-tour. It was thus an entirely unexpected by-product of Coleridge's main poetical plans. Those plans were of Miltonic size and seriousness. There is evidence, as Professor R. C. Bald has shown,[6] for believing that he was deliberately reading with the idea of writing two main works, a series of Hymns to the Sun, Moon and Elements, and an Epic on the Origin of Evil. It is hardly necessary even to say how much matter in the 'Mariner' overlaps with what might have gone into those two works.

We may even suggest that the accident, so to speak, of beginning the 'Mariner' on that November evening in 1797 released Coleridge from some of the burden of his Miltonic responsibilities and helped to split his ambitious synthesising aim of bringing all human knowledge together in the frame of one or more huge poems. I have already tried to show how, in the more ambitious poems just before this period, he was attempting, without much success, to synthesise politics, religion and philosophy in a highly Miltonic style. Now the aims and material split. It has been observed by Dr. Tillyard how very unpolitical 'The Ancient Mariner' is. 'Frost at Midnight' (dated February 1798—that is while the 'Mariner' was still being written) is, if possible, less political still. It is interesting that Coleridge's best political poem, 'France: an Ode,' is also dated February 1798: creative energy used in one direction and style seems also to have released it in other directions and styles. A political Ode in the Gray/Mason tradition, and a blank-verse meditative poem, soaring right away from its origins in Cowper, were written in among work on the 'Mariner,' which differed from both. There could be no clearer disproof of the narrowness of Coleridge's poetic range than the fact that these three poems are contemporary.

Little need be said about the context of styles to which the 'Mariner' belongs: it has plain affiliations with Gothic horrors, of which Lewis was the fashionable exponent; and it is noticeable too that in the original volume of the *Lyrical Ballads* 'The Ancient Mariner' is the only poem which derives its style from the traditional ballads as they were then available in Percy, rather than from the later ballad of broadsheet.[7] The precision, success and care, with which Coleridge later cut out many of the cruder traces of these origins—the pseudo-antique spelling, the more glaring archaisms of vocabulary, some of the marvels—is fresh evidence of the justice of his detailed judgement: but yet, when all these changes had been made, it is still remarkable how many features of ballad idiom and method the poem still retains and completely assimilates, diverting and modifying them to its own particular effects. It is partly by these means that the poem manages to escape history and yet retain tradition. Though it will not tie to a table of dates or a map, the 'Mariner' yet uses the keepings of European tradition and all the details of wind and weather which every map implies. Its imagery, both of religion and of the elements, goes deep below the surface of what we may happen to remember or happen to have seen.

But at the same time it uses to the full the vividness of visual description which was one of Coleridge's great poetic strengths. A friend of mine recently said he could not read Coleridge any more—no, not even 'The Ancient Mariner': he could not stand all the supernatural part; but only a few sentences later he went on to say that on a slow sea-voyage to Africa he got up early and walked round the deck reciting the poem to himself, and that nothing could have better fitted his mood or described what he saw than

> The fair breeze blew, the white foam flew,
> The furrow followed free.[8]

Scarcely any reader, from first acquaintance in childhood, has not felt that the first, most elementary contact with the poem leaves such isolated descriptions fixed in the memory, and it is only a step further, if it is a step at all, to feel, at the next level of relevance, the perfect attunement between the descriptions and the states of the Mariner's mind.

> Down dropt the breeze, the sails dropt down,
> 'Twas sad as sad could be;
> And we did speak only to break
> The silence of the sea![9]

None of Coleridge's poems shows more completely developed in practice the principle of description which was quoted earlier from his letter to Sotheby of 1802:

> Never to see or describe any interesting appearance in nature without connecting it, by dim analogies, with the moral world proves faintness of impression. Nature has her proper interest, and he will know what it is who believes and feels that everything has a life of its own, and that we are all *One Life*. A poet's heart and intellect should be *combined*, intimately combined and unified with the great appearances of nature and not merely held in solution and loose mixture with them, in the shape of formal similes.[10]

The full relevance of this to 'The Ancient Mariner' will begin to appear gradually in what I have to say later. The present relevance is that in the poem the method of relating nature to the moral world is not by 'dim analogies,' nor 'in the shape of formal similes' (there are very few), but by the poet's heart and intellect being intimately *combined* and unified with the great appearances of nature. The method of conjunction is immediate in the natural imagery, and it is only by understanding the imagery that the 'moral world' can be understood. For the present a single simple instance must be enough.

> And now there came both mist and snow,
> And it grew wondrous cold:
> And ice, mast-high, came floating by,
> As green as emerald.
>
> And through the drifts the snowy clifts
> Did send a dismal sheen:
> Nor shapes of men nor beasts we ken—
> The ice was all between.
>
> The ice was here, the ice was there,
> The ice was all around:
> It cracked and growled, and roared and howled,
> Like noises in a swound! [11]

In those stanzas it is *in* the descriptive phrases 'As green as emerald' and 'a dismal sheen' that the double mood of admiration and fear is conveyed: and the double character of this mood is important.

'The great appearances of nature' play an overwhelming part in the poem, and their part was emphasised and further explained in the prose

173

gloss that was added in 1817. Lowes put this side of the poem epigram-matically by saying that the chief characters in 'The Ancient Mariner' are 'Earth, Air, Fire and Water.'[12] By chief 'characters' we must under-stand also chief channels of action—for it is through the elements that the Mariner is acted upon.

The function of the elements and heavenly bodies is not merely to *image* the Mariner's spiritual states (though indeed they do this), but also to provide in the narrative structure of the poem the link between the Mariner as ordinary man, and the Mariner as one acquainted with the invisible world, which has its own sets of values.

This link is first suggested in the idea that the Albatross has a power of control over the elements: it is continued in the idea of the plaguing spirit that followed the ship nine fathoms deep from the land of mist and snow. The skeleton ship with the figures of Death and Life-in-Death is linked to the phenomena of the tropical sunset:

> The Sun's rim dips; the stars rush out:
> At one stride comes the dark;
> With far-heard whisper, o'er the sea,
> Off shot the spectre bark.[13]

The angelic spirits who inspire the dead men to work the ship are sent to release the ship from the control of the daemons of the elements; and the spirit from the South Pole works under their orders. The two voices in Parts V and VI are two fellow daemons of the Polar Spirit, two 'in-visible inhabitants of the element,' as the gloss calls them. And finally the ship is brought back to port under the undisputed control of angelic spirits, but accompanied by a wind.

Across this whole system of daemons of the elements and angelic spirits lies the framework of ordinary Catholic theology—Christ and Mary Queen of Heaven, and in the ending the ordinary Catholic prac-tices of confession, absolution and church-going.

The inter-relation of the different spiritual beings is one of the hardest points in the poem to be clear or confident about; and it is best, ap-proaching the more doubtful through the less, to begin by discussing the poem's more obvious bearings on the 'moral world,' and indeed to establish first that it has a bearing on the moral world at all. For even this has sometimes been disputed. We must start from Coleridge's one main comment on the poem, as it is reported in the *Table Talk* under 31 May 1830:

Mrs. Barbauld once told me that she admired the Ancient Mariner very much, but that there were two faults in it,—it was improbable, and had no moral. As for the probability, I owned that that might admit some question; but as to the want of a moral, I told her that in my own judgment the poem had too much; and that the only, or chief fault, if I might say so, was the obtrusion of the moral sentiment so openly on the reader as a principle or cause of action in a work of such pure imagination. It ought to have had no more moral than the Arabian Nights' tale of the merchant's sitting down to eat dates by the side of a well, and throwing the shells aside, and lo! a genie starts up, and says he *must* kill the aforesaid merchant *because* one of the date shells had, it seems, put out the eye of the genie's son.

The story of the Merchant and the Genie in *The Arabian Nights* is briefly this. A merchant is travelling in a desert with nothing to eat but some biscuits and dates in a wallet. He sits down to eat dates and throws the stones about: a huge and terrible genie appears, with a great scimitar, and says he will cut off the merchant's head. Why? Because one of the stones was flung into the eye of the genie's son and killed him. The merchant pleads that it was quite accidental: but the genie is relentless. Finally the genie allows the merchant one year's respite. He is free to go home to provide for his wife and children, and to order his affairs. This he does, with great justice and generosity and, after a struggle, he returns to the same spot in the desert, as arranged with the genie, exactly one year later. Here he falls in with three old men, mysterious strangers, to whom he tells his story; the genie then appears again. And each of the strangers in turn makes a bargain with the genie that if he can tell the genie a story more marvellous than he has ever heard before, the genie is to remit one-third of the merchant's punishment. The stories cap each other for marvellousness; the genie is honest to the bargain; the merchant goes free and triumphant home, and the three old men go off mysteriously into the desert as they came.

Now this story has not got a 'moral' in the sense that there is a clear explicit detachable maxim which neatly sums up the didactic drift of it. But it seems equally clear that one cannot possibly read the story without being very aware of moral issues in it; aware that its whole development is governed by moral situations, and that without them there wouldn't really be a story. The arbitrariness of the genie; the awful consequences to the merchant of what was originally, on his side, a pure accident; the thoughts of the merchant for his family; these are moral matters. The generosity and exactness with which he arranged his affairs in the year of respite is developed very fully in the story: and much is made of the struggle about his bargain to return, and of the punctuality and faithfulness with which he kept it. It is very difficult indeed, in reading the story, not to see in his final release, as the result of the three old men's tales, a reward for his honourableness and care in all his dealings. And when one has got so far, it is not difficult to see that— always allowing for the fact that no 'maxim' conveys the *whole* moral of a story—some such maxim as this, deduced from it, is not irrelevant: 'The arbitrary character of fate may be overcome by human honour and goodness; and there may be mysterious powers in the world which aid these virtues.' In the *Arabian Nights* version this moral, or anything like it, is not in Coleridge's words 'obtruded too openly.' But to deny altogether that it (or something like it) is there (when the whole story depends on the genie's arbitrariness, the merchant's honourableness and his final release) would seem to me a grotesque example of wilful blindness.

We do not know how well Coleridge remembered the story or how accurately his nephew reported what he said. But as the *Table Talk* passage stands, it is surely clear that Coleridge never said or meant that the 'Mariner' neither had nor was meant to have a moral bearing or a 'moral sentiment.' He said the fault was *'the obtrusion of the moral senti-ment so openly* . . . in a work of such pure imagination.' And this seems to point to his possible dissatisfaction with the summary of the 'moral' as a kind of didactic epigram towards the end:

> He prayeth well, who loveth well
> Both man and bird and beast.
>
> He prayeth best, who loveth best
> All things both great and small;
> For the dear God who loveth us,
> He made and loveth all.[14]

It is obvious that those lines do rub the point home and that they may, when detached from their context, be degraded to the status of a motto in 'almanac art,' or used to express the quite worthy desire to put out crumbs for the dicky-birds on a cold and frosty morning. But coming in context, after the richness and terror of the poem, it is no more a banal moral apothegm, but a moral which has its meaning *because it has been lived.*

All recent full discussions of 'The Ancient Mariner' have taken this for granted. In what follows I owe a great deal to three such discussions, one by Dr. Tillyard;[15] one by Dr. Bowra;[16] and one by the American writer and critic Mr. Robert Penn Warren.[17] All agree, however much they differ from each other, that the poem has a very serious moral and spiritual bearing on human life: and they are surely right. For Coleridge, talking in 1830, could not possibly have meant to exclude all moral relevance from the working of the 'pure imagination' when his whole developed critical theory stressed again and again the union of heart and head, the special power of the poet to bring 'the whole soul of man into activity.'[18]

Coleridge has set us a special problem of critical method. It is obvious that his own creative experience must have deeply affected his critical theories and practice: but he never fully brought the two into relation; he rarely adduced his own poems as instances, and never expounded them. Furthermore, his important critical work was all a good deal later than most of his important creative work. We cannot thus be sure how much of his critical opinion may fairly be carried back into 1797–8 and brought to bear on his own greatest poetry. It is very hard to be fair, and not to pick out what suits us and reject the rest. It is, for instance, tempting to use Coleridge's later distinctions between allegory and symbol in interpreting 'The Ancient Mariner'; but they had not been expressed in 1797–8. In fact, we may be misled if we start the critique of the 'Mariner' and 'Kubla Khan' with this disjunction of allegory from symbol in mind. For all allegory involves symbolism, and in proportion as symbolism becomes developed and coherent it tends towards allegory. This is one of the problems involved in Mr. Warren's exciting essay: he starts as a 'symbolist' criticising all the 'allegorisers' and ends up in something so organised and precise that Coleridge, anyway, would probably have called it an allegorisation. But Mr. Warren would be quite willing to accept that, provided only that his kind of allegory is seen to be distinct from simple 'two-dimensional' allegory.

The poem's very richness at once tempts and defeats definiteness of interpretation; as we commit ourselves to the development of one strand of meaning we find that in the very act of doing so we are excluding something else of importance.

An example of this difficulty occurs on the threshold of interpretation, in the opinion we form about the Mariner's relation to ordinary human beings and the relation of the voyage to ordinary human life. Dr. Tillyard, struck (as everybody must be struck) by the similarities in spirit between the poem and the seventeenth-century voyages—

> We were the first that ever burst
> Into that silent sea—

as voyages of adventure and discovery, and using, to support his argument, the later Coleridge passage in the *Biographia* about the range of hills which must be crossed by an inquiring spirit, maintains that the Mariner himself is a mental and spiritual adventurer, 'an unusually enquiring spirit,' that he together with the rest of the crew are, from the accepted social point of view, *self-appointed* outcasts and criminals; and that the sea-voyage indicates 'spiritual adventure' which they go out of their way to seek.[19]

But how is this present in the poem? The beginning of the Mariner's own account of the voyage contains no hint that he thought of the voyage as a high spiritual enterprise at variance with current limited social ideas, a conscious seeking of adventure. The ship starts off in an atmosphere of communal agreement and pleasure:

> The ship was cheered, the harbour cleared,
> Merrily did we drop
> Below the kirk, below the hill,
> Below the lighthouse top.[20]

The voyage, it seems, began normally, commonly, happily, the crew at one both with the society they left and with each other. In the literature of sea-going the antecedents are rather to be found in such voyages as that described by Herodotus—certainly used by Coleridge when he wrote

> The Sun now rose upon the right— [21]

the voyage in which the Phoenician seamen doubled the Cape without knowing that there was a Cape.[22] Adventure came upon them unaware.

The Mariner, said Wordsworth in rude complaint, 'does not act, but is continually acted upon.' There is, surely, an important element of truth in this, though it does not in the least derogate from the poem's merits.[23] There are only three points in the poem at which the Mariner may be said to 'act'; these are—the shooting of the Albatross; the blessing of the water-snakes; and the biting of his arm. Each of these actions has a very different character. The shooting of the Albatross comes quite suddenly and unexplained; superficially it is unmotivated and wanton. The Mariner himself never makes any explicit attempt to

178

explain it: nor does the poem contain, from his point of view, any defence of it. We shall return to this. In the first phase of his recovery, in the crisis at the centre of the poem, when he blesses the water-snakes, he does so *unaware*, and this word 'unaware' is deliberately repeated and occurs each time significantly, emphatically, at the end of the line. That is to say, he did not really know what he was doing; he could find no adequate spring of action in himself, and retrospectively attributed his undeliberate blessing to a supernatural influence on him:

> Sure my kind saint took pity on me.[24]

He himself thought he was more acted upon than acting. Against this must be set the one clear occasion in the poem on which the Mariner does deliberately act. In Part III, when all the crew, including himself, have been stricken dumb by the drought, it is he who sees the sail; it is he who, by a prodigious effort, bites his arm, sucks the blood and finds voice to cry out. This is his one tremendous effort: it is a moment of terrible hope for him and for the whole crew. But the hope is blasted, not just negatively, but positively, appallingly, blasted. The crew all die cursing him with their eyes, and he alone survives.

This is crucial to the whole poem's dramatic effect and, by inference, also to its moral effect. On the one occasion when the Mariner does consciously, deliberately and with all his effort *act,* his action leads ironically to the climax of the disaster. The irony is enforced by the two lines that end this Part:

> And every soul, it passed me by,
> Like the whizz of my cross-bow![25]

The disastrous anticlimax of this action and this hope is made to throw back to the earlier, unexplained act of the shooting. One main element in the poem's theme is that the Mariner's experience involves a tangle of error, incomprehensibility and frustration. He is certainly not a great courageous spiritual adventurer, though he has a great spiritual experience. He started his voyage in unison with the ordinary world in a common set of values: he comes back as half outcast and half participator. In the poem as a whole a deliberate contrast is certainly presented between the background of the wedding and the Mariner's tale. The interruptions of the Wedding-Guest are meant to point this contrast. His constant fear is that the Mariner is a ghost come back from the dead or even himself some kind of infernal spirit. The contrast is not so much between two types of personality, the normal/conventional and the abnormal/adventurer, but between two aspects of reality, and two potentialities of experience, the visible bodily world of human beings marrying and giving in marriage and an invisible world of spirits and the dead where quite a different system of values is to be learnt. The effect of the interruptions of the Wedding-Guest is to show how these two kinds of reality are always co-existent: the total effect of the poem is to show them interpenetrating. As it has been said, in one aspect the poem is a prothalamium, and there is even the hint that though the wedding-guests who make the 'loud uproar' have got their values wrong, yet the bride and bride-maids singing in the garden-bower are somehow touched by the Mariner's spiritual knowledge: and certainly the guest who has heard the tale cannot join the ordinary merry-making: 'He went like one that hath been stunned.'

The words 'error' and 'incomprehensibility,' used just now of the Mariner's experience, were then a temporary and partial formulation of what must now be developed. The Mariner leaves his killing of the Albatross without any full explanation; he does not, cannot or dare not attempt to give his motives. But the description of the bird, its nature and power, taken with the prose gloss, makes it clear that the killing of it was a ghastly violation of a great sanctity, at least as bad as a murder. The bird's human associations appear in the fact that it was hailed as a Christian soul in God's name, it answered the Mariner's hollo, ate human food, and played with the crew. The gloss calls it 'the pious bird of good omen.'[26] Thus it images not only its own obvious place in the natural order, but a system of both human and religious values which is declared to have power over the ship and its crew through its connection with the weather. Furthermore, a function of the bird as a Christian emblem is also hinted at later on, when its corpse is hung round the Mariner's neck 'instead of the cross.'

We have to consider our terminology for talking of an image used in such a complex way. Mr. Warren systematically and boldly uses the terms 'symbol' and 'symbolism,' and develops his theory of a symbol as 'focal, massive, and concrete'; Dr. Bowra also accepts the term 'symbol.' The terminology is not what matters so much as the degree of precision and equation that the use of a terminology allows. Mr. Warren is here somewhat confused: at one point he seems to equate the killing of the bird with the murder of a human being (arguing by a long analogy from Poe), and at another point to say that the killing 'symbolises' the Fall. If these two things are to be held together, it is clear that the symbol

180

must be functioning not merely towards different objects but in different ways: for the killing cannot *equate* with both a murder and the Fall, which are very different kinds of things. It seems best to avoid the term 'symbol' in order to avoid this risk of incompatible equation. What happens in the poem is that the images gather their bearing by progressively rich associations, by gradual increment, and that exact equation is never fully demanded, even though the associations are ordered and controlled. The killing of the Albatross thus becomes a violation of a great sanctity at the animal, human, and spiritual levels: but these levels are only gradually declared as the poem proceeds, just as the Mariner only gradually discovered the consequences of what he had done. Our enlightenment runs parallel with his.

Any possible link with the Fall is of a different kind from the link with murder; for if such a link is there, it lies in the corruption of the human will by original sin and must be imported into the poem from outside, to explain the Mariner's motive, when he is not able or willing to explain it himself. His sin may or may not be partly the sin of pride and self-assertion against the order of the universe. As the poem stands it is a sin of ignorance, and links to that half-adumbrated sin of Cain, that he 'neglected to make a proper use of his senses etc.' It was a wicked ignorance because accompanied by a wildly thoughtless failure to consider what might be the truth about the order of the universe.

This failure to reach the truth, and, to him, the incomprehensibility of what was going on, is made more apparent when the rest of the crew become accomplices in his crime. They do not know whether the fog and mist (along with the Albatross who brought them) are good or bad, or whether the bird belongs more to them or to the breeze: nor do they know whether the sun is good or bad. This is made fully apparent in that wonderful pair of stanzas in which the thought and verse are in shape identical, but with opposite content:

> And I had done a hellish thing,
> And it would work 'em woe:
> For all averred, I had killed the bird
> That made the breeze to blow.
> Ah wretch! said they, the bird to slay,
> That made the breeze to blow!
>
> Nor dim nor red, like God's own head,
> The glorious Sun uprist:
> Then all averred, I had killed the bird

> That brought the fog and mist.
> 'Twas right, said they, such birds to slay,
> That bring the fog and mist.[27]

The best approach to clarifying these stanzas (and the poem as a whole) is through the nature of the sun.

In the very next stanza the misunderstanding and incomprehensibility are allied to the wonder at novelty which the poem took over from the sixteenth-century voyages:

> We were the first that ever burst
> Into that silent sea.

This is one of the places in which the parallel between the physical voyage and the spiritual experience is most perfectly realised. An experience you don't understand produces first a shock of new glorious delight and then turns out to be something else. It is the worst kind of ethical and spiritual mistake—accepting wrong values.

On the naturalistic level this turns on the character of the tropic sun: and much here depends on the syntax.

> Nor dim nor red, like God's own head,
> The glorious sun uprist:

The syntax of these two lines makes it possible to interpret—

> *Either* (a) That God's head *is* dim and red, but the glorious sun uprose unlike it.
>
> *Or* (b) That the glorious sun rose like God's head which is *not* dim and red.

Interpretation (b) is made rather more likely, and (a) rather more unlikely, by the comma after 'red,' and this comma is apparently present in all texts. *Lyrical Ballads,* 1800, reads:

> Nor dim nor red, like an Angel's head,

with a comma after 'head.'[28] There seems no apparent reason, either internally in the poem, or externally, why an angel's head should be dim and red. This temporary variant seems to point to accepting interpretation (b) with the common reading.

The very fact that Coleridge ever changed 'God's own' to 'an Angel's' seems to suggest that what he had in mind was the nimbus, aureole or 'glory' of Christian iconography, and that this is picked up in the word 'glorious.' The rising sun was bright, golden and rayed, quite different from the small, clear-edged, bloody sun which becomes the image of evil two stanzas later. At the naturalistic level, both for the mariners and for Coleridge, the tropic sun changed from being a beautiful, pleasant, 'good' thing to being an unpleasant, evil thing: this change is a natural quality of the tropic sun, irrespective of the eye of the beholder. The naturalistic error of the crew was not to know that the tropic sun has this double character: and this naturalistic error is an image of their moral and spiritual error. This brings clearly to the front a main feature of 'the great appearances of nature' in the poem. It has been remarked for some time that the evil and disaster in the poem occur under the light of the sun, and the different phases of the redemption occur under the light of the moon. And Mr. Warren has developed this 'symbolism of the two lights' further than it had been taken before, by the introduction of his 'secondary' theme which I shall come to in a moment.

In Part II the becalming and the drought all occur under the influence of the sun; it is under the bloody sun that the deep rots, and that the creatures of the deep are slimy things that crawl with legs upon the slimy sea. We have already noticed how the spectre-bark appears in conjunction with the tropical sunset.

Part IV begins with the crisis of extreme isolation, with the frustrated desire for death, and then moves into the first phase of recovery and redemption.

The parallels here again between the spiritual and the natural—the physical imagery not just illuminating but actually conveying the spiritual state—are what most characterise the poem. It is clearest in the landless waste of the sea, the most awful loneliness:

> Alone, alone, all, all alone,
> Alone on a wide wide sea!
> And never a saint took pity on
> My soul in agony.[29]

The transition also from the barren desire for death to the first state of redemption is brought in through the magnificent imagery of the moon and stars. From the helpless repetition of

> the sky and the sea, and the sea and the sky[30]

—the dead, static, unchanging monotony of the spiritual isolation without a specified light—there is a shift by means of the wonderful stanza

> The moving Moon went up the sky,
> And no where did abide:
> Softly she was going up,
> And a star or two beside—[31]

From death to life, or rather from death-in-life, which is so much worse than death that death is longed-for and unattainable. From death-in-life to life. From the flat, unchanging waste of the sea and the sky and the sky and the sea to the ordered, even movement, with grace and hope, of the moon and stars.

The prose gloss at this point is that one long sentence of astounding beauty:

> In his loneliness and fixedness he yearneth towards the journeying Moon, and the stars that still sojourn, yet still move onward; and every where the blue sky belongs to them, and is their appointed rest, and their native country and their own natural homes, which they enter unannounced, as lords that are certainly expected and yet there is a silent joy at their arrival.

The emphasis there seems unmistakable; that the moon and the stars express order and joy. And the word 'joy' was a key word for Coleridge to express the fullest and richest happiness in experience.[32]

By this moonlight we see the colouring of the water-snakes, and the blessing of them is by this moonlight:

> Beyond the shadow of the ship,
> I watched the water-snakes:
> They moved in tracks of shining white,
> And when they reared, the elfish light
> Fell off in hoary flakes.[33]

The beams of the moon have just before been said to fall 'Like April hoar-frost spread.' In Dorothy Wordsworth's Journal and again and again in Coleridge's descriptive prose this comparison between moonlight and hoar-frost or 'hoariness' occurs. It was one of their common, agreed comparisons.

The blessing under moonlight is the critical turning-point of the poem. Just as the Albatross was not a mere bird, so these are not mere

184

water-snakes—they stand for all 'happy living things.' The first phase of redemption, the recovery of love and the recovery of the power of prayer, depends on the Mariner's recognition of his kinship again with other natural creatures: it is an assertion and recognition of the other central principle in the letter to Sotheby:

> that everything has a life of its own, and that we are all *One Life*.

And at that point the reminder of the sin against this principle is gone—

> The Albatross fell off, and sank
> Like lead into the sea.[34]

At this point we must pause and look back; for we have passed over a difficulty in the imagery of the sun and moon. If the moon is to be associated always with the good and the redemption, why is it that the crew die by the star-dogged moon at the end of Part III? It is difficult to explain this and yet support the idea of a consistently developing imagery in terms of the penance and redemption and reconciliation theme alone; and it is this point, together with others allied to it, that chiefly made me sympathetic to the idea behind Mr. Warren's secondary theme of the 'Imagination.'

The poem up to this point, that is Parts I to IV and the opening stanzas of Part V, taken together with the ending, Part VII, is relatively easy to interpret as a tale of crime, punishment and reconciliation, with the recovery of love in the blessing of the water-snakes as its climax. But the remainder of Part V and the whole of Part VI do not seem at first sight to have quite the same coherence and point. It is here that readers may still find 'unmeaning marvels' and an elaborated supernatural machinery which dissipates concentration. There are wonderful details in the verse, some of the finest descriptions of all; but they may seem to fall apart and to have too little bearing on each other and on the whole. Many published accounts of the poem do not adequately face the implications of the detail in these Parts. It is therefore best to summarize shortly what happens.

The Mariner hears a roaring wind and sees the fires and lightning in the sky. But the ship moves on untouched by the wind, and the re-animated dead men work it: a troop of blessed spirits has entered into them. These spirits make various music. The ship goes on, moved from beneath by the spirit of the South Pole. Through the Two Voices the

Mariner learns that it is this Polar Spirit who requires vengeance for the Albatross's death, and that he will have more penance to do.

Part VI. The Voices say that the ocean is under the power of the moon. The ship is now moved northward by the angelic power while the Mariner is in his trance. He wakes to see the final curse in the eyes of the dead men. Then that spell is snapped, and he feels at last a sweet breeze on himself alone. He arrives at his home port, steeped in moonlight. Then, as the gloss says: 'The angelic spirits leave the dead bodies, And appear in their own forms of light.' This acts as the signal which brings out the boat from land.

In Part VII a dreadful rumbling sound comes under the water and the ship sinks.

A quite normally accepted and simple interpretation of Parts V and VI treats them as a further necessary extension of the expiation theme. In the blessing of the water-snakes the Mariner has reconciled himself to the creatures, but it remains for him to reconcile himself also with the Creator:[35] therefore he has to suffer once more (this time from the curse of the dead men's eyes) and to win the power of recognising the beauty of the angelic music.

This is broadly acceptable; but it takes us very little distance in understanding the complicated machinery. Is there any serious import in the answers to such questions as these: What is the function of the Polar Spirit? In one aspect he appears as the friend and avenger of the 'pious bird of good omen,' and yet he is made to work under obedience to the angelic troop, who are thus plainly, in the spiritual hierarchy, superior to him; and he is bought off by the promise that the Mariner's penance shall continue. It might have seemed better to have made the angelic troop themselves the protectors of the Albatross and made them require the further penance. Why should the ship be moved first by the Polar Spirit and then by the angelic power? Again, what is the significance of the two winds in Parts V and VI? Put the problem in another way: are the avenging by the tutelary spirits of the South Sea and the reanimation of the dead bodies to work the ship here just out of politeness, because Wordsworth suggested them?[36] The first main problem here is to decide whether there is any meaning in the two different kinds of supernatural being.

The whole discussion of this problem has been clarified and ennobled by Mr. Warren's long essay, which I now wish to summarise. He maintains that the poem has 'two basic themes, both of them very rich and provocative.' The primary theme, which is 'the outcome of the fable

taken at its face value as a story of crime and punishment and reconciliation,' is the 'the theme of sacramental vision, or the theme of the
"One Life." ' The secondary theme is 'concerned with the context of
values in which the fable is presented' and is 'the theme of the imagination.' The two themes are finally fused in the poem.[37] He aims to
establish the existence of this secondary theme by two lines of argument
—first, that there are parts of the poem not otherwise easily intelligible,
such as Parts V and VI; and second, that the symbolism of the poem is
richer and more coherent than the redemption, visionary, theme alone
requires. Mr. Warren elaborates the contrast of the 'two lights' in great
detail.

He points out quite rightly and fully (p. 87) the 'pervasive presence
of the moon and moonlight in Coleridge's work,' especially in association
with creativeness. In 'Sonnet to the Autumnal Moon,' 1788, she is called,
the 'Mother of wildly-working visions,'[38] and in 'Songs of the Pixies,'
1796, 'Mother of wildly-working dreams.'[39] 'Christabel' and 'The Ancient Mariner' are bathed in moonlight: the moon is over the deep
romantic chasm of 'Kubla Khan'; it is prominent in 'The Nightingale,'
'Cain' and 'Dejection.'

Mr. Warren maintains that the association is so recurrent and persistent in Coleridge's writing, between creation or the activity of the
secondary imagination and the moonlight, half-lights, dim lights, gloom,
luminiscent clouds and so on, that the association between them can
justifiably be regarded as habitual; and that as it goes back even into
his very early poems, it can without injustice be taken as established
(even if not consciously) at the time of writing the 'Mariner.' He quotes
from the *Biographia* passage in which Coleridge recalled the origin of
the *Lyrical Ballads* themselves:

> The sudden charm, which accidents of light and shade, which moon-
> light or sun-set, diffused over a known and familiar landscape, . . . These
> are the poetry of nature.[40]

The Albatross, besides being associated with human nature on the
level of the primary theme, is also associated with the moon, mist, cloud
and fog-smoke, on the level of the secondary theme of the imagination:

> In mist or cloud, on mast or shroud,
> It perched for vespers nine;
> Whiles all the night, through fog-smoke white,
> Glimmered the white Moon-shine.[41]

Furthermore the bird is associated with the breeze, which Mr. Warren takes to be the 'creative' wind, for which there are countless parallels in other poets.

> The sun is kept entirely out of the matter. The lighting is always in-direct, for even in the day we have only 'mist or cloud,'—the luminous haze, the symbolic equivalent of moonlight. But not only is the moon associated with the bird, but the wind also. Upon the bird's advent a 'good south wind sprung up behind.' And so we have the creative wind, the friendly bird, the moonlight of imagination, all together in one symbolic cluster.[42]

He thus establishes what he calls a 'symbolic cluster,' including the wind, bird, mist and moon, which belong to the imagination and all the imaginative side of man's activity. And in his shooting, the Mariner not only commits a crime against the other, natural and spiritual, order of the world, but also a crime against creative imagination; and part of the penalty is the loss of the wind.

The dual character of the ice which I have already noted at the first arrival of the ship near the South Pole—the emerald and the dismal sheen—also expresses the dual character of the imagination, that it is partly a blessing and partly a curse to him who lives by it. It is this curs-ing side of the imagination which accounts for the particular vengeance of the Polar Spirit on the Mariner as distinct from the punishment ex-acted by the sun. And this dual character and special vengeance also explain why the moon is allowed to be the light by which the crew die. And further, in his capacity of Wanderer, the Mariner is to be thought of as the 'cursed poet' of the later Romantics. By contrast to the moon and mist of the Imagination, the sun and the glaring light are, for Mr. Warren, the light of the Understanding, the mere reflective faculty, which 'partakes of DEATH';[43] and just as the Mariner and also the crew failed to see the significance of the bird in the mist, so they also fail to understand the nature of the sun, not only at the naturalistic level, as we have already seen, but also because they are taking the lower faculty of the Understanding as their inadequate guide to life.[44]

Warren's essay must be read complete, with its notes, to see how inadequate is this broad outline of its argument. There are two main questions about it which most urgently need asking: how far does it succeed in giving a coherent and convincing explanation of the miscella-neous detail in the difficult parts of the poem? And in what sense does it establish that there is a theme which *is* 'the theme of the imagination'?

The answers to both these questions depend upon the view we take of symbols and symbolism.

I suggest that if we accept the term 'symbol' we must allow symbols a freer, wider, less exact reference; and that therefore it is probably wiser to drop the term altogether. Mr. Warren himself fully allows for the possibility (even likelihood) that Coleridge did not *consciously* use symbols at all. This is consistent with Coleridge's recognition of the unconscious element in the workings of genius: but it does not therefore follow that there was a latent precision waiting for critics to elucidate it. Mr. Warren seems in the last resort to be a precisionist more because he wishes to make clear to himself and others some features of the richness he has found in the poem than because he believes that the poem actually works upon its readers by the methods of precision. There is a natural and proper dread of the long-traditional praise of the poem's 'atmosphere,' because that praise has so often accompanied the belief that there is scarcely any content or meaning at all, and that all is thin, vague and 'magical.' But a rich certainty is not the only alternative to a poor uncertainty.

The first of the two questions, that about the miscellaneous detail, can only be answered here by two examples. In dealing with Part V, Warren agrees with Bowra and others that 'in the reanimation of the bodies of the fellow mariners, there is implicit the idea of regeneration and resurrection'; but then he finds himself compelled to write:

> But the behaviour of the reinspirited bodies, taken in itself, offers a difficulty. Taken at the natural level, the manipulating of the sails and ropes serves no purpose. Taken at the symbolic level, this activity is activity without content, a 'lag' in the poem, a 'meaningless marvel.' [45]

Nor does he later succeed in giving an adequate explanation of the need for this behaviour, even when not 'taken in itself'; for he concentrates more on the angelic troop than on what it makes the bodies do.

At this point Warren's scheme of symbolism does not serve us. But if we look to the total effect of the poem on its readers, there is little doubt that ll. 329–44 add something not adequately expressed elsewhere, especially the stanza:

> The body of my brother's son
> Stood by me, knee to knee:
> The body and I pulled at one rope,
> But he said nought to me.

This brings home, as nothing else does, the horror of the deaths, the violation of family ties which the action has involved; it dramatises to the Mariner's consciousness the utter ruin of the merry, unified community which had set out on the voyage. The curse in the stony eyes (ll. 436–41) is made far more appalling by this specially intimate experience of the fact that intimacy was gone for ever. And this is achieved at a point where the 'system' of the poem is decidedly weak.

The second point of detail is the rumbling and the sinking of the ship in Part VII; Warren skates over this rather hastily:

> There is the terrific sound which sinks the ship and flings the stunned Mariner into the Pilot's boat. In the logic of the symbolic structure this would be, I presume, a repetition of the wind or storm motif: the creative storm has a part in reestablishing the Mariner's relation to other men. Even if the destruction of the ship is regarded, as some readers regard it, as a final act of the Polar Spirit, to show, as it were, what he could do if he had a mind to, the symbolic import is not altered, for the Spirit belongs to the cluster of imagination which has the terrifying and cataclysmic as well as benign aspect.[46]

He then argues that the sinking of the ship is not an act of the Polar Spirit, but of the angelic troop.

> At the level of the primary theme, the angelic troop wipe out the crime (i.e, the 'criminal' ship and the dead bodies); at the level of the secondary theme, they do so by means of the 'storm' which belongs to the symbolic cluster of the imagination.[47]

But this is surely to abandon a coherent symbolism altogether and to fall back on simple interpretation of the narrative in the light of decisions already made; for the clusters of symbols established earlier have borne some intelligible relation (either traditionally or in Coleridge's habitual associations) to what they symbolise: the creative wind is traditionally intelligible, and the moon and half-lights have special associations for Coleridge. But the method of the ship's destruction does not conform to the 'logic' of such symbolism as this; and Warren's use of 'I presume' points to his uneasiness about it.[48] A submarine rumbling followed by a violent explosion is in a different key; it has a different sort of effect on the reader from that of the other items which Warren groups together as associated with the Imagination.

What seems to have happened is that Mr. Warren, delighted by the relative coherence of the moon-bird-mist-wind cluster, has forced other items into congruence with it, by minimising differences in their character and in their emotional effects. But such forcing would not have been necessary if he had started out with a less rigid theory of symbolic reference. That his own mind was working from the less precise towards the more precise, even in the course of thinking out his essay, is apparent in the way he speaks of the light of the sun. On p. 93 he writes of the sun:

> It is the light which shows the familiar as familiar, it is the light of practical convenience, it is the light in which pride preens itself, it is, to adopt Coleridge's later terminology, the light of the 'understanding,' it is the light of that 'mere reflective faculty' that 'partook of Death.'

His mind is here moving out of what is richly and variously suggestive into what is precise and technical. I suggest that he went through a similar mental process in reaching the interpretation of the moon, the bird and the mist, and that in the result the 'theme of the imagination' is something narrower and more technical than the poem can carry. For by the imagination Warren does mean the technical, creative poet's imagination of Coleridge's later theory, and he says (p. 103) that the poem is 'in particular about poetry itself.' This leads to the conception of the Mariner as the *poète maudit*.

The fact, however, is that there was for Coleridge no such stable and exact association between moonlight, half-light, shifting lights-and-shadows, etc. and the specifically poetic and creative imagination. These were indeed associated with and productive of creative and visionary moods, but they were also associated with the more tender emotions and the more fruitful virtues, such as those of love. These lines, addressed to Tranquillity in 1801

> And when the gust of Autumn crowds,
> And breaks the busy moonlight clouds,
> Thou best the thought canst raise, the heart attune,
> Light as the busy clouds, calm as the gliding moon.[49]

are part of the definition of a mood of moral insight which originally had a topically political context. This description of Hartley in a letter to Tom Poole in 1803 is expressive of the creativeness of a child's whole living personality, which may indeed bear analogies to poetic creativeness but yet, in a child, certainly cannot be identified with it:

Hartley is . . . a strange strange Boy—'*exquisitely wild*'! An utter Visionary! like the Moon among thin Clouds, he moves in a circle of Light of his own making—he alone, in a Light of his own. Of all human Beings I never yet saw one so naked of *Self*.[50]

Again, the famous lines of 'Dejection: an Ode'

> This light, this glory, this fair luminous mist,
> This beautiful and beauty-making power[51]

describe not the 'shaping spirit of Imagination' itself, but the Joy which is the prerequisite condition of it. One more example brings us back closely to Mr. Warren's more limited application of the 'symbolism' of the moon. In the lines 'To William Wordsworth,' written after hearing the first version of *The Prelude* read aloud, Coleridge describes himself while listening as being like the sea under the influence of the moon:

> In silence listening, like a devout child,
> My soul lay passive, by thy various strain
> Driven as in surges now beneath the stars,
> With momentary stars of my own birth,
> Fair constellated foam, still darting off
> Into the darkness; now a tranquil sea,
> Outspread and bright, yet swelling to the moon.[52]

Here there is no doubt that the moon is an image of Wordsworth's imagination seen in its power over others. By contrast, at the other extreme of reference, is the Note-Book entry

> Socinianism, moonlight; methodism, a stove. O for some sun to unite heat and light![53]

And in the intermediate, neutral area Coleridge once summed up his fascinated interest in the natural phenomena of a night-sky by applying to it the phrase of Boccaccio, *vestito d'una pallidezza affumicata*.[54]

It would be endless to quote all Coleridge's uses of imagery from the moon and stars, clouds, the night-sky and uncertain lights; these examples give some idea of the range. It is certain that, before and after the time of 'The Ancient Mariner,' such images were used for creativeness both of a wider and of a more specially poetic kind; but they were used also for much else, especially in conjunction with the subtler processes of the mind and the more delicate modes of feeling. They were used especially for the mysteries and uncertainties of mental life which Coleridge was beginning to explore more fully as he became more dissatisfied with the crude associationism represented by Hartley and its 'inanimate cold world,' and as his general ideals of life moved further from those of 'the poor loveless ever-anxious crowd.' It seems to me that the imagery of the mist and the moon and the Albatross in 'The Ancient Mariner' belongs with this area of experience in general and with Coleridge's exploration of it; indeed the whole poem is part of the exploration, it is part of the experience which led Coleridge into his later theoretic statements (as of the theory of the Imagination) rather than a symbolic adumbration of the theoretic statements themselves.

Within the poem, and most obviously in the motto later added from Burnet ('Harum rerum notitiam semper ambivit ingenium humanum, nunquam attigit.'), the emphasis is on the mystery and the richness of the mystery. Through the development of the imagery we are gradually led into the realisation that the values of 'the land of mist and snow' are of the greatest possible concern, but that they are indescribable. They are certainly contrasted with the values which belong to the specious day-to-day clarity of the sun, but they are left to establish themselves in us mysteriously and indefinitely, as Burnet's world of spirits is mysterious and indefinite. Mr. Warren has permanently enriched our understanding of the poem by insisting on its statement of the 'context of values' in which the crime and punishment and reconciliation occur; his symbolist 'equations' serve to point out elements which may be involved in this context; but the decision to 'adopt Coleridge's later terminology' in stating the equivalents symbolised has, in the long run, the effect of making the poem seem more technical and diagrammatic than Mr. Warren himself first found it, or than Coleridge could ever have admitted it to be.

NOTES

1. The other leading references are conveniently given in J. L. Lowes, *The Road to Xanadu* (London, 1931), pp. 222–4, 528–31. Cf. *Biographia Literaria*, Ch. xiv.

2. *The Complete Poetical Works of Samuel Taylor Coleridge*, ed. E. H. Coleridge (Oxford, 1912), I, 289, ll. 67–72.

3. *PW*, pp. 285-6, *n*. 1.

4. This review is reprinted in *Coleridge's Miscellaneous Criticism*, ed. T. M. Raysor (Cambridge, Mass., 1936), pp. 370-8.

5. For fuller details see Lowes, pp. 243-60.

6. R. C. Bald, 'Coleridge and *The Ancient Mariner*,' *Nineteenth Century Studies*, ed. Herbert Davis and Others (Cornell University Press, 1940), pp. 15ff.

7. See the Percy version of 'The Wandering Jew'; 'Sir Cauline' for some of the vocabulary; 'Young Waters' and 'King Estmere' especially for past tenses with 'did.' William Taylor's translation of Bürger's 'Lenore' must not be forgotten.

8. ll. 103-4; all quotations from the 'Mariner' are from the text in *PW*, I, 187-209.

9. ll. 107-10.

10. *Letters of S. T. Coleridge*, ed E. H. Coleridge (London, 1895), I, 403-4.

11. ll. 51-62.

12. Lowes, pp. 74ff.

13. ll. 199-202.

14. ll. 612-17.

15. E. M. W. Tillyard, *Five Poems*, pp. 66-86.

16. C. M. Bowra, *The Romantic Imagination*, Ch. iii.

17. 'A Poem of Pure Imagination,' in *The Rime of the Ancient Mariner* (New York, 1946).

18. *BL*, II, 12.

19. *Five Poems*, pp. 70-1.

20. ll. 21-4.

21. l. 83.

22. Hdt. IV, 42, 3-4. Coleridge would certainly have known the passage in the original, and also, as Lowes shows (p. 127), the quotation and application of it in Bryan Edwards's *History . . . of the British Colonies in the West Indies*.

23. Wordsworth's famous, disingenuous and ungenerous note on the 'Mariner' was published in *Lyrical Ballads* (1800), I, on an unnumbered page after the text; quoted in full, Lowes, p. 520.

24. l. 286.

25. ll. 222-3.

26. Coleridge's 'Argument' to the edition of 1800 said the Mariner killed the bird 'cruelly and in contempt of the laws of hospitality.'

27. ll. 91-102.

28. *Lyrical Ballads* (1800), I, 162. The important comma after 'Angel's head' is omitted in *PW*, I, 190, *apparatus criticus*. Warren at this point seems to be mistaken: he accepts interpretation (b) for the text, but then goes on to argue that the mariners have a wrong view of God because 'dim and red' are qualities of the 'other light' group, and belong with the luminous haze, etc. But surely 'dim and red' are an anticipation of the evil 'bloody sun' that soon follows. Warren is far too exact in requiring every 'dim' light to be 'good'; and he underestimates the truth to physical fact about the tropic sun. See also Leo Kirschbaum, *The Explicator*, Vol. VII, No. i, Oct. 1948. I thank

Mr. James Maxwell for this reference, which, in fact, introduced me to Warren's book.

29. ll. 232–5.

30. l. 250.

31. ll. 263–6.

32. See, e.g., 'Dejection: an Ode.'

33. ll. 272–6.

34. ll. 290–1.

35. See, e.g., Bowra, *op. cit.*, pp. 70–1.

36. The Fenwick Note to 'We Are Seven,' *Poetical Works*, ed. E. de Selincourt, I, 360–1; see also Lowes, pp. 222–3.

37. Warren, p. 71.

38. l. 2; *PW*, I, 5.

39. Warren here gives the publication date; the lines were written in 1793; *PW*, I, 40–4. The phrase quoted is in fact applied to Night, not to the Moon; ll. 85–7 are more relevant:

> What time the pale moon sheds a softer day
> Mellowing the woods beneath its pensive beam:
> For mid the quivering light 'tis ours to play.

40. *BL*, II, 5.

41. ll. 75–8.

42. Warren, p. 91.

43. Warren, p. 79 and *passim*, quoting *BL*, I, 98.

44. Assuming that the sun does represent the Understanding, I think Mr. Warren makes his own case more difficult than he need when he comes to explain the appearance of the sun in a good context, when the angelic spirits fly up from the bodies into it. For surely to Coleridge the Understanding was never altogether unnecessary in the whole scheme of the mind's action. It was never altogether superseded, but was always a necessary ground of advance towards the Reason and the Imagination.

45. Warren, p. 97.

46. Warren, p. 100.

47. *ibid.*

48. And his writing of the Mariner being flung into the boat by the sound suggests some hasty reading here.

49. *PW*, I, 361.

50. *Unpublished Letters of S. T. Coleridge*, ed. E. L. Griggs (London, 1932), I, 292.

51. *PW*, I, 365.

52. ll. 95–101; *PW*, I, 408. Cf. Satyrane's First Letter in *The Friend*, 23 Nov. 1809, quoted in *PW ad loc*. The patches of phosphorescent light in the sea-foam are an image of Coleridge's troubled, but bright, reception of those moments in *The Prelude* in which he himself was involved.

53. *Anima Poetae*, ed. E. H. Coleridge (London, 1895), p. 26.

54. *ibid.*, p. 46.

T. S. ELIOT

———

Byron

THE facts of a large part of Byron's life have been well set forth, in the last few years, by Sir Harold Nicolson and Mr. Quennell, who have also provided interpretations which accord with each other and which make the character of Byron more intelligible to the present generation. No such interpretation has yet been offered in our time for Byron's verse. In and out of universities, Wordsworth, Coleridge, Shelley and Keats have been discussed from various points of view: Byron and Scott have been left in peace. Yet Byron, at least, would seem the most nearly remote from the sympathies of every living critic: it would be interesting, therefore, if we could have half a dozen essays about him, to see what agreement could be reached. The present article is an attempt to start that ball rolling.

There are several initial difficulties. It is difficult to return critically to a poet whose poetry was—I suppose it was for many of our contemporaries, except those who are too young to have read any of the poetry of that period—the first boyhood enthusiasm. To be told anecdotes of one's own childhood by an elderly relative is usually tedious; and a return, after many years, to the poetry of Byron is accompanied by a similar gloom: images come before the mind, and the recollection of some verses in the manner of *Don Juan,* tinged with that disillusion and cynicism only possible at the age of sixteen, which appeared in a school periodical. There are more impersonal obstacles to overcome. The bulk of Byron's poetry is distressing, in proportion to its quality; one would

---

From *On Poetry and Poets*, copyright 1937, 1957 by T. S. Eliot (Farrar, Straus and Cudahy, Inc., and Faber and Faber Ltd., London), pp. 193–206. Reprinted by permission of the publishers.

suppose that he never destroyed anything. Yet bulk is inevitable in a poet of Byron's type; and the absence of the destructive element in his composition indicates the kind of interest, and the kind of lack of interest, that he took in poetry. We have come to expect poetry to be something very concentrated, something distilled; but if Byron had distilled his verse, there would have been nothing whatever left. When we see exactly what he was doing, we can see that he did it as well as it can be done. With most of his shorter poems, one feels that he was doing something that Tom Moore could do as well or better; in his longer poems, he did something that no one else has ever equalled.

It is sometimes desirable to approach the work of a poet completely out of favour, by an unfamiliar avenue. If my avenue to Byron is a road that exists only for my own mind, I shall be corrected by other critics: it may at all events upset prejudice and encourage opinion to form itself anew. I therefore suggest considering Byron as a Scottish poet—I say 'Scottish,' not 'Scots,' since he wrote in English. The one poet of his time with whom he could be considered to be in competition, a poet of whom he spoke invariably with the highest respect, was Sir Walter Scott. I have always seen, or imagined that I saw, in busts of the two poets, a certain resemblance in the shape of the head. The comparison does honour to Byron, and when you examine the two faces, there is no further resemblance. Were one a person who liked to have busts about, a bust of Scott would be something one could live with. There is an air of nobility about that head, an air of magnanimity, and of that inner and perhaps unconscious serenity that belongs to great writers who are also great men. But Byron—that pudgy face suggesting a tendency to corpulence, that weakly sensual mouth, that restless triviality of expression, and worst of all that blind look of the self-conscious beauty; the bust of Byron is that of a man who was every inch the touring tragedian. Yet it was by being so thorough-going an actor that Byron arrived at a kind of knowledge: of the world outside, which he had to learn something about in order to play his role in it, and of that part of himself which was his role. Superficial knowledge, of course: but accurate so far as it went.

Of a Scottish quality in Byron's poetry, I shall speak when I come to *Don Juan*. But there is a very important part of the Byronic make-up which may appropriately be mentioned before considering his poetry, for which I think his Scottish antecedence provided the material. That is his peculiar diabolism, his delight in posing as a damned creature— and in providing evidence for his damnation in a rather horrifying way. Now, the diabolism of Byron is very different from anything that the

Romantic Agony (as Mr. Praz calls it) produced in Catholic countries. And I do not think it is easily derived from the comfortable compromise between Christianity and paganism arrived at in England and characteristically English. It could come only from the religious background of a people steeped in Calvinistic theology.

Byron's diabolism, if indeed it deserves the name, was of a mixed type. He shared, to some extent, Shelley's Promethean attitude, and the Romantic passion for Liberty; and this passion, which inspired his more political outbursts, combined with the image of himself as a man of action to bring about the Greek adventure. And his Promethean attitude merges into a Satanic (Miltonic) attitude. The romantic conception of Milton's Satan is semi-Promethean, and also contemplates Pride as a *virtue*. It would be difficult to say whether Byron was a proud man, or a man who liked to pose as a proud man—the possibility of the two attitudes being combined in the same person does not make them any less dissimilar in the abstract. Byron was certainly a vain man, in quite simple ways:

> I can't complain, whose ancestors are there,
> Erneis, Radulphus—eight-and-forty manors
> (If that my memory doth not greatly err)
> Were their reward for following Billy's banners. . . .

His sense of damnation was also mitigated by a touch of unreality: to a man so occupied with himself and with the figure he was cutting nothing outside could be altogether real. It is therefore impossible to make out of his diabolism anything coherent or rational. He was able to have it both ways, it seems; and to think of himself both as an individual isolated and superior to other men because of his own crimes, and as a naturally good and generous nature distorted by the crimes committed against it by others. It is this inconsistent creature that turns up as the Giaour, the Corsair, Lara, Manfred and Cain; only as Don Juan does he get nearer to the truth about himself. But in this strange composition of attitudes and beliefs the element that seems to me most real and deep is that of a perversion of the Calvinist faith of his mother's ancestors.

One reason for the neglect of Byron is, I think, that he has been admired for what are his most ambitious attempts to be poetic; and these attempts turn out, on examination, to be fake: nothing but sonorous affirmations of the commonplace with no depth of significance. A good specimen of such imposture is the well-known stanza at the end of Canto XV of *Don Juan*:

Between two worlds life hovers like a star,
  'Twixt night and morn, upon the horizon's verge.
How little do we know that which we are!
  How less what we may be! The eternal surge
Of time and tide rolls on, and bears afar
  Our bubbles; as the old burst, new emerge,
Lashed from the foam of ages; while the graves
Of empire heave but like some passing waves.

verses which are not too good for the school magazine. Byron's real
excellence is on a different level from this.

The qualities of narrative verse which are found in *Don Juan* are no
less remarkable in the earlier tales. Before undertaking this essay I had
not read these tales since the days of my schoolboy infatuation, and I
approached them with apprehension. They are readable. However absurd we find their view of life, they are, as tales, very well told. As a
tale-teller we must rate Byron very high indeed: I can think of none
other than Chaucer who has a greater readability, with the exception of
Coleridge whom Byron abused and from whom Byron learned a great
deal. And Coleridge never achieved a narrative of such length. Byron's
plots, if they deserve that name, are extremely simple. What makes the
tales interesting is first a torrential fluency of verse and a skill in varying
it from time to time to avoid monotony; and second a genius for divaga-
tion. Digression, indeed, is one of the valuable arts of the story-teller.
The effect of Byron's digressions is to keep us interested in the story-
teller himself, and through this interest to interest us more in the story.
On contemporary readers this interest must have been strong to the
point of enchantment; for even still, once we submit ourselves to the
point of reading a poem through, the attraction of the personality is
powerful. Any few lines, if quoted in almost any company, will probably provide a momentary twitch of merriment:

Her eye's dark charm 'twere vain to tell,
But gaze on that of the Gazelle,
It will assist thy fancy well;
As large, as languishingly dark,
But Soul beam'd forth in every spark. . . .

but the poem as a whole can keep one's attention. *The Giaour* is a long
poem, and the plot is very simple, though not always easy to follow. A
Christian, presumably a Greek, has managed, by some means of which
we are not told, to scrape acquaintance with a young woman who be-

longed to the harem, or was perhaps the favourite wife of a Moslem named Hassan. In the endeavour to escape with her Christian lover Leila is recaptured and killed; in due course the Christian with some of his friends ambushes and kills Hassan. We subsequently discover that the story of this vendetta—or part of it—is being told by the Giaour himself to an elderly priest, by way of making his confession. It is a singular kind of confession, because the Giaour seems anything but penitent, and makes quite clear that although he has sinned, it is not really by his own fault. He seems impelled rather by the same motive as the Ancient Mariner, than by any desire for absolution—which could hardly have been given: but the device has its use in providing a small complication to the story. As I have said, it is not altogether easy to discover what happened. The beginning is a long apostrophe to the vanished glory of Greece, a theme which Byron could vary with great skill. The Giaour makes a dramatic entrance:

> Who thundering comes on blackest steed,
> With slackened bit and hoof of speed?

and we are given a glimpse of him through a Moslem eye:

> Though young and pale, that sallow front
> Is scathed by fiery passion's brunt . . .

which is enough to tell us, that the Giaour is an interesting person, because he is Lord Byron himself, perhaps. Then there is a long passage about the desolation of Hassan's house, inhabited only by the spider, the bat, the owl, the wild dog and weeds; we infer that the poet has skipped on to the conclusion of the tale, and that we are to expect the Giaour to kill Hassan—which is of course what happens. Not Joseph Conrad could be more roundabout. Then a bundle is privily dropped into the water, and we suspect it to be the body of Leila. Then follows a reflective passage meditating in succession on Beauty, the Mind, and Remorse. Leila turns up again, alive, for a moment, but this is another dislocation of the order of events. Then we witness the surprise of Hassan and his train—this may have been months or even years after Leila's death—by the Giaour and his banditti, and there is no doubt but that Hassan is killed:

> Fall'n Hassan lies—his unclosed eye
> Yet lowering on his enemy. . . .

Then comes a delightful change of metre, as well as a sudden transition, just at the moment when it is needed:

> The browsing camels' bells are tinkling:
> His mother look'd from her lattice high—
> She saw the dews of eve besprinkling
> The pasture green beneath her eye,
> She saw the planets faintly twinkling:
> ' 'Tis twilight—sure his train is nigh.'

Then follows a sort of exequy for Hassan, evidently spoken by another Moslem. Now the Giaour reappears, nine years later, in a monastery, as we hear one of the monks answering an inquiry about the visitor's identity. In what capacity the Giaour has attached himself to the monastery is not clear; the monks seem to have accepted him without investigation, and his behaviour among them is very odd; but we are told that he has given the monastery a considerable sum of money for the privilege of staying there. The conclusion of the poem consists of the Giaour's confession to one of the monks. Why a Greek of that period should have been so oppressed with remorse (although wholly impenitent) for killing a Moslem in what he would have considered a fair fight, or why Leila should have been guilty in leaving a husband or master to whom she was presumably united without her consent, are questions that we cannot answer.

I have considered the Giaour in some detail in order to exhibit Byron's extraordinary ingenuity in story-telling. There is nothing straightforward about the telling of the simple tale; we are not told everything that we should like to know; and the behaviour of the protagonists is sometimes as unaccountable as their motives and feelings are confused. Yet the author not only gets away with it, but gets away with it *as narrative*. It is the same gift that Byron was to turn to better account in *Don Juan*; and the first reason why *Don Juan* is still readable is that it has the same narrative quality as the earlier tales.

It is, I think, worth noting, that Byron developed the verse *conte* considerably beyond Moore and Scott, if we are to see his popularity as anything more than public caprice or the attraction of a cleverly exploited personality. These elements enter into it, certainly. But first of all, Byron's verse tales represent a more mature stage of this transient form than Scott's, as Scott's represent a more mature stage than Moore's. Moore's *Lalla Rookh* is a mere sequence of tales joined together by a ponderous prose account of the circumstances of their narration (modelled upon the *Arabian Nights*). Scott perfected a straightforward story with the type of plot which he was to employ in his novels. Byron combined exoticism with actuality, and developed most effectively the use of *suspense*. I think also that the versification of Byron is the ablest: but in this kind of verse it is necessary to read at length if one is to form an impression, and relative merit cannot be shown by quotation. To identify every passage taken at random as being by Byron or by Moore would be connoisseurship beyond my powers; but I think that anyone who had recently read Byron's tales would agree that the following passage could not be by him:

> And oh! to see the unburied heaps
> On which the lonely moonlight sleeps—
> The very vultures turn away,
> And sicken at so foul a prey!
> Only the fierce hyaena stalks
> Throughout the city's desolate walks
> At midnight, and his carnage plies—
> Woe to the half-dead wretch, who meets
> The glaring of those large blue eyes
> Amid the darkness of the streets!

This is from *Lalla Rookh*, and was marked as if with approval by some reader of the London Library.

Childe Harold seems to me inferior to this group of poems (*The Giaour, The Bride of Abydos, The Corsair, Lara,* etc.). Time and time again, to be sure, Byron awakens fading interest by a purple passage, but Byron's purple passages are never good enough to do the work that is expected of them in *Childe Harold*:

> Stop! for thy tread is on an Empire's dust

is just what is wanted to revive interest, at that point; but the stanza that follows, on the Battle of Waterloo, seems to me quite false; and quite representative of the falsity in which Byron takes refuge whenever he *tries* to write poetry:

> Stop! for thy tread is on an Empire's dust!
> An Earthquake's spoil is sepulchred below!
> Is the spot mark'd with no colossal bust?
> Nor column trophied for triumphal show?
> None; but the moral's truth tells simpler so,
> As the ground was before, so let it be;—

> How that red rain hath made the harvest grow!
> And is this all the world has gained by thee,
> Thou first and last of fields! king-making victory?

It is all the more difficult, in a period which has rather lost the appreciation of the kind of virtues to be found in Byron's poetry, to analyse accurately his faults and vices. Hence we fail to give credit to Byron for the instinctive art by which, in a poem like *Childe Harold,* and still more efficiently in *Beppo* or *Don Juan,* he avoids monotony by a dexterous turn from one subject to another. He has the cardinal virtue of being never dull. But, when we have admitted the existence of forgotten virtues, we still recognize a falsity in most of those passages which were formerly most admired. To what is this falsity due?

Whatever it is, in Byron's poetry, that is 'wrong,' we should be mistaken in calling it rhetoric. Too many things have been collected under that name; and if we are going to think that we have accounted for Byron's verse by calling it 'rhetorical,' then we are bound to avoid using that adjective about Milton and Dryden, about both of whom (in their very different kinds) we seem to be saying something that has meaning, when we speak of their 'rhetoric.' Their failures, when they fail, are of a higher kind than Byron's success, when he succeeds. Each had a strongly individual idiom, and a sense of language; at their worst, they have an interest in the *word.* You can recognize them in the single line, and can say: here is a particular way of using the language. There is no such individuality in the line of Byron. If one looks at the few single lines, from the Waterloo passage in *Childe Harold,* which may pass for 'familiar quotations,' you cannot say that any of them is great poetry:

> And all went merry as a marriage bell . . .
> On with the dance! let joy be unconfined

Of Byron one can say, as of no other English poet of his eminence, that he added nothing to the language, that he discovered nothing in the sounds, and developed nothing in the meaning, of individual words. I cannot think of any other poet of his distinction who might so easily have been an accomplished foreigner writing English. The ordinary person talks English, but only a few people in every generation can write it; and upon this undeliberate collaboration between a great many people talking a living language and a very few people writing it, the continuance and maintenance of a language depends. Just as an artisan who can talk English beautifully while about his work or in a public bar, may compose a letter painfully written in a dead language bearing some resemblance to a newspaper leader, and decorated with words like 'maelstrom' and 'pandemonium': so does Byron write a dead or dying language.

This imperceptiveness of Byron to the English word—so that he has to use a great many words before we become aware of him—indicates for practical purposes a defective sensibility. I say 'for practical purposes' because I am concerned with the sensibility in his poetry, not with his private life; for if a writer has not the language in which to express feelings they might as well not exist. We do not even need to compare his account of Waterloo with that of Stendhal to feel the lack of minute particulars; but it is worth remarking that the prose sensibility of Stendhal, being sensibility, has some values of poetry that Byron completely misses. Byron did for the language very much what the leader writers of our journals are doing day by day. I think that this failure is much more important that the platitude of his intermittent phlosophizing. Every poet has uttered platitudes, every poet has said things that have been said before. It is not the weakness of the ideas, but the schoolboy command of the language, that makes his lines seem trite and his thought shallow:

Mais que Hugo aussi était dans tout ce peuple. The words of Péguy have kept drifting through my mind while I have been thinking of Byron:

> 'Non pas vers qui chantent dans la mémoire, mais vers qui dans la mémoire sonnent et retentissent comme une fanfare, vibrants, trépidants, sonnant comme une fanfare, sonnant comme une charge, tambour éternel, et qui batta dans les mémoires fraçaises longtemps après que les réglementaires tarbours auront cessé de battre au front des régiments.'

But Byron was not 'in *this* people,' either of London or of England, but in his mother's people, and the most stirring stanza of his Waterloo is this:

> And wild and high the 'Cameron's gathering' rose!
> The war-note of Lochiel, which Albyn's hills
> Have heard, and heard, too, have her Saxon foes;—
> How in the noon of night that pibroch thrills,
> Savage and shrill! But with the breath which fills
> Their mountain-pipe, so fill the mountaineers
> With the fierce native daring which instils

The stirring memory of a thousand years,
And Evan's, Donald's fame rings in each clansman's ears!

All things worked together to make *Don Juan* the greatest of Byron's poems. The stanza that he borrowed from the Italian was admirably suited to enhance his merits and conceal his defects, just as on a horse or in the water he was more at ease than on foot. His ear was imperfect, and capable only of crude effects; and in this easy-going stanza, with its habitually feminine and occasionally triple endings, he seems always to be reminding us that he is not really trying very hard and yet producing something as good or better than that of the solemn poets who take their verse-making more seriously. And Byron really is at his best when he is not trying too hard to be poetic; when he tries to be poetic in a few lines he produces things like the stanza I have already quoted, beginning:

Between two worlds life hovers like a star.

But at a lower intensity he gets a surprising range of effect. His genius for digression, for wandering away from his subject (usually to talk about himself) and suddenly returning to it, is, in *Don Juan,* at the height of its power. The continual banter and mockery, which his stanza and his Italian model serve to keep constantly in his mind, serve as an admirable antacid to the high-falutin which in the earlier romances tends to upset the reader's stomach; and his social satire helps to keep him to the objective and has a sincerity that is at least plausible if not profound. The portrait of himself comes much nearer to honesty than any that appears in his earlier work. This is worth examining in some detail.

Charles Du Bos, in his admirable *Byron et le besoin de la fatalité,* quotes a long passage of self-portraiture from *Lara.* Du Bos deserves full credit for recognizing its importance; and Byron deserves all the credit that Du Bos gives him for having written it. This passage strikes me also as a masterpiece of self-analysis, but of a self that is largely a deliberate fabrication—a fabrication that is only completed in the actual writing of the lines. The reason why Byron understood this self so well, is that it is largely his own invention; and it is only the self that he invented that he understood perfectly. If I am correct, one cannot help feeling pity and horror at the spectacle of a man devoting such gigantic energy and persistence to such a useless and petty purpose: though at the same time we must feel sympathy and humility in reflecting that it is a vice to which most of us are addicted in a fitful and less presevering way; that is to say, Byron made a vocation out of what for most of us is an irregular weakness, and deserves a certain sad admiration for his degree of success. But in *Don Juan*, we get something much nearer to genuine self-revelation. For Juan, in spite of the brilliant qualities with which Byron invests him—so that he may hold his own among the English aristocracy—is not an heroic figure. There is nothing absurd about his presence of mind and courage during the shipwreck, or about his prowess in the Turkish wars: he exhibits a kind of physical courage and capacity for heroism which we are quite willing to attribute to Byron himself. But in the accounts of his relation with women, he is not made to appear heroic or even dignified; and these impress us as having an ingredient of the genuine as well as of the make-believe.

It is noticeable—and this confirms, I think, the view of Byron held by Mr. Peter Quennell—that in these love-episodes Juan always takes the passive role. Even Haidee, in spite of the innocence and ignorance of that child of nature, appears rather as the seducer than the seduced. This episode is the longest and most carefully elaborate of all the amorous passages, and I think it deserves pretty high marks. It is true that after Juan's earlier initiation by Donna Julia, we are hardly so credulous as to believe in the innocence attributed to him with Haidee; but this should not lead us to dismiss the description as false. The *innocence* of Juan is merely a substitute for the *passivity* of Byron; and if we restore the latter we can recognize in the account some authentic understanding of the human heart, and accept such lines as

> Alas! They were so young, so beautiful,
>   So lonely, loving, helpless and the hour
> Was that in which the heart is always full,
>   And having o'er itself no further power,
> Prompts deeds eternity cannot annul. . . .

The lover of Donna Julia and of Haidee is just the man, we feel, to become subsequently the favourite of Catherine the Great—to introduce whom, one suspects, Byron had prepared himself by his eight months with the Countess of Oxford. And there remains, if not innocence, that strange passivity that has a curious resemblance to innocence.

Between the first and second part of the poem, between Juan's adventures abroad and his adventures in England, there is a noticeable difference. In the first part the satire is incidental; the action is picaresque, and of the best kind. Byron's invention never fails. The shipwreck, an episode too well-known to quote, is something quite new and quite successful, even if it be somewhat overdone by the act of cannibalism in which it culminates. The last wild adventure occurs directly after Juan's arrival in England, when he is held up by footpads on the way to London; and here again, I think, in the obituary of the dead highwayman, is something new in English verse:

> He from the world had cut off a great man,
> Who in his time had made heroic bustle.
> Who in a row like Tom could lead the van,
> Booze in the ken, or at the spellken hustle?
> Who queer a flat? Who (spite of Bow-street's ban)
> On the high toby-spice so flash the muzzle?
> Who on a lark, with black-eyed Sal (his blowing)
> So prime, so swell, so nutty, and so knowing?

That is first-rate. It is not a bit like Crabbe, but it is rather suggestive of Burns.

The last four cantos are, unless I am greatly mistaken, the most substantial of the poem. To satirize humanity in general requires either a more genial talent than Byron's, such as that of Rabelais, or else a more profoundly tortured one, such as Swift's. But in the latter part of *Don Juan* Byron is concerned with an English scene, in which there was for him nothing romantic left; he is concerned with a restricted field that he had known well, and for the satirizing of which an acute animosity sharpened his powers of observation. His understanding may remain superficial, but it is precise. Quite possibly he undertook something that he would have been unable to carry to a successful conclusion; possibly there was needed, to complete the story of that monstrous house-party, some high spirits, some capacity for laughter, with which Byron was not endowed. He might have found it impossible to deal with that remarkable personage Aurora Raby, the most serious character of his invention, within the frame of his satire. Having invented a character too serious, in a way too real for the world he knew, he might have been compelled to reduce her to the size of one of his ordinary romantic heroines. But Lord Henry and Lady Adeline Amundeville are persons exactly on the level of Byron's capacity for understanding; and they have a reality for which their author has perhaps not received due credit.

What puts the last cantos of *Don Juan* at the head of Byron's works is, I think, that the subject matter gave him at last an adequate object for a genuine emotion. The emotion is hatred of hypocrisy; and if it was reinforced by more personal and petty feelings, the feelings of the man who as a boy had known the humiliation of shabby lodgings with an eccentric mother, who at fifteen had been clumsy and unattractive and unable to dance with Mary Chaworth, who remained oddly alien among the society that he knew so well—this mixture of the origin of his attitude towards English society only gives it greater intensity. And the hypocrisy of the world that he satirized was at the opposite extreme from his own. Hypocrite, indeed, except in the original sense of the word, is hardly the term for Byron. He was an actor who devoted immense trouble to *becoming* a role that he adopted; his superficiality was something that he created for himself. It is difficult, in considering Byron's poetry, not to be drawn into an analysis of the man: but much more attention has already been devoted to the man than to the poetry, and I prefer, within the limits of such an essay as this, to keep the latter in the foreground. My point is that Byron's satire upon English society, in the latter part of *Don Juan,* is something for which I can find no parallel in English literature. He was right in making the hero of his house-party a Spaniard, for what Byron understands and dislikes about English society is very much what an intelligent foreigner in the same position would understand and dislike.

One cannot leave *Don Juan* without calling attention to another part of it which emphasizes the difference between this poem and any other satire in English: the Dedicatory Verses. The Dedication to Southey seems to me one of the most exhilarating pieces of abuse in the language:

> Bob Southey! You're a poet—Poet Laureate,
> And representative of all the race;
> Although 'tis true that you turn'd out a Tory at
> Last, yours has lately been a common case;
> And now, my Epic Renegade! what are ye at? . . .

kept up without remission to the end of seventeen stanzas. This is not the satire of Dryden, still less of Pope; it is perhaps more like Hall or Marston, but they are bunglers in comparison. This is not indeed English satire at all; it is really a *flyting*, and closer in feeling and intention to the satire of Dunbar:

> Lene larbar, loungeour, baith lowsy in lisk and lonye;
> Fy! skolderit skyn, thow art both skyre and skrumple;
> For he that rostit Lawrance had thy grunye,

And he that hid Sanct Johnis ene with ane womple,
And he that dang Sanct Augustine with ane rumple,
Thy fowll front had, and he that Bartilmo flaid;
The gallowis gaipis eftit thy graceles gruntill,
As thow wald for ane haggeis, hungry gled.

To some this parallel may seem questionable, but to me it has brought a keener enjoyment, and I think a juster appreciation of Byron than I had before. I do not pretend that Byron is Villon (nor, for other reasons, does Dunbar or Burns equal the French poet), but I have come to find in him certain qualities, besides his abundance, that are too uncommon in English poetry, as well as the absence of some vices that are too common. And his own vices seem to have twin virtues that closely resemble them. With his charlatanism, he has also an unusual frankness; with his pose, he is also a *poète contumace* in a solemn country; with his humbug and self-deception he has also a reckless raffish honesty; he is at once a vulgar patrician and a dignified toss-pot; with all his bogus diabolism and his vanity of pretending to disreputability, he is genuinely superstitious and disreputable. I am speaking of the qualities and defects visible in his work, and important in estimating his work: not of the private life, with which I am not concerned.

RONALD BOTTRALL

Byron and the Colloquial Tradition
in English Poetry

MATTHEW ARNOLD ended his famous essay with these words: 'Wordsworth and Byron stand out by themselves. When the year 1900 is turned,
and our nation comes to recount her poetic glories in the century which
has then just ended, the first names with her will be these.' But Byron's
reputation had already begun to fall when Arnold was writing and it
reached its lowest point at the turn of the century; there is, indeed, little
sign of its being rehabilitated. Mr. Herbert Read, who likes categories,
has constructed a main line of English poetry. I should like in this paper
to fill in a gap in his line with three poets whom he passed over: Dryden,
Pope and Byron. I wish also to distinguish a colloquial tradition in
English poetry, and in establishing this I shall use as criteria rhythm
and word order rather than the Wordsworthian criterion of diction.

   When there is a live tradition of acted poetic drama there is, or ought
to be, a keen sense of the rhythms of colloquial speech; when there is
no contemporary poetic drama this rhythmic sense, of vital importance
in poetry, may be blunted or lost, as to a great extent it was in the
nineteenth century. Middle English and Tudor poetry outside the
Chaucerian tradition depends largely on the colloquial rhythm of the
language: Langland and Skelton write on a free rhythmical base. And
within the tradition there is magnificent colloquial writing from Chaucer
himself, not only in the couplet *Tales* but also, more remarkably, in the
intricate rime royal stanzas of *Troilus and Criseyde*. Dunbar and Henry-
son had, of course, the 'flyting' tradition alive and ready to hand. Donne

From *Criterion*, XVIII (1939), pp. 204–224. Reprinted by permission of the
author.

and Herbert use colloquial rhythms to create a momentum which frequently runs against the metrical stress. Dryden, and above all, Pope, contrived an extremely subtle metrical framework by means of which they succeeded in giving full play to colloquial rhythms and at the same time making them coincide with the patterned stress. A most illuminating study could be written of the range and subtlety of the effects that Hopkins obtained by running the colloquial stress sometimes against the metrical stress, sometimes with it. This, too, has been a favourite method of T. S. Eliot in his stanza poems and of Ezra Pound in *Hugh Selwyn Mauberley*. Pound in the best of the earlier *Cantos* and Eliot in a great deal of *The Waste Land* have done yet another thing. They have not let the colloquial stress follow the metrical exigencies, nor made an under-pattern of its cross-rhythms, but they have allowed the speech rhythm itself to determine the metrical pattern, so obtaining an exact relation of thought to feeling, of rhythm to emotion.

When Donne wrote, the drama was gathering power. He drew much of his strength from the vigorous English that was being bandied about by the pamphleteers. He was working in a live medium. My business here is rather to treat of those who have written in non-dramatic eras poetry which at another time might have taken dramatic form. Such poets use a large canvas, tell a story and write vivid dialogue. We can start, I think, with Boccaccio. Chaucer imitated Boccaccio, Dryden adapted Chaucer, Pope re-wrote him too, and very significantly, the most colloquial of all—the Merchant and the Wife of Bath. Byron was a lifelong idolater of Pope and is the nearest of all English poets to Boccaccio and Chaucer in his power of telling a story.

Here surely is a new line of approach to Byron. There is singularly little good criticism of Byron, and his best critics, Matthew Arnold and Sir Herbert Grierson, have not always praised him for the right reasons. Arnold, in his excellent essay, is so harassed by his touchstone theory that he can only cite a couple of lines from the death of the gladiator as proof of Byron's greatness; and even Grierson, who better than any other critic has seen what in Byron is truly important, can fall in with convention to the extent of calling *Childe Harold* the 'noblest panoramic poem in our literature.'

It is only after his rejection by the English society of which he had been the darling that Byron begins for the first time to take himself seriously either as a man or as an artist. He is no longer the sinister dilettante of the salons, or the rake who drank out of a skull with his roystering friends at Newstead. The bucks and dandies of the latter part of the eighteenth century and of the Regency period were accustomed to boast of their vices and dissipations. Byron's Presbyterian upbringing made him so different from the rest of his class that he was not only tormented by a sense of mortal sin, but felt disgust in the very act of committing his sexual excesses. If in the third and fourth Cantos of *Childe Harold* he drags across Europe the pageant of his bleeding heart, it is because he sees himself as an injured man, borne down by a conviction of inexpiable sin, and yet a man who needs to be justified before the world. When this agony of mind subsided he was able to write in the objective and detached manner which distinguishes his best work. A parallel may be found in Ezra Pound. The dilettante poet of the pre-War côteries got a severe enough shock from the death of Gaudier, Hulme and other of his friends in battle, for the War to act as a catalyst and produce his greatest work, *Hugh Selwyn Mauberley*. The world of society which had crumbled around Byron is symbolized by the crumbling remains of great civilizations and great men which he passes in review in *Childe Harold*. His steady growth to adult sanity and almost prophetic understanding of the political and social forces of Europe can be followed in the ottava rima poems. It is a most significant fact that his readings of Rousseau, which had been so constant, are now replaced by reading of Voltaire. The change is clear if we remember that it was a narrow Presbyterianism in which he was brought up, and that it was in the Catholic faith that he had his daughter Allegra educated. The movement is from the Protestant emphasis on self to a European, inclusive and civilized outlook. In *Childe Harold,* in spite of some justification, he is exploiting his imagined wrongs in order to revenge himself on society, in *Don Juan* he is fulfilling himself in a great work of art.

Byron's relation to the eighteenth century is a matter of the first importance. In 1820 he wrote:

> 'The great cause of the present deplorable state of English poetry is to be attributed to the absurd and systematic depreciation of Pope, in which, for the last few years, there has been a sort of epidemic concurrence.'

But remarks such as this have been glossed over as a curious aberration in the arch-Romantic. Herbert Read, in his hierarchy, neatly skips over Dryden and Pope and dismisses them as merely 'intelligent.' 'Are we then to conclude,' he asks, 'that poetry and civilization cannot exist together?' And he sadly admits, 'I think we must.' For those of us who believe that poetry and civilization cannot exist apart, a new hierarchy must obviously be established. I feel, myself, that the greatest things in Byron are the things he learned from Pope. It is commonly said that Byron got the idea of using the ottava rima from Hookham Frere, and this is certainly true, if we look only at the externals of form.[1] But Frere's ottava rima has none of that which makes Byron's handling of it so inimitable—the tremendous force of a great speaking voice. This is the sort of thing in Pope that may have helped him to attain such power:

> 'My head and heart thus flowing through my quill
> Verseman or proseman, term me what you will,
> Papist or Protestant, or both between,
> Like good Erasmus in an honest mean,
> In moderation placing all my glory,
> While Tories call me Whig, and Whigs a Tory.
>   Satire's my weapon, but I'm too discreet
> To run amuck, and tilt at all I meet;
> I only wear it in a land of Hectors,
> Thieves, supercargoes, sharpers, and directors.'
>   (*Imitations of Horace*, II. i.,   *To Mr. Fortescue*).

It is not difficult to show that the best lines of Byron's satiric work in couplets are much nearer to Churchill than to Pope, but in the close of the following stanza there is more than a superficial approximation to the manner of Pope:

> Then dress, then dinner, then awakes the world!
> Then glare the lamps, then whirl the wheels, then roar
> Through street and square the flashing chariots hurl'd
> Like harness'd meteors; then along the floor
> Chalk mimics painting; then festoons are twirl'd;
> Then roll the brazen thunders of the door,
> Which opens to the thousand happy few
> An earthly paradise of *Or Molu*.

After the ponderous epic rolling of the doors in 'brazen thunders' and the expectancy aroused by 'happy few' and 'earthly paradise,' the combination of metrical and rhetorical stress falling on the tawdry and ridiculous word '*Or Molu*' is a masterpiece of ironic demolition. But Byron's debt to Pope is something larger even than this. It permeates the whole of his best work.

When there was no longer a disproportion between sentiment and object, when he could see things as they are, and could feel as a sane man feels, Byron began to cast about for a technique which should express adequately his new objectivity, his new cynical defences. The style had from his earliest years been ready to his hand in his *Letters and Journals,* but as long as he felt it necessary to impose himself on the world and salve his own hurt pride such a style could not seem to him appropriate. In the *Letters and Journals* there is an abundance of vigorous direct writing, magnificent examples of that aristocratic colloquial speech which had been the heritage of the English nobility from the Restoration down to Chesterfield and Sheridan. Byron is the last great writer to make use of it greatly. The easy, familiar way in which Whig aristocrats wrote may be seen from Lady Caroline Lamb's account of a visit from Byron, who found her with Moore and Rogers:

'I was on the sofa, filthy and heated . . . when Lord Byron was announced I flew to change my habit. When I came back, Rogers said "Lord Byron, you are a lucky man. Here has Lady Caroline been sitting in all her dirt with us, but as soon as you were announced, she fled to make herself beautiful."'

The only prose writer of the period who approaches the Byron of the *Letters and Journals* is Cobbett, and we shall do well to remember that a passage in *The Age of Bronze* (written at the same time as *Don Juan*) is lifted directly from a letter of Cobbett's to Mr. Western in the *Weekly Register.* Also in introducing a story into a late canto of *Don Juan,* Byron says:

'And here I must an anecdote relate,
But luckily of no great length or weight.'

which is very like a remark of Cobbett: 'and here I must mention (I do not know *why* I must, by the bye) an instance of my own skill in measuring land by the eye.'[2] To point the mutualness of the debt it may be noted that for a *Ride* of a few weeks earlier Cobbett took his motto from *The Age of Bronze.*

The defects of Byron's poetic oratory and false sublime have been too often exposed for it to be necessary for me to analyse them here. But it will be well for me to remark on an important influence on the third canto of *Childe Harold,* that of Shelley. This influence has by most critics been taken to be a good one, and the imitations of Wordsworth in this canto have been put down to Shelley's advice. In this canto he professes to believe that in a world of mutability only Nature is constant; but he did not really believe in a Wordsworthian Nature. Nature was

214

not to him a healer, but a series of scenic pegs on which to hang purple passages of description. The influence of Shelley is not here, but in his use of imagery.

> Once more upon the waters! yet once more!
> And the waves bound beneath me as a steed
> That knows his rider. Welcome to their roar!
> Swift be their guidance, wheresoe'er it lead!
> Though the strained mast should quiver as a reed,
> And the rent canvas fluttering strew the gale,
> Still must I on; for I am as a weed,
> Flung from the rock, on Ocean's foam, to sail
> Where'er the surge may sweep, the tempest's breath prevail.
>
> In my youth's summer I did sing of One,
> The wandering outlaw of his own dark mind;
> Again I seize the theme, then but begun,
> And bear it with me, as the rushing wind
> Bears the cloud onwards: in that Tale I find
> The furrows of long thought, and dried-up tears,
> Which, ebbing, leave a sterile track behind,
> O'er which all heavily the journeying years
> Plod the last sands of life,—where not a flower appears.

The imagery of the first stanza is vigorous, but the change of mood leads to confusion. At first the writer is master, riding the waves, then is guided by them, then is a ship tossed by the gale, and at last a weed flung from a rock to be carried hither and thither by the surge. The contradictory aspects of Byron's character are, however, expressed, and the momentum of the stanza, suggesting the way in which Byron was torn between them, justifies it. The second half of the next stanza, however, at once raises a query whether the dried-up torrent-bed is clearly realized. How can the furrows of his (memory of the) past be the track which the last journeying years plod? Which ebb, the furrows or the dried-up tears? Are 'the last sands of life' in apposition to 'years' or are they the substance of the sterile track? If the latter, then he is obviously talking ridiculously of his early twenties. Byron himself could probably not have given a convincing answer to these queries. At the time when he wrote this canto he was constantly with Shelley and much influenced by him. Hence the tangled metaphors and the concessions to Wordsworthianism. The confusion in this stanza has no justification, it is just shoddy impressionistic thinking.

If we compare the Waterloo stanzas of *Childe Harold* with the stanzas on the 'crowning carnage' in the *Vision of Judgment,* or the Napoleon stanzas of the first poem with this from the second, we can see what has happened.

> In the first year of Freedom's second dawn
> Died George the Third; although no tyrant, one
> Who shielded tyrants, till each sense withdrawn
> Left him nor mental nor external sun:
> A better farmer ne'er brushed dew from lawn,
> A worse king never left a realm undone!
> He died—but left his subjects still behind,
> One half as mad—the other no less blind.

Here there is no over-emphasis, no restrained rhetoric. It is an admirable example of Byron's skill in conceding a little so as to make his condemnation the more crushing. In *Manfred* Byron, still writing under Shelley's influence, makes his hero say:

> 'Ye toppling towers of ice!
> Ye Avalanches, whom a breath draws down
> In mountainous o'erwhelming, come and crush me!
> I hear ye momently above, beneath,
> Crash with a frequent conflict.'

In this scene Byron is drawing on his tour in the Swiss mountains, made a month before. Here is the way in which he describes his experience in his Journal to his sister, written at the time:

> 'Ascended the Wengen mountain . . . Heard the Avalanches falling every five minutes nearly—as if God was pelting the Devil down from Heaven with snowballs.'

Such a simile would have fitted naturally into the fabric of the ottava rima poems. In them he exchanged his falsetto for a speaking voice.

The technique came to Byron's hand when it was needed. The narrative skill had always been there, and in *Beppo* it reappears, with an added subtlety which makes this poem unique in English literature. It opens with twenty stanzas which hint at the theme of the story by asides on prudery, and references to Othello and gondolas. This arouses expectation as no direct statement could do. After sixteen stanzas of narrative appears the first digression on the Cavalier Servente and Venetian morals. Out of this arises a second digression on England, its language, landscape and women contrasted with those of Italy. Then comes a digression on digression leading up to comments on his new style of writing. Here he makes a neat hit at his own *Tales*:

> Oh! that I had the art of easy writing
> What should be easy reading! could I scale
> Parnassus, where the Muses sit inditing
> Those pretty poems, never known to fail,
> How quickly would I print (the world delighting)
> A Grecian, Syrian or *Ass*yrian tale;
> And sell you, mixed with western Sentimentalism,
> Some samples of the finest Orientalism.

After this the story advances slowly by means of a series of comments on Love and Youth, the Fashionable World, Napoleon and Fortune. At stanza lxix the dénouement suddenly begins with the entrance of the mysterious Turk; but in the next eleven stanzas the reader is kept in suspense while Byron digresses on polygamy and authorship. This is a magnificent piece of story-telling craft. The attention is switched back to the intrigue for a moment, and then appears to digress again on the advisability of ladies of uncertain age retiring from balls before the sun comes up; but this is no digression; it is the cue for Laura's departure. From this point the narrative moves unerringly and with great brilliance to its end. The apex is this amazing female monologue:

> They entered and for Coffee called—it came,
> A beverage for Turks and Christians both
> Although the way they make it's not the same.
> Now Laura, much recovered, or less loth
> To speak, cries 'Beppo! what's your pagan name?
> Bless me! your beard is of amazing growth!
> And how came you to keep away so long?
> Are you not sensible 'twas very wrong?

> 'And are you *really, truly,* now a Turk?
> With any other women did you wive?
> Is't true they use their fingers for a fork?
> Well, that's the prettiest Shawl—as I'm alive!
> You'll give it me? They say you eat no pork.
> And how so many years did you contrive
> To—Bless me! did I ever? No, I never
> Saw a man grown so yellow! How's your liver?

> 'Beppo! that beard of yours becomes you not;
> It shall be shaved before you're a day older:
> Why do you wear it? Oh! I had forgot—
> Pray, don't you think the weather here is colder?
> How do I look? You shan't stir from this spot
> In that queer dress, for fear that some beholder
> Should find you out, and make the story known.
> How short your hair is! Lord! how grey it's grown!'

Only Chaucer of the English narrative poets could have achieved this vivacity and sureness of tone at a climax, while at the same time exposing the whole situation through the attitude of the speaker. Byron was working out a technique to do much the same work as Chaucer had done before him—to sum up a society and an era. Byron is much narrower in his range and in his sympathy than Chaucer, but he is far wider than Shelley or even Wordsworth.

As the ottava rima poetry of Byron is linked up with Chaucer on its narrative side, it is linked with Dryden and Pope in its satiric method. Byron has little of the finality of Dryden and none of the subtlety and finesse of Pope, but he learnt from them a sureness of tone which is seen in none of his other writings. Byron only once in ottava rima attempted the relentless, clinching rhythms of a Dryden verse 'character'—in the stanzas on Brougham in Canto I of *Don Juan*. The fact that he suppressed these lines, brilliant as they are, makes it clear that he felt incapable of making a frontal attack in Dryden's manner without losing Dryden's urbanity. His satire is much less personal than that of Pope. In *Don Juan* he is attacking a hypocritical code of living, not, like Pope, pillorying a victim against the background of an ordered society. Byron generally prefers a manner of large tolerance, and gets his satirical effects by an easy irony. The confident familiar tone of *The Vision of Judgment* is sustained from start to finish without a false emphasis or a false image. Even when he writes of Southey, whom he detested, he gets his effects by a burlesque of awkwardly hesitant speech:

> He said—(I only give the heads)—he said,
> He meant no harm in scribbling; 't was his way
> Upon all topics; 't was, besides, his bread,
> Of which he butter'd both sides; 't would delay
> Too long the assembly (he was pleased to dread),
> And take up rather more time than a day,
> To name his works—he would but cite a few—
> 'Wat Tyler'—'Rimes on Blenheim'—'Waterloo.'

The renegade and toadying character of Southey is fixed in these deprecating and slippery rhythms. There is, too, in the *Vision* not a little of the narrative art of *Beppo*. From Southey's entrance Byron makes the poem move with heightened vigour to its end, as he does *Beppo* after the advent of the husband. The King speaks only once:

> The Monarch, mute till then, exclaimed, 'What! What!
> *Pye* come again? No more—no more of that!'

The same satirical trick of repetition to emphasize vacuity is here used that we find in Pope's Sir Plume:

> 'My Lord, why, what the devil?
> Z—ds! damn the Lock! 'fore Gad, you must be civil!
> Plague on't! 'tis past a jest—nay, pr'ythee, pox!
> Give her the hair'—he spoke and rapped his box.

The close of the poem, in perfect urbanity, when George is allowed to slip into Heaven, is the highest art.

The *Vision* is probably greater than any single canto of *Don Juan* because of its homogeneity of theme and sureness of tone, but both this poem and *Beppo* are most profitably considered as annexes to *Don Juan*, which is to my mind, with the possible exception of *The Prelude*, the greatest long poem in English since *The Dunciad*. Sir Arthur Quiller-Couch spoke truly when he said that *Don Juan* is the second English epic; but it is an epic via the eighteenth century and *Tom Jones*. Byron persistently calls his work an epic, as does Fielding.

> 'If you must have an epic (he says) there's *Don Juan* for you; it is
> an epic as much in the spirit of our day as the *Iliad* was in Homer's.
> Love, religion and politics form the argument . . . and, depend upon it,
> my moral will be a good one; not even Dr. Johnson should be able to
> find a flaw in it.'

Byron has the same kind of moral seriousness as Fielding, but, like Fielding, though more obviously, he lacks the 'idea of intense moral struggle' needed to give something beyond a virtuoso structure to his epic. Fielding, as is well known, constructed a plot of immense complexity, accurate even to the calendar and to days of the week, but Byron hated system. 'When a man talks of his system, it is like a woman talking of her virtue. I let them talk on.' One ought, after all this emphasis on moral seriousness, to be able to trace in *Don Juan* a consistent attitude, but in the earlier cantos one feels too often that an incident is put in because it is funny, or a stanzas because it is witty. Nevertheless, Byron took *Don Juan* with ever increasing seriousness:

'I take a vicious and unprincipled character, and lead him through those ranks of society whose high external accomplishments cover and cloke internal and secret vices, and I paint the natural effects of such characters; and certainly they are not so highly coloured as we find them in real life. . . . It is impossible you can believe the higher classes of society worse than they are in England, France and Italy, for no language can sufficiently paint them.'

He began, doubtless, with a general idea of lampooning conventional morality, but he went on to write an epic of modern Europe. He grows with the poem and the poem does not fall off but becomes greater as it goes on. *Don Juan* is a summing up of the post-Revolution and pre-Napoleonic era by one who had been of it, but was seeing it pass. It is an exposure of the failure of the Whig aristocratic tradition by a peer who was prepared to fight against the vested interests of his own class. In both *Tom Jones* and *Don Juan*, the natural man who acts according to impulse is contrasted with the hypocrite, or the hypocritical society, which acts according to convention. The antithesis is between conduct and inclination or intention. In both, evil in the hero is mainly sexual, or at worst, anything vaguely against the social usage; but the evil of society is seen as a fundamental and rooted inability to be honest and truthful, or to care for the individual human life. In his earlier work when Byron attacks hypocrisy, one has a feeling that it is with an uneasy recollection of his own posing in the first cantos of *Childe Harold*. Byron by making Don Juan a Spaniard achieves a brilliant appearance of objectivity. In the great cantos after his arrival in England, which to my mind make a profoundly moral poem, Byron is able to write about England as he has never written before—from an external position. He is able to attack the cult of sentimentality and romantic pessimism for which he was in part responsible. The thirty stanzas of exordium to Canto XIV and the twenty-six to Canto XII are sustained pieces of social criticism only surpassed in English verse by Pope's *Satires* and *Moral Essays*.

A great deal of English poetry from 1780 to 1870 and most of it from 1870 to 1900 was written on the assumption that if only an experience is felt sincerely enough and intensely enough it will find its own words, which will be the best words, and its own form, which will be the best form. The presence of the 'daimon' of inspiration is enough. This accounts for much of the slovenliness and 'inattention' of Shelley, Browning and Swinburne. All three of them were technically competent, and at least one, in a narrow way, a great technician, but they really saw the problems of the subject, the material and the form as *one* problem; once mastered by the conviction of 'genuine' inspiration they treated the formal problem as an unavoidable but inessential corollary. In the worst work of Coleridge, Shelley and Browning indeed a mere outline of a poem is given; the reader has to do the formal work for himself. With Swinburne the problem is somewhat different; technique (by which he meant a double sestina rather than a villanelle) is an end in itself. Byron's greatness in the ottava rima poems is that he evolved a form perfectly adapted to his subject and his material, and so was able to use the whole range of the language with a virility and momentum such as is found nowhere else in nineteenth century poetry. The amazing variety of tone and the tremendous rhythmic energy of *Don Juan* come from Byron's complete understanding of the spoken language. In his controversy with Bowles Byron continually emphasizes the importance of execution, and he came to hate 'flowers of poetry'[3] and to despise 'the mart For what is sometimes called poetic diction.' He went back to Pope to learn precision of statement and the problems of relating technique to material, and to Dryden to learn how the complete resources of the language might be enlisted.

T. S. Eliot in a very interesting essay[4] cites the following stanza as an example of Byron's colloquial power:

> He from the world had cut off a great man,
> Who in his time had made heroic bustle.
> Who in a row like Tom could lead the van,
> Booze in the ken, or at the spellken hustle?
> Who queer a flat? Who (spite of Bow-street's ban)
> On the high toby-spice so flash the muzzle?
> Who on a lark with black-eyed Sal (his blowing)
> So prime—so swell—so nutty—and so knowing?

It is brilliant, but it is a *tour de force*. Byron is doing far more cleverly the sort of thing that Harrison Ainsworth was doing in 'Nix my doll pals, fake away' or Henley in 'Villon's straight tip to all cross coves' with its famous refrain 'Booze and the blowens cop the lot.' Byron in exile was showing that he still remembered the thieves' cant which he heard when he was a dandy and used to spar with Gentleman Jackson and Molineaux. When Eliot compares this stanza to Burns he is being most misleading. Burns was using a vernacular which was his native speech, Byron was faking a brilliant *pastiche*. What Byron has in common with Burns is not his use of a vivid vernacular or his homely turn of phrase, but his method of familiar, ironical address, his generous regard for the common people and his large humanity.

The language of Byron was aristocratic, and though it had a great tradition behind it, this language is charged with a lower poetic potentiality than the Scots of Burns. There is thus far less explosive force in Byron's phrasing than in that of Burns, but there is an equally powerful use of the rhythms of colloquial speech. In *Don Juan* Byron is writing as he spoke to his friends and equals, and at the same time writing great verse.

> Where's Brummell? Dished. Where's Long Pole Wellesley?
>   Diddled.
> Where's Whitbread? Romilly? Where's George the Third?
> Where is his will? (That's not so soon unriddled).
> And where is 'Fum' the Fourth, our 'royal bird'?
> Gone down, it seems, to Scotland, to be fiddled
> Unto by Sawney's violin, we have heard:
> 'Caw me, caw thee'—for six months hath been hatching
> This scene of royal itch and loyal scratching.

> Where is Lord This? And where my Lady That?
> The Honourable Mistresses and Misses?
> Some laid aside like an old Opera hat,
> Married, unmarried and remarried; (this is
> An evolution oft performed of late).
> Where are the Dublin shouts and London hisses?
> Where are the Grenvilles? Turned as usual. Where
> My friends the Whigs? Exactly where they were.

The huddled speed of question and answer, parenthesis, court gossip, innuendo, thrust and repartee, is breath-taking. Every phrase keeps, however, the normal word-order, and the rhythms of everyday speech run with and into the intricate stanza, giving an extraordinary effect of energy harnessed and then liberated at the highest pressure. Here Byron displays the whole rhythmic potentiality of colloquial English.

A remark of Goethe, 'So bald er reflectirt ist er ein Kind,' has often been brought against Byron since Arnold quoted it. Goethe, in fact, did not intend it to be taken as a general criticism, he was speaking of Byron's irritability in the face of hostile criticism; but Arnold's wider application of the remark is in part justified. The 'thought' that we find in *Childe Harold,* the 'metaphysics' of *Cain,* are those of an under-graduate, if not of a child; but Byron could forge out *poetic* thought.

> Don Juan saw that Microcosm on stilts,
> Yclept the Great World; for it is the least,
> Although the highest: but as swords have hilts
> By which their power of mischief is increased,
> When Man in battle or in quarrel tilts,
> Thus the low world, north, south, or west, or east,
> Must still obey the high—which is their handle,
> Their Moon, their Sun, their gas, their farthing candle.

We have only to compare this with the tangled metaphors quoted earlier from *Childe Harold* to note a fundamental difference. Here the metaphors are not loosely impressionistic, they are used structurally to build up a fine piece of poetic logic. Through such eighteenth century poems as Pope's *Elegy to the Memory of an Unfortunate Lady,* this stanza may even be brought into relation with Metaphysical poetry.

T. S. Eliot speaks of Byron's 'imperceptiveness to the word' and his 'schoolboy command of language.' This, I confess, I cannot understand. Byron was certainly, in his way, at least as perceptive to the word as Swinburne was in his. It is true that his interest was rather in the fundamental rhythmic movement of speech than in the word, but that was, at the time, to the good. Augustan theories of diction were too much obsessed by the word, and a Wordsworthian theory of poetics, carried to its logical end, could only debilitate and desiccate the language. Byron by bringing to his verse the colloquial force of his prose vivified and renewed the English poetic tradition. Unfortunately his example has been of little profit. He was ignored equally by Tennyson and the Pre-Raphaelites. Browning was faced with a problem of a similar kind—of turning into poetry unpoetic material and relating poetry to speech. But he approached it from another angle, from that of the word and the monologue form. He tried to give his verse the appearance of speech by introducing colloquial phrases in jerky, broken periods, not by re-creating the fundamentals of speech rhythm. The result is very much nearer the sort of thing that happens when one contemplates a knotty problem in one's mind, with half-formed words, than it is to conversational speech.

Early in the nineteenth century, with De Quincey and Landor, prose begins to usurp some of the functions of verse. Before Dryden, verse had commonly done a good deal of the work of prose, because prose was

223

still an unformed and undisciplined medium, and until the time of Browning verse had been able successfully to overlap the work of prose in many fields. Browning suffers from standing at this transitional point. A great deal of what he wrote could have been as well written in prose, and so it would have been better to have written it in prose. He included too much; nor did he clearly realize at what he was aiming. One sympathizes with Browning's intentions, but one can rarely applaud his results. No external form grew up in his hands out of an inner compulsion, as the ottava rima did in Byron's. The lack of any real philosophical or moral depth of purpose in his work cannot be disguised by the tortured surface. His colloquialisms are too often there because he felt it was his duty to write colloquially. His failure to grasp even the primary implications of the adjustment of technique to material is obvious if we note that he took over the jaunty and successful jingle of *The Pied Piper* to tell the high-flown and would-be eerie story of *The Flight of the Duchess*. A distinguished academic critic says that the grotesque rhymes of *The Grammarian's Funeral* suggest the halting steps of the bearers as they climb the mountain:

> Image the whole, then execute the parts—
>> Fancy the fabric
> Quite, ere you build, ere steel strike fire from quartz,
>> Ere mortar dab brick.

This is the end of a paragraph, whose whole weight falls on 'dab brick.' I confess that I cannot get out of my mind Pope's 'dabchick,' which

>> waddles through the copse
> On feet and wings, and flies, and wades, and hops.

Browning has often been praised for his skill in keeping a colloquial word-order in a close-rhyming form:

> Where the quiet-coloured end of evening smiles,
>> Miles and miles
> On the solitary pastures where our sheep
>> Half asleep
> Tinkle homeward through the twilight, stray or stop
>> As they crop—
> Was the site once of a city great and gay,
>> (So they say).

The sentimental lilt of the verse is fake colloquialism, as the attitude is fake Arcadianism. Compare this with Suckling's 'Of thee, (kind boy) I ask no red and white' or with Wyatt's 'What should I say?—Since faith is fled,' and the rhymes will be seen to be obtrusive, not concealed; they do not work with the colloquial movement, but against it. The truth is that instead of setting himself to solve the problems of relating material to technique, of his facts to their effectual presentation, Browning took the easiest way. He fell in with the popular demand, posed as a profound thinker and repeated the surface complexity of his successes. Instead, therefore, of his technique and subject matter growing with his intelligence, as did Byron's, all three stagnated.

Pound confesses to have learnt much from Browning, and Eliot also admits a debt. But although Eliot is confining himself nowadays to drama he seems rather to be moving away from colloquial rhythms than towards them. To me the method of *Murder in the Cathedral* is a sad watering down of the methods of *The Waste Land* and *Sweeney Agonistes*. Eliot is making the same mistake as Byron made in *Marino Faliero* and *Sardanapalus,* which were written at the same time as *Don Juan*. In these plays, in an attempt to be 'as simple and severe as Alfieri,' he broke down his poetic language to a condition where it was at a far lower tension than his prose. Who then has learnt from Byron? Or who today is attempting the same kind of thing? Sir Herbert Grierson in the first of his two admirable essays makes an attempt to answer the second question. He says, Kipling.

To find Kipling as 'le Byron de nos jours' is something of a shock. But Grierson was writing in 1920. Now, I should say, the answer is W. H. Auden, and a parallel which I had often made in my mind is authenticated by Auden's *Letter to Lord Byron* in the recent *Letters from Iceland*. At first, the more one thinks of the parallel, the more apparent it seems, even to the political background. But the resemblance is superficial. Auden's best work is based, richly and valuably, on the rhythms of colloquial speech; but its scope is narrow, Byron's is notable above all for its breadth. Byron has an infinitely greater range of tone and feeling; not merely a greater range of dislike, but a greater range of sympathy. With Auden we are in a world of private jokes and private heroisms, of preparatory schoolmasters and parlour communists. Grierson was not so wide of the mark after all when, in 1920, he mentioned Kipling. Both writers have had similar effects on their reading public. If Kipling pre-supposes Simla, Brighton and public-school jingoism, Auden presupposes Bloomsbury, Hampstead and public-school Marxism. Byron pre-supposes the aristocracy and the intelligentsia of modern Europe, and the middle and working classes as well. I have a great admiration for much of Auden's earlier work, particularly *Paid on both Sides* and *Address for a Prize-Day*, but a critical method needs critical opposition, and this Auden has not had. The rough, abrupt edges of his first two volumes were far more vital than the prettiness and fake simplicity into which he has smoothed a good deal of his later work. This is due partly to laziness, for Auden has an unfortunate technical slickness which makes him tend to write a new poem rather than get an old one right. He is moving away from his early integrity and one now suspects him of consciously writing down to the crowd. Byron says that he was 'born for opposition' and *Don Juan* aroused storms of protests from many of the friends who had survived the shipwreck of his married life. Auden, however, is now steadily cheered for saying the right thing, as Kipling was before him, and one feels that this has caused him, in his hurry to get right with the right side, to superimpose his politics on his poetry. In Auden, as in Kipling, there is a lack of cohesion between the political attitude and the poetic expression of it, and I find in much of Auden's work an uncertainty of tone and attitude, an inner uncertainty, which is discernible too in Kipling.

Auden's *Letter* to Byron is most disarming reading. It is even written in rime royal because Auden fears that ottava rima may trip him up. Not infrequently we catch the Byron manner:

> The porter at the Carlton is my brother,
> He'll wish me a good evening if I pay,
> For tips and men are equal to each other.
> I'm sure that *Vogue* would be the first to say
> Que le Beau Monde is socialist to-day;
> And many a bandit, not so gently born
> Kills vermin every winter with the Quorn.

This is ingenious, particularly the last couplet, but it is the externals only of Byron that Auden has caught. *Don Juan* leaves a conviction of breadth and seriousness. The total effect of Auden's long *Letter* is that of amusing but unimportant gossip. In the *Letter* Auden gives as his highest praise to Byron that he is the 'master of the airy manner.' If this is Auden's final word, then he has learnt nothing that Byron has to teach. Byron, however, grew with *Don Juan,* and I do not see why Auden should not grow also and become the fine poet which he potentially is. But he will not do so by taking the line of least resistance. It was a conscious self-discipline, as well as a moral urge, that enabled Byron to write in *Don Juan* not only a satire on the aristocratic classes of Europe but a great modern epic. When Napoleon fell, Byron and Goethe became the two dominating names in Europe. What above all impressed Byron's contemporaries was the tremendous impact of his personality. Perhaps Byron did something in *Don Juan* which cannot be done again except by someone with the same force of character.

NOTES

1. Byron, too, read widely in the Italian mock-heroic poets and learnt not a little from Pulci, Berni and Casti. But his translation of the first Canto of the *Morgante Maggiore*, painstaking as it is, is quite lifeless.

2. *Rural Rides*, Weston to Kensington, 26th October, 1826.

3. *Conversations of Lord Byron with the Countess of Blessington*, pp. 264-5.

4. See above, T. S. Eliot, 'Byron.'

ERNEST J. LOVELL, JR.

Irony and Image in *Don Juan*

IT IS clear that much of Byron's poetry must be judged to be imperfect, for reasons well known and generally accepted. Much of his work is flawed because, for the achievement of many poetic effects, he lacked the necessary delicately tuned ear. We must, I believe, agree with the general sense of Eliot's judgment (although its *ex cathedra* tone and the absence of essential qualification may well annoy us) that Byron's ear was 'imperfect, and capable only of crude effects.' He lacked the indispensable gift necessary for writing consistently excellent lyric poetry, a heightened sensitivity to the subtleties of sound combination. The degree to which this deficiency could betray him is clearly illustrated by 'Fare Thee Well,' a stock anthology piece. The defect is less fatal in the early verse tales, and they will still hold the excited attention of undergraduates. Yet the melodramatic heroes of *The Giaour* or *The Bride of Abydos* are without interest for most of us, except for their historical and autobiographical importance. Their minds and characters are immature, their stories without moral significance. We cannot take them seriously: Byron's life is more interesting.

The last two cantos of *Childe Harold* represent an advance, of course (although there are passages in the tales of keen psychological insight and effective picturesque description). But these two cantos suffer from qualities whose presence is clearly implied by the success with which most of Byron's romantic poetry may be translated into a foreign

From *The Major English Romantic Poets: A Symposium in Reappraisal*, ed. Clarence D. Thorpe, Carlos Baker, and Bennett Weaver; © 1957 by Southern Illinois University Press, pp. 129-48. Reprinted by permission of the publisher.

language. As Samuel C. Chew has noted, such poetry bears translation 'with little loss of effect.' The reasons are clear. The diction of *Childe Harold* is essentially the diction of good prose and frequently the language of summary, abstraction, or generalization, often expressing a call to action and hence rhetorical or persuasive. Both diction and imagery, therefore, are often curiously limited in their power to evoke rich and complex overtones of meaning, although the poem at its worst fails even to achieve the precision of good prose. To summarize these well-known difficulties—and there are others—is not to imply, however, that *Childe Harold* is without all value for our time. It is merely to say that its chief value lies in its substance, not its form, which today has little to teach us.

Manfred, on the other hand, is a work of near perfection in the sense that it accomplishes nearly perfectly what it sets out to do—embody the essence of the romantic Byronic spirit, not omitting its theatrical or melodramatic aspects. The blank verse is unusually firm, sure, and certain of itself and sets off to advantage the intervening lyrics. The chief flaw I find is that the several characters are sometimes insufficiently distinguished one from another in the tone of their speeches. Their accents are too similar (reflecting Byron's limited power to create characters other than Byronic), almost as if the poem were an expressionistic debate between opposing aspects of the poet's mind. From the successive failures of the hero's quest, however, the structure of the poem derives both unity and balanced symmetry, qualities present to a much less impressive degree in *Childe Harold,* which is improved by editorial selection. But the style of *Manfred* depends so completely on the personality of the poet and our knowledge of him that it defies instructive formal analysis: the impassioned words derive their passion and power, as the best of Byron's romantic poetry normally does, from the strength of the poet's feelings. Few works so well illustrate the cliché that the style is the man. The miracle is that the man, or one half of him, shines so brightly through the simple, occasionally commonplace diction, a fact which illustrates again that poetry may be written without excessive concern for the problems of surface texture—provided the poet has something to say and feels strongly enough about it.

Both the chief difficulties already mentioned, Byron's relative insensitivity to the sounds of words and his rather consistent reliance upon direct statement and the diction of prose, also reduce the quality of the plays, although to a lesser extent than in most of the nondramatic work. The dramas, however, suffer in a way *Childe Harold* does not from

Byron's inability, shared with many of the Romantic poets, to create a host of richly diverse characters. He seems to have lacked that capacity for empathy which is essential to the writing of great drama. Although he wrote more good plays, probably, than any of his contemporaries (G. Wilson Knight has compared his dramatic achievement favorably with that of Shakespeare), the clear fact is that Byron is not of the first rank in the drama. The judgment of Paul Elmer More still holds true: 'He lacked the dramatic art.'

What, then, apart from the derivative Popean poems, are we left with? The three great satires, obviously, *Beppo, The Vision of Judgment,* and *Don Juan,* in that order of ascending excellence. Believing that every poet is to be judged finally by his best work and assuming that the virtues of *Beppo* and *The Vision* are frequently those of Byron's greatest masterpiece, I have limited the remainder of these remarks to *Don Juan,* and more particularly to the elements of unity, irony, and imagery in *Don Juan,* a work of great originality and undeniable excellence, essentially unlike anything before it. It has much to say to the mid-twentieth century, an age which, distrusting the grandiose, sentimental, and otherwise oversimplified quite as much as Byron did, has sought the poetic means of expressing its characteristic emotional complexity, as Byron also did, in the oblique, liberating forces of irony and ambiguity. *Don Juan* is, in fact, one of the most pertinent of all poems for us today, reminding us, at a time when we are in particular need of reminder, that a poem is made for people other than its creator, and so first must entertain them, with an artistic recreation of the stuff of their own life, and finally must heal them, with a revelation of its essential meaning, that the community may know itself and so avoid deceiving itself. These are among the primary assumptions of *Don Juan.*

II

The prerequisite to any consideration of the art of *Don Juan* is an analysis of its unity, denied or overlooked often enough to make its explication at this time a task of prime critical importance. Unity denied, the poem is reduced at once to a picaresque series of loosely jointed fragments, however brilliant. It must be clearly demonstrated, therefore, that there is a controlling, unifying principle at work throughout and, more particularly, that each main narrative episode, without exception, is somehow integral to a larger structure.

That unifying principle, I suggest, is the principle of thematic unity —here, the basically ironic theme of appearance versus reality, the difference between what things seem to be (or are said or thought to be) and what they actually are. Thematic unity established, it can then be seen readily that the most significant structure is a complex and carefully considered organization of ironically qualified attitudes and that manner and matter, consequently, are flawlessly fused; for irony is here integral to both theme and mode. It is inherent in the theme, hence it functions also as a necessary principle of narrative structure; and it is, at the same time, the primary device for manipulating manner or mode, to achieve a variety of richly mixed, fully orchestrated tonal qualities, which are themselves reconciled by and subordinated to the dominant theme. In terms of substance, this means that the diverse materials and the clash of emotions gathered together in the poem are harmonized finally by Byron's insight into the difference between life's appearance and its actuality, into the highly mixed motives which ordinarily control men and women, and into their genius for self-deception and rationalization.

A summary, then, of the consistently organic relation between episode and theme is the essential prelude to any purely stylistic discussion of *Don Juan*. Such a summary of the narrative or dramatic expression of theme will make clear, in the course of it, that Byron's irony is neither shallow, cynical, insincere, incidental, nor typically romantic, whether the latter type be understood as self-irony, self-pitying disillusion, or the willful destruction of the dramatic illusion. It is, instead, ordinarily the precise, necessary, fully orchestrated, and artistically functional expression of his own hard-won point of view, almost never a mere attitude adopted for its own sake, the tone of it almost never that of the simple irony of a reversed meaning.

At the risk of grossly oversimplifying the rich complexity of a great poem, then, one may begin by recalling the original hypocrisy of Juan's education, incomplete and thus false to the actual facts of life. Indeed, the entire poem may be read as a richly humorous investigation of the results stemming from a canting, maternal education which attempted to deny the very physical foundations of life. Because Juan has been so ill-educated, he is correspondingly ill-equipped to deal with Julia, understanding neither his own emotional state nor hers, until too late, and so is sent ironically on his travels, 'to mend his former morals,' while Inez, undaunted, takes to teaching Sunday school. Before this, however, in a passage of far-reaching irony, Juan, transformed temporarily into a nympholeptic nature poet, has engaged in obscure Wordsworthian communings with nature, ludicrously deceiving himself and over-spiritualizing the natural world. This self-delusion neatly balances and underlines that of Julia, who, overspiritualizing her passion, engages in the deliberately engendered hypocrisy of Platonic love. Here, as well as elsewhere, the appearance-versus-reality theme focuses on the moral danger of denying the physical basis of life and love, although Byron does not overlook the ideal end of either. The tone of all this comic but quite meaningful irony is deepened, finally, by the criminal hypocrisy of Inez in using her own son, unknown to him, to break up Julia's marriage. Indeed, one form taken by the philosophic irony underlying the first canto suggests that cant and hypocrisy may endanger the very continuity of civilized tradition. But the crowning stroke, after the irony of Julia's tirade while her husband searches her bedroom, is that she who has so viciously deceived herself with so much talk about spiritual love should be sent to live in a convent, where presumably she may contemplate the spiritual forever.

Byron points again at the wrongheadedness of such ill-founded love, hypocritically denying its own physical basis, when he allows Juan to become seasick in the midst of protesting his eternal devotion to Julia while rereading her pathetic letter. One may profitably compare Auden's dramatization of the tension between an asserted life-long fidelity in love and the mutabilities of physical experience, in 'As I Walked Out One Evening.' But if life and love must be viewed 'really as they are,' so also must death. When the ship's company would resort self-deceptively to prayers and 'spirits' for identical reasons, to enable them to face the reality of drowning, Juan keeps them from the 'spirit room,' symbolically, at pistol point, while Byron without preaching attacks an easy crisis religion. The sentimental illusion of Julia's spiritual love, however, is dissipated for good with the appropriate final disposition of her famous letter. Its end is quite equal to that accorded Damian's note to May, in *The Merchant's Tale*, and it has much the same function—to strip the tinsel savagely and finally from false sentiment and reveal it for what it is. It is also at once grimly, ironically appropriate that the loser in the drawing of lots should be Juan's tutor, representative of that hypocritical race, instruments of Inez, who are responsible finally for Juan's being where he is. The chief satire of the shipwreck episode, however, is not directed against either the sentimental falsification of the great traditions or of the experience of love, but against the over-spiritualization of nature, against 'this cant about nature' preached gravely by those who, concerned too exclusively with the 'beauties of nature,' would overlook its destructive aspects.

Byron's use of ironic qualification within a lyric context, to achieve the illusion of increased comprehensiveness and complexity, is especially noteworthy in his treatment of Haidée's romantic paradise, which could no more exist on half-truths than Milton's Garden of Innocence. It is also a significant paradox that Juan and Haidée, lacking a common language, communicate nevertheless more precisely than if they shared the same tongue. But the tone of the Haidée episode is much more nearly similar to that of *Romeo and Juliet*, qualified and enriched as it is by such discordant elements as those supplied by the witty Mercutio and the bawdy Nurse, than it is to that of *Paradise Lost*. Byron has qualified the lyricism of the episode explicitly with the character of Zoe, who cooked eggs and 'made a most superior mess of broth' while Haidée's world turned back its clock to paradise (II, 139, 144-45, 148, 153). Zoe, a graduate of 'Nature's good old college,' the perfect complement to the innocence of Haidée, pure 'child of Nature,' is thus an important ally in enabling Byron to avoid overspiritualizing the romantic love of Juan and Haidée and abstracting one element of the experience to imply that it is the whole.

> I'll tell you who they were, this female pair,
>> Lest they should seem princesses in disguise;
> Besides, I hate all mystery, and that air
>> Of clap-trap, which your recent poets prize;
> And so, in short, the girls they really were
>> They shall appear before your curious eyes,
> Mistress and maid; the first was only daughter
> Of an old man, who lived upon the water.

Space allowing, one might pursue here the full thematic and tonal implications of such ambiguities as those resulting from Byron's skillful fusion of tragedy, comedy, and satire in the character of Lambro (which permits, among other far-reaching effects, a subtle divorce of the Rousseauistic union of virtue and taste). Or one could explore Lambro's resemblance to the old Byronic hero as well as to Byron himself (see III, 18, 51-57) and hence his implied kinship to Juan. The boy or child imagery descriptive of Juan and the mother imagery descriptive of Haidée (see II, 143, 148) add another element of richness to the characterization. And the ironic frame, audaciously suspended and un-noticed over eighty-five stanzas (III, 61-IV, 35), which results from

Lambro's unknown presence, encloses with telling effect the famous lyric on the isles of Greece (ironically enframed a second time by the Southeyan poet who sings it), the equally famous Ave Maria stanzas, and the stanzas to Hesperus. Here Byron achieves an effect quite as complex as that resulting in *The Waste Land* from Eliot's use of the same lines from Sappho, for more directly satiric purposes. Although it is impossible to discuss here these subtle, significant variations of tone and theme, or the consequent added dimensions, it may be said that nowhere else, perhaps, as in the third canto has Byron so skillfully manipulated the knife-edge dividing comedy and tragedy, or suggested more fully, within a successfully maintained romantic frame and setting, the ambiguities and rich complexities of actual existence.

Having successfully established and developed the central theme of appearance versus reality, Byron presumably felt free to permit himself a farcical variation on it: Juan disguised as a woman in a Turkish harem. But the harem episode also lays bare the romanticized Turkish travel book, the Oriental tale, and, perhaps, the romantic submissiveness of Byron's own early Oriental heroines. For Juan is literally a 'slave to the passions.' Who but Byron could have taken the old cliché, read it literally, and so have turned its seamy side inside out—to reveal the ridiculous nature and self-defeating characteristics of purely sensual love, allowing us, notwithstanding—by means of the magnificently mixed tone—to pity its symbol as a woman! But Gulbeyaz, the enslaved specialist in love who should have known better, also represents the final self-deception of one who thinks that love, the free gift of self-surrender, may be bought and commanded. And to the extent that love, Juan's chief interest and most serious occupation, is equated in the poem with all of life, Byron is saying, without heroics, that life itself is impossible without freedom, however attractive a loving or benevolent despot may seem to be, or whatever luxuries may seem to surround the 'escape from freedom.'

Byron prepared for his ironic demolition of modern war, 'Glory's dream unriddled,' in his portrait of the Sultan, disguised as lord of all he surveys except his latest favorite wife and the Empress Catherine, whose boudoir he so well might have graced, as Byron points out, to the furtherance of both 'their own true interests.' The two courts of the opposing rulers, each so seriously concerned with 'love,' form of course an ironic frame for the bloody siege of Ismael, the narrative vehicle of Byron's attack on the false heroics of war. Although the irony is too pervasive to describe, it may be recalled that the immediate theme is not an unqualified pacifism but the hypocrisy and cant of war ('the crying sin of this double-dealing and false-speaking time'), with especial attention to the unsavory paradox of a Christian war of conquest and the attendant Christian mercies of the invading Russians, shortly to become members of the Holy Alliance. But Byron's satire does not depend on a simple reversal of the hypocrisy of war; his tone is carefully qualified, as it ordinarily is, with the result that the satire is never thin or one-dimensional. Successfully avoiding the easy resolution of a comment on the general meaninglessness of war, he can thus frankly recognize its excitement, the intense loyalties and the heroism it evokes, and the paradoxical acts of generosity it calls forth.

Juan at the court of Catherine completes the ironic frame of the war cantos and allows Byron to play his own variation on the old theme of 'to the brave the fair'—the sickening lust of the gentle sex to possess a uniform and see 'Love turn'd a lieutenant of artillery'—only to show that such generous reward of the returning hero will debilitate him and that such a surrender of arms (to other arms) may well bring him nearer death, even, than his wars did. Meanwhile the relations between Catherine and Juan are without hypocrisy, and are known to all. Juan even has an official title. Gross as Catherine's appetites are, they are not so reprehensible as the hypocrisy of Inez's letter (X, 31–34), which serves the further purpose of recalling, without naming, Julia's hypocrisy of Platonic love and Byron's insistence on the necessity of recognizing the physical basis of love. The Catherine episode qualifies the latter insight by making the obvious point that the merely physical, lacking spiritual warmth, will sicken even the greatest lover and force him to more temperate climates.

As Juan moves on across the Continent, Byron ironically deflates the tradition of the picturesque tour (XI, 58–64), chiefly by rhyming a roll call of famous cities and a list of natural resources. When Juan reaches England, where hypocrisy and cant achieve a dazzling multiplicity of aspects, Byron's satiric exposition of the difference between appearance and reality rises, without shrillness, to its greatest heights. He reveals pretense to be the pervading rottenness of an entire culture—beginning with the irony of the attempted highway robbery, shortly after Juan arrives in the land of freedom, law, and order, and closing with the magnificent final irony of the Duchess of Fitz-Fulke disguised as the ghost of the Black Friar, emblematic of a land where the sensual comes draped in the robes of the spiritual, while a country girl in a red cape is brought before the lord of the manor charged with immorality.

It is a land where the wealthy, to escape the press of the city, crowd together in the country. Assembled in all their boredom and frivolity at Norman Abbey, weighty with the great traditions of the past, they may well remind us of Eliot's similarly ironic juxtaposition of the richly traditional setting and spiritual poverty in *The Waste Land*. In Juan's England, even the food masquerades in foreign dress, fit nourishment for a hypocritical people. Things in *Don Juan*, then, are never what they seem, not even the title character, the 'natural' man at home in every 'artificial' society, the exile and wanderer never haunted by a sense of quest. He finds equilibrium in the 'changeable' sex and his moments of eternity in the symbol of the physical here and now. He is the world's most famous lover, yet he never seduces a woman. Although he treads a rake's progress, he does so without becoming cynical or worldly minded. He is a man famous in love and war, yet a child in search of a mother (who will also be mistress and goddess), and he finds her, repeatedly, in woman after woman!

III

An effort, however inadequate, has already been made to indicate that the functional irony of *Don Juan* is seldom the simple irony of a reversed meaning. To abstract the meaning of the narrative in an attempt to suggest the pervasive unity of the main theme and establish the organic relation of each of the chief episodes to it, may suggest that some oversimplification has taken place. As a corrective, therefore, it may be well to say again that Byron repeatedly used irony as a qualifying device within the larger frame of his satire, and so saved it regularly from oversimplification, thinness, and monotony of tone. The point, which deserves to be emphasized, may be illustrated by a brief analysis of the richly mixed tone characteristic of Byron's feminine portraits. It is significant that *Don Juan* combines and reconciles within itself the extremes of the love poem and of the satire, mingling and fusing attitudes of almost pure approval and almost complete disapproval—at once a great hymn to love and a satire on women, and frequently concerned with the comedy of love. Thus the satire may merge so successfully with comedy or at other times with tragedy that it is often hardly recognizable as 'serious' satire: seldom or never is it narrowly satiric or expressive of unqualified disapproval. The tone, in other words, is also never 'pure.'

Consider Julia, for example. Is she a hypocritical self-deceiver viciously leading herself and Juan on with the cant of Platonic love, or is she a woman betrayed originally into marriage with an old man, led deliberately into a trap by Inez, and sentenced finally by society to a convent, to pay for a single indiscretion? Is she a tragically pathetic figure or a comically shrew-tongued termagant? Byron, it seems, can have it several ways at once, as he does also (though in different wise and reconciling other extremes) with Haidée, the island goddess who is also Juan's mistress, mother, and nurse, attended by the earthy figure of Zoe. There is also the richly ambiguous Lambro, at once an affectionately comic parody of the Byronic hero and the unwitting agent of tragedy, who sheds his own ambiguous light over the entire episode. Byron, of course, was quite aware of the romantic character of the Haidée episode, and so repeatedly qualified and enriched its tone with heterogeneous materials, creating an atmosphere of lyrical tenderness, but at the same time intellectually awake to the physical actualities. In the final tragedy he asserts the validity of the romantic vision, but he is aware too (as the violent shift in tone at IV, 74, indicates) that life must go on, as dangerous, as ludicrous, or as humiliating as ever, despite tragedy or the death of romance. Thus Byron was able to explore fully the experience of ideal, romantic love without ever forcing his romanticism. Although he bases the dream squarely on a physical foundation, supporting and guarding the lyrical motif with numerous discordant elements, his is not in any sense the self-contradictory attitude of romantic irony. The romance is not canceled out but intensified.

Byron's treatment of Gulbeyaz offers an instructive contrast to that of Haidée and illustrates how skillfully he can qualify and develop a tone which is basically comic. The Sultana, who loses the game of love by reason of the very device which made it possible for her to win, Juan's disguise, is the woman comically scorned by Juan in petticoats. But she is at the same time genuinely pathetic in her frustrated tears, which turn, note, metaphysically and murderously, into a tempest that nearly drowns Juan finally, sewed up in a sack. (Byron develops a tear-tempest figure over several stanzas, V, 135-37.)

In the portrait of Adeline, however, neither predominantly romantic as Haidée nor comic as Gulbeyaz, but present for purposes of pure satire, Byron uses ironic qualification with perhaps even greater skill. Here his chief concern was social satire, focusing on English hypocrisy, and Adeline, clearly, was to be one of its chief exponents. We see her entertaining her country guests in a bid for their votes, then ridiculing them when they have left. We see her indeed as acquiescent hostess to all the hypocrisy and pretense assembled at Norman Abbey; and we see her inevitably deceiving herself, with the subtle deceit of an ill-understood friendship for Juan. But in ironic qualification of all this deception, she has most of the solid virtues and all the charm of the polished society which she reflects and symbolizes at its best. And, paradoxically, it is this very quality of polished smoothness which gives rise, simultaneously, to Byron's satire and to his sympathetic approval. The coldly polished manners of these frozen Englishmen, with their philosophy of *nil admirari*, reduce them to a comically bored, colorless sameness; but it is the same quality of self-discipline which accounts for the achievements and virtues of Adeline, making her a perfectly gracious hostess, a musician, and a poetess, able to admire Pope without being a bluestocking. Despite the effort required and the vacancy in her heart, she can love her lord, nevertheless, 'conjugal, but cold.' And although she is falling in love with Juan, she refuses to admit it even to herself. But such restraint and self-discipline, Byron knew, is won at the price of bottling up and suppressing the emotions beneath a layer of ice, thus doubly distilling them and ironically intensifying their explosive qualities, enabling them the more effectively to break down the cold and icy walls of polished restraint (XIII, 36-39). Even Adeline's hypocrisy with her country guests arises out of a kind of sincerity, her *mobilité*. Thus recognizing the complex origins of hypocritical social conduct at the very time that he is attacking hypocrisy, achieving a triumph of mixed tone, Byron can acknowledge the attractiveness of Adeline, one of his most subtle projections of the appearance-versus-reality theme. He elevates her to something like a symbol of one aspect of the English character, and allows her, 'the fair most fatal Juan ever met,' his richly endowed and highly ambiguous 'Dian of the Ephesians' (XIV, 46), to merge finally, with his other goddesses of love, into the complex and all-embracing figure of 'Alma Venus Genetrix' (XVI, 109).

Don Juan does therefore show a significant thematic unity. Its most significant structure is a considered organization of attitudes expressed by means of a rich variety of ironically qualified tones, and each of the chief narrative episodes bears an organic relation, clear but subtly varied, to the larger theme. There remains to be considered the instrument which Byron forged to render it, 'style' in the limited sense.

IV

It is surely one of the monstrous ironies of our time, the present critical Age of Irony and Ambiguity, the Period of the Poetic Paradox, that Byron, the master of these, should have been so neglected by the new critics. For *Don Juan* shows remarkably detailed affinities (excepting one important quality) with the recent poetry of our century and with the "respectable" forebears which its critics point to with pride. One might easily show, for example, how consistently *Don Juan* meets the tests of 'modernity' formulated and applied by Selden Rodman as a guide in selecting poems for his *New Anthology of Modern Poetry* (1946):

> imagery patterned increasingly on everyday speech
> absence of inversions, stilted apostrophes, conventional end-rhymes, 'poetic' language generally . . .
> freedom from the ordinary logic of sequence, jumping from one image to the next by 'association' [evident in the digressions of *Don Juan*] . . .
> emphasis on the ordinary, in reaction against the traditional poetic emphasis on the cosmic . . .
> concern with the common man, almost to the exclusion of the 'hero' or extraordinary man [see *Don Juan*, I, i]
> concern . . . with the social order as against 'heaven' and 'nature'

Or consider the point by point correspondence between the commonly recognized qualities of Byron's 'medley' style and those described in the following discussion from C. Day Lewis' *A Hope for Poetry*:

> Both Eliot and Edmund Wilson have called attention to the kinship between the French Symbolists and the English metaphysicals. Wilson outlines the similarities: 'The medley of images; the deliberately mixed metaphors; the combination of passion and wit—of the grand and the prosaic manners; the bold amalgamation of material with spiritual.' And again, speaking of Corbière's poetry, he calls it 'a poetry of the outcast: often colloquial and homely, yet with a rhetoric of fantastic slang; often with the manner of slapdash doggerel, yet sure of its own morose artistic effects.' Exclude the word 'morose,' and the passage gives an exact description of Auden's work. That combination 'of the grand and the prosaic manners,' a constant alternation of the magniloquent and the colloquial, is a quality shared by Donne, Wilfred Owen and Auden . . . .

Or, one might add, by Byron.

This 'constant alternation of lyricism and flatness . . . , the salient characteristic of post-war technique' (making deliberate use of slang, prosaic words, commonplace images, and bathos to produce verse of an 'uneven, conversational surface'), Day Lewis traces to the 'emotional complexity to which the modern poet is so often subject.' Byron again might have been mentioned, for the trait is fundamental in him. Rooted in his essentially modern sensibility, it made sustained lyrical writing and absolute purity of tone as difficult for him as they now are for many of his poetic descendants. It has now become a critical cliché that Auden shows important similarities to Byron (Auden's long 'Letter to Lord Byron' made the comparison inevitable; Byron's continuing influence is evident in *Nones*). Yvor Winters, however, significantly unsympathetic with much in contemporary poetry, is the only critic, I believe, who has ever suggested, and he briefly and unflatteringly, that Byron stands at the head of that long line of masters of the double mood and the conversational-ironic manner which comes down through Laforgue, Pound, and Eliot to the most recent poetaster of ironic discord. It is a significant and little-known fact, too, that Byron was one of the favorite poets of Joyce.[1]

Why, then, the pronounced critical disfavor from a quarter which so obviously might offer its homage? The new critics have insisted rightly enough on the importance of a richly qualified tone, on the complexity and comprehensiveness which may result in a poetry of synthesis or inclusion, invulnerable itself to irony because incorporating the principle of irony within itself and avoiding oversimplification and sentimentality by uniting or reconciling impulses ordinarily opposed. With all this Byron would have been in sympathy. Like many of the poets in present favor, he frequently juxtaposed discordant elements in a deliberate effort to crash through the cant of his day ('the mart / For what is sometimes called poetic diction, / And that outrageous appetite for lies'), awaken his etherized reader, and shock him out of his complacency into some new perception or fresh insight. But the new critics, in large number, have gone on to insist that the chief or sole instrument of the irony must be the metaphor or simile and that the synthesis must take place within the single image, which, as Pound's influential definition noted, will present 'an intellectual and emotional complex in an *instant* of time' (italics mine). Thus Eliot writes: 'We have come to expect poetry to be something very concentrated, something distilled; but if Byron had distilled his verse, there would have been nothing whatever left.' It becomes a matter of some importance, therefore, to inquire into the spatial limits of the area of fusion. How great an area may be allowed, how small a one is actually demanded before the fusion or reconciliation is achieved successfully, before it will produce, in Pound's words, 'that sense of sudden liberation; that sense of freedom from time limits and space limits; that sense of sudden growth, which we experience in the presence of the greatest works of art'? Byron's successful practice, attested for over a century by critic and general reader alike, although in the present terms unanalyzed, would seem to offer an answer. For Byron's peculiar distinction was to achieve a style which, within the self-imposed limits of a conversational metric and manner, could not only express the author's many-sided awareness of the world, in all its immense complexity, but also speak clearly to the common reader. Byron successfully reconciles within his verse quite discordant elements, yet does so without excessive verbal density or compression and the consequent obscurity, without forcing the image to bear an unbearable weight of meaning, which in fact many a modern poem buckles beneath. He achieved, in other words, almost all the virtues of ambiguity and comprehensiveness which may accompany a poetry of synthesis (proving himself, incidentally, to possess 'a mechanism of sensibility which could devour any kind of experience,' as Eliot said of the metaphysicals), yet achieved them without benefit of the metaphysical image and certainly without screwing up the tension of the poem to a painful degree. The careless ease of *Don Juan,* often remarked, is the necessary counterweight or safety valve to the audacity of the ironic juxtapositions and is the mark of the balanced point of view, recently enshrined by the new critics, and of the poetic voice under easy control (and *in* control of its materials), explosive as its effects typically are. In short, the comprehensiveness of vision, chief justification of the metaphysical image, is achieved without the use of violently compressed or telescoped imagery and without sacrificing the sense of wholeness, the clear subordination of imagistic detail, itself a form of reconciliation, to theme and larger purpose.

It is important to remember, furthermore, that Byron's compositional unit is not the single line or succinctly phrased image, but the stanza, within which he frequently brings together the same elements of ironic incongruity so much in present favor. It may be objected, perhaps, that so to assemble them is to dilute them or relieve them of their electrifying tension. But, obviously, the typical stanza does possess its charge, characteristically an ironic demolition which produces its own shock and has its own characteristic voltage, much more appropriate to the long conversational poem than the image of high intellectual tension which may be well enough suited to the typical short poem of our day. Indeed, prevailing taste and present critical theory are often inimical to and inadequately prepared to deal with the long poem of conversational tone. The critical tools are still to be developed, or rediscovered. Over-intensity, of course, would have paralyzed Byron's satiric purpose, impeded the flow of his thought, and been incongruous within his conversational manner. When his imagery functions ironically to qualify an idea or thrust it under a clear comic light, the irony is under conscious *control*, and the imagery is necessarily so ordered as to cut off any associations, ironical extensions, or ambiguities except those deliberately sought. His imagery is usually thinner, less allusive, with a slighter degree of intensity or extension, and without the depth or density of much twentieth-century verse. It nonetheless accomplishes its purpose perfectly and does so, in its larger context, without oversimplifying.

It is not characteristic of *Don Juan*, of course, to see a world in a grain of sand, an infinity of suggestiveness in the particular image or symbol extending to embrace simultaneously several different levels of thought, to end with a fusion, or blurring, of the actual and the ideal. Such a use of the image would frequently have produced a fundamental contradiction in the very purpose of the poem, which rests on the clear difference between appearance and reality and makes that difference its main theme, the principle of its stanzaic structure (typically a microcosm and image of the whole poem), and the *raison d'être* for its ironic manner. Thus Byron often refrained from reconciling discordant elements even within the single stanza (achieving unity within a larger structure of attitudes), choosing instead to use the image to illustrate or qualify the idea, linking image and idea, not divorcing them in an effort to make the image substitute for the idea. The method, to be sure, is that of Pope, whom Auden calls his master; and, as Louis MacNeice has pointed out, it is also the method of ordinary conversation, which uses images 'to drive home a meaning, to make a point, to *outline* a picture (for an outline is distinct from a suggestion).' But the method is not that which uses imagery as mere decoration.

It is perhaps finally a matter of congruity. Byron's satiric purpose was first to portray his world, still disconcertingly ours, as he saw it in all its complexity and then to attack the element of pretense or deception in it. Seriously concerned with this larger purpose, he knew that to give undue regard to the parts, fusing imagery at white (and unapproachable) heat, spotting little island nodes of 'pure' poetry in the great ebb and flow of his conversational epic, would detract attention from his main theme, obscure his meaning, and magnify the subordinate elements of imagery out of their proper focus. So Byron used the humorous figure, the extended or multiple simile, the conversational metaphor, accumulating images instead of compressing them, much as certain neoclassical poets did: to draw the mind back a little from the main action or idea, place it in clearer focus, qualify, and so light it up in proper perspective, 'to show things really as they are.' To illustrate more specifically, we can see him using imagery drawn from classical mythology in order to suggest the godlike eternity in time at the otherwise very human heart of his heroines and so indicate the element of strangeness at the center of the physical or the sexual, and the mystery at the heart of the comedy of love (V, 96; XVI, 49, 109). Conversely, he can use simple, almost commonplace garden imagery to establish a tone of lyric tenderness and suggest the fragility and transience of his heroines (VI, 65), or, as with Dudù, to suggest natural innocence in the midst of artificiality (VI, 53). He can describe the sea in Canto II in terms of the treacherously human and so personalize a great and otherwise impersonal natural force (42, 49), pointing by the same means at the human causes contributing to the tragedy and at the mistaken pantheistic creed of some of his contemporaries (34, 52). In the midst of a satiric attack on hypocritical social convention he can use traditional imagery of various kinds, frequently drawing upon ancient or modern history, and so suggest that although a rebel, even a 'revolutionary' reformer, he is not a man adrift in time, cut off from a sterile and meaningless past, but one who values the continuity of the great traditions, desiring not their destruction but their modification (XII, 78; XIII, 11). Byron had not heard that a poem must be disjointed if it is adequately to express an age out of joint, but he can, nevertheless, ironically juxtapose images suggestive of both classical and nineteenth-century civilization and so give to the satire of the contemporary scene increased depth, order, and perspective (IV, 75–79; XI, 7). Or he can use imagery drawn from his personal life and so leaven the 'objective' narrative of Juan, the public myth of himself allowing him to use imagery which is personal but seldom private or cryptic. We see him using deliberately discordant images to qualify the tragedy of the shipwreck episode (II, 92), the romance of the Haidée episode, or the comedy of the harem scene (V, 92), thus establishing a state of tension between image and dramatic situation. He can explore a figure at length in order to set forth the ambiguities in such a character as Adeline's (XIII, 36–38) or the subconscious urges of Dudù (VI, 75–77), accumulate figures as an aid to securing suspense (I, 102–4), or use an image for purposes of greater concentration or precision. He is master of the purely derogatory image (III, 94–95), but he can also use imagery playfully so as to avoid confusing the satirical and the hysterical tones, referring to the lust of Catherine, for example, as follows:

> She could repay each amatory look you lent
> > With interest, and in turn was wont with rigour
> To exact of Cupid's bills the full amount
> At sight, nor would permit you to discount.

On the other hand, he is quite able to use imagery which allows a mingling of the approbative and the satirical attitudes and permits him to disassociate himself from both parties, as in the famous Daniel Boone stanzas (VIII, 60–67).

The style of *Don Juan* thus provides an answer to several problems which still confront the modern poet: offering first of all a means of accommodation within a single form, without oversimplification and yet without obscurity, of a wealth of material drawn from all levels of existence. It is a style which has solved the problem of communication, and solved it moreover, in important part, even by means of a number of devices needlessly out of present favor and lacking which poetry is the poorer—such devices or modes as narrative, comedy, rhetoric, and invective, which allowed Byron not only to speak out in full voice or whisper subtly and devastatingly but also to canvass the whole range of tones between. A completely uninhibited style, flexible beyond anything before it, it is able at once to give the impression of dramatic conversation, using rhythms close to the movement of modern speech, and also to allow the nearly complete lyric, humorous, or meditative expression of the whole man behind it. To paraphrase Eliot's recent appeal for a new poetic drama, it is a style which not having lost touch with colloquial speech can bring poetry into the world in which the reader lives and to which he returns when he puts down his book. By means of it, Byron was able to explore many levels of his personal experience and complex sensibility, giving full expression to his own personality, but able, in addition, always to place the personal reference or image in perspective, inserting flat, colloquial statements, deliberately banal or flashy, and so to achieve not only a release from the merely personal but also a simultaneous extension of his field of reference.

All this he achieved, furthermore, without ever sacrificing common humanity or passion or attempting to purify his poetry of its human associations. He would not have understood the current neoformalism, nor sympathized much with it if he had. If we may believe Louise Bogan, writing in *The New Yorker* (June 9, 1951), 'Glances at life, as a matter of fact, are now thought to be vulgar and naive, and emotion becomes increasingly suspect as problems of surface texture receive primary emphasis.' Now Byron had as much reason as any man to suspect emotion, but he did not therefore squeeze it out of his poetry. What we receive finally from *Don Juan* is the many-faceted image of Byron himself, looking freely and with intelligent interest *outward* on the human situation as he saw it and remembering always that the first concern of any writer is to entertain, to make his work interesting. He was quite incapable of that cold vanity which leads a poet, having convinced himself that 'the question of communication, of what the reader will get from it, is not paramount,' to sing for himself alone; and the example of Byron's vigorous satire, necessarily looking outward, but never neglecting the inner man, could be a healthy counterinfluence upon the inward lookers and private singers of our day, as well as upon those who so scrupulously erase the living author in order to build a 'flawless' structure. The felt and serious present need for the return of intelligible personality to poetry is well illustrated by the recent work of the English neo-Romantics.

The peculiar appropriateness, for our time, of a flexible style such as that of *Don Juan*, with its strong colloquial element, may be indicated in the words of C. Day Lewis, although he gave only passing reference to Byron. Concluding a lecture delivered in 1947 in praise of *The Colloquial Element in English Poetry*, exemplified by certain poems of Donne, Browning, Hardy, Frost, and MacNeice, he said,

> There is a time for pure poetry, and a place for the undiluted grand manner, but I doubt if they are here and now, when the press of events, the crowding novelties, the so rapidly changing features of the world in which we live seem to demand of the poet that he should more than ever be responsive, fluid, adaptable; that his utterance should be human rather than hierophantic; that he should study to make his technique as supple and elastic as he may, to mould it to the intricate contours of modern experience.

The example of *Don Juan*, finally, may well provide another service, less purely stylistic, to modern poetry: teach it how to put irony, neither self-defeating, static, sterile, nor depressive of the will to action, back into the service of propaganda, that the main stream of poetry may become again a poetry of action, helping man to take confidence again in himself and his society without being at all blinded to the defects or limitations of either. *Don Juan* offers an example of a poetry which allows an indignant exposure of the world's folly and the hypocritical deceptiveness of man, whose failure to see or act upon the difference between appearance and reality is at once comic and tragic. But it is also a poetry which is of the world and free of despair, avoiding the extreme position of the congenital disillusioned idealist. It counsels man to live in his world and be reconciled with it, if only the more effectively to correct it. It is a poetry of satirical attack upon the world which is at the same time, miraculously, a poetry of acceptance, not rejection. It is a poetry of clear present use.

NOTES

1. See also the tributes paid to *Don Juan* by Yeats, writing to H. J. C. Grierson, February 21, 1926 *(Letters of W. B. Yeats)*, and by Virginia Woolf in her *Diary*, August 8, 1918. Yeats wrote, 'I am particularly indebted to you for your essay on Byron [in *The Background of English Literature*]. My own verse has more and more adopted . . . the syntax and vocabulary of common personal speech. The passages you quote [which included *Don Juan*, II, 177, 181, 183-85, 188] are perfect personal speech. The overchildish or over pretty or feminine element in some good Wordsworth and in much poetry up to our date comes from the lack of natural momentum in the syntax.' Yeats concluded that Byron was 'the one great English poet' who constantly sought this quality, although he did not always achieve it.

Virginia Woolf saw in the style of Byron's poem 'a method [which] is a discovery by itself. It's what one has looked for in vain—an elastic shape which will hold whatever you choose to put into it. Thus he could write out his mood as it came to him; he could say whatever came into his head. He wasn't committed to be poetical; and thus escaped his evil genius of the false romantic and imaginative. When he is serious he is sincere: and he can impinge upon any subject he likes. He writes 16 cantos without once flogging his flanks. He had, evidently, the able witty mind of what my father Sir Leslie would have called a thoroughly masculine nature. . . . Still, it doesn't seem an easy example to follow; and indeed like all free and easy things, only the skilled and mature really bring them off successfully. But Byron was full of ideas—a quality that gives his verse a toughness and drives me to little excursions over the surrounding landscape or room in the middle of my reading.'

For W. H. Auden's most recent comments on *Don Juan*, see *The New Yorker*, XXXIV (April 26, 1958), 133-150, and *The Listener*, LIX (May 22, 1958), 876. The latter is an account of Auden's lecture given at Oxford on May 12, 1958, and later broadcast by BBC.

C. S. LEWIS

Shelley, Dryden, and Mr. Eliot

FEW poets have suffered more than Shelley from the modern dislike of
the Romantics. It is natural that this should be so. His poetry is, to an
unusual degree, entangled in political thought, and in a kind of political
thought now generally unpopular. His belief in the natural perfectibility
of man justly strikes the Christian reader as foolishness; while, on the
other hand, the sort of perfection he has in view is too ideal for dialectical materialists. His writings are too generous for our cynics; his life is
too loose for our 'humanist' censors. Almost every recent movement of
thought in one way or another serves to discredit him. From some points
of view, this reaction cannot be regarded as wholly unfortunate. There
is much in Shelley's poetry that has been praised to excess; much even
that deserves no praise at all. In his metre, with all its sweetness, there
is much ignoble fluidity, much of mere jingle. His use of language is
such that he seldom attains for long to the highest qualities of distinction, and often sinks to a facility and commonplace almost Byronic.
He is not a *safe* poet; you cannot open his works to refute one of his
enemies with any sense of confidence. But reaction must not be allowed
to carry us too far; and when Mr. Eliot offers up Shelley as a sacrifice to
the fame of Dryden it is time to call a halt. To be sure, Mr. Eliot has
his own purpose in that comparison: he is combating the view of the
last century that Shelley must necessarily be a greater poet than Dryden
because his subjects are more obviously poetical—because the one
writes lyrics and the other satire, because one is in the coffee-house
and the other in the clouds.[1] But we must not fall over, like Luther's
drunk man, one the other side of the horse. Those who prefer Shelley

From *Rehabilitations and Other Essays* (Oxford University Press, 1939),
pp. 3-34.

to Dryden need not do so on the grounds which Mr. Eliot has envisaged; and to prove this I will now maintain that Shelley is to be regarded, on grounds which Mr. Eliot himself will allow, as a more masterly, a more sufficient, and indeed a more *classical* poet than Dryden.

The days are, or ought to be, long past in which any well-informed critic could take the couplet poets of our 'Augustan' school at their own valuation as 'classical' writers. This would be quite as grave an error as the romantic criticism which denied them to be men of genius. They are neither bad poets nor classical poets. Their merits are great, but neither their merits nor their limitations are those of ancient literature or of that modern literature which is truly classical. It would be hard to find any excellence in writing less classical than wit; yet it is in wit that these poets admittedly excel. The very forms in which the greatest and most characteristic of classical poetry is cast—the epic and the tragedy—are the forms which they attempt with least success. Their favourite form is Satire, a form not invented by the Greeks, and even in Roman hands not very like *MacFleknoe* or the *Dunciad*. But it is needless to labour the point. To any one who still thinks Pope a classical poet we can only say 'Open your Sophocles, your Virgil, your Racine, your Milton'; and if that experiment does not convince him, we may safely dismiss him for a blockhead.

Of the school in general, then, we may say that it is a good, unclassical school. But when we turn to Dryden, we must, I think, say more than this. We must admit that we have here a great, flawed poet, in whom the flaws, besides being characteristically unclassical, are scarcely forgivable even by the most romantic or revolutionary standards.

I have said 'a great, flawed poet.' Of the greatness I wish to make no question; and it is a greatness to which the name of *genius* is peculiarly applicable. The most abiding impression which Dryden makes upon us is that of exuberant power. He is what Middle English critics would have called 'boisteous.' He excels in beginnings. 'A milk white hind immortal and unchanged'—'In pious times ere priestcraft did begin'—there is no fumbling at the exordium. He leaps into his first paragraph as an athlete leaps into the hundred yards' track, and before the fascination of his ringing couplets gives us leisure to take breath we have been carried into the heart of his matter. The famous 'magnanimity' of his satire is another aspect of this same quality of power. His strength is so great that he never needs—or never gives us the impression of needing—to use it all. He is justly praised by Mr. Eliot for 'what he has made of his material,' for his 'ability to make the small into the great, the

248

prosaic into the poetic':[2] not that the value of a literary result is in a direct ratio to its difficulty—a theory with absurd consequences—but that the sheer strength of the poet is more easily judged when it is thus isolated. Of this transforming power I know no better example than the résumé of the political situation which opens *Absalom and Achitophel*. Not only is the prosaic made poetical, but the obscure and complicated is made clear and simple. A child can hardly fail to understand the state of Israel as Dryden describes it; and yet surprisingly little of that situation, as Dryden saw it, has been omitted. If anything is misrepresented, the misrepresentation is deliberate.

Mr. Eliot himself selects, to illustrate this transforming power, a passage from *Alexander's Feast* and another from *Cymon and Iphigenia*. The first is that in which the tipsy Alexander 'Fought all his battles o'er again; And thrice he routed all his foes, and thrice he slew the slain.' Certainly, if the thing was to be done at all, this is the way to do it. The sudden irruption of the country-dancing fourteener among the nobler, if never very subtle, rhythms of the ode, most happily expresses the transition from heroics to a tavern scene. Dryden has brought off his effect—and it is an effect which will be dear to all who hate the heroic and cannot see any civil or religious ceremony without wishing that some one may slip. For a critic like Mr. Eliot, however, the question must surely be not only whether a given effect has been attained, but also whether, and why, it ought to have been attempted. Certain classicists would resent the intrusion of the comic into the greater ode at all, as an offence against decorum. I am sure that Mr. Eliot remembers, and almost sure he approves, the delicious reproaches levelled against Racine by French critics for venturing within the remotest hailing distance of comedy in certain scenes of *Andromaque*; and the greater ode is as lofty a form as tragedy. But even if we allow the comic note, can we excuse comedy of quite this hackneyed and heavy-handed type? That Alexander in his cups should resemble exactly the first drunken braggart whom you may meet in a railway refreshment room, appears to Mr. Eliot to add 'a delicate flavour.'[3] But what is there delicate about it? Indelicacy, in the sense of grossness and crudity of apprehension, ἀγροικία, is surely the very essence of it. It does not seem to have crossed Dryden's mind that when Alexander got drunk he may have behaved like a drunk gentleman or a drunk scholar and not like an 'old soldier.' No: this is not a subtle or delicate joke. If it is to be defended at all, it must be defended as a 'good plain joke.' As such, Mr. Eliot apparently likes it, and I do not: and this is of very little consequence. What is important is that the passage raises in our minds a rather disturbing doubt about Dryden's poetical purity of intention. The joke may be good or bad in itself. Let us suppose that it is good;— the question remains whether even a good joke, of this tavern type, really contributes to the total effect of the ode. Does Dryden really care whether it contributes or not? Is he, in fine, a man ready, for every ray of accidental beauty that may come in his way, to sacrifice the integrity of his work—a dabbler in 'good passages'—a man who can produce good poetry but not good poems?

As regards *Alexander's Feast* I am content to leave the question open: when once it has been raised we shall have no difficulty in answering it for the rest of Dryden's more considerable works. What do we enjoy in *Absalom and Achitophel*? Undoubtedly, the incidental merits. Of the poem taken as a whole, as a ποίημα, Johnson has said the last word.

> 'There is an unpleasing disproportion between the beginning and the end. We are alarmed by a faction formed of many sects, various in their principles, but agreeing in their purpose of mischief, formidable for their numbers, and strong by their supports; while the King's friends are few and weak. The chiefs on either part are set forth to view: but when expectation is at the height, the King makes a speech, and
> Henceforth a series of new times began.'

No doubt, the very nature of the case compelled Dryden to this fault; but that excuses the man without mending the poem. I do not argue *why* the work is botched, but *that* it is. It is even part of my case that the defect in *Absalom* was unavoidable. It is a radical defect, consubstantial with Dryden's original conception. It is no mere accident. The work is not merely maimed, it is diseased at the heart. Like many human invalids, it is not lacking in charms and happy moments; but classicists like Mr. Eliot (and myself) should not accept any amount of littered poetry as a poem. If we turn to *The Hind and the Panther* we find the same irredeemable defect in an aggravated form. Of course it is full of 'good things'; but of the plan itself, the nerve and structure of the poem, what are we to say if not that the very design of conducting in verse a theological controversy allegorized as a beast fable suggests in the author a state of mind bordering on aesthetic insanity? If the poet had succeeded it would indeed provide a noble example of the transforming power which Mr. Eliot claims for him. But he has not. *The Hind and the Panther* does not exist, as *Phèdre* or *Persuasion* or *The Alchemist* exist. It is not a poem: it is simply a name which we give for convenience to a number of pieces of good description, vigorous satire, and 'popular' controversy, which have all been yoked together by external violence.

It may be objected that I am selecting poems merely occasional, specimens at least of 'applied' poetry, which cannot fairly be judged by the highest standards. But this is dangerous argument for the defenders of Dryden. The two poems I have quoted are among his most considerable works: they contain much of his noblest, and much of his most piquant, poetry. If these have to be thrown to the wolves as mere applied poetry for which special indulgence is sued, it will be hard, on what remains, to support the plea that Dryden is a poet comparable to Shelley. But I pass over this difficulty. Let us turn to work more purely 'poetical,' and specially to the *Fables* which no one asked him to write. Here, if anywhere, we may hope to find the real 'maker' at last instead of the mere fountain of brilliant 'passages.' Here, perhaps, Dryden will become the master, not the slave, of inspiration.

It falls out very happily that Mr. Eliot should have chosen from one of these fables a passage in illustration of the 'transforming power.' It is the satire on the militia in *Cymon and Iphigenia.*

> The country rings around with loud alarms,
> And raw in fields the rude militia swarms, &c.

Of this, Mr. Eliot observes 'the comic is the material, the result is poetry.'[4] Yes, but comic poetry. The passage, if not so lustily comic as the picture of Alexander's tipsy valour, is a humorous passage; and I do not know why it shows more power to make comic poetry of comic material than to make idyllic poetry of idyllic material. Yet it shows power enough, and I will not press the point; but I cannot help wondering that Mr. Eliot should think it worth while to quote this amusing description (a 'beauty' surely not very recondite), and yet not worth while to tell us why it should be in *Cymon and Iphigenia* at all. To what artistic end, precisely, is this satire on militias inserted in a romantic fable? I am afraid it is there only because Dryden wanted to write it. Doubtless, the fault is here much more venial than in *Alexander's Feast.* The joke itself is less hackneyed, and the lower tone of the fable admits a laxer kind of relevance than the ode. Perhaps, justified as an 'episode' the lines are excusable: and if, in this place, Dryden 'will have his joke,' have it he shall, for me. But there is worse behind. In *Sigismonda and Guiscardo* Dryden reveals so much of himself that I question whether any one who has read it with attention can fail to see, once and for all, the *alte terminus haerens* which divides Dryden from the class of great poets. Here he sets out to tell a tragic and 'heroic' story. It is not a story of the highest order. It suffers from that overstrain and tendency to falsetto which is the infallible mark of the prosaic mind desperately determined to be 'poetical.' You could not make an *Oedipus* or a *Lear* out of it; you might make a *Cid*. But it is, at least, a story worth telling. And now mark what Dryden does with it. He does not intend to forgo a single thrill of the tragic ending. He intends to purge our emotions. We are to see the heroine 'devoutly glue' her lips to the heart of her murdered husband, and our respect is to be demanded for her 'Mute solemn sorrow without female noise.' That is the note on which the poem is to end. And yet, with such an end in view, this old poet goes out of his way to insert at the beginning of his story a ribald picture of his heroine as the lascivious widow of conventional comedy. I will not quote the pitiful lines in which Dryden winks and titters to his readers over these time-honoured salacities. The reader may turn to the passage for himself. And when he has read on to the bitter end of it, to that couplet where even Dryden's skill in language deserts him and we sink to the scribbled meanness of

> On either side the kisses flew so thick
> That neither she nor he had breath to speak,

then let him remind himself that all this is the beginning of a tragic story, and that Dryden will presently try to make sublime this same woman whom he is here turning into a Widow Wadman. For such sin against the essential principles of all poetry whatever, no excuse can be made. It cannot be accident. Dryden is the most conscious of writers: he knows well what he is doing. He destroys, and is content to destroy, the kind of poem he sat down to write, if only he can win in return one guffaw from the youngest and most graceless of his audience. There is in this a poetic blasphemy, an arrogant contempt for his own art, which cannot, I think, be paralleled in any other great writer.

It would show a serious misunderstanding if Dryden's partisans pleaded at this point that I was enslaved to some Victorian canon of solemnity as the essence of poetry and judging Dryden by an alien standard. I have no quarrel with comic or cynical or even ribald poetry. I have no quarrel with Wycherley, I admire Congreve, I delight in Prior and still more in *Don Juan*. I delight in Dryden himself when he is content to talk bawdy in season and consider 'Sylvia the fair in the bloom of fifteen' a very pretty piece. But in these fables—as also in the heroic tragedies which are similarly blemished—it is Dryden, not I, who has chosen that the heroic should be trumps, and has lost the game by rules of his own choosing. It was Dryden, not I, who decided to write *Annus Mirabilis* as a serious and lofty historical poem on what he regarded as the 'successes of a most just and necessary war.' If, after that decision, he describes the enemy as

> Vast bulks which little souls but ill supply,

then we have every right to tell that a nation of reasonable men, not to say men of courage and honour, are very ill-celebrated by the insinuation that their enemies are lubbers. This kind of thing runs through all Dryden's attempts at the graver and more enthusiastic kinds of poetry, and it must be remembered that such attempts make up a large part of his work. The sin is so flagrant that I cannot understand how so cultivated a critic as Mr. Eliot has failed to see the truth; which truth had now better be stated quite frankly. Dryden fails to be a satisfactory poet because being rather a boor, a gross, vulgar, provincial, misunderstanding mind, he yet constantly attempts those kinds of poetry which demand the *cuor gentil*. Like so many men of that age he is deeply influenced by the genuinely aristocratic and heroic poetry of France. He admires the world of the French tragedians—that exalted tableland where rhetoric and honour grow naturally out of the life lived and the culture inherited. We in England had had an aristocratic tradition of our own, to be sure; a tradition at once more sober and more tenderly romantic than the French, obeying a code of honour less dissociated from piety. The Duke and Duchess of Newcastle were perhaps its last exponents. But Dryden seems to know nothing of it. He and his audiences look to Versailles, and feel for it that pathetic yet unprofitable yearning which vulgarity so often feels for unattainable graces. But the yearning does not teach them the secret. Where their model was brilliant they are flashy; where the *Cid* was brave, Almansor swaggers; refinements of amorous casuistry out of the heroic romances are aped by the loves of grooms and chambermaids. One is reminded of a modern oriental, who may have the blood of old paynim knighthoods in him, but who prefers to dress himself up as a cheap imitation of a European gentleman.

The worst thing about such challenging praise as Mr. Eliot offers Dryden—praise, I believe, with which Dryden would be seriously embarrassed—is that it forces the rest of us to remember Dryden's faults. I have dealt with them, as I see them, plainly, not maliciously. The man is irremediably ignorant of that world he chooses so often to write about. When he confines himself to satire, he is at home; but even here, the fatal lack of architectonic power seldom allows him to make a satisfactory poem. That is the case against Dryden. It would have been pleasanter to state the case for him—to analyse, in order to praise, the masculine vigour of his English, the fine breezy, sunshiny weather of the man's mind at its best—his poetical health; the sweetness (unsurpassed in its own way) of nearly all his versification. But we cannot allow him to be used, and so used, as a stick to beat Shelley.

I have now to show that Shelley, with all his faults of execution, is a poet who must rank higher than Dryden with any critic who claims to be classical; that he is superior to Dryden by the greatness of his subjects and his moral elevation (which are merits by classical standards), and also by the unity of his actions, his architectonic power, and his general observance of *decorum* in the Renaissance sense of the word; that is, his disciplined production not just of poetry but of the poetry in each case proper to the theme and the species of composition. But it is hardly possible in the present age to approach these questions without first removing some popular prejudices.

In the first place there is the prejudice which leads many people to mutter the word 'Godwin' as soon as Shelley is mentioned. They are quite sure that Godwin wrote a very silly book; they are quite sure that the philosophic content of much Shelleyan poetry is Godwinian; and they conclude that the poetry must be silly too. Their first premiss I cannot discuss, since a regrettable gap in my education has left me still the only critic in England who has not that familiar knowledge of *Political Justice* which alone can justify confident adverse criticism. But the second I can.[5] It is quite clear to any reader of general education—it must be clear, for example, to Mr. Eliot—that the influence of Dante and Plato is at least as dominant in Shelleys' thought as that of Godwin—unless, indeed, Godwin shared the opinions of Dante and Plato, in which case Godwin cannot have been so very silly. Thus, I do not know what Godwin says about free love; but I see that the passage in *Epipsychidion* beginning

True love in this differs from gold and clay

may well derive from *Purgatorio* xv. 49, and thus ultimately from Aristotle's *Ethics* 1169 A. I do not myself agree with Shelley's application of the doctrine to sexual promiscuity; but then Plato, and many communists, would, and neither Shelley nor Godwin need be made the scapegoat. Thus again, in *Prometheus Unbound* I see that the main theme—the myth of a universal rebirth, a restoration of all things—is one which may occur in any age and which falls naturally into place beside Isaiah or the Fourth Eclogue, and that to pin it down to Godwin is a provincialism. Something it may owe to Godwin; but its debts to Aeschylus and, as Mr. Tillyard has shown, to Plato's *Politicus* are at least equally interesting. If Shelley were an ignoramus who had read no book but *Political Justice,* or a dullard who could invent nothing, we might be driven to suppose that his Asia was merely a personification of Godwinian benevolence; but when we know that he had read of divine love and beauty in Plato and remember that he wrote the *Hymn to Intellectual Beauty,* the identification becomes merely perverse. And finally, whatever Godwin may really have said, one of the chief tenets attributed to him is explicitly rejected at the end of Act III. Let us hear no more of Godwin.[6]

Another prejudice is harder to combat because it is ill-defined. It usually expresses itself by the damning epithet 'adolescent'; it began with Arnold's phrase about the 'ineffectual angel.' Shelley is supposed to be not merely *seely* in the Elizabethan sense, but *silly* in the modern sense; to believe ludicrously well of the human heart in general, and crudely ill of a few tyrants; to be, in a word, insufficiently disillusioned. Before removing this misunderstanding, I must point out that if it were granted it would not place him below Dryden. Dryden is equally ignorant of the world, though in the opposite direction, as his sorry joke about Alexander would be sufficient to show. Whenever he attempts to be lofty he betrays himself. There are senile and vulgar illusions no less than illusions adolescent and heroical; and of the two, I see no reason for preferring the former. If I must, in either event, be blindfold, why should I choose to have my eyes bandaged with stinking clouts rather than with cloth of gold? The fashion indeed is all for the stinking clouts, and it is easy to see why. Men (and, still more, boys) like to call themselves disillusioned because the very form of the word suggests that they have had the illusions and emerged from them—have tried both worlds. The claim, however, is false in nine cases out of ten. The world is full of impostors who claim to be disenchanted and are really unenchanted: mere 'natural' men who have never risen so high as to be in danger of the generous illusions they claim to have escaped from. Mr. Mencken is the perfect example. We need to be on our guard against such people. They talk like sages who have passed through the half-truths of humanitarian benevolence, aristocratic honour, or romantic passion, while in fact they are clods who have never yet advanced so far. Ἀπειροκαλία is their disease; and Dryden himself is not free from it. He has not escaped from those enchantments which some find in Shelley; he has tried desperately to taste the like, and failed, and the fustian remains in his poetry like a scar on his face. He indeed deserves pity, since he has struggled against the disease, unlike our modern impostors who glory in it and call it health; but this does not alter the conclusion that he cannot be set against Shelley as one who knows against one who is deluded. If we granted the doctrine of Shelley's amiable ignorance of the one half of life, it would still but balance Dryden's banausic ignorance of the other.

But I do not grant the doctrine, and I do not see how it can be accepted by any one who has read Shelley's poetry with attention. It is simply not true to say that Shelley conceives the human soul as a naturally innocent and divinely beautiful creature, interfered with by external tyrants. On the contrary no other heathen writer comes nearer to stating and driving home the doctrine of original sin. In such an early work as *The Revolt of Islam* those who come 'from pouring human blood' are told to

> Disguise it not—we have one human heart—
> All mortal thoughts confess a common home. (viii. xix.)

and again,

> Look on your mind—it is the book of fate—
> Ah! it is dark with many a blazoned name
> Of misery—*all are mirrors of the same.* (xx.)

This is weak, exclamatory poetry, I grant you, but my concern is with the *sentens*. When Shelley looks at and condemns the oppressor he does so with the full consciousness that he also is a man just like that: the evil is within as well as without; all are wicked, and this of course is the significance of the allegorical passage in *Prometheus Unbound*, where the Furies say to Prometheus

> We will live through thee, one by one,
> Like animal life, and though we can obscure not

The soul which burns within, that we will dwell
Beside it, like a vain loud multitude
Vexing the self-content of wisest men:
That we will be dread thought beneath thy brain
And foul desire round thine astonished heart,
And blood within thy labyrinthine veins
Crawling like agony.
Prom.   Why ye are thus now.

The same doctrine, more briefly and suggestively expressed, occurs in the *Triumph of Life,* where he explains the failure of the wise, the great, and the unforgotten by saying

                              their lore
Taught them not this, to know themselves; their might
Could not repress *the mystery within,*
And for the morn of truth they feigned, deep night
Caught them ere evening. (211-15).

We mistake Shelley wholly if we do not understand that for him, as certainly as for St. Paul, humanity in its merely natural or 'given' condition is a body of death. It is true that the conclusion he draws is very different from that of St. Paul. To a Christian, conviction of sin is a good thing because it is the necessary preliminary to repentance; to Shelley it is an extremely dangerous thing. It begets self-contempt, and self-contempt begets misanthropy and cruelty. In *The Revolt of Islam* the passage I have already quoted leads up to the statement that it is this self-contempt which arms Hatred with a 'mortal sting.' The man who has once seen the darkness within himself will soon seek vengeance on others; and in *Prometheus* self-contempt is twice mentioned as an evil. I do not think we can seriously doubt that Shelley is right. If a man will not become a Christian, it is very undesirable that he should become aware of the reptilian inhabitants in his own mind. To know how bad we are, in the condition of mere nature, is an excellent recipe for becoming much worse. The process is very accurately described in some of the most memorable lines Shelley ever wrote:

          'Tis a trick of this same family
          To analyse their own and other minds.
          Such self-anatomy shall teach the will
          Dangerous secrets: for it *tempts our powers,*
          Knowing what must be thought and may be done,

> Into the depth of darkest purposes:
> So Cenci fell into the pit; even I
> Since Beatrice *unveiled me to myself,*
> *And made me shrink from what I cannot shun,*
> *Show a poor figure to my own esteem,*
> *To which I grow half reconciled* . . . .
>
> (Cenci, II. ii. 108 et seq.)

The lines which I have italicized provide an excellent short history of thought and sentiment in the early twentieth century, and the whole passage is a measure of the difference between Byron and Shelley. Byron, speaking through his Byronic heroes, is in the very article of that process which Shelley describes, and rather proud of it. He suffers the predicament; Shelley observes and understands it. He understands it, I think, a good deal better than most of his modern critics.

Shelley's poetry presents a variety of kinds, most of them traditional. The elegy and the greater ode come down to him from the *exemplaria graeca* through eighteenth-century practice; the metrical structure of the latter is indeed rooted in a misunderstanding of Pindar, but a misunderstanding which had become itself a precedent by Shelley's time. *Swellfoot* is almost an attempt to revive the Old Comedy—an attempt which should interest Mr. Eliot since Shelley in it faces the cardinal problem of much of Mr. Eliot's poetry: namely, whether it is possible to distinguish poetry about squalor and chaos from squalid and chaotic poetry. I do not think it a great success. The lyrical drama is in part Aeschylean; in part, I think, Shelley's redemption of a bad eighteenth-century form. It derives from, and redeems, the drama of Mason, just as *The Prelude* and *Excursion* derive from, and confer new power upon, the eighteenth-century treatise-poem. Shelley's lyric is a greater novelty, but heavily indebted on the metrical side to Dryden himself. The fantastic tale or idyll (as in *Alastor* or the *Witch of Atlas*) probably derives from the mythological epyllion of the Elizabethans. In all these kinds Shelley produces works which, though not perfect, are in one way more satisfactory than any of Dryden's longer pieces: that is to say, they display a harmony between the poet's real and professed intention, they answer the demands of their forms, and they have unity of spirit. Shelley is at home in his best poems, his clothes, so to speak, fit him, as Dryden's do not. The faults are faults of execution, such as over-elaboration, occasional verbosity, and the like: mere stains on the surface. The faults in Dryden are fundamental discrepancies between the real and the assumed poetic character, or radical vices in the design:

diseases at the heart. Shelley could almost say with Racine, 'When my plan is made my poem is done'; with Dryden the plan itself usually foredooms the poem's failure.

Thus *Alastor* is a poem perfectly true to itself. The theme is universally interesting—the quest for ideal love. And both the theme and the treatment are fully suited to Shelley's powers. Hence the poem has an apparent ease, a noble obviousness, which deceives some readers. Mr. Eliot himself is too experienced a writer to be guilty of the delusion that he could write like Shelley if he chose; but I think many of Mr. Eliot's readers may suffer from it. They mistake the inevitability of *Alastor*, which really springs from the poet's harmony with his subject, for the facility of commonplace, and condemn the poem precisely because it is successful. Of course it has its faults—some of the scenery is over-written, and the form of line which ends with two long monosyllables comes too often. But these are not the sort of defects that kill a poem: the energy of imagination, which supports so lofty, remote, and lonely an emotion almost without a false note for seven hundred lines, remains; and it deserves to be admired, if in no higher way, at least as we admire a great suspension-bridge. I address myself, of course, only to those who are prepared, by toleration of the theme, to let the poem have a fair hearing. For those who are not, we can only say that they may doubtless be very worthy people, but they have no place in the European tradition.

Perhaps this muscular sustaining power is even more noticeable in the *Witch of Atlas,* for there Shelley goes more out of himself. In *Alastor* the congeniality of the theme was fully given in Shelley's temper; in the *Witch* he is going successfully beyond the bounds of his temper—making himself something other than he was. For in this poem we have, indeed, Shelley's ordinary romantic love of the fantastical and ideal, but all keyed down, muted, deftly inhibited from its native solemnity and intensity in order to produce a lighter, more playful effect. The theme, at bottom, is as serious as ever; but the handling 'turns all to favour and to prettiness.' The lightness and liquidity of this piece, the sensation which we feel in reading it of seeing things distinctly, yet at a vast distance, cannot be paralleled in any poem that I know. We must go to another art, namely to music, to find anything at all similar; and there we shall hardly find it outside Mozart. It could not, indeed, have been written if Shelley had not read the Italians; but it is a new modification, and in it all the light-hearted dancing perfection of Ariosto is detached from Ariosto's hardness and flippancy (though not from his irony) and used with a difference—disturbed by overtones, etherialized.

The whole poem is a happy reproof to that new Puritanism which has captured so many critics and taught us to object to pleasure in poetry simply because it is pleasure. It is natural, though regrettable, that such people should be exasperated by this mercurial poem; for to them it is miching mallecho (as Shelley said of *Peter Bell*) and means, as so much of his poetry means, mischief. They know very well that they are being laughed at; and they do not like to be told how

> Heaven and Earth conspire to foil
> The over-busy gardener's blundering toil.

If Shelley had written only such poems he would have shown his genius: his artistry, the discipline and power of obedience which makes genius universal, are better shown elsewhere. *Adonais* naturally occurs to the mind, for here we see Shelley fruitfully submitting to the conventions of a well-established form. It has all the traditional features of the elegy—the opening dirge, the processional allegory, and the concluding consolation. There is one bad error of taste. The Muse, lamenting Adonais, is made to lament her own immortality,

> I would give
> All that I am to be as thou now art!
> But I am chained to Time, and cannot thence depart.
> (xxvi.)

This is to make a goddess speak like a new-made human widow, and to dash the public solemnity of elegy with the violent passions of a personal lyric. How much more fitting are the words of the Roman poet:

> Immortales mortales flere si foret fas,
> Flerent divae Camenae Naevium poetam.

But it is a slip soon recovered, and not to be compared with the prolonged indecorum of Dryden's satiric conceits in his elegy for Mrs. Anne Killigrew:

> To the next realm she stretch'd her sway
> For Painture near adjoining lay
> A plenteous province, and alluring prey.
> A chamber of Dependencies was fram'd
> (As conquerors will never want pretence,
> When arm'd, to justify th' offence)
> And the whole fief, in right of poetry, she claim'd.
> The country open lay without defence, &c.

There are eighteen lines of it, and I do not know whether any major poet other than Dryden ever played such silly tricks at a funeral. No one demands that every poet should write an elegy: let each man be a master of his own trade. But the fact remains that when Shelley intends to do so, he does so; Dryden, equally intending, does not—*nimium amator ingenii sui*. I do not now speak of the unexampled rapture of Shelley's close. I might do so if I were to argue with Dryden, for he loves this ecstasy and quotes with approval *furentis animi vaticinatio*; being often a romantic in wish, though seldom happily romantic in the event. But I do not know whether Mr. Eliot shares Dryden's admiration for 'those enthusiastic parts of poetry'; and I would prefer to argue from positions that are, or ought in logic to be, admitted by Mr. Eliot. But I have slipped into that sentence 'If I were to argue with Dryden' unawares. Let no one suppose I am such a coxcomb as to think that my defence of Shelley could stand against Dryden's humane and luminous and Olympian dialectic; or, indeed, that it would be required in the presence of one who would almost certainly shame and anticipate me with such generous praise of Shelley as he has given to Shakespeare, or Milton, or Tasso, and a frank acknowledgment (he made more than one) of his own offences against the laws of poetry. Whoever else is a Drydenian in Mr. Eliot's way, I have no fear lest Dryden himself should be one.

Of course Shelley too had his failures. *The Revolt of Islam* does not really exist much more than *The Hind and the Panther* exists, and the ruin is less redeemed by fine passages. The *Letter to Maria Gisborne* is little better than a draft—a thing scrawled as quickly as the pen would cover the paper and really unfit for the printer. *Peter Bell the Third* is a more doubtful case. I am not prepared to endure either its squalors or its obscurity by any such moderate promise of enjoyment as it holds out; but perhaps the creator of Sweeney ought to have more patience both with the one and with the other. I do not greatly admire—but perhaps some of Mr. Eliot's weaker disciples should—this little picture:

> As he was speaking came a spasm
>   And wrenched his gnashing teeth asunder:
> Like one who sees a strange phantasm
> He lay—there was a silent chasm
>   Between his upper jaw and under.

Epipsychidion raises in an acute form a problem with which Mr. Eliot has been much occupied: I mean the problem of the relation between our judgement on a poem as critics, and our judgement as men on the ethics, metaphysics, or theology presupposed or expressed in the poem. For my own part, I do not believe that the poetic value of any poem is identical with the philosophic; but I think they can differ only to a limited extent, so that every poem whose prosaic or intellectual basis is silly, shallow, perverse, or illiberal, or even radically erroneous, is in some degree crippled by that fact. I am thus obliged to rate *Epipsychidion* rather low, because I consider the thought implied in it a dangerous delusion. In it Shelley is trying to stand on a particular rung of the Platonic ladder, and I happen to believe firmly that that particular rung does not exist, and that the man who thinks he is standing on it is not standing but falling. But no view that we can adopt will remove *Epipsychidion* from the slate. There is an element of spiritual, and also of carnal, passion in it, each expressed with great energy and sensibility, and the whole is marred, but not completely, by the false mode (as Mr. Eliot and I would maintain) in which the poet tries to blend them. It is particularly interesting to notice the internal, perhaps unconscious, control which arises amidst the very intensity of the experience and tightens up the metrical form: the first forty lines are almost 'stopped couplets' and the whole movement is much closer to Dryden's couplet than to that of Keats.

But we are now rapidly approaching that part of our subject where the difference between Mr. Eliot and myself ceases. In his essay on Dante, Mr. Eliot says that he thinks the last canto of the *Paradiso* 'the highest point that poetry has ever reached.'[7] I think the same—and since it is so pleasant to agree, let me add irrelevantly that I think as he does about the *Bhagavad-Gita*.[8] And a few pages later Mr. Eliot singles Shelley out as the one English poet of his century (I would have said the one English poet yet recorded) 'who could even have begun to follow' Dante's footsteps;[9] and he generously allows that Shelley, at the end of his life, was beginning to profit by his knowledge of Dante. I do not know how much of Shelley's work Mr. Eliot would admit by this concession. I suppose he would admit, at the very least, the *Triumph of Life*. If any passage in our poetry has profited by Dante, it is the unforgettable appearance of Rousseau in that poem—though admittedly it is only the Dante of the *Inferno*. But I am not without hope that Mr. Eliot might be induced to include more. In this same essay he speaks of a modern 'prejudice against beatitude as material for poetry.'[10] Now Dante is eminently the poet of beatitude. He has not only no rival, but none second to him. But if we were asked to name the poet who

most nearly deserved this inaccessible *proxime accessit,* I should name
Shelley. Indeed, my claim for Shelley might be represented by the
proposition that Shelley and Milton are, each, the half of Dante. I do
not know how we could describe Dante better to one who had not read
him, than by some such device as the following:

'You know the massive quality of Milton, the sense that every word
is being held in place by a gigantic pressure, so that there is an architectural sublime in every verse whether the matter be sublime at the
moment or not. You know also the air and fire of Shelley, the very
antithesis of the Miltonic solidity, the untrammelled, reckless speed
through pellucid spaces which makes us imagine while we are reading
him that we have somehow left our bodies behind. If now you can
imagine (but you cannot, for it must seem impossible till you see it
done) a poetry which combined these two all-but incompatibles—a
poetry as bright and piercing and aereal as the one, yet as weighty, as
pregnant and as lapidary as the other, then you will know what Dante
is like.'

To be thus half of Dante (Caesar is my authority for such a rarefied
critical symbolism) is fame enough for any ordinary poet. And Shelley, I
contend, reaches this height in the fourth act of *Prometheus.*

Genetically considered, the fourth act, we know, is an afterthought:
teleologically it is that for which the poem exists. I do not mean by this
that the three preceding acts are mere means; but that their significance
and beauty are determined by what follows, and that what came last in
the writing (as it comes last in the reading) is 'naturally prior' in the
Aristotelian sense. It does not add to, and therefore corrupt, a completed structure; it gives structure to that which, without it, would be
imperfect. The resulting whole is the greatest long poem in the nineteenth century, and the only long poem of the highest kind in that
century which approaches to perfection.

The theme is one of sane, public, and perennial interest—that of rebirth, regeneration, the new cycle. Like all great myths its primary appeal is to the imagination: its indirect and further appeal to the will and
the understanding can therefore be diversely interpreted according as
the reader is a Christian, a politician, a psycho-analyst, or what not.
Myth is thus like manna; it is to each man a different dish and to each
the dish he needs. It does not grow old nor stick at frontiers racial,
sexual, or philosophic; and even from the same man at the same moment
it can elicit different responses at different levels. But great myth is

rare in a reflective age; the temptation to allegorize, to thrust into the story the conscious doctrines of the poet, there to fight it out as best they can with the inherent tendency of the fable, is usually too strong. *Faust* and the *Niblung's Ring*—the only other great mythical poems of modern times—have in this way been partially spoiled. The excellence of Shelley is that he has avoided this. He has found what is, for him, the one perfect story and re-made it so well that the ancient version now seems merely embryonic. In his poem there is no strain between the literal sense and the imaginative significance. The events which are needed to produce the λύσις seem to become the symbols of the spiritual process he is presenting without effort or artifice or even consciousness on his part.

The problem was not an easy one. We are to start with the soul chained, aged, suffering; and we are to end with the soul free, rejuvenated, and blessed. The selection of the Prometheus story (a selection which seems obvious only because we did not have to make it) is the first step to the solution. But nearly everything has still to be done. By what steps are we to pass from Prometheus in his chains to Prometheus free? The long years of his agony cannot be dramatically represented, for they are static. The actual moment of liberation by Heracles is a mere piece of 'business.' Dramatic necessity demands that the Titan himself should do or say something before his liberation—and if possible something that will have an effect on the action. Shelley answers this by beginning with Prometheus's revocation of the curse upon Jupiter. Now mark how everything falls into place for the poet who well and truly obeys his imagination. This revocation at once introduces the phantasm of Jupiter, the original curse on the phantasm's lips, and the despair of Earth and Echoes at what seems to be Prometheus's capitulation. We thus get at one stroke a good opening episode and a fine piece of irony, on the dramatic level; but we also have suggested the phantasmal or nightmare nature of the incubus under which the soul (or the world) is groaning, and the prime necessity for a change of heart in the sufferer, who is in some sort his own prisoner. Prometheus, we are made to feel, has really stepped out of prison with the words, 'It doth repent me.' But once again structural and spiritual necessities join hands to postpone his effective liberation. On the structural side, the play must go on; on the other, we know, and Shelley knows, how long a journey separates the first resolve, from the final remaking, of a man, a nation, or a world. The Furies will return, and the act closes with low-toned melodies of sadness and of hopes that are as yet remote and notional.

The whole of the next act, in story, is occupied with the difficult efforts of Asia to apprehend and follow a dream dreamed in the shadow of Prometheus: the difficult journey which it leads her; her difficult descent to the depths of the earth; and her final reascension, transformed, to the light. Difficulty is, so to speak, the subject of this act. The dramatic advantage of splitting the sufferer's role into two parts, those of Prometheus and Asia, and of giving the latter a task to perform in the liberation, is sufficiently obvious. But we hardly need to notice this. Most of us, while we read this act, are too absorbed, I fancy, by the new sensation it creates in us. The gradual ineluctable approach of the unknown, where the unknown is sinister, is not an uncommon theme in literature; but where else are we to find this more medicinable theme— these shy approaches, and sudden recessions, and returnings beyond hope, and swellings and strengthenings of a far-off, uncertainly prognosticated good? And again, it is a necessity for Shelley, simply because he has placed his fiend in the sky, to make Asia go down, not up, to fetch this good; but how miraculously it all fits in! Does any reader, whether his prepossessions be psychological or theological, question this descent into hell, this return to the· womb, this death, as the proper path for Asia to take? Our imaginations, constrained by deepest necessities, accept all that imagery of interwoven trees and dew and moss whereby the chorus drench the second scene with darkness, and the softness and damp of growing things: by the same necessity they accept the harsher images of the final precipitous descent to Demogorgon's cave, and the seated darkness which we find there. It is out of all this, silver against this blackness, that the piercing song of Asia's reascension comes; and if any one who has read that song in its setting still supposes that the poet is talking about Godwin or the Revolution, or that Shelley is any other than a very great poet, I cannot help him. But for my own part I believe that no poet has felt more keenly, or presented more weightily the necessity for a complete unmaking and remaking of man, to be endured at the dark bases of his being. I do not know the book (in profane literature) to which I should turn for a like expression of what von Hügel would have called the 'costingness' of regeneration.

The third act is the least successful: Shelley's error was not to see that he could shorten it when once he had conceived the fourth. Yet some leisure and some slackened tension are here allowable. We are certainly not ready for the fourth act at once. Between the end of torment and the beginning of ecstasy there must be a pause: peace comes before beatitude. It would be ridiculous, in point of achievement, to compare this weak act in Shelley's play with the triumphant conclusion of the *Purgatorio*; but structurally it corresponds to the position of the earthly paradise between purgatory and heaven. And in one scene at least it is worthy of its theme. The dialogue between Ocean and Apollo (at 'the mouth of a great river in the island Atlantis') is among his best things: a divine indolence soaks it, and if there are better lines in English poetry there are none that breathe a more heartfelt peace than Ocean's:

> It is the unpastured sea hungering for calm:
> Peace, monster. I come now. Farewell.

The fourth act I shall not attempt to analyse. It is an intoxication, a riot, a complicated and uncontrollable splendour, long, and yet not too long, sustained on the note of ecstasy such as no other English poet, perhaps no other poet, has given us. It can be achieved by more than one artist in music: to do it in words has been, I think, beyond the reach of nearly all. It has not, and cannot have, the solemnity and overwhelming realism of the *Paradiso*, but it has all its fire and light. It has not the 'sober certainty of waking bliss' which makes Milton's paradise so inhabitable—but it sings from regions in our consciousness that Milton never entered.

Some anti-romantic repudiations of such poetry rest, perhaps, on a misunderstanding. It might be true, as the materialists must hold, that there is no possible way by which men can arrive at such felicity; or again, as Mr. Eliot and I believe, that there is one Way, and only one, and that Shelley has missed it. But while we discuss these things, the romantic poet has added meaning to the word Felicity itself. Whatever the result of our debate, we had better attend to his discovery lest we remain more ignorant than we need have been of the very thing about which we debated.

NOTES

1. *Selected Essays*, 1932, p. 295.
2. Op. cit., p. 296.
3. Op. cit., p. 297.
4. Ibid.
5. It will be noticed that even if the premises were true, the inference is invalid. A similar paralogism has occurred about Mr. Housman (of course,

since his death) in the form, 'Kipling is bad. Some lines of Housman are like some lines of Kipling. Therefore Housman is bad.'

6. That is, nothing more in the usual strain. For a reprint of *Political Justice* (a book very difficult to find) I am all agog: it is not likely to be so dull as our critical tradition proclaims.

7. Op. cit., p. 227.

8. Op. cit., p. 244.

9. Op. cit., p. 250.

10. Ibid.

F. R. LEAVIS

Shelley

IF Shelley had not received some distinguished attention in recent years (and he has been differed over by the most eminent critics) there might, perhaps, have seemed little point in attempting a restatement of the essential critical observations—the essential observations, that is, in the reading and appreciation of Shelley's poetry. For they would seem to be obvious enough. Yet it is only one incitement out of many when a critic of peculiar authority, contemplating the common change from being 'intoxicated by Shelley's poetry at the age of fifteen' to finding it now 'almost unreadable,' invokes for explanation the nature of Shelley's 'ideas' and, in reference to them, that much-canvassed question of the day, 'the question of belief or disbelief':

> 'It is not so much that thirty years ago I was able to read Shelley under an illusion which experience has dissipated, as that because the question of belief or disbelief did not arise I was in a much better position to enjoy the poetry. I can only regret that Shelley did not live to put his poetic gifts, which were certainly of the first order, at the service of more tenable beliefs—which need not have been, for my purposes, beliefs more acceptable to me.'

This is, of course, a personal statement; but perhaps if one insists on the more obvious terms of literary criticism—more strictly critical terms—in which such a change might be explained, and suggests that the terms actually used might be found unfortunate in their effect, the impertinence will not be unpardonable. It does, in short, seem worth endeavour-

From *Revaluation: Tradition and Development in English Poetry* (George W. Stewart, Publisher, Inc., and Chatto and Windus Ltd., London, 1949), pp. 203-32. Reprinted by permission of the publishers.

ing to make finally plain that, when one dissents from persons who, sympathizing with Shelley's revolutionary doctrines and with his idealistic ardours and fervours—with his 'beliefs,' exalt him as a poet, it is strictly the 'poetry' one is criticizing. There would also appear to be some reason for insisting that in finding Shelley almost unreadable one need not be committing oneself to a fashionably limited taste—an inability to appreciate unfashionable kinds of excellence or to understand a use of words that is unlike Hopkins's or Donne's.

It will be well to start, in fact, by examining the working of Shelley's poetry—his characteristic modes of expression—as exemplified in one of his best poems.

> Thou on whose stream, mid the steep sky's commotion,
> Loose clouds like earth's decaying leaves are shed,
> Shook from the tangled boughs of Heaven and Ocean,
>
> Angels of rain and lightning: there are spread
> On the blue surface of thine aëry surge,
> Like the bright hair uplifted from the head
>
> Of some fierce Maenad, even from the dim verge
> Of the horizon to the zenith's height,
> The locks of the approaching storm.

The sweeping movement of the verse, with the accompanying plangency, is so potent that, as many can testify, it is possible to have been for years familiar with the Ode—to know it by heart—without asking the obvious questions. In what respects are the 'loose clouds' like 'decaying leaves'? The correspondence is certainly not in shape, colour or way of moving. It is only the vague general sense of windy tumult that associates the clouds and the leaves; and, accordingly, the appropriateness of the metaphor 'stream' in the first line is not that it suggests a surface on which, like leaves, the clouds might be 'shed,' but that it contributes to the general 'streaming' effect in which the inappropriateness of 'shed' passes unnoticed. What again, are those 'tangled boughs of Heaven and Ocean'? They stand for nothing that Shelley could have pointed to in the scene before him; the 'boughs,' it is plain, have grown out of the 'leaves' in the previous line, and we are not to ask what the tree is. Nor are we to scrutinize closely the 'stream' metaphor as developed: that 'blue surface' must be the concave of the sky, an oddly smooth surface for a 'surge'—if we consider a moment. But in this poetic surge, while we let ourselves be swept along, there is no considering, the image doesn't challenge any inconvenient degree of realization, and the oddness is lost. Then again, in what ways does the approach of a storm ('loose clouds like earth's decaying leaves,' 'like ghosts from an enchanter fleeing') suggest streaming hair? The appropriateness of the Maenad, clearly, lies in the pervasive suggestion of frenzied onset, and we are not to ask whether her bright hair is to be seen as streaming out in front of her (as, there is no need to assure ourselves, it might be doing if she were running before a still swifter gale: in the kind of reading that got so far as proposing to itself this particular reassurance no general satisfaction could be exacted from Shelley's imagery).

Here, clearly, in these peculiarities of imagery and sense, peculiarities analysable locally in the mode of expression, we have the manifestation of essential characteristics—the Shelleyan characteristics as envisaged by the criticism that works on a philosophical plane and makes judgments of a moral order. In the growth of those 'tangled boughs' out of the leaves, exemplifying as it does a general tendency of the images to forget the status of the metaphor or simile that introduced them and to assume an autonomy and a right to propagate, so that we lose in confused generations and perspectives the perception or thought that was the ostensible *raison d'être* of imagery, we have a recognized essential trait of Shelley's: his weak grasp upon the actual. This weakness, of course, commonly has more or less creditable accounts given of it— idealism, Platonism and so on; and even as unsentimental a judge as Mr. Santayana correlates Shelley's inability to learn from experience with his having been born a 'nature preformed,' a 'spokesman of the *a priori*,' 'a dogmatic, inspired, perfect and incorrigible creature.'[1] It seems to me that Mr. Santayana's essay, admirable as it is, rates the poetry too high. But for the moment it will be enough to recall limitations that are hardly disputed: Shelley was not gifted for drama or narrative. Having said this, I realize that I had forgotten the conventional standing of *The Cenci*; but controversy may be postponed: it is at any rate universally agreed that (to shift tactfully to positive terms) Shelley's genius was 'essentially lyrical.'

This predicate would, in common use, imply a special emotional intensity—a vague gloss, but it is difficult to go further without slipping into terms that are immediately privative and limiting. Thus there is certainly a sense in which Shelley's poetry is peculiarly emotional, and when we try to define this sense we find ourselves invoking an absence of something. The point may be best made, perhaps, by recalling the observation noted above, that one may have been long familiar with the *Ode to the West Wind* without ever having asked the obvious questions; questions that propose themselves at the first critical inspection. This poetry induces—depends for its success on inducing—a kind of attention that doesn't bring the critical intelligence into play: the imagery feels right, the associations work appropriately, if (as it takes conscious resistance not to do) one accepts the immediate feeling and doesn't slow down to think.

Shelley himself can hardly have asked the questions. Not that he didn't expend a great deal of critical labour upon his verse. 'He composed rapidly and attained to perfection by intensive correction. He would sometimes write down a phrase with alterations and rejections time after time until it came within a measure of satisfying him. Words are frequently substituted for others and lines interpolated.' The *Ode to the West Wind* itself, as is shown in the repository[2] of fragments the preface to which supplies these observations, profited by the process described, which must be allowed to have been in some sense critical. But the critical part of Shelley's creative labour was a matter of getting the verse to feel right, and feeling, for Shelley as a poet, had—as the insistent concern for 'rightness,' the typical final product being what it is, serves to emphazise—little to do with thinking (though Shelley was in some ways a very intelligent man).

We have here, if not sufficient justification for the predicate 'essentially lyrical,' certainly a large part of the reason for Shelley's being found essentially poetical by the succeeding age. He counted, in fact, for a great deal in what came to be the prevailing idea of 'the poetical'—the idea that had its latest notable statement in Professor Housman's address, *The Name and Nature of Poetry*. The Romantic conceptions of genius and inspiration[3] developed (the French Revolution and its ideological background must, of course, be taken into account) in reaction against the Augustan insistence on the social and the rational. When Wordsworth says that 'all good poetry is the spontaneous overflow of powerful feelings' he is of his period, though the intended force of this dictum, the force it has in its context and in relation to Wordsworth's own practice, is very different from that given it when Shelley assents, or when it is assimilated to Byron's 'poetry is the lava of the imagination, whose eruption prevents an earthquake.'[4] But Byron was for the young Tennyson (and the Ruskin parents)[5] the poet, and Shelley (Browning's 'Sun-treader') was the idol of the undergraduate Tennyson and his fellow Apostles, and, since the poetry of 'the age of Wordsworth' became canonical, the assent given to Wordsworth's dictum has commonly been Shelleyan.

The force of Shelley's insistence on spontaneity is simple and un-equivocal. It will be enough to recall a representative passage or two from the *Defence of Poetry*:

'for the mind in creation is as a fading coal, which some invisible in-fluence, like an inconstant wind, awakes to transitory brightness; this power arises from within, like the colour of a flower which fades and changes as it is developed, and the conscious portions of our nature are unprophetic either of its approach or its departure.'

'Inspiration' is not something to be tested, clarified, defined and de-veloped in composition,

'but when composition begins, inspiration is already on the decline, and the most glorious poetry that has ever been communicated to the world is probably a feeble shadow of the original conceptions of the poet. . . . The toil and delay recommended by critics can be justly interpreted to mean no more than a careful observation of the inspired moments, and an artificial connexion of the spaces between their suggestions, by the intertexture of conventional expressions; a necessity only imposed by the limitedness of the poetical faculty itself. . . .'

The 'poetical faculty,' we are left no room for doubting, can, of its very nature, have nothing to do with any discipline, and can be associated with conscious effort only mechanically and externally, and when Shelley says that Poetry

'is not subject to the control of the active powers of the mind, and that its birth and recurrence have no necessary connexion with consciousness or will'

he is not saying merely that the 'active powers of the mind' are in-sufficient in themselves for creation—that poetry cannot be written merely by taking thought. The effect of Shelley's eloquence is to hand poetry over to a sensibility that has no more dealings with intelligence than it can help; to a 'poetic faculty' that, for its duly responsive vibrat-ing (though the poet must reverently make his pen as sensitive an instrument as possible to 'observe'—in the scientific sense—the vibra-tions), demands that active intelligence shall be, as it were, switched off.

Shelley, of course, had ideas and ideals; he wrote philosophical essays, and it need not be irrelevant to refer, in discussing his poetry, to Plato, Godwin and other thinkers. But there is nothing grasped in the poetry—no object offered for contemplation, no realized presence to persuade or move us by what it is. A. C. Bradley, remarking that 'Shelley's ideals of good, whether as a character or as a mode of life, resting as they do on abstraction from the mass of real existence, tend to lack body and individuality,' adds: 'But we must remember that Shelley's strength and weakness are closely allied, and it may be that the very abstractness of his ideal was a condition of that quivering intensity of aspiration towards it in which his poetry is unequalled.'[6] That is the best that can be respectably said. Actually, that 'quivering intensity,' offered in itself apart from any substance, offered instead of any object, is what, though it may make Shelley intoxicating at fifteen makes him almost unreadable, except in very small quantities of his best, to the mature. Even when he is in his own way unmistakably a distinguished poet, as in *Prometheus Unbound*, it is impossible to go on reading him at any length with pleasure; the elusive imagery, the high-pitched emotions, the tone and movement, the ardours, ecstasies and despairs, are too much the same all through. The effect is of vanity and emptiness (Arnold was right) as well as monotony.

The force of the judgment that feeling in Shelley's poetry is divorced from thought needs examining further. Any suspicion that Donne is the implied criterion will, perhaps, be finally averted if for the illuminating contrast we go to Wordsworth. Wordsworth is another 'Romantic' poet; he too is undramatic; and he too invites the criticism (Arnold, his devoted admirer, made it) that he lacks variety. 'Thought' will hardly be found an assertive presence in his best poetry; in so far as the term suggests an overtly active energy it is decidedly inappropriate. 'Emotion,' his own word, is the word most readers would insist on, though they would probably judge Wordsworth's emotion to be less lyrical than Shelley's. The essential difference, however—and it is a very important one—seems, for present purposes, more relevantly stated in the terms I used in discussing Wordsworth's 'recollection in tranquillity.' The process covered by this phrase was one of emotional discipline, critical exploration of experience, pondered valuation and maturing reflection. As a result of it an organization is engaged in Wordsworth's poetry, and the activity and standards of critical intelligence are implicit.

An associated difference was noted in the sureness with which Wordsworth grasps the world of common perception. The illustration suggested was *The Simplon Pass* in comparison with Shelley's *Mont Blanc*. The element of Wordsworth in *Mont Blanc* (it is perceptible in these opening lines) serves only to enhance the contrast:

> The everlasting universe of things
> Flows through the mind, and rolls its rapid waves,
> Now dark—now glittering—now reflecting gloom—
> Now lending splendour, where from secret springs
> The source of human thought its tribute brings
> Of waters—with a sound but half its own,
> Such as a feeble brook will oft assume
> In the wild woods, among the mountains lone,
> Where waterfalls around it leap for ever,
> Where woods and winds contend, and a vast river
> Over its rocks ceaselessly bursts and raves.

The metaphorical and the actual, the real and the imagined, the inner and the outer, could hardly be more unsortably and indistinguishably confused. The setting, of course, provides special excuse for bewildered confusion; but Shelley takes eager advantage of the excuse and the confusion is characteristic—what might be found unusual in *Mont Blanc* is a certain compelling vividness. In any case, Wordsworth himself is explicitly offering a sense of sublime bewilderment, similarly inspired:

> Black drizzling crags that spake by the wayside
> As if a voice were in them, the sick sight
> And giddy prospect of the raving stream,
> The unfettered clouds and region of the heavens,
> Tumult and peace, the darkness and the light—
> Were all like workings of one mind, the features
> Of the same face . . .

He is, of course, recollecting in tranquillity; but the collectedness of those twenty lines (as against Shelley's one hundred and forty) does not belong merely to the record; it was present (or at least the movement towards it was) in the experience, as those images, 'one mind,' 'the same face'—epitomizing, as they do, the contrast with Shelley's ecstatic dissipation—may fairly be taken to testify.

This comparison does not aim immediately at a judgment of relative value. *Mont Blanc* is very interesting as well as idiosyncratic, and is not obviously the product of the less rare gift. There are, nevertheless, critical judgments to be made—judgments concerning the emotional quality of Wordsworth's poetry and of Shelley's: something more than mere description of idiosyncrasy is in view. What should have come out in the comparison that started as a note on Wordsworth's grasp of the outer world is the unobtrusiveness with which that 'outer' turns into 'inner': the antithesis, clearly, is not altogether, for present purposes, a simple one to apply. What is characteristic of Wordsworth is to grasp surely (which, in the nature of the case, must be delicately and subtly) what he offers, whether this appears as belonging to the outer world—the world as perceived, or to inner experience. He seems always to be presenting an object (wherever this may belong) and the emotion seems to derive from what is presented. The point is very obviously and impressively exemplified in *A slumber did my spirit seal*, which shows Wordsworth at his supreme height. Here (compare it with the *Ode to the West Wind*, where we have Shelley's genius at its best; or, if something more obviously comparable is required, with Tennyson's *Break, break, break*) there is no emotional comment—nothing 'emotional' in phrasing, movement or tone; the facts seem to be presented barely, and the emotional force to be generated by them in the reader's mind when he has taken them in—generated by the two juxtaposed stanzas, in the contrast between the situations or states they represent.

Shelley, at his best and worst, offers the emotion in itself, unattached, in the void. 'In itself' 'for itself'—it is an easy shift to the pejorative implications of 'for its own sake'; just as, for a poet with the habit of sensibility and expression described, it was an easy shift to deserving them. For Shelley is obnoxious to the pejorative implications of 'habit': being inspired was, for him, too apt to mean surrendering to a kind of hypnotic rote of favourite images, associations and words. 'Inspiration,' there not being an organization for it to engage (as in Wordsworth, whose sameness is of a different order from Shelley's, there was), had only poetical habits to fall back on. We have them in their most innocent aspect in those favourite words: *radiant, aërial, odorous, daedal, faint, sweet, bright, winged, -inwoven,* and the rest of the fondled vocabulary that any reader of Shelley could go on enumerating. They manifest themselves as decidedly deplorable in *The Cloud* and *To a Skylark*, which illustrate the dangers of fostering the kind of inspiration that works only when critical intelligence is switched off. These poems may be not unfairly described as the products of switching poetry on.[7] There has been in recent years some controversy about particular points in *To a Skylark*, and there are a score or more points inviting adverse criticism. But this need hardly be offered; it is, or should be, so plain that the poem is a mere tumbled out spate ('spontaneous overflow') of poeticalities, the place of each one of which Shelley could have filled with another without the least difficulty and without making any essential difference. They are held together by the pervasive 'lyrical emotion,' and that this should be capable of holding them together is comment enough on the nature of its strength.

Cheaper surrenders to inspiration may easily be found in the collected Shelley; there are, for instance, gross indulgences in the basest Regency album taste.[8] But criticism of Shelley has something more important to deal with than mere bad poetry; or, rather, there are badnesses inviting the criticism that involves moral judgments. It must have already appeared (it has virtually been said) that surrendering to inspiration cannot, for a poet of Shelley's emotional habits, have been very distinguishable from surrendering to temptation. The point comes out in an element of the favoured vocabulary not exemplified above: *charnel, corpse, phantom, liberticide, aghast, ghastly* and so on. The wrong approach to emotion, the approach from the wrong side or end (so to speak), is apparent here; Shelley would clearly have done well not to have indulged these habits and these likings: the viciousness and corruption are immediately recognizable. But viciousness and corruption do not less attend upon likings for tender ('I love Love'),[9] sympathetic, exalted and ecstatic emotions, and may be especially expected to do so in a mind as little able to hold an object in front of it as Shelley's was.

The transition from the lighter concerns of literary criticism to the diagnosis of radical disabilities and perversions, such as call for moral comment, may be conveniently illustrated from a favourite anthology-piece, *When the lamp is shattered*:

> When the lamp is shattered
> The light in the dust lies dead—
> When the cloud is scattered
> The rainbow's glory is shed.
> When the lute is broken,
> Sweet tones are remembered not;
> When the lips have spoken,
> Loved accents are soon forgot.
>
> As music and splendour
> Survive not the lamp and the lute,
> The heart's echoes render
> No song when the spirit is mute:—
> No song but sad dirges,
> Like the wind through a ruined cell;
> Or the mournful surges
> That ring the dead seaman's knell.

When hearts have once mingled
Love first leaves the well-built nest;
  The weak one is singled
To endure what it once possessed.
    O Love! who bewailest
The frailty of all things here,
  Why choose you the frailest
For your cradle, your home, and your bier?

  Its passions will rock thee
As the storms rock the ravens on high;
  Bright reason will mock thee,
Like the sun from a wintry sky.
    From thy nest every rafter
Will rot, and thine eagle home
  Leave thee naked to laughter,
When leaves fall and cold winds come.

The first two stanzas call for no very close attention—to say so, indeed, is to make the main criticism, seeing that they offer a show of insistent argument. However, reading with an unsolicited closeness, one may stop at the second line and ask whether the effect got with 'lies dead' is legitimate. Certainly, the emotional purpose of the poem is served, but the emotional purpose that went on being served in that way would be suspect. Leaving the question in suspense, perhaps, one passes to 'shed'; 'shed' as tears, petals and coats are shed, or as light is shed? The latter would be a rather more respectable use of the word in connexion with a rainbow's glory, but the context indicates the former. Only in the vaguest and slackest state of mind—of imagination and thought—could one so describe the fading of a rainbow; but for the right reader 'shed' sounds right, the alliteration with 'shattered' combining with the verse-movement to produce a kind of inevitability. And, of course, suggesting tears and the last rose of summer, it suits with the general emotional effect. The nature of this is by now so unmistakable that the complete nullity of the clinching 'so,' when it arrives—of the two lines that justify the ten preparatory lines of analogy—seems hardly worth stopping to note:

The heart's echoes render
No song when the spirit is mute.

Nor is it surprising that there should turn out to be a song after all, and a pretty powerful one—for those who like that sort of thing; the 'sad dirges,' the 'ruined cell,' the 'mournful surges' and the 'dead seaman's knell' being immediately recognizable as currency values. Those who take pleasure in recognizing and accepting them are not at the same time exacting about sense.

The critical interest up to this point has been to see Shelley, himself (when inspired) so unexacting about sense, giving himself so completely to sentimental banalities. With the next stanza it is much the same, though the emotional *clichés* take on a grosser unction and the required abeyance of thought (and imagination) becomes more remarkable. In what form are we to imagine Love leaving the well-built nest? For readers who get so far as asking, there can be no acceptable answer. It would be unpoetically literal to suggest that, since the weak one is singled, the truant must be the mate, and, besides, it would raise unnecessary difficulties. Perhaps the mate, the strong one, is what the weak one, deserted by Love, whose alliance made possession once possible, now has to endure? But the suggestion is frivolous; the sense is plain enough—enough, that is, for those who respond to the sentiment. Sufficient recognition of the sense depends neither on thinking, nor on realization of the metaphors, but on response to the sentimental commonplaces: it is only when intelligence and imagination insist on intruding that difficulties arise. So plain is this that there would be no point in contemplating the metaphorical complexity that would develop if we could take the tropes seriously and tried to realize Love making of the weak one, whom it (if we evade the problem of sex) leaves behind in the well-built nest, a cradle, a home and a bier.

The last stanza brings a notable change; it alone in the poem has any distinction, and its personal quality, characteristically Shelleyan, stands out against the sentimental conventionality of the rest. The result is to compel a more radical judgment on the poem than has yet been made. In 'Its passions will rock thee' the 'passions' must be those of Love, so that it can no longer be Love that is being apostrophized. Who, then, is 'thee'? The 'frailest'—the 'weak one'—it would appear. But any notion one may have had that the 'weak one,' as the conventional sentiments imply, is the woman must be abandoned: the 'eagle home,' to which the 'well-built nest' so incongruously turns, is the Poet's. The familiar timbre, the desolate intensity (note particularly the use of 'bright' in 'bright reason'), puts it beyond doubt that Shelley is, characteristically, addressing himself—the 'pardlike Spirit beautiful and swift,' the 'Love in desolation masked,' the 'Power girt round with weakness.'

Characteristically: that is, Shelley's characteristic pathos is self-regarding, directed upon an idealized self in the way suggested by the tags just quoted.[10] This is patently so in some of his best poetry; for instance, in the *Ode to the West Wind*. Even there, perhaps, one may find something too like an element of luxury in the poignancy (at any rate, one's limiting criticism of the Ode would move towards such a judgment); and that in general there must be dangers and weakness attending upon such a habit will hardly be denied. The poem just examined shows how gross may be, in Shelley, the corruptions that are incident. He can make self-pity a luxury at such a level that the conventional pathos of album poeticizing, not excluding the banalities about (it is plainly so in the third stanza) the sad lot of woman, can come in to gratify the appetite.

The abeyance of thought exhibited by the first three stanzas now takes on a more sinister aspect. The switching-off of intelligence that is necessary if the sentiments of the third stanza are to be accepted has now to be invoked in explanation of a graver matter—Shelley's ability to accept the grosser, the truly corrupt, gratifications that have just been indicated. The antipathy of his sensibility to any play of the critical mind, the uncongeniality of intelligence to inspiration, these clearly go in Shelley, not merely with a capacity for momentary self-deceptions and insincerities, but with a radical lack of self-knowledge. He could say of Wordsworth, implying the opposite of himself, that

> he never could
> Fancy another situation
> From which to dart his contemplation
> Than that wherein he stood.

But, for all his altruistic fervours and his fancied capacity for projecting his sympathies, Shelley is habitually—it is no new observation—his own hero: Alastor, Laon, The Sensitive Plant

> (It loves, even like Love, its deep heart is full,
> It desires what it has not, the Beautiful)

and Prometheus. It is characteristic that he should say to the West Wind

> A heavy weight of hours has chained and bowed
> One too like thee: tameless, and swift, and proud,

and conclude:

Be thou, Spirit fierce,
My spirit! Be thou me, impetuous one!

About the love of such a nature there is likely at the best to be a certain innocent selfishness. And it is with fervour that Shelley says, as he is always saying implicitly, 'I love Love.' Mr. Santayana acutely observes: 'In him, as in many people, too intense a need of loving excludes the capacity for intelligent sympathy.' Perhaps love generally has less in it of intelligent sympathy than the lover supposes, and is less determined by the object of love; but Shelley, we have seen, was, while on the one hand conscious of ardent altruism, on the other peculiarly weak in his hold on objects—peculiarly unable to realize them as existing in their own natures and their own right. His need of loving (in a sense that was not, perhaps, in the full focus of Mr. Santayana's intention) comes out in the erotic element that, as already remarked in these pages, the texture of the poetry pervasively exhibits. There is hardly any need to illustrate here the tender, caressing, voluptuous effects and suggestions of the favourite vocabulary and imagery. The consequences of the need, or 'love,' of loving, combined, as it was, with a notable lack of self-knowledge and a capacity for ecstatic idealizing, are classically extant in *Epipsychidion*.

The love of loathing is, naturally, less conscious than the love of Love. It may fairly be said to involve a love of Hate, if not of hating: justification enough for putting it this way is provided by *The Cenci*, which exhibits a perverse luxury of insistence, not merely upon horror, but upon malignity. This work, of course, is commonly held to require noting as, in the general account of Shelley, a remarkable exception: his genius may be essentially lyrical, but he can, transcending limitations, write great drama. This estimate of *The Cenci* is certainly a remarkable instance of *vis inertiae*—of the power of conventional valuation to perpetuate itself, once established. For it takes no great discernment to see that *The Cenci* is very bad and that its badness is characteristic. Shelley, as usual, is the hero—here the heroine; his relation to Beatrice is of the same order as his relation to Alastor and Prometheus, and the usual vices should not be found more acceptable because of the show of drama.

Nor is this show the less significantly bad because Shelley doesn't know where it comes from—how he is contriving it. He says in his *Preface* that an idea suggested by Calderon is 'the only plagiarism which I have intentionally committed in the whole piece.' Actually, not only is the 'whole piece' Shakespearian in inspiration (how peculiarly dubious an affair inspiration was apt to be for Shelley we have seen), it is full of particular echoes of Shakespeare—echoes protracted, confused and woolly; plagiarisms, that is, of the worst kind. This Shakespearianizing, general and particular is—and not the less so for its unconsciousness—quite damning. It means that Shelley's drama and tragedy do not grow out of any realized theme; there is nothing grasped at the core of the piece. Instead there is Beatrice-Shelley, in whose martyrdom the Count acts Jove—with more than Jovian gusto:

> I do not feel as if I were a man,
> But like a fiend appointed to chastise
> The offences of some unremembered world.
> My blood is running up and down my veins;
> A fearful pleasure makes it prick and tingle:
> I feel a giddy sickness of strange awe;
> My heart is beating with an expectation
> Of horrid joy.

The pathos is of corresponding corruptness. The habits that enable Shelley to be unconscious about this kind of indulgence enable him at the same time to turn it into tragic drama by virtue of an unconscious effort to be Shakespeare.

There are, of course, touches of Webster: Beatrice in the trial scene is commonly recognized to have borrowed an effect or two from the White Devil. But the Shakespearian promptings are everywhere, in some places almost ludicrously assorted, obvious and thick. For instance, Act III, Sc. ii starts (stage direction: 'Thunder and the sound of a storm') by being at line two obviously Lear. At line eight Othello comes in and carries on for ten lines; and he reasserts himself at line fifty. At line fifty-five Hamlet speaks. At line seventy-eight we get an effect from *Macbeth*, to be followed by many more in the next act, during which, after much borrowed suspense, the Count's murder is consummated.

The quality of the dramatic poetry and the relation between Shelley and Shakespeare must, for reasons of space, be represented—the example is a fair one—by a single brief passage (Act V, Sc. iv, l. 48):

> O
> My God! Can it be possible I have
> To die so suddenly? So young to go
> Under the obscure, cold, rotting, wormy ground!
> To be nailed down into a narrow place;

To see no more sweet sunshine; hear no more
Blithe voice of living thing; muse not again
Upon familiar thoughts, sad, yet thus lost—
How fearful! to be nothing! Or to be . . .
What? Oh, where am I? Let me not go mad!
Sweet Heaven, forgive weak thoughts! If there should be
No God, no Heaven, no Earth in the void world;
The wide, gray, lampless, deep, unpeopled world!

This patently recalls Claudio's speech in *Measure for Measure* (Act III, Sc. i):

Ay, but to die, and go we know not where;
To lie in cold obstruction and to rot;
This sensible warm motion to become
A kneaded clod; and the delighted spirit
To bathe in fiery floods, or to reside
In thrilling region of thick-ribbed ice;
To be imprisoned in the viewless winds,
And blown with restless violence round about
The pendent world; or to be worse than worst
Of those that lawless and incertain thoughts
Imagine howling:—'tis too horrible!
The weariest and most loathed worldly life
That age, ache, penury, and imprisonment
Can lay on nature is a paradise
To what we fear of death.

The juxtaposition is enough to expose the vague, generalizing externality of Shelley's rendering. Claudio's words spring from a vividly realized particular situation; from the imagined experience of a given mind in a given critical moment that is felt from the inside—that is lived—with sharp concrete particularity. Claudio's 'Ay, but to die . . .' is not insistently and voluminously emotional like Beatrice's ('wildly')

O
My God! Can it be possible . . .

but it is incomparably more intense. That 'cold obstruction' is not abstract; it gives rather the essence of the situation in which Claudio shrinkingly imagines himself—the sense of the warm body (given by 'cold') struggling ('obstruction' takes an appropriate effort to pronounce) in vain with the suffocating earth. Sentience, warmth and motion, the essentials of being alive as epitomized in the next line, recoil from death, realized brutally in the concrete (the 'clod' is a vehement protest, as 'clay,' which 'kneaded' nevertheless brings appropriately in, would not have been). Sentience, in the 'delighted spirit,' plunges, not into the delightful coolness suggested by 'bathe,' but into the dreadful opposite, and warmth and motion shudder away from the icy prison ('reside' is analogous in working to 'bathe'). The shudder is there in 'thrilling,' which also—such alliteration as that of 'thrilling region' and 'thick-ribbed' is not accidental in a Shakespearian passage of this quality —gives the sharp reverberating report of the ice as, in the intense cold, it is forced up into ridges or ribs (at which, owing to the cracks, the thickness of the ice can be seen).

But there is no need to go on. The point has been sufficiently enforced that, though this vivid concreteness of realization lodged the passage in Shelley's mind, to become at the due moment 'inspiration,' the passage inspired is nothing but wordy emotional generality. It does not grasp and present anything, but merely makes large gestures towards the kind of effect deemed appropriate. We are told emphatically what the emotion is that we are to feel; emphasis and insistence serving instead of realization and advertising its default. The intrusion of the tag from Lear brings out the vague generality of that unconscious set at being Shakespeare which Shelley took for dramatic inspiration.

Inspection of *The Cenci,* then, confirms all the worst in the account of Shelley. Further confirmation would not need much seeking; but, returning to the fact of his genius, it is pleasanter, and more profitable, to recall what may be said by way of explaining how he should have been capable of the worst. His upbringing was against him. As Mr. Santayana says: 'Shelley seems hardly to have been brought up; he grew up in the nursery among his young sisters, at school among the rude boys, without any affectionate guidance, without imbibing any religious or social tradition.' Driven in on himself, he nourished the inner life of adolescence on the trashy fantasies and cheap excitements of the Terror school. The phase of serious tradition in which, in incipient maturity, he began to practise poetry was, in a subtler way, as unfavourable: Shelley needed no encouragement to cultivate spontaneity of emotion and poetical abeyance of thought. Then the state of the world at the time must, in its effect on a spirit of Shelley's sensitive humanity and idealizing bent, be allowed to account for a great deal—as the sonnet, *England in 1819,* so curiously intimates:

An old, mad, blind, despised, and dying king,—
Princes, the dregs of their dull race, who flow
Through public scorn,—mud from a muddy spring,—
Rulers who neither see, nor feel, nor know,
But leech-like to their fainting country cling,
Till they drop, blind in blood, without a blow,—
A people starved and stabbed in the untilled field,—
An army, which liberticide and prey
Makes as a two-edged sword to all who wield,—
Golden and sanguine laws which tempt and slay;
Religion Christless, Godless—a book sealed;
A Senate,—Time's worst statute unrepealed,—
Are graves, from which a glorious Phantom may
Burst, to illumine our tempestuous day.

The contrast between the unusual strength (for Shelley) of the main body of the sonnet and the pathetic weakness of the final couplet is eloquent. Contemplation of the actual world being unendurable, Shelley devotes himself to the glorious Phantom that may (an oddly ironical stress results from the rime position) work a sudden miraculous change but is in any case as vague as Demogorgon and as unrelated to actuality —to which Shelley's Evil is correspondingly unrelated.

The strength of the sonnet, though unusual in kind for Shelley, is not of remarkably distinguished quality in itself; the kindred strength of *The Mask of Anarchy* is. Of this poem Professor Elton says:[11] 'There is a likeness in it to Blake's [gift] which has often been noticed; the same kind of anvil-stroke, and the same use of an awkward simplicity for the purposes of epigram.' The likeness to Blake is certainly there—much more of a likeness than would have seemed possible from the characteristic work. It lies, not in any assumed broadsheet naïveté or crudity such as the account cited might perhaps suggest, but in a rare emotional integrity and force, deriving from a clear, disinterested and mature vision.

When one fled past, a maniac maid,
And her name was Hope, she said:
But she looked more like Despair,
And she cried out in the air:

'My father Time is weak and gray
With waiting for a better day;
See how idiot-like he stands,
Fumbling with his palsied hands!

> He has had child after child,
> And the dust of death is piled
> Over every one but me—
> Misery, oh, Misery!'
>
> Then she lay down in the street,
> Right before the horses' feet,
> Expecting, with a patient eye,
> Murder, Fraud, and Anarchy.

These stanzas do not represent all the virtue of the poem, but they show its unusual purity and strength. In spite of 'Murder, Fraud, and Anarchy,' there is nothing of the usual Shelleyan emotionalism—no suspicion of indulgence, insistence, corrupt will or improper approach. The emotion seems to inhere in the vision communicated, the situation grasped: Shelley sees what is in front of him too clearly, and with too pure a pity and indignation, to have any regard for his emotions as such; the emotional value of what is presented asserts itself, or rather, does not need asserting. Had he used and developed his genius in the spirit of *The Mask of Anarchy* he would have been a much greater, and a much more readable, poet.

But *The Mask of Anarchy* is little more than a marginal throw-off, and gets perhaps too much stress in even so brief a distinguishing mention as this. The poetry in which Shelley's genius manifests itself characteristically, and for which he has his place in the English tradition, is much more closely related to his weaknesses. It would be perverse to end without recognizing that he achieved memorable things in modes of experience that were peculiarly congenial to the European mind in that phase of its history and are of permanent interest. The sensibility expressed in the *Ode to the West Wind* is much more disablingly limited than current valuation allows, but the consummate expression is rightly treasured. The Shelleyan confusion appears, perhaps, at its most poignant in *The Triumph of Life,* the late unfinished poem. This poem has been paralleled with the revised *Hyperion,* and it is certainly related by more than the *terza rima* to Dante. There is in it a profounder note of disenchantment than before, a new kind of desolation, and, in its questioning, a new and profoundly serious concern for reality:

> . . . their might
> Could not repress the mystery within,
> And for the morn of truth they feigned, deep night

Caught them ere evening . . .

For in the battle Life and they did wage,
She remained conqueror . . .

'Whence camest thou? and whither goest thou?
How did thy course begin?' I said, 'and why?

Mine eyes are sick of this perpetual flow
Of people, and my heart sick of one sad thought—
Speak!'

     as one between desire and shame
Suspended, I said—If, as it doth seem,
Thou comest from the realm without a name

Into this valley of perpetual dream,
Show whence I came and where I am, and why—
Pass not away upon the passing stream.

But in spite of the earnest struggle to grasp something real, the sincere revulsion from personal dreams and fantasies, the poem itself is a drifting phantasmagoria—bewildering and bewildered. Vision opens into vision, dream unfolds within dream, and the visionary perspectives, like those of the imagery in the passage of *Mont Blanc,* shift elusively and are lost; and the failure to place the various phases or levels of visionary drift with reference to any grasped reality is the more significant because of the palpable effort. Nevertheless, *The Triumph of Life* is among the few things one can still read and go back to in Shelley when he has become, generally, 'almost unreadable.'

Shelley's part in the later notion of 'the poetical' has been sufficiently indicated. His handling of the medium assimilates him readily, as an influence, to the Spenserian-Miltonic line running through *Hyperion* to Tennyson. Milton is patently present in *Alastor,* the earliest truly Shelleyan poem; and *Adonais*—

Afar the melancholy thunder moaned,
Pale Ocean in unquiet slumber lay

—relates him as obviously to *Hyperion* as to *Lycidas.* Indeed, to compare the verse of *Hyperion,* where the Miltonic Grand Style is transmuted by the Spenserianizing Keats, with that of *Adonais* is to bring out the essential relation between the organ resonances of *Paradise Lost* and the pastoral melodizing [12] of *Lycidas.* Mellifluous mourning in *Adonais* is

286

a more fervent luxury than in *Lycidas,* and more declamatory ('Life like a dome of many-coloured glass'—the famous imagery is happily conscious of being impressive, but the impressiveness is for the spell-bound, for those sharing the simple happiness of intoxication); and it is, in the voluptuous self-absorption with which the medium enjoys itself, rather nearer to Tennyson.

But, as was virtually said in the discussion of imagery from the *Ode to the West Wind,* the Victorian poet with whom Shelley has some peculiar affinities is Swinburne.

NOTES

1. See the essay on Shelley in *Winds of Doctrine.*

2. *Verse and Prose from the Manuscripts of Percy Bysshe Shelley.* Edited by Sir John C. E. Shelley-Rolls, Bart., and Roger Ingpen.

3. See *Four Words* (now reprinted in *Words and Idioms),* by Logan Pearsall Smith.

4. *Letters and Journals,* ed. R. E. Prothero, vol iii, p. 405 (1900). (I am indebted for this quotation to Mr. F. W. Bateson's *English Poetry and the English Language.)*

5. 'His ideal of my future,—now entirely formed in conviction of my genius, —was that I should enter at college into the best society, take all the best prizes every year, and a double first to finish with; marry Lady Clara Vere de Vere; write poetry as good as Byron's, only pious; preach sermons as good as Bossuet's, only Protestant; be made, at forty, Bishop of Winchester, and at fifty, Primate of England.' *Praeterita,* vol. i, p. 340 (1886).

6. *Oxford Lectures on Poetry,* p. 167.

7. Poesy's unfailing river
    Which through Albion winds forever
    Lashing with melodious wave
    Many a sacred Poet's grave . . .
          Lines Written Among the Euganean Hills.

8. See, for instance, the poem beginning, 'That time is dead for ever, child.'

9. See the last stanza of 'Rarely, rarely comest thou.'

10. Cf. Senseless is the breast, and cold,
     Which relenting love would fold;
     Bloodless are the veins and chill
     Which the pulse of pain did fill;
     Every little living nerve
     That from bitter words did swerve
     Round the tortured lips and brow,
     Are like sapless leaflets now,
     Frozen upon December's brow.
          Lines Written Among the Euganean Hills.

11. *Survey of English Literature, 1780–1830*, Vol. II, p. 202.
12.

> O Golden tongued Romance, with serene lute!
> Fair plumed Syren, Queen of far-away!
> Leave melodizing on this wintry day,
> Shut up thine olden pages, and be mute:

Keats. *Sonnet: on sitting down to read King Lear once again.*

FREDERICK A. POTTLE

The Case of Shelley

THE CASE of Shelley requires us to come to grips with the problem posed
by the decline of a first-rate reputation. It would be easier to discuss if it
followed a more conventional formula; if, for example, it were true to
say that Shelley was ignored in his lifetime, idolized by the Victorians,
and not seriously attacked till the New Critics took him in hand. As a
matter of fact, he was not ignored in his lifetime, and some extremely
able depreciation of his poetry appeared in the Victorian era. The
critics of the period 1814–1822 paid a surprising amount of attention
to him, generally concurring in the verdict that he was a poet of great
but misguided powers.[1] This attitude did not give way to one of complete approval, but continued to characterize much of the most respected criticism of the century down almost to its end. The classic
statement of the position is perhaps that of Wordsworth, made only five
years after Shelley's death: 'Shelley is one of the best *artists* of us all:
I mean in workmanship of style.'[2] This is high praise from a man whose
praise in such matters counts, but it is far from being unmixed praise.
By saying *artist* rather than *poet*, and by emphasizing the word, Wordsworth meant to qualify: Shelley, he is saying, was a very able craftsman
but he chose to write about the wrong things. Matthew Arnold and
Leslie Stephen disagreed about the nature of Wordsworth's virtues but
they were essentially in agreement as to the nature of Shelley's defects.
Those defects, they said, were unreality and unsubstantiality. To Arnold,
Shelley was a beautiful *and ineffectual* angel; to Stephen, Shelley's
poetry was too often the rainbow-colored mist into which the stagnant

Originally printed in *Publications of the Modern Language Association of
America*, LXVII (1952), pp. 589–608. Revised for this volume by the author.

pool of Godwin's paradoxes had been transmuted.[3] Poe, Melville, George Henry Lewes, Swinburne, and Francis Thompson were ardent Shelleyans, Browning an ardent Shelleyan who later admitted some qualifications. Lamb, Hazlitt, Carlyle, Kingsley, and Mark Twain were violent anti-Shelleyans; the admiration of Emerson, Tennyson, and William Morris was less than hearty.[4] During this time, generally speaking, the objections to Shelley's subject-matter shade off from loathing to unexcited disapproval or to the mere recognition of a limitation; while at the same time the emotions roused by his personality can be seen generally changing from hatred to affection, or at least to respect. To the earliest critics Shelley was a monster of immorality and impiety; to the later (even to many who did not care much for his poetry) he was an angel, a pure unearthly spirit. And a remarkable paradox emerges: though respected critics continually reiterate their lack of full satisfaction with the subject-matter of Shelley's poems, it is conceded as a matter of course everywhere in England and America, long before the end of the century, that he is one of the greatest English poets.

But not quite like the others in that company. From the first appearance of Shelley's poems down at least to the year 1917 (and I can hardly have been the last to experience it) his poems had a unique power to intoxicate and to enthral sensitive young men and women, to operate upon them with the force of a sudden conversion. And this power of conversion had unpleasant consequences. Many people, as the range of their literary experience widened, grew ashamed of the extravagance of their youthful discipleship and transferred their disgust to the poetry that had caused it. Others never did extend their range much but remained one-poet men all their lives. The Shelleyans have included an alarming number of crackpots, cranks, fanatics, and bores. A discouraging amount of the writing on Shelley at all periods has been polemical, violently for or violently against.

The more tidy experiential arrangement would be to give the entire summary of Shelley's reputation down to the present day before advancing any theory. But because we have already uncovered what appears to be a central, permanent, and legitimate cause of disagreement among critics of Shelley, I shall pause to dissect it out before going on to isolate others which seem to require historical explanations. In the power of Shelley's poetry to make conversions we have a clue to the paradox of the Victorian criticism. Shelley is a passionately religious poet. His theory of poetry, which he himself developed at length in his *Defence of Poetry*, identifies poetry with prophecy. As Arthur Clutton-

Brock pointed out, he has been misunderstood by many critics because, being violently unorthodox, he has always been read as a secular poet, not for what he is. No one would have complained of the unreality of his poetry or of its want of substance if his subject-matter, like Crashaw's, had been the Christian religion instead of that religion which he was always trying to discover and to express for himself.[5] He believed literally that there is a spirit in Nature, and that Nature therefore is never a mere 'outward world.' When he invoked the breath of Autumn's being, he was not indulging in an empty figure. The breath ('spiritus') that he invoked was to him as real and as awful as the Holy Ghost was to Milton. He believed that this spirit works within the world as a soul contending with obstruction and striving to penetrate and transform the whole mass. He looked forward to that far-off day when the 'plastic stress' of this power shall have mastered the last resistance and have become all in all, when outward nature, which now suffers with man, shall have been redeemed with him. This is the faith of the prophet, the faith held by the authors of Isaiah and of the Revelation, though of course their theologies differed widely and fundamentally from Shelley's. Shelley's main passion as a poet was not, in the ordinary sense, to reform the world; it was to create an apocalypse of the world formed and realized by Intellectual Beauty or Love.[6]

I am sure that Clutton-Brock is right in insisting that the way to understand, perhaps even to be moved by, Shelley's alleged unsubstantiality and lack of intellectual content is to realize that he is a prophetic poet. I do not know that any one has yet pointed out that it is also the way to understand another quality of his poetry which people of the present day find even more troublesome: I mean his alleged unmanliness, what it is now the fashion to call his maudlin self-pity. Those who knew Shelley intimately (and they included some men of very masculine character) all testify to the manliness, cheerfulness, and courageousness of his private life. He seems, after he attained to maturity, to have been very much the kind of man who keeps his personal troubles to himself. Though I agree with Mr. T. S. Eliot that his letters are not very good reading, I find them after 1814 on the whole manly and not without qualities of shrewdness and humor. Some of his short lyric poems are personal, really do give utterance to a private sense of weakness and unhappiness, but they are fewer than is commonly supposed, and, so far as I can remember, *Lines Written Among the Euganean Hills* is the only one of them that he ever published. In most of his despondent verse it is the general and properly public woe of the *vates,* the prophet, that is being expressed. For the prophet cannot merely rest in saying that the earth shall be full of the knowledge of the Lord, as the waters cover the sea; having been overwhelmed with the loveliness of that vision, he must cry, 'How long, Lord?' Over against the ecstatic apocalypse, in every prophetic tradition, there stands the despondent psalm; over against the power of the divine afflatus, the weakness of uninspired humanity. 'Thou art the God of my *strength*,' says the Psalmist, 'why hast thou put me from thee? and why go I so *heavily* while the enemy oppresseth me?' And again, 'Why art thou so *heavy*, O my soul?' Shelley's psalm employs the same vocabulary to express the same situation: '. . . The impulse of thy *strength* . . . O uncontrollable! A *heavy* weight of hours has chained and bowed . . .'

No matter how unitarian critics may be in theory, practical criticism in the long run judges poetry for both aesthetic and moral value: or, to use Arnold's terminology, for 'felicity and perfection of diction and manner' and for 'truth and seriousness of substance and matter.' The standards for aesthetic value (as I shall say later) appear to be relative to the evaluating sensibility; those for moral value to be more nearly uniform from age to age. The total judgment, as Arnold says, 'strikes a balance.'[7] But since there is no common denominator for the two kinds of value, the total judgment is a compromise. And not merely a compromise; it is always a *personal* compromise. Two critics may be in substantial agreement as to the amount of aesthetic and moral value in a given poem and yet may emerge with the opposed verdicts 'Good' and 'Bad' because they weight the two factors differently. In the long run, however, and generally speaking, criticism gives greater weight to aesthetic value in poetry than it does to moral value. Poets (Shelley is an example) who continue to be vigorously attacked for their subject-matter will go on being rated great poets as long as readers in general feel and testify to the 'felicity and perfection of their diction and manner.'

We have uncovered the problem of belief in poetry, always a troublesome one and peculiarly troublesome in the case of Shelley. For it is hard to see how one can read a prophetic poet without vivid feelings of some sort about the prophecy that is being made. The prophetic poet has a message and he believes passionately in it. He strains forward towards his apocalyptic vision; his perception of the world 'as it is' is affected by what he believes it may become. What are you going to do about a prophet whose poetic gifts you consider to be of the first order but whose prophecy strikes you as heretical or silly?

In such a case, no matter what test you set up, whether Arnold's 'truth and seriousness' or Eliot's that the view of life presented must be 'coherent, mature, and founded on the facts of experience,'[8] different critics, and good critics too, are going to emerge with different answers. It is not merely that we cannot agree on what is true; we cannot even agree on what is respectable. There will always be serious and qualified critics, who, like Wordsworth and Arnold, will grant that Shelley was a great artist, but will condemn him for the ideas he has presented, the view of the world that inheres in his writings. But if that were the whole of the case against Shelley, there would be no reason for saying that his reputation is declining. We should merely have the same state of affairs that has existed from the beginning. There never was so complete and general an acceptance of Shelley's subject-matter as there apparently was, let us say, of Pope's. There has always been a numerous and respectable body of anti-Shelleyans, but until recently Shelley's reputation maintained itself against their strictures. And the reason is clear. So long as Shelley was widely recognized, both by those who liked his poetry and by those who did not, as one of the best artists of us all—or, to use Eliot's words, as having poetic gifts of the first order—attacks on the cogency of his thought would not have succeeded in damping his fame. Opposed to every Eliot who decried his thought would have been a Bradley or a C. S. Lewis to argue eloquently that Shelley's thought *is* coherent, mature, and founded on the facts of experience.[9] And there would have been others to assert that even if Shelley's view of life is somewhat thin and unsubstantial, he offers, especially in his lyrics, such an over-plus of aesthetic value as to make up for the defect.

To return now to the survey. The period from about 1895 to 1920 marked the highest point of the tide of Shelley's reputation. The problem of belief became a great deal less troublesome. Two of the most distinguished practitioners of literature during that time, Hardy and Shaw, were out-and-out Shelleyans: men who not only respected Shelley's art but who also found his ideas congenial. Shaw's religion, in fact, was by his own confession derived in large part from Shelley, and it resembled Shelley's closely. Yeats in his first period was a committed Shelleyan, regarding *Prometheus Unbound* as 'a sacred book' and *A Defence of Poetry* as 'the profoundest essay on the foundation of poetry in English.'[10] Some of the best academic critics of the time, for example, Bradley and Elton, wrote sympathetically and persuasively of the positive virtues of Shelley's poetry, without more qualification than is to be expected in any serious and patient evaluation. The consensus of this late-Victorian or late-Romantic criticism was that Shelley's minor works were his major works; that admirable as his longer works may be, they show his limitations in a way that his lyrics do not; that Shelley was England's greatest lyric poet.

The rise of the New Humanists marked the turn of the tide. Paul Elmer More's essay on Shelley appeared in 1910, but it is my impression that the water-line did not begin visibly to retreat until the publication of Irving Babbitt's *Rousseau and Romanticism* in 1919. From that time to this the reputation of Shelley has continued steadily to ebb.

I wish I knew whether the assault of the New Humanists really had anything in common with that of the New Critics. I should rather guess that it had little more than the fact that T. S. Eliot was educated at Harvard in the prime of Irving Babbitt, and that Eliot admired the work of Paul Elmer More. The New Humanists were not practitioners of any literature except the literature of criticism; they were academics, and their attack was essentially moralistic. Though their standards of value were somewhat different from Arnold's, their methods were similar. The New Criticism is something very different. Like Wordsworth's prefaces, it is essentially the manifesto of a new idiom in poetry; it has its origin in the works of practitioners like Pound, Eliot, the later Yeats, Ransom, Tate, and Warren. It will be sufficient for the purposes of this paper to say that the New Humanists' attack on Shelley, though it was vigorously continued and has not yet ceased, soon merged with and became trifling in comparison with the attack of those younger contemporary practitioners of literature who devote themselves also to criticism, and of critics who followed their lead.

It is very important to realize that the present revolt from Shelley was not academic in origin, but was a revolt of practitioners of literature. It is not necessary to name the significant modern writers who are anti-Shelleyan; one had better save time and say that they all are. And the more significant modern academic criticism, as I have said, took its lead from the practitioners, and is remarkably like that of the practitioners. Brooks and Leavis are in substantial agreement on the subject of Shelley with Ransom, Tate, and Warren. Indeed, the central modern critical document on Shelley may be taken to be Leavis' essay in *Revaluation*.

Because modern criticism is so polemical, it is not easy to discover what it really wants to do with Shelley. One distinguished modern practitioner of whom I asked the question told me with warmth that he wished Shelley to be completely forgotten and as soon as possible; but he added that he knew he was unfair. Another, whom I charged with disliking Shelley, replied, 'I like Shelley very much when he will behave himself.' The second statement is probably the more candid, and indicates a wish on the part of modern critics, not to eliminate Shelley utterly from the roll of English poets, but to reduce his stature, to turn him from a major into a minor poet. And they are not content, as the nineteenth century was, to rest their case for this depreciation on the truth and seriousness of his substance and matter. When Mr. Eliot invoked the Arnoldian formula, saying that he could 'only regret that Shelley did not live to put his poetic gifts, which were certainly of the first order, at the service of more tenable beliefs,' Dr. Leavis rebuked him rather sharply.[11] Modern critics repudiate the dualism of the nineteenth century and test all poetry by a unitary standard. They may be diametrically opposed in their basic positions, some asserting that the aesthetic value of a poem is a function of its moral and theological soundness, others that when the beliefs of a poet are properly ordered in a poem, the question of their truth or falsity outside the poem does not rise, but the practical result is the same. One no longer says that a man is a great artist but lacking in wisdom. To Dr. Leavis or Mr. Tate, Shelley is not a great artist dealing with an unfortunate subject-matter; he is a bungler, a bad craftsman, and *therefore* a bad poet. This, in spite of the confusing survivals of older oppositions that turn up in the New Criticism, is something new. Our survey of Shelley's reputation has given reason to suppose that a poet can withstand a good deal of attack on the soundness of his ideas so long as a majority of the people who read him find aesthetic value of a high order in his poetry. But if a majority of the people who read him get little aesthetic value from him, his reputation is certainly going to be scaled down.

So much for the historical material. The principle which I offer for ordering it is that of aesthetic relativism, which I shall elaborate in the following set of definitions.

Poetry may be generally defined as language that expresses the qualities of experience, in distinction from language that indicates its uses. If one wishes to define more closely, one must introduce historical factors, specifications of some poetry but not of all poetry.

Poetry expresses the qualities of experience in terms of given historic sensibilities. Each historic sensibility has an idiom completely expressive of it. It *needs* that idiom and struggles to attain it. The needs of our sensibility do not operate merely at the level of the literary imagination,

they are *interests* operating at the very lowest level of perception an
shaping that largely inferential synthesis which we call 'the world as it is

The organization of sensibility is always changing or shifting. A
given moments in history, for example at the turn of the eighteent'
century and again in the third decade of the twentieth, this shift becam
remarkably accelerated.

The standards by which men evaluate poetry, when they actually d
evaluate it personally and do not quote other people, are the definition
of their own sensibilities. In dealing with contemporary poetry, critic
who are abreast of the shift strive to define the truly modern idiom an
to facilitate its emergence; in dealing with poetry of the past, the
judge in terms of the needs of their own sensibilities. When critics sa
that a poem is good, they usually mean that it meets the needs of thei
sensibilities; when they say that it is bad, that it does not.

The organization of modern sensibility can be characterized not un
fairly by a metaphor of catastrophe. The present generation is a ship
wrecked generation. It has come ashore on a desert island with very littl
baggage and with few tools. Life on this desert island is possible, bu
only as men are vigilant, strong, self-reliant, and courageous. Self-pit
is dangerous. The most that can be hoped for is so little above bar
survival that any person who reminds the men on the island of the easie
life they enjoyed before the shipwreck, or who draws glowing picture
of a better day in store for the island in the far-distant future, will b
roughly silenced. 'They ain't a thing you can do about it, so shut up.' [1]
Men in this state cannot afford the display of much emotion; they mus
be wary, tight-lipped, 'tough-minded.'

When modern sensibility demands that poetry shall deal with th
actual world, the phrase means something very different from what i
meant one hundred and fifty years ago. To men now it means the worl
as it presents itself to average perception in a culture that has bee
thoroughly imbued with the positivistic temper. Modern sensibilit
meets the dilemma of belief by using a starkly positivistic perception o
the world to adumbrate non-positivistic values. It is skeptical of al
large syntheses based on faith, indeed of all large syntheses whatsoeve
It wants no prophetic poetry, at least no poetry of millennial prophecy
It shuns commitments; if it makes them, it wants to know thoroughl
what it is letting itself in for. It is very suspicious of pronounced rhythm
in verse. It wants its poetry developed, not by explicit statement, an
not by a flood of images each relevant at only one point, but by th
developed image, a large image firmly held, displaying point after poin

of relevancy. It dislikes metaphors within metaphors. Above all, it wants no simplification or purification of experience in the interests of alleged beauty or of an alleged higher truth. It insists that since the experience of the actual world is always a complex of the pleasant and the disgusting, of the beautiful and the ugly, of attraction and horror, poetry must hold the discordant elements together, not allow them to separate. Poetry must operate through Irony, Paradox, and Understatement.

Modern criticism maintains that by these standards Shelley is a bad poet. He is sentimental: that is, he calls for a greater display of emotion than the modern reader feels to be warranted by the occasion. He employs pronounced, intoxicating, hypnotic rhythms that seem to be trying to sweep the reader into hasty emotional commitments. He seldom uses a firmly held, developed image, but pours out a flood of images which one must grasp momentarily in one aspect and then release. He is fond of figures within figures. He imposes his will on the object of experience: he does not explore 'reality,' he flies away from it. He seldom takes a gross, palpable, near-at-hand object from the world of ordinary perception and holds it for contemplation: his gaze goes up to the sky, he starts with objects that are just on the verge of becoming invisible or inaudible or intangible and he strains away even from these. He exhibits dissociation of sensibility: though he is even too much aware of the disgusting, the ugly, the painful, and the horrible, he puts all the beauty into one poem and all the ugliness into another, or he sorts them out in different portions of the same poem. He luxuriates in emotion. He embarrasses the reader by representing himself as weak, frail, bowed, bleeding, fainting, and dying.

It must be sufficiently apparent that I consider Shelley a great poet. I do not, however, share the confident belief of many of my colleagues that the anti-Shelleyanism of the New Critics is a mere fad or fashion that will soon pass away. I lecture to a large group of undergraduates each year on Shelley, and I read a good many of the critical papers which they and my graduate students write on Shelley's poetry. It is clear to me that within fifty years practically everybody will be saying about Shelley what the New Critics are saying now. The disesteem of Shelley is going to become general, and it may continue for a century or more.[13]

So much of the judgment of Shelley as I have outlined above is a valid judgment. Modern criticism, after a remarkable acceleration in shift of sensibility, is engaged in establishing the autonomy of its own idiom. Its worst enemy is the debased or effete Romantic idiom of our latter-day Shelleyans. Modern criticism is right in recognizing Shelley as the great central exemplar of the idiom and practice from which it must disengage itself. Even if it were to grant (as it ultimately will) that Shelley is a much abler poet than others with whom it is now classing him, it would still reject him. There is very little in Shelley's poetry that modern sensibility *needs*. One may put it more strongly: Shelley's poetry is poison for a modern craftsman.

The judgment of modern criticism on Shelley is in the main not only valid, it will remain valid within its own frame of reference. One should not say that it is *merely* the modern judgment of Shelley; it *is* the modern judgment of Shelley. The New Critics are doing just what all of us did in our day; if it seems radically different, it is only because there has been a great acceleration in shift of sensibility in the last thirty years. When the significant Shelley criticism of this age is collected, it will be Leavis' essay, or some essay like Leavis', that will be chosen, not anything I might write. My evaluation of Shelley (which is very different from Leavis') is already old-fashioned. The sort of thing I can do was done as well as it could be done almost forty years ago by Bradley, Clutton-Brock, and Elton.

But the judgment of modern criticism on Shelley, though valid and permanently valid, is not exclusively valid. It does not impair in the least the validity of the serious criticism that preceded it. And it will not prevent Shelley from returning to very high general esteem. I do not see how any one could read carefully the great critical essays on Shelley from Bagehot's in 1856 to Grierson's in 1946 and still predict that the history of Shelley's reputation will be like Cowley's. It will probably be much more like Pope's. Though the Romantics and the Victorians steadily depreciated Pope and even went so far as to call him no poet at all, they continued to accord him practically the status of a major poet by showing that they were unable to ignore and forget him. By shifting the area of their attention, they were even able to read him. Though they were repelled by the satires and the *Essay on Man*, they found they could enjoy *The Rape of the Lock, Eloisa to Abelard,* and the *Elegy to the Memory of an Unfortunate Lady.* Shelley will not be dropped from the academic curriculum, but he will probably occupy a less prominent place there than he now does, and he will be represented by different assignments. It will be possible, even in Shelley, to find some poems congenial to the modern temper. *Mont Blanc,* with its extended image, will be preferred to the *Ode to a Skylark*. Dr. Leavis has also said a good word for *The Mask of Anarchy*. Mr. Eliot, whose pronouncements on Shelley since 1933 have been generally respectful, has high praise for *The Triumph of Life*.[14]

Are we then to conclude that whatever is is right, that the experiential method merely describes the vicissitudes of reputation but never submits any critical practice to judgment? By no means. I believe that modern criticism is doing very well, but I think it could be improved and still remain true to itself.

I have no right to demand of those modern critics who are genuinely and thoughtfully absolutist that they accede to the views I am here setting forth. My views and theirs are radically incompatible. We must simply say to each other, 'Our disagreement is fundamental.' But I cannot escape the feeling that the majority of the New Critics are anything but consistent and clear-headed absolutists. It appears to me that they constantly make statements which indicate that the real cast of their thought is, like mine, subjective and experiential, and that therefore their absolutism is arbitrary and illogical. I do not think that many of them, if they forced themselves to think that far back, could tolerate the stark rationalism of the *a priori* position which they would see that their absolutism assumes. It appears to me that their absolutism is a prejudice; that it springs in part from the very human but unregenerate passion we all have for bullying other people, in larger part from not having recognized the fact that one can make real judgments without making absolute judgments; that a judgment may be firm, unqualified, and valid without being absolutely so.

Let me illustrate. An observer on the ground, standing at the right place, will announce that the track of a bomb falling from a plane is a parabola. If another person *standing at that same point* says it is something else, he is, simply wrong. But if an observer *in the plane* says that the track is a straight line, he is not wrong. In relation to the plane the track *is* a straight line. This observer's report has the same standing as that of the first observer on the ground.

I sincerely believe that many of our modern critics would not only be more comfortable, they would be a good deal more persuasive on a basis of reasoned relativism than they are on their present basis of uneasy and dogmatic absolutism. A critic who changed his base would not have to alter his critical standards in the least. He would merely give up the attempt to identify—I am partly quoting, partly paraphrasing a recent pronouncement of Mr. T. S. Eliot[15]—what is best for his own time with what is best universally and always; he would stop pretending to erect a theory good for all time upon his perception of what is needed for the present. It is a necessary and laudable task to show the limitations of Shelley's poetry by measuring it against modern sensibility. But (I should maintain) it is equally necessary and laudable to expose the limitations of modern sensibility by measuring it against Shelley's poetry.

I wish modern criticism to continue to judge literature firmly by modern standards, but if it could find ways to be less polemic, it would go down better with me, and I think it would read better a hundred years from now. It is true that our present-day critics are no more arrogant than Wordsworth and no more spiteful than Swinburne, but I should like Wordsworth's criticism better if he had not been so arrogant and Swinburne's better if he had not been so spiteful. The battle, though not over, is clearly won. Is it not possible now to relax, to be candid, to stop sneering and snarling? Is it not possible for the New Critics to admit a little *pietas*? Would it not be more seemly for critics who occupy prominent positions as professors of English to stop using the term 'professor' merely as one of abuse?

For it must be clear to any fair-minded observer that modern criticism of Shelley is not completely candid. The critics are still making a case. They are suppressing much that could be said for his poetry on their own grounds. They are practicing, and encouraging others to practice, a kind of reading of him which they would brand as superficial if applied to Donne or Yeats.

I wish modern criticism would spend less time in prescription and more in calm, patient, neutral description. Though our judgments of the value of Shelley's poems are bound to vary widely and unpredictably, all critics of all periods ought ideally to be able to *describe* his poems in the same way: ought to be able to say, 'The structure of thought of this poem is so-and-so,' or, 'The metaphors of this poem are such-and-such.' Actually, after a thorough-going shift in sensibility, critics manhandle and misread poems because, since they dislike them, they do not approach them with patience and good will.[16] We can now see how clumsy and obtuse the Victorians often were in reading Pope: they speak glibly of the lack of distinction in his ideas without bothering to understand them, and they misread his figures. We cannot blame them for not liking Pope better, but it does seem as though they could have described him more accurately. Wordsworth says that you must love a poet before he will seem worthy of your love. It is so; and love is a thing that cannot be commanded. Respect, however, can, and respect will go a long way. One can, and should, conclude that a poet is worthy of respect when one finds that a good many respectable critics have respected him and still do respect him. All accomplished poetry requires close reading and Shelley's is especially difficult. The danger the New Critics run is that of not taking Shelley seriously enough.

A critic who calls Shelley careless should be very careful to make sure he has understood him. It is true that Shelley is more careless than Wordsworth or Milton, but he is less careless than Keats or Shakespeare. Shelley appears to have been quite innocent of any instruction in English grammar: he writes just as he talked and his conversational tradition (Eton), though good, was not at all points identical with the formal written standard. Consequently his poetry anywhere may make the verb agree in number with the nearest noun rather than with the actual subject; like Byron he is capable of sentences that never conclude. His larger compositions show occasional patches that read like improvisations that he never went back to finish. But these sketchy or unfinished areas are generally peripheral; they seldom affect the main design. On the whole he deserved Wordsworth's tribute to his craftsmanship. What modern critics call carelessness in Shelley is more often the highly adroit and skilful writing of a kind of poetry which they do not understand because they do not like that kind of poetry.

The New Critics show a remarkable want of delicacy of touch in handling Shelley, and they too often misread the poems they condemn. The tactic of bringing up *Romeo and Juliet* to demolish *The Indian Serenade* is a good deal like training a sixteen-inch gun on a cat-boat. The poem was never meant to compete in that class. It is playful and extravagant; it is a dramatic poem; it follows a well-known convention. One is not to assume that the person speaking is really fainting or failing or dying or even that he thinks he is; he is a young man (an East-Indian young man, at that) singing a serenade. Faced with a witty seventeenth-century love-poem of extravagant compliment, the modern critic knows just how to handle it; faced with Romantic extravagance, he loses all lightness of touch and becomes priggish and solemn.

Or take Dr. Leavis' contention that Shelley's metaphors sprout other metaphors that are suggested merely by the *words* he has just used. 'What,' says he, referring to the opening lines of the second stanza of the *Ode to the West Wind*, 'are those "tangled boughs of Heaven and Ocean"? They stand for nothing that Shelley could have pointed to in the scene before him; the "boughs," it is plain, have grown out of the "leaves" in the previous line . . .' Because things cannot be given precise and limited location by a gesture of the forefinger, it does not follow that they are non-existent. Clouds, it is true, have no visible means of support, but they are actually just as much subject to gravity as leaves are. If they 'hang' high in the heavens, forming a solid and relatively stationary canopy, it is because they are being held there by a tangle of sunbeams, air, and water vapor ('Ocean'). A critic who believes that it is bad poetic practice to cite transparent and diffused substances as parts of a visual image will undoubtedly find a great deal to object to in Shelley, for this is one of Shelley's favorite devices. But it is the old and familiar objection of vaporousness or 'abstraction,' not verbalism. That Shelley puts figures inside figures is certainly true. It may well be that in the debased Shelleyan tradition of the end of the nineteenth century and the beginning of the twentieth the secondary figures have only a verbal existence. I doubt if that ever happens with Shelley. At any rate, before I said so in any particular case, I should expect to have to approach him with good will and to spend as much time on the poem in question as I would on one by Donne or T. S. Eliot.

A final instance. Both Dr. Leavis and Mr. Tate have subjected 'When the lamp is shattered' to extended destructive analysis. Both have misread the basic figures of the poem. Dr. Leavis calls the first two lines a sentimental banality, an emotional *cliché:*

> When the lamp is shattered
> The light in the dust lies dead.

The figure, at least, is not a *cliché;* it is a brilliant one that I do not remember ever having seen in any other poem. Dr. Leavis must have read the second line as 'The light lies dead in the dust,' and have taken this to be a pretentious and ultimately dishonest way of stating the commonplace that light cannot survive its source. But Shelley has not inverted the word order: he wants the words to be read just as he wrote them. His figure (see the following one of the rainbow) deals with reflected or refracted light. In a room which is lighted by a lamp, some of the light of which you are aware comes directly from the lamp to your eye, some is reflected from walls, ceiling, and floor. The direct rays Shelley might have called 'the light in the lamp'; the reflected light he calls 'the light in the dust.' What he is saying is not something so obvious as that when the lamp is broken the light goes out; it is that when the lamp goes out, the walls and floor of the room don't go on shining with a luminescence of their own. The point of this appears in the

second stanza, where he applies the figure. The 'light in the lamp' is the
love of the spirit, the 'light in the dust' is the love of the flesh. But when
the light of the spirit goes out, the 'light in the dust' does *not* go out; it
shines on with a mournful vitality of its own. Love goes, lust remains.
When we come to 'heart' in the second stanza we see the reason for both
the 'dust' and the 'lies dead' of the first. A heart *is* 'dust'; it could in
literal fact 'lie dead.' When Shelley applies the expression figuratively
to light, he is deliberately and purposefully anticipating. This is what
Professor Wimsatt, in his useful analysis of the nature of Romantic
imagery, has called the importation of the tenor into the vehicle.[17]

Mr. Tate[18] confines his strictures to the last (the fourth) stanza of the
poem, but that stanza cannot be discussed apart from the preceding one:

> When hearts have once mingled   17
> Love first leaves the well-built nest;
>   The weak one is singled
> To endure what it once possessed.
>   O Love! who bewailest
> The frailty of all things here,
>   Why choose you the frailest
> For your cradle, your home and your bier?
>
> Its passions will rock thee   25
> As the storms rock the ravens on high;
>   Bright reason will mock thee,
> Like the sun from a wintry sky.
>   From thy nest every rafter
> Will rot, and thine eagle home
>   Leave thee naked to laughter,
> When leaves fall and cold winds come.

Mr. Tate identifies 'Its' of line 25 with 'Love's,' makes 'thee' a human
lover (a woman), and says that the ravens in line 26 are eagles in line
30. It is quite certain, I think, that the antecedent of 'Its' is 'the frailest
[heart]' of line 23, and 'thee' is Love. The poem is a bitter or ironic
contrary to 'Music, when soft voices die,' which Shelley had written in
the previous year. The 'argument' of the concluding stanza is that as
soon as lovers have enjoyed each other, they always fall out of love, but
unfortunately not at the same time. The weaker of the two (man or
woman) goes on loving after the stronger has been released. This hopeless persistence of love on one side causes love generally to seem unreasonable and ridiculous. The ultimate tenor is stated only in the three

spaced terms: 'passions,' 'reason,' and 'laughter.' Lines 18–24 adopt and develop as vehicle the old conceit that when a man and a woman are in love, it is because the god of Love is nesting in their hearts;[19] while in the concluding stanza, this conceit in turn becomes tenor to a vehicle of a nesting raven. Line 17 is the most troublesome of the poem, and perhaps should not be defended. Having committed himself, contrary to his general practice, to an elaborate extended figure, it may be thought that it was bad judgment on Shelley's part to lead into it by another heart figure which appears to be radically incompatible. The difficulty, I think, here as elsewhere in Shelley, is caused by telescoping of syntax. Lines 17–18, if one spelled out the mental connections one needs to make if one is to read the passage with the right tone, might run something like this: 'When hearts have once mingled [and separated again into the usual divided state which we express by calling them nests of the god of Love], Love first leaves the well-built nest.' The effect of the syntactical fusion on me, at least, is to reduce line 17 to the status of dead metaphor or ironic *cliché*, which is perhaps just what was intended: 'When hearts have once mingled [as one reads in sentimental poems, including my own].' But past that snag, the rest seems to me reasonably clear sailing. The poet addresses the god of Love: 'You are always complaining about human frailty, but if what you want is stability, why do you choose the frailer of two hearts to come to first and to linger in longest? You are supposed to be a noble creature, and your nest is supposed to be an eagle home; why, then, choose something much more like a raven's nest? [In Shelley's day the English raven commonly nested near the top of a tall tree; the golden eagle—the eagle *par excellence*—always built its nest on a cliff.] The passions of the frailer heart will rock you as rudely as the storm winds rock the ravens in their nest. Just as the raven, if it stays in the nest after the leaves fall, will be exposed to the bright cold sun and biting winds of winter, so, if you linger in the frail heart, you will be exposed to rational mockery and to laughter.' There are two parallel series of four terms each: on the one side, Love, frail heart, mocking reason, laughter; on the other, raven, nest in a deciduous tree, winter sun, cold winds. 'Eagle home' in line 30 I take to be bitterly ironic. Mr. Tate cites the 'confusion' of line 31: 'Are we to suppose that the other birds come by and mock the raven (eagle), or are we to shift the field of imagery and see "thee" as a woman?' This implies a rule that there shall never be any crossing-over of tenor into vehicle: extended similes must always run either *a, b, c, d* as *w, x, y, z*, or *a* as *w, b* as *x, c* as *y, d* as *z*. 'Laughter' in line 31 is mere carelessness: the figure demands 'sun and wind.' That Shelley constantly flashes back and forth between tenor and vehicle is undoubted, but I should agree with Professor Wimsatt (who of course does not guarantee this particular instance) that such practice is not carelessness but a brilliant extension of poetic possibilities.

I am not under the illusion that I have gone very far towards proving 'When the lamp is shattered' to be a good poem. I have no conviction that if Dr. Leavis and Mr. Tate accepted my reading of it they would like it any better. I doubt whether any person of advanced modern sensibility can like it very much. But I should like to think that I could make any patient and candid modern reader agree that it is a respectable poem.

I do not expect to reverse the decline in Shelley's reputation, though I confidently predict that that decline will one day be reversed. I do own my hope of persuading some of our modern critics to extend their present very narrow choice of judgments. A mature and complete criticism needs more verdicts than stark 'Good' and 'Bad.' It needs to recognize degrees of goodness and badness. Particularly, it needs to be able to discriminate poems that have seldom or never been found good by any recorded serious set of standards—metaphysical, neo-classical, romantic, present-day—from poems that have been emphatically declared good by a long line of respectable critics. Evaluation that confines itself to the sharp delineation of the present perspective is no doubt our first need, but it is only half of criticism.

NOTES

1. See Newman I. White (ed.), *The Unextinguished Hearth* (Durham, N.C., 1938).

2. An oral judgment recorded by his biographer, Christopher Wordsworth, in 1827. See Markham L. Peacock, Jr. (ed.), *The Critical Opinions of William Wordsworth* (Baltimore, 1950), under *Shelley* and *Byron*.

3. Matthew Arnold, concluding paragraphs of 'Byron' and 'Shelley' in *Essays in Criticism, Second Series;* Sir Leslie Stephen, 'Godwin and Shelley,' in *Hours in a Library.* The judgments were first published in 1881 and 1879 respectively.

4. Most of this material is conveniently collected in Newman I. White's *Shelley* (New York, 1940), especially in II, 389–418.

5. Arthur Clutton-Brock, 'Introduction' to *The Poems of Percy Bysshe Shelley*, ed. Charles D. Locock (London, 1911), I, xi–xxii. My summary is in large part direct quotation.

6. A good deal of this is taken verbally from Andrew C. Bradley's 'Shelley's View of Poetry,' in *Oxford Lectures on Poetry* (London, 1909), 152–153, and from the extension of that essay, 'Shelley and Arnold's Critique,' in *A Miscellany* (London, 1931), p. 149.

7. 'Byron,' in *Essays in Criticism, Second Series*.

8. Thomas S. Eliot, 'Shelley and Keats,' in *The Use of Poetry and the Use of Criticism* (Cambridge, Mass., 1933), pp. 87–88.

9. Professor Lewis's essay 'Shelley, Dryden, and Mr. Eliot' is reprinted in the present volume.

10. 'The Philosophy of Shelley's Poetry' in *Ideas of Good and Evil* (London, 1903), pp. 91, 93, 110–111.

11. *The Use of Poetry* (see n. 8), p. 88; Frank R. Leavis, 'Shelley,' above, pp. 268–269.

12. Red to Wyman in Norman Mailer's *The Naked and the Dead*, Part II, Sec. 5.

13. I guessed when I made this prediction that the presently dominant organization of sensibility would have about as long a reign as the neo-classic and the Romantic, but the speed of our modern methods of communication is probably bringing major shifts of sensibility closer together. Though I had not sensed it, the students at Yale had already begun to react from strict or polemic New Criticism before I wrote the present essay (end of 1951). The best of them now approach Shelley with good will and write perceptive papers on him. Academic publication of books and articles on Shelley has recently been very active. But I do not yet see among our practitioners of literature the emergence of an idiom that would justify one in concluding that the anti-Shelleyan trend has really been reversed. Shelley is not going to lack for defenders, but the defenders will be mainly academic and the justifications largely historical.

14. 'Talk on Dante,' *Kenyon Review* (XIV, 1952), pp. 178–188. Mr. Donald Davie's essay in the present volume (first published in 1953) furnishes other choices.

15. Preface to Leone Vivante's *English Poetry and Its Contribution to Knowledge of a Creative Principle* (London, 1950).

16. 'Our "Neo-classic" age is repeating those feats of its predecessor which we least applaud. It is showing a fascinating versatility in travesty. And the poets of the "Romantic" period provide for it what Shakespeare, Milton and Donne were to the early eighteenth-century grammarians and emendators—effigies to be shot at because what they represent is no longer understood' (Ivor A. Richards, *Coleridge on Imagination*, London, 1950, p. 196).

17. William K. Wimsatt, 'The Structure of Romantic Nature Imagery,' reprinted in this volume, pp. 24 ff.

18. 'Understanding Modern Poetry,' in *On the Limits of Poetry* (New York, 1948), p. 126.

19. Mr. Tate approves of this conceit as it appears in Guido Guinizelli: 'Al cor gentil ripara sempre Amore / Come alla selva augello in la vedura' (*Ibid.*, p. 78).

DONALD DAVIE

Shelley's Urbanity

(1) *The Shelleyan Sublime*

HOWEVER we look at it, Shelley affects the sublime. We may not know
what the sublime is, and yet know that, to be acceptable, it must include
'The Triumph of Life' and 'Prometheus Unbound.' Whatever we think
of these poems (and the latter at any rate makes dull reading in my
experience), there can be no doubt how high the poet aims in them,
what large pretensions he makes. In short, whatever his performance,
Shelley promises in these poems to move on a level where (for instance)
'urbanity' cannot count.

But this is what makes criticism of Shelley so difficult; he evades so
many standards. In this he is peculiar even among the poets of the sublime. His sublimity is peculiarly indefinite and impalpable. From one
point of view his poetry is certainly sensuous; but the sensuousness is
not of a sort to bring into poetry the reek and grit of common experience.
For Shelley goes as far as poetry can go, while it uses intelligible language, in cutting the hawsers which tie his fancies to the ground. His
metaphors are tied so tenuously to any common ground in experience
that it is peculiarly hard to arrive at their mooring in common logic or
association. It was this, for instance, which gave Mr. Eliot so much
trouble with an image in 'To a Skylark':

> Keen as are the arrows
> Of that silver sphere,
> Whose intense lamp narrows
> In the white dawn clear
> Until we hardly see—we feel that it is there.

From *Purity of Diction in English Verse* (Chatto and Windus Ltd., 1953),
pp. 133–59. Reprinted by permission of the publisher.

It is typical of Shelley's obscurity that as it happens I find no difficulty here, but only the accurate register of a sense-perception[1]—the fading of the morning-star. For Shelley evades as many standards as he can, and when he cannot evade them, makes their application as difficult as he can; or so it must seem to the harassed critic. And as a result we can expect to find the critics even further than usual from agreement about the nature of his achievement. All one can say is that the period of un-critical adulation is past, and that we have learnt, since Dr. Leavis' damaging scrutiny,[2] to be on our guard when Shelley is most sublime.

At any rate, if Shelley is great, in 'Prometheus Unbound,' in 'The Triumph of Life,' even in such shorter poems as 'The Cloud,' he is so by virtue of *invention*, the characteristic virtue of the sublime. And the eighteenth-century critics would agree that in poems of this sort the poet has considerable licence. We can expect (and it is only right) that the diction of an epic or a hymn will be less chaste than the diction of a familiar epistle. And we can go so far as to say that in the case of such poems the question of diction should not be introduced at all. But this is not quite true. There are always limits. As Keats remarked, 'English must be kept up'—even in the epic. And Shelley as usual goes to the limit, or over it.

'The Cloud' is a good example:

> Sublime on the towers of my skiey bowers,
>   Lightning my pilot sits;
> In a cavern under is fettered the thunder,
>   It struggles and howls at fits;
> Over earth and ocean, with gentle motion,
>   This pilot is guiding me,
> Lured by the love of the genii that move
>   In the depths of the purple sea;
> Over the rills, and the crags, and the hills,
>   Over the lakes and the plains,
> Wherever he dream, under mountain or stream,
>   The Spirit he loves remains;
> And I all the while bask in Heaven's blue smile,
>   Whilst he is dissolving in rains.

The image is audacious to begin with. There is no reason in natural philosophy to give a basis in logic to the notion that a cloud is directed by electric charges. The image depends entirely on association, and the leap of association is something of a strain. However, it is made easier

308

by the elaboration which makes the thunder a prisoner in the dungeons
of the cloud. Natural philosophy lends its aid to the logical association
of a cloud with the genii of the sea; and the lightning is supposed
amorous of the sea—a link sanctioned by neither logic nor association
(however 'free'), but carried as it were on the cloud's back. The real
difficulty comes with the 'he,' appearing three times in the last six lines.
Is this 'he' the lightning, the actual cloud, or the idea of the cloud which
is always present even in a cloudless sky? We are given no indication
that this 'he' is any other than 'the pilot,' i.e., the lightning. And yet this
is surely impossible in the last two lines:

> And I all the while bask in Heaven's blue smile,
> Whilst he is dissolving in rains.

Shelley means to say, I think, that the ideal cloud continues to bask
while the actual cloud dissolves in rains; but in fact he says that the
cloud, ideal or actual, rides high, while the lightning dissolves. And this
is lunacy.

The fault here lies in the conduct and development of a metaphor,
not, in the first place, in choice of language. And yet the two cannot be
distinguished since the metaphor only comes to grief on the loose use
of a personal pronoun. This looseness occurs time and again:

> The stars peep behind her and peer;
> And I laugh to see them whirl and flee,
> Like a swarm of golden bees,
> When I widen the rent in my wind-built tent,
> Till the calm rivers, lakes, and seas,
> Like strips of the sky fallen through me on high,
> Are each paved with the moon and these.

The grotesque 'and these' is an affront to all prosaic discipline. So again:

> I am the daughter of Earth and Water,
> And the nursling of the Sky;
> I pass through the pores of the ocean and shores;
> I change but I cannot die . . .

—where 'ocean and shores' is unthinkable in speech or prose. And finally:

> From cape to cape, with a bridge-like shape,
> Over a torrent sea,
> Sunbeam-proof, I hang like a roof,—
> The mountains its columns be.

Here the language is quite indiscriminate; the adjectival 'torrent' is a Latinate urbanity, 'sunbeam-proof' is an audacious coining, and 'The mountains . . . be' is a *naïveté*.

Obviously the conduct of the metaphor in the second stanza is a more serious flaw than any of these later examples. And obviously too, Shelley pitches his poem in a high key, to advise us not to expect nicety of discrimination and prosaic sense. The poem offers compensations. But all the same when the barbarities are so brutal and the carelessness so consistent, it may be doubted whether we can let them pass on any understanding. In poems of this sort, the weight to be given to diction and invention respectively is something that must be left to the taste of the reader. But this may serve as an example of how, even in sublime poems, the poet may take such liberties with his diction as to estrange his reader's sympathies. For one reader, at any rate, 'The Cloud' remains a poem splendid in conception but ruined by licentious phrasing.

(ii) *Shelley and the Familiar Style*

This does not dispose of Shelley's pretensions to sublimity. They confuse at almost every point the issue of his diction. In reading Wordsworth it is comparatively easy to distinguish the 'sublime' poems from the others, and to say that this poem begs the question of diction, this other does not. In the case of Shelley this is not so easily done. And yet there are poems by Shelley which plainly make no sublime pretensions. It was Ernest de Selincourt, I think, who proposed Shelley as one of the masters of the familiar style. The term, like all those which we find we need, is out of fashion; but plainly it refers to a quality of tone, of unflurried ease between poet and reader, in short to urbanity, the distinctive virtue of a pure diction.

It is worth remarking how unlikely this was, in the period when Shelley wrote. Plainly urbanity will come most easily to a poet who is sure of his audience, sure that he and his reader share a broad basis of conviction and assumption. The whole pressure of Shelley's age was against anything of the kind. Urbanity, except in the raffish version of Byron and Praed, was out of fashion among critics and readers; but that was the least of the difficulties. In the Elizabethan, the Caroline and the Augustan ages, the poet moved in a society more or less stable and more or less in agreement about social propriety. Most poets moved in circles where manners were ceremonious. The courteous usages were mostly hypocritical, but at least they were consistent; and they furnished the poet with a model urbanity which he could preserve in the tone of his writing. This was as true of the ponderous decorum of Mrs. Thrale's drawing-room as of the elaborate frivolity of the court of Charles II. Presumably, the violent dislocation of English society at the end of the eighteenth century (the Industrial Revolution) had destroyed the established codes of social behaviour. At any rate, in the Godwin household, in the family of Leigh Hunt, in the extraordinary domestic arrangements of Lord Byron, personal suffering and passion broke through into conversation and social demeanour. These were people who lived on their nerves, whom an established code of behaviour no longer protected. Therefore we cannot expect to find in the poetry of 1820 the exquisite assurance, the confident communication between poet and reader, which dignifies the slightest pieces of Thomas Carew or Thomas Parnell. We cannot expect it; but we find it. It is only natural that Spenser and Dryden, Carew and Parnell, enjoy this assurance. It is anything but natural, it seems almost impossible, that Shelley should do so.

The familiar style in this sense derives from the mean style of the Elizabethans, distinguished by them from the high style, proper to the heroic poem and the hymn, and from the base style of satire and pastoral. It is related too, to what Coleridge, in *Biographia Literaria,* called the 'neutral' style. It is distinguished from the other styles, in the nineteenth century as in the sixteenth, by being comparatively prosaic. Now, according to Johnson, a diction was pure when it was sanctioned by speech-usage on the one hand, and by literary precedent (classic and neo-classic) on the other. The poet's needs tugged him now one way, now the other; to tread a middle course, in touch with both sorts of usage, was to write a pure diction. But as the literary models varied (Juvenal for satire, Virgil for epic), so did the spoken models. The speech of a cobbler was not the model for epic, nor the speech of bishops for satire. There survived, in fact, though mostly unacknowledged, Puttenham's rule that the model for the high style was the speech of courtiers and governors; for the mean style, the speech of merchants and yeomen; for the base style, the speech of peasants and menial trades. In theory Wordsworth ignored the other criterion, literary precedent, and, as Coleridge confusedly saw, came near to asserting that the only permissible style was the mean. In any of the styles, to maintain a pure diction was to preserve 'the tone of the centre' which Arnold was to esteem in Attic prose. It is one way of explaining 'the sublime,' to say that, as England in the eighteenth century became a bourgeois state, the spoken model for the high style disappeared, and in poetry which 'affected the sublime' (the Augustan version of the high style) the question, whether the diction was pure, became meaningless. We are usually asked to acknowledge that Shelley's greatest poetry was of this sort. But there are other poems which are in the base and the mean styles; and it is among these that we have to look for Shelley the master of the familiar style.

The clearest example of Shelley's base style is the 'Letter to Maria Gisborne.' If we continue to talk in terms of Elizabethan decorum, this corresponds to 'The Shepheard's Calender,' as 'Julian and Maddalo,' in the mean style, to 'Colin Clout's Come Home Again,' as 'The Cloud,' in the high style, to 'Fowre Hymnes.' Shelley himself invites the Spenserian parallel:

> Near those a most inexplicable thing,
> With lead in the middle—I'm conjecturing
> How to make Henry understand; but no—
> I'll leave, as Spenser says, with many mo,
> This secret in the pregnant womb of time,
> Too vast a matter for so weak a rhyme.[3]

The archaism, like others ('I wist' . . . 'they swink') is used partly as Spenser used it in 'The Shepheard's Calender' or 'Mother Hubberd's Tale,' partly as Byron used it in 'Don Juan,' to draw attention to its ungainly self. But the 'Letter to Maria Gisborne' is neither Spenserian nor Byronic. It belongs to the tradition of Donne and Browning, who use the base style to unusual ends. There is no gainsaying that Shelley's verse resembles Browning's more than Donne's; it is an exercise in agility, not energy. Still, it is heartening, not hearty; and affectionate without being mawkish. It is too exuberant to be called urbane in the usual sense. But it is so, in the sense that the poet is sure of his relationship with the person he addresses, that he knows what is due to her and to himself, that he maintains a consistent tone towards her. She is not a peg to hang a poem on, nor a bosom for him to weep on, but a person who shares with him certain interests and certain friends and a certain sense of humour.

This poem is prosaic only in the relatively unimportant sense that it introduces things like hackney-coaches, Baron de Tott's Memoirs, 'self-impelling steam-wheels,' and 'a queer broken glass With ink in it.' But like Donne's verse or Browning's, Shelley's is far more figurative than normal prose. For truly lean and bare prosaic language, we turn to 'Julian and Maddalo':

I rode one evening with Count Maddalo
Upon the bank of land which breaks the flow
Of Adria towards Venice; a bare strand
Of hillocks, heaped from ever-shifting sand,
Matted with thistles and amphibious weeds,
Such as from earth's embrace the salt ooze breeds
Is this; an uninhabited sea-side,
Which the lone fisher, when his nets are dried,
Abandons; and no other object breaks
The waste, but one dwarf tree and some few stakes
Broken and unrepaired, and the tide makes
A narrow space of level sand thereon,
Where 'twas our wont to ride while day went down.

This of course represents a specifically Romantic purity—the adoption, from prose or careful conversation, of a vocabulary of natural description. At their best, the eighteenth-century poets had good reason for believing that features of natural appearance had to be dignified by figures, if they were to be pleasing and instructive; but more often their fussing with metaphors and personifications represented an impurity even by their own standards, for there can be little doubt that their practice in this particular was very far from any spoken usage. Shelley's assumption, that accuracy confers its own dignity, produced a much purer diction; and there are satisfying examples of this elsewhere in 'Julian and Maddalo,' as elsewhere in his work.[4] But what the Romantics gained with one hand they lost from the other. For if Johnson, for example, was 'intolerably poetical' when he essayed natural description, he had an enviable prosaic assurance in his dealings with the abstractions of moral philosophy. And it is in this province that Shelley's diction is woefully impure. He expressed, in *The Defence of Poetry*, his concern for these large abstractions, and his Platonic intention to make them apprehensible and 'living' in themselves. In 'The Witch of Atlas' he came near to effecting this; but more often, this programme only means that an abstraction such as Reason or Justice must always be tugged about in figurative language. The moment they appear in Shelley's verse (and they always come in droves) the tone becomes hectic, the syntax and punctuation disintegrate. In 'Julian and Maddalo,' by inventing the figure and the predicament of the maniac, Shelley excuses this incoherency and presents it (plausibly enough) as a verbatim report of the lunatic's ravings: and in this way he preserves the decorum of the conversation piece (the poem is sub-titled 'A Conversation'). As a result, the whole of this passage, tiresome and unpoetic as it is, impairs but does not ruin the whole. The urbanity is resumed in the close:

> If I had been an unconnected man
> I, from this moment, should have formed some plan
> Never to leave sweet Venice,—for to me
> It was delight to ride by the lone sea;
> And then, the town is silent—one may write
> Or read in gondolas by day or night,
> Having the little brazen lamp alight,
> Unseen, uninterrupted; books are there,
> Pictures, and casts from all those statues fair
> Which were twin-born with poetry, and all
> We seek in towns, with little to recall
> Regrets for the green country. I might sit
> In Maddalo's great palace, and his wit
> And subtle talk would cheer the winter night
> And make me know myself, and the firelight
> Would flash upon our faces, till the day
> Might dawn and make me wonder at my stay.

The conversation we have attended to in the poem is just as civilized as the intercourse of Maddalo and Julian here described. It is in keeping that Julian should know little of Maddalo and not approve of all that he knows, but should be prepared to take him, with personal reservations, on his own terms. It is the habit of gentlemen; and the poet inculcates it in the reader, simply by taking it for granted in his manner of address. The poem civilizes the reader; that is its virtue and its value.

'To Jane; the Invitation' and 'To Jane: the Recollection' were originally two halves of one poem, called 'The Pine Forest of the Cascine near Pisa.' In the second working over, 'The Invitation' gained enormously, 'The Recollection' hardly at all. The evolution of the latter poem illustrates very forcibly the process (analysed by Dr. Leavis) by which the characteristically Shelleyan attitude emerges from a Wordsworthian base. The original version is strikingly Wordsworthian in metre and diction:

> A spirit interfused around,
>   A thinking, silent life;
> To momentary peace it bound
>   Our mortal nature's strife;—
>
> And still, it seemed, the centre of
>   The magic circle there,

Was one whose being filled with love
The breathless atmosphere.

This becomes:

A spirit interfused around,
A thrilling, silent life,—
To momentary peace it bound
Our mortal nature's strife;
And still I felt the centre of
The magic circle there
Was one fair form that filled with love
The lifeless atmosphere.

As Dr. Leavis notes, the changes ('thrilling' for 'thinking,' 'being' to 'fair form,' and 'lifeless' for 'breathless') are all in the direction of eroticism. It is more pertinent to the present enquiry to notice that they all remove the discourse further from prosaic sense. One could write, in sober prose, of a *'breathless'* atmosphere; one could never describe it as *'lifeless.'* And by the same token a prose-writer can make us conceive how a person can seem to imbue a locality or a moment with a peculiar spiritual flavour; but that the emanation should be physical, an attribute of 'form' rather than 'being,' is something far more difficult. It is, of course, part of the poetic function to persuade us of realities outside the range of prosaic sense. But this can hardly be done by the familiar tone; and certainly Shelley does not do it here. He does not persuade us of the novelty, he only tricks us into it. His verse neither appeals to an old experience, nor creates a new one. These passages are a serious flaw in such a short poem.

The other piece, 'The Invitation,' is a nonpareil, and one of Shelley's greatest achievements. It maintains the familiar tone, though in highly figured language, and contrives to be urbane about feelings which are novel and remote. This poem presents the experience which 'The Recollection' tries to define and rationalize; and the definition is there, already, in the expression. Jane's influence upon the scene where she moved is here entirely credible; what Shelley afterwards tried to express, first in Wordsworthian and then in erotic terms, here persuades us from the start with no fuss or embarrassment. It is the lack of fuss, the ease and assurance, which persuades us throughout. In other words, the poem is first and foremost a triumph of tone. We can accept Jane as 'Radiant Sister of the Day,' largely because the lyrical feeling has already accommodated such seemingly unmanageable things as unpaid bills and unaccustomed visitors. It is an achievement of urbanity to move with such ease from financial and social entanglements to elated sympathy with a natural process; just as it is a mark of civilization to be able to hold these things together in one unflurried attitude.

(III) 'The Sensitive Plant' and 'The Witch of Atlas'

It is important that we should understand the reservations we have to make about 'The Recollection.' We dislike Shelley's eroticism, in the end, because it seems a vicious attitude, morally reprehensible; but we dislike it in the first place only because it produces a vicious diction, a jargon. In the end every true literary judgment is a moral judgment. But many critics go wrong, and many readers misunderstand them, because they pass too rapidly into the role of moralist. Even so, those critics are doing their duty better than others who think that moral judgment is no part of their business. I think we should value the significant ambiguity in such phrases as 'chaste diction,' 'pure diction,' 'vicious style,' 'the conduct of a fable.' But I am willing to let the ambiguity tell its own tale and to stop short, in this argument, before the point at which literary criticism moves over and becomes philosophical. It is best to think, therefore, that we condemn Shelley's eroticism (as we do) because it produces a jargon, and not because we dislike it 'in itself.'

For the Elizabethan, the love-song (the 'praise' or the 'complaint') demanded the mean style, unless it used the pastoral convention. And the best of Shelley's love-songs (not those, like 'Love's Philosophy,' which figure in the anthologies) are distinguished, like the best Caroline lyrics, by urbanity. As early as 1814, the 'Stanza, written at Bracknell' can control self-pity by controlled and judicious phrasing:

> Thy dewy looks sink in my breast;
>   Thy gentle words stir poison there;
> Thou hast disturbed the only rest
>   That was the portion of despair!
> Subdued to Duty's hard control,
>   I could have borne my wayward lot:
> The chains that bind this ruined soul
>   Had cankered then—but crushed it not.

It is not serious, of course, only album-verse; as is some of Carew. It all depends on how good the album is; in other words, on the degree of civilization in the society which calls for such trifles. And of course there is no question of comparison with Carew. But the Caroline neatness in the third and fourth lines, and the Augustan echo in the fifth, represent an urbane control which Shelley later threw away. More urbane still are the stanzas, 'To Harriet,' written in the same year:

> Thy look of love has power to calm
>   The stormiest passion of my soul;
> Thy gentle words are drops of balm
>   In life's too bitter bowl;
> No grief is mine, but that alone
> These choicest blessings I have known.
>
> Harriet! if all who long to live
>   In the warm sunshine of thine eye,
> That price beyond all pain must give,—
>   Beneath thy scorn to die;
> Then hear thy chosen own too late
> His heart most worthy of thy hate.
>
> Be thou, then, one among mankind
>   Whose heart is harder not for state,
> Thou only virtuous, gentle, kind,
>   Amid a world of hate;
> And by a slight endurance seal
> A fellow-being's lasting weal.
>
> For pale with anguish is his cheek.
>   His breath comes fast, his eyes are dim,
> Thy name is struggling ere he speak.
>   Weak is each trembling limb;
> In mercy let him not endure
> The misery of a fatal cure.
>
> Oh, trust for once no erring guide!
>   Bid the remorseless feeling flee;
> 'Tis malice, 'tis revenge, 'tis pride
>   'Tis anything but thee;
> Oh, deign a nobler pride to prove,
> And pity if thou canst not love.

Of course we cheapen the idea of urbanity by applying it to such polished nothings as these. But in their brittle elegance they represent a tradition which could have made Shelley's later love-verse a source of delight instead of embarrassment. The consciously elegant wording

317

in places suggests another poet and even another period. Indeed there is more than a hint of pastiche; but that very period-flavour represents a discipline which Shelley threw away.

He can be seen doing so in the 'Bridal Song' of 1821, which is admirable in its first version. In this first:

> O joy! O fear! what will be done
> In the absence of the sun!

—is as manly and wholesome as Suckling's 'Ballad of a Wedding.' In the last version:

> O joy! O fear! there is not one
> Of us can guess what may be done
> In the absence of the sun . . .

—is just not true. And the familiar tone of 'Come along!' which securely anchors the first version, is merely silly in the others.

As Dr. Leavis points out, it appears from parts of 'Peter Bell the Third' that Shelley quite deliberately worked erotic elements into the Wordsworthian base of many of his poems. He seems to have mistaken for prudery the master's natural frigidity. No doubt, too, the erotic jargon was bound up with his dedicated flouting of all the sexual morality of his society. For whatever reason Shelley in his love-lyrics adopted a hectic and strident tone, and the urbanity of his early pieces never bore fruit. At the same tme he threw into lyrical form more and more of his poetry. The lyric became confused with the hymn and so moved into the orbit of the sublime.

But the jargon came to be habitual with him, whatever sort of poem he wrote, until it taints them nearly all, sublime or not. One of the least tainted is 'The Sensitive Plant,' which I find one of his greatest achievements, and of great interest from the point of view of diction. In this poem and 'The Witch of Atlas' Shelley is as daring as ever in invention, making his fable as wayward and arbitrary as possible. In both poems the sensuousness is of his peculiar sort which makes the familiar remote. (He takes a common object such as a rose or a boat, and the more he describes it, the less we remember what it is.) In short, the vision in both these poems has all the difficulties of the Shelleyan sublime, impalpable and aetherial. What distinguishes these poems, however, from such a similar (and maddening) piece as 'Alastor,' is the presence, at the end of each of them, of a tough hawser of sober sense which at once pulls the preceding poem into shape and (what amounts to the same thing) gives it as much prose meaning as it will bear.

'The Sensitive Plant' is in three parts, with a conclusion. The first part presents in ecstatic detail the garden in summer, and dwells with particular weight upon one plant in the garden, which appears endowed with almost human intelligence in so far as it seeks to express the love it feels and the beauty it aspires to. Devoid of bloom and scent, it is unable to do so. But this predicament is subordinate to the poet's more general purpose, which is, in Part I, to make the garden seem like a dream. He does so with persuasive ease, partly by metrical resourcefulness (the metres induce a dream, not a pre-Raphaelite swoon), partly by deliberate confusion between the five senses, and partly by exploiting the vaporous, atmospheric and luminous features in the scene which he describes. Part II is short and concerned with the presiding human deity of the garden, a woman who is a sort of human counterpart of the Sensitive Plant. Part III begins with the death of the lady and describes how the garden, through autumn and winter into the next spring, falls into unweeded ruin.

In the scheme of this fable there is plainly room for an erotic element. The garden, for all its dream-like quality, pulses with germinating energy; and this 'love' is what the sensitive plant seeks to express:

> But none ever trembled and panted with bliss
> In the garden, the field, or the wilderness,
> Like a doe in the noontide with love's sweet want,
> As the companionless Sensitive Plant.

We know Shelley's eroticism is vicious only by the vicious diction it produces. Therefore we can have no complaints about the third line of this stanza, at the same time as we condemn the first. There the trembling and the panting and the bliss, coming thus together, are Shelleyan jargon, reach-me-down words which obviate the need for thinking and feeling precisely. The vice in question is not lasciviousness but more generally self-indulgence which betrays itself in lax phrasing as in lax conduct. Once we have read a certain amount of Shelley's verse, we recognize and dislike words from the private jargon, even when they are used with propriety:

> And the hyacinth purple, and white, and blue,
> Which flung from its bells a sweet peal anew
> Of music so delicate, soft, and intense,
> It was felt like an odour within the sense.

319

This is deliberate confusion between the senses, not used as later poets used it for definition of a compound sense-experience, nor only for intensification, but to throw over waking experience the illusion of a dream. Unfortunately 'intense' is a word we learn to suspect in Shelley, and it irritates. So again:

> The plumed insects swift and free,
> Like golden boats on a sunny sea,
> Laden with light and odour, which pass
> Over the gleam of the living grass;
>
> The unseen clouds of the dew, which lie
> Like fire in the flowers till the sun rides high,
> Then wander like spirits among the spheres,
> Each cloud faint with the fragrance it bears;
>
> The quivering vapours of dim noontide,
> Which like a sea o'er the warm earth glide,
> In which every sound, and odour, and beam,
> Move as reeds in a single stream.

Here the confusion between the senses is particularly persuasive, for it appeals to known facts about atmospheric conditions, or else to the evidence of the senses in such conditions. Unfortunately 'faint' and 'dim' are words from the jargon; and this perturbs the reader, even though both are plausible in this context.

Occasionally, too, there are flagrant violations of prosaic discipline:

> But the Sensitive Plant which could give small fruit
> Of the love which it felt from the leaf to the root,
> Received more than all, it loved more than ever,
> Where none wanted but it, could belong to the giver . . .

and:

> The snowdrop, and then the violet,
> Arose from the ground with warm rain wet,
> And their breath was mixed with fresh odour, sent
> From the turf like the voice and the instrument

—which is culpably ambiguous like Byron's lines which appalled Wordsworth:

> I stood in Venice on the Bridge of Sighs
> A palace and a prison on each hand.

And yet at the very crux of the argument lies the beautiful stanza:

> And the beasts, and the birds, and the insects were drowned
> In an ocean of dreams without a sound;
> Whose waves never mark, though they ever impress
> The light sand which paves it, consciousness.

This is memorably poetic, and yet, in the distinction between 'mark' and 'impress,' and in the logical tautness of the whole image, it is 'strong' with the prosaic strength which Dr. Johnson found in Denham.

The object of these many examples is not to pick holes in a master-piece, still less to reduce judgment to some ridiculous balancing of good stanzas against bad. They are meant to illustrate what is after all the capital difficulty in reading Shelley—his unevenness. He has hardly left one perfect poem, however short. In reading him one takes the good with the bad, or one does without it altogether. The business of private judgment on his poems is not a weighing of pros and cons but a decision whether the laxity, which is always there, lies at the centre of the poem (as it often does) or in the margin. I have no doubt that the faults of 'The Sensitive Plant' are marginal, and that at the centre it is sound and strong.

In any case, the second and third parts of the poem are an improvement on Part I. Part III, in particular, presents a rank and desolate scene as in 'Julian and Maddalo' but in greater detail. It is done more poetically than by Crabbe, but no less honestly.

The six stanzas of the 'Conclusion' are of a quite different kind. They ask to be judged on the score of diction, and they triumphantly pass the test they ask for:

> Whether the Sensitive Plant, or that
> Which within its boughs like a Spirit sat,
> Ere its outward form had known decay,
> Now felt this change, I cannot say.
>
> Whether that Lady's gentle mind,
> No longer with the form combined
> Which scattered love, as stars do light,
> Found sadness, where it left delight,
>
> I dare not guess; but in this life
> Of error, ignorance, and strife,
> Where nothing is, but all things seem,
> And we the shadows of the dream,

It is a modest creed, and yet
Pleasant if one considers it,
To own that death itself must be,
Like all the rest, a mockery.

That garden sweet, that lady fair,
And all sweet shapes and odours there,
In truth have never passed away:
'Tis we, 'tis ours are changed; not they.

For love, and beauty, and delight,
There is no death nor change: their might
Exceeds our organs, which endure
No light, being themselves obscure.

There is not a phrase here which would be out of place in unaffected prose. If that is strange praise for a piece of poetry, it is what one can rarely say of the poetry of Shelley's period. If these stanzas stood by themselves, they might seem tame and flat. In their place in the longer poem they are just what is needed to vouch for the more florid language of what has gone before.

The only comparable achievement, among Shelley's poems, is 'The Witch of Atlas.' In most editions this poem is introduced by some loose-jointed jaunty stanzas in which Shelley replies to the objection that his poem is lacking in human interest. He compares it with 'Peter Bell':

Wordsworth informs us he was nineteen years
    Considering and re-touching Peter Bell;
Watering his laurels with the killing tears
    Of slow, dull care, so that their roots to Hell
Might pierce, and their wide branches blot the spheres
    Of Heaven, with dewy leaves and flowers; this well
May be, for Heaven and Earth conspire to foil
The over-busy gardener's blundering toil.

My Witch indeed is not so sweet a creature
    As Ruth or Lucy, whom his graceful praise
Clothes for our grandsons—but she matches Peter,
    Though he took nineteen years, and she three days
In dressing. Light the vest of flowing metre
    She wears; he, proud as dandy with his stays,
Has hung upon his wiry limbs a dress
Like King Lear's 'looped and windowed raggedness'.

If you strip Peter, you will see a fellow
  Scorched by Hell's hyperequatorial climate
Into a kind of a sulphureous yellow:
  A lean mark, hardly fit to fling a rhyme at;
In shape a Scaramouch, in hue Othello.
  If you unveil my Witch, no priest nor primate
Can shrive you of that sin,—if sin there be
In love, when it becomes idolatry.

The point of the comparison with 'Peter Bell' is not very clear. The implication is that both poems are free fantasies, and that Wordsworth spoiled his by labouring it, whereas the essential virtue of such pieces is their spontaneity, and this Shelley claims to achieve. More interesting is the question how far such poems will bear scrutiny for meanings, how far such fantasies can be treated as allegorical. This I take to be the question of the last stanza above, and Shelley's answer is rather ambiguous. He begins by warning the reader not to rationalize at all, implying that Wordsworth came to grief by inviting such a reading; but then, in the teasing play with 'love' and 'idolatry,' he seems to allow that to look for an allegory is perhaps the best tribute one can give. At any rate, it seems plain that 'The Witch of Atlas,' like 'Kubla Khan' no less than 'Peter Bell,' is a flight of gratuitous fancy, a sort of iridescent bubble in which the reader looks for a 'message' only at his peril.

And of course the poem is all that Shelley says—a wayward fable, set in an unearthly landscape peopled by creatures neither human nor divine. Like 'Alastor' and 'The Sensitive Plant' it has no meaning except as a whole. It is one half of a vast metaphor with the human term left out; and this, its meaning for human life, emerges from the shape of the whole or else it is lost for ever. It was lost in 'Alastor,' and to give the meaning in an Introduction (as Shelley did then) is not enough. The meaning may fit the myth, but it is not carried in the myth, and one always forgets what 'Alastor' is about. 'The Witch of Atlas,' which is just as wayward and inhuman, takes on meaning, as much meaning as it can bear without cracking the singing voice. Shelley takes care of the meaning:

The priests would write an explanation full,
  Translating hieroglyphics into Greek,
How the God Apis really was a bull,
  And nothing more; and bid the herald stick
The same against the temple doors, and pull
  The old cant down; they licensed all to speak

> Whate'er they thought of hawks, and cats, and geese,
> By pastoral letters to each diocese.

It is absurd, of course. We cannot really believe that the ideal beauty of the vision means no more in moral terms than the regeneration of religious institutions, and their purification from superstition. But Shelley admits the absurdity, by his verse-form, at the same time as he implies that such a change must after all be *part* of any regenerated world. There is no danger of taking this too seriously, and thereby damaging the sheer creative *élan* of the poem. And by thus slipping back, at the end of the poem, into the familiar, even slangy base style of the prefatory stanzas, Shelley guards this most visionary and fantastic poem from any rough handling. He casts his myth into a sort of rough-hewn cradle of coarse sense. The device is the same as that in 'The Sensitive Plant,' except that here Shelley uses the base, where there he used the mean style. To complain that the poem is 'obscure' or 'lacking in human interest' is now out of the question. If one does so, one has missed the point, and made not a mistake only but a social blunder. To that extent Shelley's is an achievement, once again, of urbanity.

*

The poet I have considered here is a poet of poise and good breeding. Shelley was the only English Romantic poet with the birth and breeding of a gentleman, and that cannot be irrelevant. What is more surprising is the evidence that in other poems Shelley failed chiefly for want of the very tact which is here conspicuous. I am at a loss to explain how a poet so well aware of what he was doing should also have written 'The Cenci.' But if urbanity depends on the relation between poet and public, then it may be that Shelley's failures in tact were connected with his being unread and neglected. In her notes on the poems of 1821, Mrs. Shelley hinted as much:

> Several of his slighter and unfinished poems were inspired by these scenes, and by the companions around us. It is the nature of that poetry, however, which overflows from the soul, oftener to express sorrow and regret than joy; for it is when oppressed by the weight of life, and away from those he loves, that the poet has recourse to the solace of expression in verse.

It is, alas, too true that many of Shelley's poems are the products of self-pity looking for 'solace' or compensation; and it is not strange that the 'slighter and unfinished poems,' inspired by 'the companions around us,' should be some of Shelley's best work. This is not the poetry 'which overflows from the soul,' but the considered expression of an intelligent man.

NOTES

1. Cf. from 'Ode to Naples':
      'The isle-sustaining ocean-flood,
   A plane of light between two heavens of azure.'
2. See above, pp. 268ff.
3. Or, as Sidney says (Astrophel and Stella): 'Too high a theme for my low style to show.'
4. Notably in "Lines" (1815), 'The Sunset' (1816), 'Summer and Winter' (1820) and 'Evening: Ponte al Mare, Pisa' (1821).

DOUGLAS BUSH

Keats and His Ideas

THE anti-romantic reaction of the last few decades left two poets relatively undamaged and even elevated—Blake, who had scarcely attained
a secure place in the nineteenth-century hierarchy, and Keats, whom
the nineteenth century had taken a long time to recognize in his true
colors. The slowness with which the real Keats had emerged was not
entirely the fault of poets, critics, and general readers, since they did
not have all the materials for a just estimate; in addition to the all-important letters, the revised *Hyperion* was not printed until 1856 and
was not generally available until 1867. While Keats's influence on the
poetry of the century was probably more constant and conspicuous than
that of any other romantic, his personal and poetical reputation under-
went perhaps more changes than that of any other. At first his loyal
friends propagated the notion that he had been hounded to death by
the reviewers, a notion sentimentalized and embalmed in *Adonais* (in
our age we may have gone a bit too far in minimizing the effect of the
reviews). For some people the picture of a lily-livered aesthete was
corrected by Lord Houghton's *Life, Letters, and Literary Remains*
(1848), but the Keats of manly strength and sanity was attenuated or
distorted through his becoming a tutelary genius of Pre-Raphaelite
aestheticism. Then his personal and, less directly, his poetical character
suffered again from the publication of the letters to Fanny Brawne,
which upset even some of his special admirers. In our time, with a full

From *The Major English Romantic Poets: A Symposium in Reappraisal,* ed.
Clarence D. Thorpe, Carlos Baker, and Bennett Weaver; © 1957 by
Southern Illinois University Press, pp. 231–45. Reprinted by permission of
the publisher.

body of poems and letters, with a better perspective, and with information enlarged in all directions, we think we have arrived at real knowledge and understanding of Keats the man, the thinker, and the poet.

At the same time it can hardly be said that modern criticism has reached even a provisional judgment of Keats's poetical stature to which all students would subscribe. In 1925 Amy Lowell's loving, lavish, and amorphous work contributed to our view of the man, but the author's poetical predilections made her unable to see in the poet much more than an early Imagist. In the same year Mr. Murry, in his *Keats and Shakespeare*, so exalted the poet-prophet that—with all the fine insights that have marked his Keatsian criticism in general—he somewhat blurred the difference between the poetry Keats wrote and the Shakespearian kind of poetry he wanted to write. The next year brought a parallel sort of opposition: H. W. Garrod expounded the traditional Keats, the poet of sensuous luxury, and C. D. Thorpe presented the first full and satisfactory analysis of the new philosophic Keats, the deeply thoughtful and troubled student of life and poetry. A partly similar antithesis appears in two large treatments of recent years, N. F. Ford's *The Prefigurative Imagination of John Keats* (1951) and E. R. Wasserman's *The Finer Tone* (1953), although they are allied in their concern with Keats's romantic striving toward a vision beyond mortal limits. For Mr. Ford, Keats's chief poems, from *Endymion* onward, celebrate sexual love and sensuous beauty, immediate sensation being intensified by the ideal of a postmortal elysium in which earthly happiness is repeated in a finer tone; in Mr. Wasserman's subtle and, it must be said, relentless explication of Keats's symbolism, the 'finer tone' is so philosophic that even *The Eve of St. Agnes* becomes metaphysical. Recent criticism, less full than the stream of the 1920's and 1930's, has been less concerned with general estimates than with analysis of particular poems, especially the odes. The question of Keats's stature, as I said, remains a question. It is clear that he has had little influence on the most representative modern poetry (though the pioneer Wilfred Owen was a devotee); while the neo-metaphysical poets would not find him usable, the neo-romantics may. On the other hand, some modernist poets and critics, in slighting or damning most of the romantic poets, have paid high tribute to Keats.

This paper is restricted—so far as it is possible to observe the restriction—to a survey of Keats's ideas, and the subject raises a number of related queries. We might ask what 'ideas' in poetry are, and we remember that even Matthew Arnold pronounced 'For ever wilt thou love, and she be fair' a moral idea. But, if we are not philosophers or aestheticians, it is better to assume that we know what ideas are and to consider more practical matters. Are the ideas in Keats's poetry central in our experience of the poems, or do they have only the historical and peripheral value of explaining elements in poetry that is cherished for quite different reasons? Does Keats's best work give modern readers the total effect of major poetry, or is it superlative minor poetry that stirs only our sensuous faculties, or can we divide it into major and minor on the strength of its ideas? Does his poetry live in itself and speak to us directly, or is it in part sustained by our respect for his personality and the rightness of his self-knowledge and aspirations? Does the poet get into his poetry the realistic experience and understanding of life revealed in the letters, or does he fall short of the full maturity and wisdom of the letter-writer? This paper does not undertake to answer such questions; it cannot do much more than amplify them.

As soon as we try to weigh Keats's aesthetic and philosophical ideas in relation to the poetry, we encounter at least two general elements of complication. One is the obvious fact that he did not start with a full-fledged set of convictions, that both poems and letters are a product and a record of some years of rapid development. The other complication is the no less obvious fact that even in his ripest maturity Keats had not achieved a settled and unified creed but was continually divided against himself. We must take account of both facts, though it involves the repeating of commonplaces.

Some of Keats's central ideas were present, if only in embryo, in his very early verse. The poems of 1814–16, with their frequent symbols of liberty and tyranny, give evidence of a schoolboy liberalism which was only to mature in later years. More important—and heightened by his sense of imprisonment in London and in medical studies—was a devotion to poetry and nature, and an eager recognition of their affinity, that resemble the intoxication of a young man in love with love. In *To George Felton Mathew* (November, 1815) and, with much more fervent elaboration, in *I Stood Tip-Toe* (latter half of 1816), Keats associates classical myth with poetry and nature; for him as for Hunt, myth is partly a Wordsworthian revelation of truth and beauty in nature, partly an ideal version of human experience (which was Wordsworthian too). Although as yet Keats's actual poetic world is mainly one of luxurious sensation and fancy, he is already possessed by the romantic faith in the imagination. Here, and in *Sleep and Poetry* of the same period, the poet, raised above reason through nature and art and the senses, must and can transcend human limitations and 'burst our mortal bars.' Only once, at this time, does Keats in some sense achieve that goal, in the sonnet on Chapman's *Homer* (October, 1816), which ends with the 'gigantic tranquility' of a vision perfectly fulfilled and expressed.

Sleep and Poetry is the first full disclosure of conflicts between Keats's opposed instincts and ambitions. In the same paragraph he would 'die a death Of luxury' and also win immortality by seizing like a strong giant 'the events of this wide world.' Dwelling happily in the realm of Flora and old Pan, he is resolved that he must pass these joys 'for a nobler life,' where he may find 'the agonies, the strife Of human hearts.' (The evolution Wordsworth had gone through is self-compulsive antici- pation for Keats.) High visions of the mysterious and fearful world of imagination give way to a disillusioned sense of actuality, yet a vast idea rolls before him and he sees 'The end and aim of Poesy.' Under the banner of Wordsworth, Hunt, and Hazlitt, he attacks the Popeian tra- dition, but with his own special emphasis—'beauty was awake!' How- ever, as if conscious of reaching beyond his grasp, Keats subsides, in the rest of the poem, into the untroubled pleasures of friendship and Hunt's pictures. But later, in the spring of 1817, art and nature of a less merely sensuous kind arouse partly parallel tensions: the grandeur of the Elgin Marbles brings home to him the heavy weight of mortality, and both they and the sea become symbols of an inspiring if unattainable beauty and greatness.

The ideas so far observed have been expresed in Keats's verse. When we follow the letters, meagre at first, up to the completion of *Endymion* (November, 1817), we find some more or less similar and some new attitudes. Haydon's resolute loyalty to his art in the face of difficulty draws an echo from Keats,[1] and that conviction is to be reaffirmed and enlarged, under the growing stress of experience, in many subsequent letters. In this same letter (May 10–11, 1817), Keats would like to think of Shakespeare as his tutelary genius; he is conscious of a horrid mor- bidity of temperament; and he sees the sun, moon, stars, and earth 'as materials to form greater things—that is to say ethereal things.' The sense of mortality is oppressive (55,60); life is 'a continual struggle against the suffocation of accidents' (59). In the notable letter to Bailey of November 22, 1817, when *Endymion* is done, we have the first enun- ciation of the doctrine of negative capability (though it is not so named until December 21), and the first clear statement, a very strong and all-comprehending statement, of Keats's conception of poetry and life:

I am certain of nothing but of the holiness of the Heart's affections and the truth of Imagination—What the imagination seizes as Beauty must be truth—whether it existed before or not—for I have the same Idea of all our Passions as of Love they are all in their sublime, creative of essential Beauty. (67)

For evidence of this 'favorite Speculation'—a main tenet of European romanticism—he refers to the first book of *Endymion* and the ode to Sorrow of the fourth book; and he cites Adam's dream ('he awoke and found it truth'). Then comes 'O for a Life of Sensations rather than of Thoughts'—that is 'O for the life of the artist rather than of the consecutive logical thinker.' As artist, Keats can live in the moment, in the setting sun or in the sparrow picking about the gravel. But the next sentence brings him to the resources of the human spirit in meeting misfortune.

Explicit or implicit in this famous letter are some of Keats's enduring articles of faith and also some of his central tensions or 'unreconciled opposites.' If we put the letter beside the just completed *Endymion*, it is perhaps not too much to say that the brief piece of prose is, as a statement of ideas, more arresting than the diffuse and wayward poem. For *Endymion* reflects not so much the fruitful pressure of conflicting and equally realized impulses, but the confusion that results from half-unconscious instincts breaking through a self-imposed and only half-realized ideal. The 'Platonic' idealism of Keats's parable, the idea that the way to the One lies through loving apprehension of the Many, was a sincere conviction, but his metaphysical notion of unity or reality was much less real than his sensuous response to the actual and concrete (which is not to deny, with N. F. Ford, the allegorical intention). Keats conceives of Beauty, but he loves particular beauties, natural and erotic. The final identifying of Cynthia with the Indian maid is an equation in Platonic algebra, not an experience; and the handling of this climactic incident has far less authenticity than Endymion's moods of disillusionment in his quest of the Ideal. In the 'Hymn to Pan,' though Keats has some feeling for the One or the All, the strength of the Hymn is rather in its catalogue of particulars. The episodes of Alpheus and Arethusa and of the reviving of young lovers are romantically decorative and inadequate examples of humanitarian 'friendship' and service. And while, according to the letter to Bailey, the 'Ode to Sorrow' is intended to illustrate the belief that 'all our Passions,' as well as love, are 'in their sublime, creative of essential Beauty,' the Ode is too merely pretty (and, in the Bacchic pageant, too merely pictorial) to fulfill any such intention. In short, the young poet's sensuous and erotic instincts are much stronger than his Platonic instincts; and *Endymion* is assuredly an uncertain 'first Step towards the chief attempt in the Drama—the playing of different Natures with Joy and Sorrow' (90; January 30, 1818).

A large proportion of Keats's great utterances on poetry and life are contained in the letters of 1818, and we may, abandoning chronology, recall some of them. The general axioms set forth in the letter to Taylor of February 27 (107) are ideals that Keats says he has not yet attained: namely, that 'Poetry should surprise by a fine excess and not by Singularity'; that 'Its touches of Beauty should never be half way,' that they should leave the reader not breathless but filled with a luxurious content; and 'That if Poetry comes not as naturally as the Leaves to a tree it had better not come at all.' Such anxioms are more or less alien from those of most modern poets, but, since they fit more or less perfectly the finest poems Keats was to write, we can only say that the house of poetry has many mansions.

Other principles, no less axiomatic for Keats, are often affirmed in other letters. One prime essential is intensity (Keats's striving, by every technical means, toward that complex end has been concretely demonstrated by W. J. Bate). Yet intensity seems to operate on such different planes that in itself it carries only an elementary criterion of value. In December, 1817, Keats had invoked *King Lear* as a great example of the intensity that is 'the excellence of every Art' and is 'capable of making all disagreeables evaporate, from their being in close relationship with Beauty and Truth' (70). We might accept that as an informal and incomplete but incontrovertible statement of aesthetic theory. In his letter, however, Keats had just been complaining, in a manner hardly preparatory for *Lear*, that West's picture had 'nothing to be intense upon; no women one feels mad to kiss, no face swelling into reality.' Then in January, 1818, sitting down to read *King Lear* once again, Keats could feel 'the fierce dispute, Betwixt Hell torment [later 'damnation'] and impassion'd Clay'—and in February he could begin such a decorative tissue of romantic pathos as *Isabella*.

Throughout 1818—though not so much of course in the accounts of the Scottish tour—the letters, and some poems copied in the letters, reveal positive or conflicting attitudes that are characteristic of Keats's mature view of himself, the world, and poetry. He recognizes the mixture of beauty and cruelty in nature, the mixture of good and evil in men, the superiority of disinterested goodness to works of genius, the necessity and the moral benefits of facing pain and trouble. As artist he fluctuates—and is aware of his fluctuations—between belief in the poetic efficacy of a wise passiveness, of sensuous and imaginative receptivity, and belief in the active pursuit of rational knowledge and philosophy. Some of these ideas get full expression in the letter to Reynolds of May 3, 1818. Here Keats sees all departments of knowledge as 'excellent and calculated towards a great whole'; knowledge reduces a thinking man's heat and fever, eases the burden of the mystery, and strengthens the soul, though perhaps it may not 'console us for the death of a friend and the ill "that flesh is heir too."' There follows the fragment of an ode to Maia, which is hardly a plea for philosophic knowledge. Then comes the extended comparison of Wordsworth and Milton. In the Keatsian hierarchy Shakespeare was of course the great exemplar of the supreme poetic endowment and attitude, negative capability, while Wordsworth and Milton were the great exemplars of poetry with a purpose and a message (and both had the attraction, for a young poet, of being more imitable than Shakespeare). Keats finds—if one may go on summarizing the familiar—greater concern with humanity and the human heart in Wordsworth than in Milton, though the fact testifies less to greater individual power than to a general march of intellect. (Keats's comments on Milton show, not unnaturally, no modern comprehension of Milton's thought and themes.) He speaks also of the axioms in philosophy that must be proved upon our pulses, of the wisdom that comes only from sorrow (and the skeptic in him adds that that may be folly). Finally, there is the account of the several chambers in the mansion of life, 'the infant or thoughtless Chamber,' 'the Chamber of Maiden-Thought,' where pleasant wonders become darkened by a sense of human misery and heartbreak—the point Wordsworth had reached in *Tintern Abbey*. But against this steadily deepening awareness of human suffering might be set such a remark as this, inspired by northern scenes: 'they can never fade away—they make one forget the divisions of life; age, youth, poverty and riches; and refine one's sensual vision into a sort of north star which can never cease to be open lidded and stedfast over the wonders of the great Power' (154). At moments the senses can reconcile what the mind and the heart cannot.

In the many letters that come after this time, most of the critical and ethical ideas are reaffirmations, with similar or altered focus and emphasis, of those already encountered. The impersonal, non-moral imagination of the poet of negative capability is opposed to 'the wordsworthian or egotistical sublime' (226–27; October 27, 1818). This universally sympathetic and creative power is associated sometimes with particular objects and experiences, sometimes with 'the mighty abstract Idea . . . of Beauty in all things' (239; October, 1818). 'I never can feel certain of any truth but from a clear perception of its Beauty' (258; December, 1818). Keats summarizes Hazlitt on the non-moral character of the poetic imagination as differing from pure reason and the moral sense. Even the cruelty of a beast, or a quarrel in the street, may give pleasure, because the imagination enjoys excitement and energy, 'the sense of power abstracted from the sense of good' (307–9, 315–17; March, 1819). But while the hawk and the stoat fulfill their predatory instincts, man is capable of the distinterested goodness that was supremely mani-fested in Socrates and Jesus; there is a continual birth of new heroism among human creatures. The working of human energies and human reasonings, though erroneous, may be fine, and in this consists poetry, though it is thereby less fine than philosophy, as an eagle is less fine than a truth (316). Keats lays much stress on enduring the buffets of the world, a theme that is elaborated in the picture of life and its adversities as a 'vale of Soul-making' (334; April, 1819). This idea seems to be the very opposite of negative capability, since the chameleon poet has no identity, no ethical character, whereas men are not souls 'till they acquire identities, till each one is personally itself.' In this view of life as a series of trials Keats finds 'a system of Salvation' more rational and acceptable than the Christian. Though he can still wonder more and more at Shakespeare and *Paradise Lost,* and 'look upon fine Phrases like a Lover' (368), he still ranks fine doing above fine writing (373). Then comes a reaction against Milton that leads to the abandoning of the second *Hyperion,* a recoil from Miltonic 'art' to 'other sensations' (384, 425; September, 1819).

These have been scanty reminders of the growth and recurrence of some leading aesthetic and ethical ideas in Keats's letters, and we must observe, with equal brevity, how far they are embodied in the mature poems. Of the first *Hyperion* it is perhaps safe to say that—in spite of difficulties that critics have inclined to overlook—we comprehend intel-lectually, and in some degree emotionally, the ethical-aesthetic theme, but that the poem's chief power over us comes rather from the inlaid beauties of image and phrase and rhythm. For we are hardly stirred more by the sorrows of the fallen Titans than we are by such pictures as that of the dreaming oaks; even these incidental, 'non-human' images refine 'our sensual vision into a sort of north star.' Oceanus' speech is certainly Keats's own testimony to the principle of beauty and the grand march of intellect in human history. The beauty, however, that Oceanus has beheld in the young god of the sea, and that Clymene has heard in the music of the Apollo who is not yet a god, seems to be beauty in the conventional romantic sense, the sense that it frequently bears in the letters. Yet Keats had quite early evolved the larger and deeper conception of beauty created by all our passions in their sublime, that is, a vision, refined by intense apprehension, of all the varied and painful stuff of actual life. It is of course the attainment, through Mnemosyne, of this vision of suffering that makes Apollo a god, a 'soul,' a true poet. Oceanus had approached that idea—

> O folly! for to bear all naked truths,
> And to envisage circumstance, all calm,
> That is the top of sovereignty—

but he had done so only parenthetically, as a prelude to the delivery of bad news, and that was not the theme of his speech. The speech as a whole might be said to represent the young Keats, Apollo's deification the mature Keats; and—granted that Apollo's 'Knowledge enormous' takes in the downfall of the Titans—the fragmentary poem really establishes no substantial connection between the aesthetic or romantic and the ethical or tragic ideals of beauty. Nor is Keats able to dramatize Apollo's passing through the Chamber of Maiden-Thought and the vale of soul-making; his transformation is simply asserted.[2]

The total effect of *The Eve of St. Agnes* is in a way not unlike that of *Hyperion.* The theme—if we hesitate to climb all the rungs of Mr. Wasserman's metaphysical ladder—is young love in a world of hostility and age and death, but we are no more, and perhaps less, moved by the young lovers' feelings than we are by the sculptured dead in icy hoods and mails, the colored window, and a hundred other incidental items in the romantic setting, items of material, sensuous empathy. One is reluctant even to hint at disparagement of a uniquely rich and magical tapestry, and yet one remembers that comment on Robert Burton's account of love which might seem to have come from another man: Keats sees 'the old plague spot; the pestilence, the raw scrofula' in the human mingling of 'goatish winnyish lustful love with the abstract adoration of the deity.'[3] Although Mr. Wasserman's view of *The Eve of St. Agnes* is not incompatible with Mr. Gittings' realistic—and dubious—argument for its genesis in the poet's having an affair with Isabella Jones, we may, looking only at the poem, see it as an example of romantic idealism shunning the inward troubles of 'impassion'd clay.'

The great odes of the spring were variations on one theme, a theme complex enough as Keats consciously conceived it and further complicated and intensified by his half-unconscious doubts of his own aesthetic resolution. The *Ode to Psyche* is devoid of explicit 'ideas,' except as its animating idea is the power of the imagination to preserve and transmute direct sensuous experience. That theme causes no conflict in *Psyche*; but conflict is central in the *Nightingale* and the *Grecian Urn*. In these two odes Keats feels not so much the joy of the imaginative experience as the painful antithesis between transient sensation and enduring art. He cannot wholly accept his own argument, because both his heart and his senses are divided. The power of the imagination, the immortality of art, offer no adequate recompense for either the fleeting joys or the inescapable pains of mortality. Keats's early desire to burst our mortal bars, to transcend the limitations of human understanding, becomes in the *Nightingale* the desire for death, the highest sensation, or an anguished awareness of the gulf between life and death. In the end the imagination cannot escape from oppressive actuality; far from attaining a vision of ultimate truth, it achieves only a momentary illusion.

In the *Grecian Urn*, the sensations evoked are almost wholly concerned with young love (the great fourth stanza is logically a digression), and again Keats cannot convince himself that love and beauty on marble are better than flesh-and-blood experience, however brief and unhappy that may be. It is the underlying lack of satisfaction that inspires the unrelated picture of the little town, for ever empty of humanity, a picture almost forced upon the poet, as it were, by his recognition of the negative side of his theme. But he overrides his emotional skepticism (though it comes up again in 'Cold Pastoral'), and ends with the positive statement of his most famous 'idea,' a statement that has been much questioned on the score of both meaning and artistic propriety. The meaning (and the meaning of similar utterances in the letters) may be simpler than some of the explanations of it. In a world of inexplicable mystery and pain, the experience of beauty is the one sure revelation of reality; beauty lives in particulars, and these pass, but they attest a principle, a unity, behind them. And if beauty is reality, the converse is likewise true, that reality, the reality of intense human experience, of suffering, can also yield beauty, in itself and in art. This is central in the poet's creed, if not all explicit in this poem, yet the undercurrent here prevents the urn's assertion from being the Q.E.D. it is intended to be. If the *Grecian Urn* and the *Nightingale* rise above *Psyche* and *Melancholy*, the reason is not only their artistic superiority but the complexity of their unresolved tensions. They were begun, so to speak, by the poet of sensuous luxury, but were taken over by the poet who had learned on his pulses the knowledge given to Apollo and could not escape from it.

Lamia, written in the late summer of this year, is, like *The Eve of St. Agnes,* a highly decorative story of romantic love, with a difference. The emotional simplicity of a tale of happy fruition has given place to a mixture of passion, dissonance, and tragedy; Romeo and Juliet have become, in a sense, Troilus and Cressida. *Lamia* is Keats's only completed poem that has caused real disagreement in regard to its theme and intention. To group various interpretations (some of them rendered in concretely and impossibly allegorical terms), *Lamia* is (1) a literal romantic narrative, with ethical overtones perhaps but with no general parable, a poem in which Keats was concentrating his forces on technique and popular appeal; (2) a condemnation of cold philosophic reason; (3) a condemnation of feeling and the senses; (4) a condemnation of a divorce between reason and feeling; (5) an incoherent expression of Keats's unresolved conflicts, emotional and philosophical; (6) a contrast between the immortal and perfect love of Hermes and the nymph and the mortal, imperfect love of Lycius and Lamia. It is assuredly not easy to harmonize the implicit or explicit contradictions in both the narrative and the author's comments within the poem, and inner conflicts that had troubled Keats before had lately been heightened by the course of his passion for Fanny Brawne and the problems of his mind and career. Keats had long had ambivalent feelings toward women and love, and 'Bright star' and *The Eve of St. Agnes* had been quickly followed by *La Belle Dame sans Merci;* as poet, he had long fluctuated between the ideals of sensation and thought and between the ideals of poetic contemplation and humanitarian action. If we see in *Lamia* the condemnation of a sensuous dreamer (to put 'the moral' crudely), we feel more sure of our ground because of our external knowledge of his ethical growth and his state of mind. Lycius' quest has stopped far short of Endymion's, and the beauty he embraces is sterile and corrupt. But does the poem, as a statement of its theme (whatever we take that to be), really come home to us, or does it remain mere romantic narrative and picture-making, on a lower level for the most part than *Hyperion* and *The Eve of St. Agnes?*

Keats's last important poems sharply define his poetic dilemma. There could scarcely be a greater contrast than there is between *To Autumn* (September 19, 1819) and *The Fall of Hyperion. To Autumn* is Keats's most perfect poem, but it has none of the tensions of the *Nightingale* and the *Grecian Urn*. Critics have said that the rich serenity of the ode has been 'earned,' in the sense that it finally composes and transcends its author's inner turmoil. The verdict, however, seems to depend more on biography than on the poem itself, and might equally well be rendered— if we look only at the poetic texts—in regard to the fragmentary ode to Maia, which was written at the beginning of Keats's troubled maturity. *To Autumn* does embody acceptance of the process of fruition and decay, yet can we extend that idea—as Keats does not—from the life of nature to the life of man? While the poem is the product of his ripest art, it expresses a recurrent mood; it is less a resolution of the perplexities of life and poetic ambition than an escape into the luxury of pure—if now sober—sensation.

That the ode was not a final resolution is made clear by the revised *Hyperion*. The *Fall*—on the one hand a new experiment in technique, a partial exchange of Milton for Dante—is Keats's last confessional poem, a last desperate effort to define the nature and function of poetry and his own position. The poem is much more difficult to interpret in detail than the odes, though recent criticism has largely neglected explication. After three years of experience and mature thought Keats is returning to the problem set forth in *Sleep and Poetry,* a problem which then had been mainly of the future but had, with increasing complexity and intensity, disturbed him ever since. In the simplest terms, there is the question of poetry versus humanitarian action, and—even if we exclude the cancelled lines—the question of the humanitarian poet versus 'the dreamer.' The poet of the *Fall*—there is no longer the *persona* of Apollo —is allowed to gain the height reserved for

> those to whom the miseries of the world
> Are misery, and will not let them rest.

But, he asks, since there are thousands of such, why is he here alone? The others, says Moneta, are not poets, visionaries and 'dreamers weak,' but active servants of humanity who do not desire or need to come. What benefit can poets do to the great world? Other men have their work, 'sublime or low'; each has his distinct joys and distinct pains;

> Only the dreamer venoms all his days,
> Bearing more woe than all his sins deserve.

337

Is Keats saying that the poet of negative capability, who lives all men's lives, is subject to a curse, a futile fever of the imagination remote from normal, healthy life?

The debate is not directly continued—unless we admit the cancelled lines, which attempt to distinguish between the true poet and the dreamer—but something like a final answer is given through what the narrator discerns in Moneta's unveiled face and eyes,

> a wan face
> Not pined by human sorrows, but bright-blanch'd
> By an immortal sickness which kills not;
> It works a constant change, which happy death
> Can put no end to; deathwards progressing
> To no death was that visage; it had past
> The lily and the snow . . . .

Here, or in the whole episode, seem to be concentrated, and perhaps reconciled on a new plane, some of Keats's central perplexities—the fluidity of experience and the enduring truth of art; a vision of life that embraces but transcends all suffering, that unifies all diverse and limited human judgments *sub specie aeternitatis;* the supreme sensation and insight of death without death itself. Moneta's face and eyes reflect, in calm benignity, the knowledge that had rushed upon Apollo, and Keats is reaffirming the godlike supremacy of the poetic vision, but his conception has risen above mere negative capability to what suggests, to one critic[4] at least, Christ taking upon himself the sorrows of the world.

Whether or not Keats had thus moved toward the Christian 'idea,' at any rate his poetic criteria, which had never been low, had reached a level where not a great deal of the world's poetry could pass the test. There is no question of the modern validity of many of his aesthetic principles and observations, since many of his phrases have become part of our critical language. And, as parallels to his doctrine of negative capability, for example, we might recall Mr. Eliot's emphasis on the impersonality of the artist, or Yeats's 'intellectual innocence.' As for Keats himself, it may be added, it is not clear, at least to me, how far he had succeeded, or would have succeeded, in harmonizing his conception of negative capability, of the amoral artist, with his conception of the soul's need of acquiring, through the trials of experience, a positive ethical identity—and here we might recall Yeats's posing of 'the choice' between 'Perfection of the life, or of the work.'

Even if in the *Fall of Hyperion* Keats was not repudiating much of himself, he leaves us uncertain about his final judgment of his own poetry. Our concern here has been with his ideas, and his poetry would be exactly what it is if all the letters had been lost. Some of his ideas and problems are directly embodied in the poems, sometimes they are between the lines, sometimes—as in *To Autumn*—they are temporarily forgotten or put aside. But their positive or negative importance is great. For most readers and some critics Keats remains a poet of miraculous sensuous apprehension and magical expression, and in much or most of his poetry his negative capability seems to stop well short of Shakespearian exploration of life and man, to be mainly confined to aesthetic sensation and intuition. But even if we share that conventional estimate, we must say that his poetry is not all of a piece. Keats's Shakespearian or humanitarian ambitions, his critical and self-critical insights, his acute awareness of the conditions enveloping the modern poet, his struggles toward a vision that would comprehend all experience, joy and suffering, the natural and the ideal, the transient and the eternal—all this made him capable of greater poetry than he actually wrote, and makes him, more than his fellow romantics, our contemporary. And if these 'ideas' did not get into his poems very often or very far, their overshadowing presence distinguishes his major from his minor achievements. Though his poetry in general was in some measure limited and even weakened by the romantic preoccupation with 'beauty,' his finest writing is not merely beautiful, because he had seen 'the boredom, and the horror' as well as 'the glory.'

NOTES

1. *Letters of John Keats,* ed. Maurice B. Forman, 4th edition (Oxford University Press, 1952), p. 28. Hereafter page numbers in this edition are indicated in parentheses in the text.

2. Although the two *Hyperions* have been relatively neglected in recent criticism, one may refer to Kenneth Muir's perceptive study in *Essays in Criticism,* II (1952), 54–75.

3. *Complete Works of John Keats,* ed. H. B. Forman (Glasgow, 1900–1901), III, 268.

4. D. G. James, *The Romantic Comedy* (London: Oxford University Press, 1948), pp. 149–50.

W. JACKSON BATE

Keats's Style: Evolution toward Qualities of Permanent Value

WITH the decline of neoclassicism, poetry was faced with some relatively new problems and a new uneasiness about its value and function. The problems and the uneasiness have persisted; and the principal ways of meeting them have not changed radically from those the greater romantics adopted. Whether we like our legacy or not, the present literary generation is very much the heir of the romantics.

On the other hand, of course, much of the poetry as well as critical effort of the last forty years has been written in a spirit of conscious protest against the idiom of romantic poetry. Some of the rather confused distinctions which this militant protest created at its start seem now to have become domesticated into academic orthodoxy, and we have begun to take them for granted, as we do most domestic phenomena, without any very searching revision of our first impressions. We especially follow the confusion of poetic form with mere idiom, and feel that we are describing or analyzing poetry according to the first when we are really thinking only of the latter. We hold academic symposia now on differences in the 'metaphysical,' 'Augustan,' 'romantic,' and 'modern modes'; and the word 'mode,' because it is open and fluid, gives us the feeling that we are being comprehensive. But it usually turns out to be restricted to special problems of metaphor, syntax, and phrasing. Like good Alexandrian rhetoricians, we have begun to play close to the ground.

No brief discussion of the style of a romantic poet can hope to improve

From *The Major English Romantic Poets: A Symposium in Reappraisal*, ed. Clarence D. Thorpe, Carlos Baker, and Bennett Weaver; © 1957 by Southern Illinois University Press, pp. 217–30. Reprinted by permission of the publisher.

on the situation. There are, after all, genuine differences between the idiom of the romantics and the poetry of the last forty years; and some of them are quite fundamental. But any discussion that could make place for these acknowledged differences, and then subsume them within larger considerations would involve a more pluralistic, leisurely, less compartmentalized procedure that would permit us to review the total achievement of a poet. This is particularly the case with Keats. He has worn very well. He has continued to stir the imagination of poets and critics for a century and a half. On the other hand, the idiom of much of his earlier poetry is hardly at the present time a model or even much of an encouragement. Indeed, to a good many younger readers, some of it is not even very congenial. Of course the language of his greatest poetry has always held a magnetic attraction; for there we reach, if only for a brief while, a high plateau where in mastery of phrase he has few equals in English poetry, and only one obvious superior. A very important part of the more general significance of Keats is the fact that he was able to reach that level. But this, by itself, is not enough to explain the large, at times almost personal, relevance that we feel. He is a part of our literary conscience. Leaving aside the poignant appeal (and with it the sense of difference) of his own peculiar circumstances—the fact that he started with so little, the manner in which he struggled his way into poetry, his early death, and the like—we sense that this gifted young poet was working his way through problems that any honest poet of the last century and a half has faced.

Nothing less than a fairly capacious and imaginative consideration of his achievement, then, could get very far in capturing, or even beginning to suggest, the relevance of Keats's art to poetry since his death, and especially during the last generation. Still, the assigned purpose of this essay is to concentrate briefly on the stylistic character of Keats's poetry. Hard put to compartmentalize in this way, I should be forced to resort to the term 'honesty.' Certainly this is what now appeals to us most when we think of Keats as a whole, especially in the context of the letters. And we feel this impression confirmed in his stylistic development. Considering his short life, there is no parallel to the diversity of styles with which he experimented. Yet it was never experimentation for its own sake. The experimentation moves constantly toward great honesty—greater openness to concrete life and the claims of experience, toward greater fullness and richness of expression, and at the same time a growing strength of control and sensitivity to the formal claims of poetic art.

II

The early verse of Keats, down through the writing of *Isabella* (early in 1818), shows little selectivity of subject in either its themes or its imagery when it is measured by a really high standard. The impulse towards self-absorption in the object is associated with having the 'soul,' as he said, 'lost in pleasant smotherings.' It finds its outlet, that is, in a luxurious abandonment to the conventionally 'poetic' objects and images that intrigued a youthful romantic poet, and that Keats found ready at hand in the verse of his mentor, Leigh Hunt, and in the poets Hunt held up as a model. This sort of poetry, as it is developed by Hunt and the youthful Keats, and as it is continued throughout the poorer verse of the nineteenth century, is essentially a reaction, of course, against neo-classic conventions: an attempt to substitute for the stock themes and stock diction of the preceding century a conception of 'poetic' material even more confined, a diction equally liable to stereotype, and a versification—as Keats later learned—of equal monotony.

We need not retrace in any detail the characteristics of Keats's early diction and imagery: his use of *y*-ending adjectives ('sphery,' 'lawny,' 'bloomy,' 'surgy,' and the like); the unfortunate predilection for adverbs made from participles ('lingeringly,' 'dyingly,' 'cooingly'), and for abstract nouns that have little intellectual content ('languishment,' 'designments,' 'soft ravishment'); the use of such conventional props in his imagery as 'Pink robes, and wavy hair,' the 'silvery tears of April,' and monotonously recurring nymphs with 'downward' glances, the habitual appearance of objects with 'pillowy' softness, and the frequently embarrassing attempts to introduce action ('madly I kiss/The wooing arms') into this smothering world of rose-leaves, doves, 'almond vales,' and 'blooming plums/Ready to melt between an infant's gums.'

These characteristics and their sources have been frequently discussed, are familiar to every student of English poetry, and have little interest to present-day readers except as a steppingstone in Keats's chronological development. And they are accompanied not only by a lack of structural control but by a deliberately cultivated slackness of manner—except in his early sonnets, written in the Petrarchan form and employing diverse and not too effective structural peculiarities drawn from Hunt, occasionally Wordsworth, and the Miltonic imitators of the late eighteenth century. One is almost tempted to conclude that if Pope, in his versification, went in one direction and employed a device to secure economy and tightness, then Hunt—and the youthful Keats—not only discarded it but, in some instances, deliberately adopted an opposite device. Examples of this would take us into the by-roads of prosody—particularly caesural-placing, where Keats followed Hunt very closely. It is perhaps enough to note how forcibly Keats, even more than Hunt, broke the couplet. In fact, when a pause is needed at the end of a line, he frequently put it at the end of the *first* line of the couplet, and then tried to run on the second line, without break, into the next couplet:

> Full of sweet dreams, and health, and quiet breathing./
> Therefore, on every morrow, are we wreathing
> A flowery band to bind us to the earth,/
> Spite of despondence, of the inhuman dearth
> Of noble natures, of the gloomy days,/
> Of all the unhealthy and o'er-darken'd ways
> Made for our searching: yes, in spite of all,/
> Some shape of beauty moves away the pall
> From our dark spirits. Such the sun, the moon,/
> Trees old, and young, sprouting a shady boon
> For simple sheep . . . .
>
> *Endymion, 1, 4–15*

The style of *Isabella*, written a few months after Keats became twenty-three, shows an embarrassed and confused attempt by Keats to rid himself of the influences of Hunt and of the 'sickening stuff' he later associated with Hunt's taste. 'I shall have,' he wrote, 'the Reputation of Hunt's elevé. His corrections and amputations will by the knowing ones be traced.' He had grown 'tired' of the 'slipshod' *Endymion;* his opinion of it was 'very low,' and he wanted to 'forget' it. Abandoning the loose, run-on couplet he had taken over from Hunt, Keats selected the tight ottava rima stanza (perhaps better fitted for satire, because of the snap of its concluding couplet); and though the story has limited possibilities, to say the least, and though there is still (as he himself was to say) a mawkish sentimentality of phrase and image, the versification shows an energetic struggle to impose a disciplined control.

III

It is during the year or more following the writing of *Isabella* that the maturer style of Keats developed so rapidly. Among the primary characteristics of this style is a suggestive power of image capable of securing from the reader an unusually intense emotional and imaginative identification. This quality has become widely recognized in recent years, particularly since the implications of Keats's own conception of the poet's character, and of his puzzling term, 'Negative Capability,' have been discussed. We need not here make distinctions between the romantic theory of sympathetic identification, in which the poet takes on, through participation, the qualities and character of his object, and the more recent theory of *Einfühlung* (or empathy), with its suggestion that many of these qualities are merely the subjective creation of the poet or observer, and are bestowed upon the object rather than descried in it. The poetry of Keats contains abundant examples that might be used to substantiate either, or both at once, as a guiding characteristic of his verse.

Certainly, in the verse written before *Hyperion*, a subjective element —more empathic than sympathetic—often characterizes this imaginative identification ('sweet peas, on *tiptoe* for a flight,' the foam crawling along the back of the wave with a 'wayward indolence'). But a more sympathetic in-feeling is equally apparent (minnows 'staying their wavy bodies 'gainst the stream,' lions with 'nervy tails,' or the organic in-feeling in 'Ere a lean bat could plump its wintry skin'). The verse from *Hyperion* through the great odes is replete with such imagery, ranging from 'The hare *limp'd trembling* through the frozen grass' to the agonies of the huge figures in *Hyperion:* 'horrors, portion'd to a giant nerve,/Oft made Hyperion ache'; or

> *through all his bulk* an agony
> *Crept* gradual, from the feet unto the crown,
> Like a lithe serpent *vast and muscular,*
> Making *slow way*, with head and neck *convuls'd*
> *From over strainèd might* . . .
>
> (1, 259–63)

Such lines remind us of the passages in both Shakespeare and Milton that evoked so strong a sympathetic participation in Keats—as, for example, when he wrote in the margin beside *Paradise Lost*, IX, 179 ff., where Satan enters the serpent without arousing him from sleep:

Satan having entered the Serpent, and inform'd his brutal sense— might seem sufficient—but Milton goes on '*but his sleep disturbed not.*' Whose spirit does not ache at the smothering and confinement . . . the '*waiting close?*' Whose head is not dizzy at the possible speculations of Satan in the serpent prison? No passage of poetry ever can give a greater pain of suffocation.

Or again there is his enthusiastic mention, in one of his letters (November 22, 1817), of Shakespeare's image of the sensitive retreat of a snail:

> As the snail, whose tender horns being hit,
> Shrinks back into his shelly cave with pain.

And we may recall Charles Cowden Clarke's story of Keats's reaction, while reading the *Faerie Queene* as a boy, to the phrase, 'sea-shouldering whales': as if raising himself against the pressure of the waves, 'he hoisted himself up, and looked burly and dominant. . . .'

This kinaesthetic gift of image, if one wishes to call it that, this organically felt participation, is further revealed in Keats's ability to bring into focus several diverse sense-impressions of an object, and—in transmuting them into a single image or series of images—present a more valid, rounded, and fully realized apperception. This unifying interplay of sense-impressions should not be confused with synaesthesia. Keats's imagery, to be sure, is perhaps as richly packed with examples of suggestive synaesthesia as any that can be found ('*fragrant* and enwreathèd light,' 'pale and silver silence,' 'scarlet pain,' 'the *touch* of *scent*'), and Keats's use of it had more effect on the synaesthetic imagery of later English poetry than any other one model. But the really distinctive quality in Keats—and a quality his Victorian imitators rarely attained—is less the *substitution* than it is the *substantiation* of one sense by another in order to give, as it were, additional dimension and depth, as in 'the *moist scent* of flowers,' 'embalmèd darkness,' or in making incense tangibly 'soft' and visible:

> I cannot see what flowers are at my feet,
> Nor what *soft* incense *hangs* upon the boughs.

A further example is Keats's predilection for tactile qualities: his craving for touch ('Touch,' he wrote, 'has a memory'), and for a firm grasp of the concrete as it exists in space. Thus images directly or indirectly connected with the sense of taste are sustained and deepened, in their vitality, through associations with tactile and muscular response: the 'purple-stainèd mouth,' the nightingale singing of summer 'in *full-throated* ease,' or the closing stanza of the *Ode on Melancholy,* with its

> *aching* Pleasure nigh,
> Turning to poison while the *bee-mouth sips* . . .
> Though seen of none save him whose *strenuous tongue*
> Can *burst* Joy's *grape against his palate* fine . . . .

This tactile strength gives a three-dimensional grasp to Keats's images. Perhaps the most notable instance is the famous 'wealth of *globèd* peonies,' in the same ode: here the hand is virtually enclosing the peony, further assuring itself of the three-dimensional roundness.

There is, in short, a *centering* in Keats's imagery of the various qualities of an object into a single apperception; and as a result the object emerges as a totality with its several aspects resolved into a unified whole rather than delineated or suggested separately. The use of strong tactile associations that give a firmer hold, a more definitely felt outline, is one means by which this centering of impressions, into an amalgamated whole, is secured and anchored. His general amassing and condensing of sense-impressions is another. And the result is an imagery that is less 'synaesthetic,' in the ordinary sense, than it is a gifted illustration of what Hazlitt meant by 'gusto'—that is, a state in which the imagination, through sympathetic excitement, draws out and expresses the total character of its object. In this intense identification, the impressions made on one sense 'excite by affinity those of another'; the object is grasped as a vital whole. And accompanying this sympathetic gusto, with its resolving of diverse impressions into a unified and immediate experience, is a discerning ability to sense organic motion, with a vivid fellow-feeling, and as an unfolding and continuing process. One is reminded of Severn's account:

'a wave . . . billowing through a tree,' as he described the uplifting surge of air among swaying masses of chestnuts or oak foliage, or when, afar off, he heard the wind coming across woodlands. 'The tide! the tide!' he would cry delightedly, and spring on to some stile, or upon the bough of a wayside tree, and watch the passage of the wind upon the meadow grasses or young corn, not stirring till the flow of air was all around him, while an expression of rapture made his eyes gleam and his face glow.

IV

It is especially through a rapidly developed mastery of idiom and versification that Keats acquired the control of impact and the formal sense of structure that restrains the concrete richness of his mature verse and thus contributes to its massive and interwoven firmness. It is here that the powerful influence of Milton—against which he was later to react in some ways—had so salutary an effect, lifting him far beyond the weak and fitful devices with which he had tried to tighten his versification in

346

Isabella. The first *Hyperion,* begun a few months after *Isabella,* immediately reveals that no apprentice, at once so gifted and eager, ever sat at the feet of Milton; certainly none ever learned from Milton more quickly and with greater ultimate profit. To be sure, much that he took over consists merely of the obvious mannerisms that all Miltonic imitators have used. One example is the frequent use of the adjective in place of the adverb ('Shook *horrid* with such aspen malady,' 'Crept *gradual,* from the foot unto the crown'). And there are the 'Miltonic inversions' with which Keats later thought *Hyperion* was disfigured: the epithet after the noun ('omens drear,' 'palace bright,' 'metal sick'), and the verb before the subject ('Pale wox I,' 'There saw she direst strife'). But other devices less mannered and more generally helpful were adopted. Among them should be noted the Milton ellipsis ('still snuff'd the incense, teeming up/From man to the sun's God; yet unsecure'); a condensed asyndeton ('some also shouted; Some wept, some wail'd, all bow'd with reverence'); and a use of repetition more effective than the crude repetition that Keats had taken over from Fairfax in his attempt to tighten *Isabella.* In versification, Keats closely followed Milton, and acquired metrical qualities that were to remain as a strengthening support in his verse. Chief among these are an increased slowing and weighting of the line with spondees, and also the use of the majestic sixth-syllable caesura, which Keats alone among Milton's imitators seems to have had the ear to catch. A growing sense of stanzaic structure is apparent in the *Eve of St. Agnes,* which, in contrast to other eighteenth- and nineteenth-century poems in the Spenserian stanza, often preserves the quatrain division that Spenser himself used in the stanza (*abab bcbc c*). In his sonnets, Keats now abandoned the Petrarchan form, which had been the dominant sonnet form since Milton; and he went back instead to the Shakespearian rhyme scheme, consisting of three heroic, or elegiac, quatrains and a couplet. But the sonnet was now only an incidental and casual form for Keats. If his poetic temper was still mainly lyrical, it was becoming too richly weighted to be couched in the brief space of the sonnet. In fact, he not only wished for a more lengthy form, which would permit a more leisurely development, but he desired a different rhyme pattern. In the first eight lines of the Petrarchan form, the three couplets (*a bb aa bb a*), he felt, had a 'pouncing' quality, the second line of each couplet leaping out, as it were, to match the first. In the Shakespearian form, on the other hand, the three alternate-rhyming quatrains (the heroic, and in the eighteenth century the traditional 'elegiac' quatrain) often had an 'elegiac' languor as well; and the concluding couplet, with which even Shakespeare had difficulty, 'has seldom a pleasing effect' (May 3, 1819). Keats wanted, therefore, 'a better sonnet stanza than we have,' and wrote an experimental sonnet, 'If by dull rhymes,' the theme of which is

> Let us find out, if we must be constrained,
> Sandals more interwoven and complete
> To fit the naked foot of Poesy.

After experimenting in the *Ode to Psyche*, he finally developed a ten-line stanza (in the later ode, *To Autumn*, eleven lines). This stanza is essentially constructed from the *disjecta membra* of both sonnet forms, and was possibly influenced also by some of the ten-line ode-stanzas common in the eighteenth century. Avoiding the 'pouncing rhymes' of the Petrarchan octave, the continual alternate rhyming of the Shakespearian form, and its concluding couplet, this new ode-stanza—though there are variations—consists basically of one alternate-rhyming quatrain (*abab*) from the three that make up the Shakespearian sonnet, with the addition of something like the ordinary sestet (*cde cde*) of the Petrarchan form. And here, in these closely knit and restraining stanzas, Keats certainly achieved a lyrical form 'more interwoven and complete.' In the odes, moreover, may be seen a masterful use of the assonance and vowel-interplay, first employed in *Hyperion* and continued throughout the *Eve of St. Agnes* and many of the sonnets, with an intricacy hardly equalled in the history of English verse. Keats informed his friend, Benjamin Bailey, that he had a 'principle of melody in verse,' upon which he had his own motives, particularly in the management of open and close vowels:

> Keats's theory was that the vowels should be . . . interchanged like differing notes in music, to prevent monotony . . . . I well remember his telling me that, had he studied music, he had some notions of the combinations of sounds, by which he thought he could have done something as original as his poetry.

And when Keats turned to the writing of *Hyperion*, in the autumn of 1818, he began to make use of an elaborate patterning both of open and close vowels and also of assonance. This use of assonance and vowel-arrangement is extraordinarily complex at times, and cannot be described in any detail in this essay. A few examples of assonance patterning, however, may be cited:

1   2   3   1   2   3

And still she slept an azure-lidded sleep.

1 2   3 1   2   3

Nor let the beetle, nor the death-moth be.

Or, to take a somewhat more complicated example:

1   1   2   2

And bid old Saturn take his throne again.

3 4   3   4

Patterns of vowel repetition occur, in an even more complex manner, throughout series of more than one line, and easily substantiate Saintsbury's assertion that the deliberate and frequent use of assonance in English poetry starts with Keats.

v

With the great odes, we are probably at the apex of Keats's poetic art. A discussion of the relevance of Keats's stylistic craftsmanship to the present day could quite justifiably turn into simply an explication of one or two of these odes. But the procedure taken here, rightly or wrongly, has been to stress the rather rapid experimentation with styles, the interests that led to it, and some of the more general aspects of Keats's development in this series of experiments. Hence, there would be place for only the briefest explication; and considering the care with which the odes have been examined, especially in the last twenty years, a short impressionistic explication would be presumptuous. Nor could we get very far in discussing the form of these odes even in general terms unless we spent time in reminding ourselves of the underpart of the iceberg—of what was going on in the mind of Keats throughout the year before the great odes and especially the last two or three months of it.

But we can certainly note in these odes—especially the *Ode on a Grecian Urn* and the *Ode to a Nightingale*—what I can only call a successful intrusion of the dramatic. In each we are dealing with a miniature drama. In each the poet seeks at the start—in the *Ode to a Nightingale* shortly after the start—to identify himself with an object that can lift himself beyond a world of flux. In each there is a gradual disengagement, an inability to follow completely the implications of sympathetic

349

absorption, and a return back (implicit in the *Grecian Urn,* more obvious in the *Nightingale*) to the world of process and the claims of the human heart. So, a century later with Yeats, there may be the paeans to Byzantium; but the drama lies in the return back—the descent down the ladder, as in 'The Circus Animals' Desertion'—to the human condition, and the assertive, unstilled desires of the dying animal, from which 'all ladders start.' The structure of the odes cannot be considered apart from this drama. Nor can the massive richness and the courageous openness to the full concrete expression, be considered apart from the drama, especially at a time like the present when fear of the welter, the quick unpredictable decay or change of concrete life has so intimidated the imagination of writers. There is courage here, in this welcome of concrete amplitude by Keats; and the courage is not apart from the poetic art.

The poems of the summer and early autumn of 1819 add important nuances to the situation. The questioning, before the odes, of the value and function of poetry in such a world as we find ourselves becomes more articulate in the letters. Energetic changes in style and form follow. *Lamia* drops, for the time being, many of the stylistic qualities of Keats from *Hyperion* through the odes. We have now a fairly open allegory, in some ways impetuously ironic and mocking in tone, which had, he hoped, a new energy that would 'take hold of people in some way—give them either pleasant or unpleasant sensations.' As if in a deliberate attempt to put things at arm's length, he surprisingly reverts to the crisp heroic couplet (the 'rocking-horse' meter he had once shied away from) of Dryden and Pope, though with a vivid color all of his own. The couplet is not so closed as in Dryden or Pope; but there are many closer similarities of a minor prosodic nature. Whatever else may be said of *Lamia,* it treats the effect of a Circian enchantment upon the impressionable mind of a young man (Lycius) who is open to the appeal of a magic world, and who is unable to withstand reality when it is pointed out to him. This general theme is closely related to the style which Keats, within two months, has suddenly evolved in contrast to the odes.

But at the same time he has begun to disengage himself from this new style, and to turn to still another, though the fragmentary form of the *Fall of Hyperion*—the revised *Hyperion*—hardly shows it to advantage. For, leaving aside all the psychological difficulties of this impetuous period, he was dealing with a discarded fragment. Little can be said about the style of this recast and warmed-up fragment except about meter and idiom. Stripped of its original allegory, the poem indicts the 'dreamer' who makes poetry a means of escape from the concrete world. Keats strips the poem, too, of many of its Miltonic mannerisms. In the place of the grandeur of the first *Hyperion*, we have now a more mellow blank verse, Virgilian and half-pastoral in tone:

> Still was more plenty than the fabled horn
> Thrice emptied could pour forth, at banqueting
> For Proserpine return'd to her own fields,
> Where the white heifers low.
>
> *I, 35–38*

> When in mid-May the sickening East Wind
> Shifts sudden to the South, the small warm rain
> Melts out the frozen incense from all flowers.
>
> *I, 97–99*

Despite the uncertainty of the poem as a whole, there is a relaxed, even confident, quietness in the opening hundred lines or so of this revision. This opening can be said to suggest a style unlike anything else in the nineteenth century: a style towards which Keats might well have moved —or through which he would have passed to something else—had he continued to write for a few more years. Meanwhile, Keats's last great poem—the ode *To Autumn*—is, of course, a return to the full and dense richness that characterized the great odes of the preceding May, but a richness now harmonized and lifted to a serenity quite unequalled elsewhere in romantic poetry.

VI

The range and variety of Keats's style are perhaps greater than can be found in other nineteenth-century English poets. This is a large tribute; the brevity of Keats's career makes it larger. This variety partly explains Keats's continued appeal despite changes of taste during the past century. Victorian poets, for example, could find in Keats a veritable treasure house of the qualities they valued. Even when the romantic emphasis on 'suggestiveness' in poetry—on qualities in poetry that will stimulate the imagination into a creative activity of its own—developed into a cult of subjective revery, with the poem serving merely as a backdrop to one's own personal mood, Keats, particularly in the early verse, could furnish the Victorians with as striking a precedent or model as Shelley. More specialized developments in Victorian poetry could find in him an even better stimulus than Wordsworth, Coleridge, Byron, or Shelley. Among two such developments one may mention a tendency— as in Tennyson, or in a different and cruder way, Swinburne—to sacrifice metaphor and concentrated imagery almost completely in order to exploit the musical qualities of verse; and Keats, as was said earlier— though without sacrificing metaphor and image—offers as dexterous and skillful a use of sound, especially in assonance, as can be found in English verse since the beginning of the romantic era. Similarly, the pre-Raphaelites, with their interest in single pictures, and in their effort to string a poem about a set of hangings or tapestries, usually to the neglect of any organic development of the poem as a whole, could find in Keats better examples to imitate than in any other romantic. Because Keats's images often attain remarkable clarity, as well as the condensation and the suggestive magic that the pre-Raphaelites liked, his poetry, more than that of the other romantics, remained popular with the Imagists when they revolted against pre-Raphaelite vagueness.

In the shift in stylistic taste, of which the revival of metaphysical poetry was a symptom, Keats was left relatively unscathed during the general barrage directed at nineteenth-century poetry. One explanation is the tensely braced and formal tightness of his mature verse, particularly the odes, which is hard to match in other verse of the century. Another is a growing experimental use of disparates and of sketched, suggestive metaphor in his phrasing: 'branchèd thoughts, new grown'; lightning viewed as 'crooked strings of fire' that 'singe away the swollen clouds'; or the now famous cancelled stanza of the *Ode on Melancholy:*

> Though you should build a bark of dead men's bones,
> And rear a phantom gibbet for a mast,
> Stitch creeds together for a sail, with groans
> To fill it out, blood stainèd and aghast;
> *Although your rudder be a dragon's tail*
> *Long sever'd, yet still hard with agony . . . .*

This active associative suggestion through compressed metaphor, when joined with an emphatic in-feeling that is comparatively weaker in metaphysical poetry, provides us with an idiom that at its best approximates that of Shakespeare. The combination, at least, is rare since Shakespeare.

The point is the variety, and a variety that consists not only in a successive series of styles but also in the diverse appeal of formal and stylistic qualities that are coalesced in the greatest poetry of Keats. It has stood him very well throughout some rather serious changes in stylistic taste during the past century, and throughout the growing, self-conscious fastidiousness that Johnson describes as 'elegance refined into impatience.' It is possible that what we think of as current tastes in poetry may continue for another generation, further refined. In this case the best of Keats will retain its relevance. But it may be that we are about to undergo another shift, a shift into a new romanticism, more sophisticated, of course, and more formally conscious than the old, but, I can only hope, with equal courage and openness to amplitude of emotion and experience. Indeed it may be a natural human craving for courage and openness, sharpened by long claustrophobia, that will have prodded us into such a shift and sustained it.

Should this be so, it would be difficult to imagine any poet since the mid-seventeenth century who could mean more. The help, the encouragement—the desire of which leads us constantly to reshuffle and re-evaluate our predecessors, when we are not doing so simply as an academic exercise—will not, of course, come from using even the greatest verse of Keats as a model. He that imitates the *Iliad*, said Edward Young, is not imitating Homer. The relevance is in what we catch from the example.

CLEANTH BROOKS

Keats's Sylvan Historian*

THERE is much in the poetry of Keats which suggests that he would have approved of Archibald MacLeish's dictum, 'A poem should not mean/ But be.' There is even some warrant for thinking that the Grecian urn (real or imagined) which inspired the famous ode was, for Keats, just such a poem, 'palpable and mute,' a poem in stone. Hence it is the more remarkable that the 'Ode' itself differs from Keats's other odes by culminating in a statement—a statement even of some sententiousness in which the urn itself is made to say that beauty is truth, and—more sententious still—that this bit of wisdom sums up the whole of mortal knowledge.

This is 'to mean' with a vengeance—to violate the doctrine of the objective correlative, not only by stating truths, but by defining the limits of truth. Small wonder that some critics have felt that the unravished bride of quietness protests too much.

T. S. Eliot, for example, says that 'this line ['Beauty is truth,' etc.] strikes me as a serious blemish on a beautiful poem; and the reason must be either that I fail to understand it, or that it is a statement which is untrue.' But even for persons who feel that they do understand it, the line may still constitute a blemish. Middleton Murry, who, after a discussion of Keats's other poems and his letters, feels that he knows what

---

* This essay had been finished some months before I came upon Kenneth Burke's brilliant essay on Keats's 'Ode ('Symbolic Action in a Poem by Keats,' *Accent*, Autumn, 1943). I have decided not to make any alterations, though I have been tempted to adopt some of Burke's insights, and, in at least one case, his essay has convinced me of a point which I had considered but rejected—the pun on 'breed' and 'Brede.'

From *The Well Wrought Urn*, copyright 1947 by Cleanth Brooks (Harcourt, Brace and Co., Inc., 1947), pp. 139–52. Reprinted by permission of the publisher and the author.

Keats meant by 'beauty' and what he meant by 'truth,' and that Keats used them in senses which allowed them to be properly bracketed together, still, is forced to conclude: 'My own opinion concerning the value of these two lines *in the context of the poem itself* is not very different from Mr. T. S. Eliot's.' The troubling assertion is apparently an intrusion upon the poem—does not grow out of it—is not dramatically accommodated to it.

This is essentially Garrod's objection, and the fact that Garrod does object indicates that a distaste for the ending of the 'Ode' is by no means limited to critics of notoriously 'modern' sympathies.

But the question of real importance is not whether Eliot, Murry, and Garrod are right in thinking that 'Beauty is truth, truth beauty' injures the poem. The question of real importance concerns beauty and truth in a much more general way: what is the relation of the beauty (the goodness, the perfection) of a poem to the truth or falsity of what it seems to assert? It is a question which has particularly vexed our own generation—to give it I. A. Richards' phrasing, it is the problem of belief.

The 'Ode,' by its bold equation of beauty and truth, raises this question in its sharpest form—the more so when it becomes apparent that the poem itself is obviously intended to be a parable on the nature of poetry, and of art in general. The 'Ode' has apparently been an enigmatic parable, to be sure: one can emphasize *beauty* is truth and throw Keats into the pure-art camp, the usual procedure. But it is only fair to point out that one could stress *truth* is beauty, and argue with the Marxist critics of the 'thirties for a propaganda art. The very ambiguity of the statement, 'Beauty is truth, truth beauty' ought to warn us against insisting very much on the statement in isolation, and to drive us back to a consideration of the context in which the statement is set.

It will not be sufficient, however, if it merely drives us back to a study of Keats's reading, his conversation, his letters. We shall not find our answer there even if scholarship does prefer on principle investigations of Browning's ironic question, 'What porridge had John Keats.' For even if we knew just what porridge he had, physical and mental, we should still not be able to settle the problem of the 'Ode.' The reason should be clear: our specific question is not what did Keats the man perhaps want to assert here about the relation of beauty and truth; it is rather: was Keats the poet able to exemplify that relation in this particular poem? Middleton Murry is right: the relation of the final statement in the poem to the total context is all-important.

Indeed, Eliot, in the very passage in which he attacks the 'Ode' has indicated the general line which we are to take in its defense. In that passage, Eliot goes on to contrast the closing lines of the 'Ode' with a line from *King Lear*, 'Ripeness is all.' Keats's lines strike him as false; Shakespeare's, on the other hand, as not clearly false, and as possibly quite true. Shakespeare's generalization, in other words, avoids raising the question of truth. But is it really a question of truth and falsity? One is tempted to account for the difference of effect which Eliot feels in this way: 'Ripeness is all' is a statement put in the mouth of a dramatic character and a statement which is governed and qualified by the whole context of the play. It does not directly challenge an examination into its truth because its relevance is pointed up and modified by the dramatic context.

Now, suppose that one could show that Keats's lines, *in quite the same way*, constitute a speech, a consciously riddling paradox, put in the mouth of a particular character, and modified by the total context of the poem. If we could demonstrate that the speech was 'in character,' was dramatically appropriate, was properly prepared for—then would not the lines have all the justification of 'Ripeness is all'? In such case, should we not have waived the question of the scientific or philosophic truth of the lines in favor of the application of a principle curiously like that of dramatic propriety? I suggest that some such principle is the only one legitimately to be invoked in any case. Be this as it may, the 'Ode on a Grecian Urn' provides us with as neat an instance as one could wish in order to test the implications of such a maneuver.

It has seemed best to be perfectly frank about procedure: the poem is to be read in order to see whether the last lines of the poem are not, after all, dramatically prepared for. Yet there are some claims to be made upon the reader too, claims which he, for his part, will have to be prepared to honor. He must not be allowed to dismiss the early characterizations of the urn as merely so much vaguely beautiful description. He must not be too much surprised if 'mere decoration' turns out to be meaningful symbolism—or if ironies develop where he has been taught to expect only sensuous pictures. Most of all, if the teasing riddle spoken finally by the urn is not to strike him as a bewildering break in tone, he must not be too much disturbed to have the element of paradox latent in the poem emphasized, even in those parts of the poem which have none of the energetic crackle of wit with which he usually associates paradox. This is surely not too much to ask of the reader—namely, to assume that Keats meant what he said and that he chose his words with care. After all, the poem begins on a note of paradox, though a mild one: for we ordinarily do not expect an urn to speak at all; and yet, Keats does more than this: he begins his poem by emphasizing the apparent contradiction.

The silence of the urn is stressed—it is a 'bride of quietness'; it is a 'foster-child of silence,' but the urn is a 'historian' too. Historians tell the truth, or are at least expected to tell the truth. What is a 'Sylvan historian'? A historian who is like the forest rustic, a woodlander? Or, a historian who writes histories of the forest? Presumably, the urn is sylvan in both senses. True, the latter meaning is uppermost: the urn can 'express/A flowery tale more sweetly than our rhyme,' and what the urn goes on to express is a 'leaf-fring'd legend' of 'Tempe or the dales of Arcady.' But the urn, like the 'leaf-fring'd legend' which it tells, is covered with emblems of the fields and forests: 'Overwrought,/With forest branches and the trodden weed.' When we consider the way in which the urn utters its history, the fact that it must be sylvan in both senses is seen as inevitable. Perhaps too the fact that it is a rural historian, a rustic, a peasant historian, qualifies in our minds the dignity and the 'truth' of the histories which it recites. Its histories, Keats has already conceded, may be characterized as 'tales'—not formal history at all.

The sylvan historian certainly supplies no names and dates—'What men or gods are these?' the poet asks. What it does give is action—of men *or* gods, of godlike men or of superhuman (though not daemonic) gods—action, which is not the less intense for all that the urn is cool marble. The words 'mad' and 'ecstasy' occur, but it is the quiet, rigid urn which gives the dynamic picture. And the paradox goes further: the scene is one of violent love-making, a Bacchanalian scene, but the urn itself is like a 'still unravish'd bride,' or like a child, a child 'of silence and slow time.' It is not merely like a child, but like a 'foster-child.' The exactness of the term can be defended. 'Silence and slow time,' it is suggested, are not the true parents, but foster-parents. They are too old, one feels, to have borne the child themselves. Moreover, they dote upon the 'child' as grandparents do. The urn is fresh and unblemished; it is still young, for all its antiquity, and time which destroys so much has 'fostered' it.

With Stanza II we move into the world presented by the urn, into an examination, not of the urn as a whole—as an entity with its own form—but of the details which overlay it. But as we enter that world, the paradox of silent speech is carried on, this time in terms of the objects portrayed on the vase.

The first lines of the stanza state a rather bold paradox—even the dulling effect of many readings has hardly blunted it. At least we can easily revive its sharpness. Attended to with care, it is a statement which is preposterous, and yet true—true on the same level on which the original metaphor of the speaking urn is true. The unheard music is sweeter than any audible music. The poet has rather cunningly enforced his conceit by using the phrase, 'ye soft pipes.' Actually, we might accept the poet's metaphor without being forced to accept the adjective 'soft.' The pipes might, although 'unheard,' be shrill, just as the action which is frozen in the figures on the urn can be violent and ecstatic as in Stanza I and slow and dignified as in Stanza IV (the procession to the sacrifice). Yet, by characterizing the pipes as 'soft,' the poet has provided a sort of realistic basis for his metaphor: the pipes, it is suggested, are playing very softly; if we listen carefully, we can hear them; their music is just below the threshold of normal sound.

This general paradox runs through the stanza: action goes on though the actors are motionless; the song will not cease; the lover cannot leave his song; the maiden, always to be kissed, never actually kissed, will remain changelessly beautiful. The maiden is, indeed, like the urn itself, a 'still unravished bride of quietness'—not even ravished by a kiss; and it is implied, perhaps, that her changeless beauty, like that of the urn, springs from this fact.

The poet is obviously stressing the fresh, unwearied charm of the scene itself which can defy time and is deathless. But, at the same time, the poet is being perfectly fair to the terms of his metaphor. The beauty portrayed is deathless because it is lifeless. And it would be possible to shift the tone easily and ever so slightly by insisting more heavily on some of the phrasings so as to give them a darker implication. Thus, in the case of 'thou canst not leave/Thy song,' one could interpret: the musician cannot leave the song even if he would: he is fettered to it, a prisoner. In the same way, one could enlarge on the hint that the lover is not wholly satisfied and content: 'never canst thou kiss,/ . . . yet, do not grieve.' These items are mentioned here, not because one wishes to maintain that the poet is bitterly ironical, but because it is important for us to see that even here the paradox is being used fairly, particularly in view of the shift in tone which comes in the next stanza.

This third stanza represents, as various critics have pointed out, a recapitulation of earlier motifs. The boughs which cannot shed their leaves, the unwearied melodist, and the ever-ardent lover reappear. Indeed, I am not sure that this stanza can altogether be defended against the charge that it represents a falling-off from the delicate but firm precision of the earlier stanzas. There is a tendency to linger over the scene sentimentally: the repetition of the word 'happy' is perhaps symptomatic of what is occurring. Here, if anywhere, in my opinion, is to be found the blemish on the ode—not in the last two lines. Yet, if we are to attempt a defense of the third stanza, we shall come nearest success by emphasizing the paradoxical implications of the repeated items; for whatever development there is in the stanza inheres in the increased stress on the paradoxical element. For example, the boughs cannot 'bid the Spring adieu,' a phrase which repeats 'nor ever can those trees be bare,' but the new line strengthens the implications of speaking: the falling leaves are a gesture, a word of farewell to the joy of spring. The melodist of Stanza II played sweeter music because unheard, but here, in the third stanza, it is implied that he does not tire of his song for the same reason that the lover does not tire of his love—neither song nor love is consummated. The songs are 'for ever new' because they cannot be completed.

The paradox is carried further in the case of the lover whose love is 'For ever warm and still to be enjoy'd.' We are really dealing with an ambiguity here, for we can take 'still to be enjoy'd' as an adjectival phrase on the same level as 'warm'—that is, 'still virginal and warm.' But the tenor of the whole poem suggests that the warmth of the love depends upon the fact that it has not been enjoyed—that is, 'warm and still to be enjoy'd' may mean also 'warm *because* still to be enjoy'd.'

But though the poet has developed and extended his metaphors furthest here in this third stanza, the ironic counterpoise is developed furthest too. The love which a line earlier was 'warm' and 'panting' becomes suddenly in the next line, 'All breathing human passion far above.' But if it is *above* all breathing passion, it is, after all, outside the realm of breathing passion, and therefore, not human passion at all.

(If one argues that we are to take 'All breathing human passion' as qualified by 'That leaves a heart high-sorrowful and cloy'd'—that is, if one argues that Keats is saying that the love depicted on the urn is above only that human passion which leaves one cloyed and not above human passion in general, he misses the point. For Keats in the 'Ode' is stressing the ironic fact that all human passion *does* leave one cloyed; hence the superiority of art.)

The purpose in emphasizing the ironic undercurrent in the foregoing lines is not at all to disparage Keats—to point up implications of his poem of which he was himself unaware. Far from it: the poet knows precisely what he is doing. The point is to be made simply in order to make sure that we are completely aware of what he *is* doing. Garrod, sensing this ironic undercurrent, seems to interpret it as an element over which Keats was not able to exercise full control. He says: 'Truth to his main theme [the fixity given by art to forms which in life are impermanent] has taken Keats farther than he meant to go. The pure and ideal art of this "cold Pastoral," this "silent form," *has* a cold silentness which in some degree saddens him. In the last lines of the fourth stanza, especially the last three lines . . . every reader is conscious, I should suppose, of an undertone of sadness, of disappointment.' The undertone is there, but Keats has not been taken 'farther than he meant to go.' Keats's attitude, even in the early stanzas, is more complex than Garrod would allow: it is more complex and more ironic, and a recognition of this is important if we are to be able to relate the last stanza to the rest of the 'Ode.' Keats is perfectly aware that the frozen moment of loveliness is more dynamic than is the fluid world of reality *only* because it is frozen. The love depicted on the urn remains warm and young because it is not human flesh at all but cold, ancient marble.

With Stanza IV, we are still within the world depicted by the urn, but the scene presented in this stanza forms a contrast to the earlier scenes. It emphasizes, not individual aspiration and desire, but communal life. It constitutes another chapter in the history that the 'Sylvan historian' has to tell. And again, names and dates have been omitted. We are not told to what god's altar the procession moves, nor the occasion of the sacrifice.

Moreover, the little town from which the celebrants come is unknown; and the poet rather goes out of his way to leave us the widest possible option in locating it. It may be a mountain town, or a river town, or a tiny seaport. Yet, of course, there is a sense in which the nature of the town—the essential character of the town—is actually suggested by the figured urn. But it is not given explicitly. The poet is willing to leave much to our imaginations; and yet the stanza in its organization of imagery and rhythm does describe the town clearly enough; it is small, it is quiet, its people are knit together as an organic whole, and on a 'pious morn' such as this, its whole population has turned out to take part in the ritual.

The stanza has been justly admired. Its magic of effect defies reduction to any formula. Yet, without pretending to 'account' for the effect in any mechanical fashion, one can point to some of the elements active in securing the effect: there is the suggestiveness of the word 'green' in 'green altar'—something natural, spontaneous, living; there is the suggestion that the little town is caught in a curve of the seashore, or nestled in a fold of the mountains—at any rate, is something secluded and something naturally related to its terrain; there is the effect of the phrase 'peaceful citadel,' a phrase which involves a clash between the ideas of war and peace and resolves it in the senses of stability and independence without imperialistic ambition—the sense of stable repose.

But to return to the larger pattern of the poem: Keats does something in this fourth stanza which is highly interesting in itself and thoroughly relevant to the sense in which the urn is a historian. One of the most moving passages in the poem is that in which the poet speculates on the strange emptiness of the little town which, of course, has not been pictured on the urn at all.

The little town which has been merely implied by the procession portrayed on the urn is endowed with a poignance beyond anything else in the poem. Its streets 'for evermore/ Will silent be,' its desolation forever shrouded in a mystery. No one in the figured procession will ever be able to go back to the town to break the silence there, not even one to tell the stranger there why the town remains desolate.

If one attends closely to what Keats is doing here, he may easily come to feel that the poet is indulging himself in an ingenious fancy, an indulgence, however, which is gratuitous and finally silly; that is, the poet has created in his own imagination the town implied by the procession of worshipers, has given it a special character of desolation and loneliness, and then has gone on to treat it as if it were a real town to which a stranger might actually come and be puzzled by its emptiness. (I can see no other interpretation of the lines, 'and not a soul to tell/ Why thou art desolate can e'er return.') But, actually, of course, no one will ever discover the town except by the very same process by which Keats has discovered it: namely, through the figured urn, and then, of course, he will not need to ask why it is empty. One can well imagine what a typical eighteenth-century critic would have made of this flaw in logic.

It will not be too difficult, however, to show that Keats's extension of the fancy is not irrelevant to the poem as a whole. The 'reality' of the little town has a very close relation to the urn's character as a historian. If the earlier stanzas have been concerned with such paradoxes as the ability of static carving to convey dynamic action, of the soundless pipes to play music sweeter than that of the heard melody, of the figured lover to have a love more warm and panting than that of breathing flesh and blood, so in the same way the town implied by the urn comes to have a richer and more important history than that of actual cities. Indeed, the imagined town is to the figured procession as the unheard melody is to the carved pipes of the unwearied melodist. And the poet, by pretending to take the town as real—so real that he can imagine the effect of its silent streets upon the stranger who chances to come into it—has suggested in the most powerful way possible its essential reality for him—and for us. It is a case of the doctor's taking his own medicine: the poet is prepared to stand by the illusion of his own making.

With Stanza V we move back out of the enchanted world portrayed by the urn to consider the urn itself once more as a whole, as an object. The shift in point of view is marked with the first line of the stanza by the apostrophe, 'O Attic shape . . .' It is the urn itself as a formed thing, as an autonomous world, to which the poet addresses these last words. And the rich, almost breathing world which the poet has conjured up for us contracts and hardens into the decorated motifs on the urn itself: 'with brede/Of marble men and maidens overwrought.' The beings who have a life above life—'all breathing human passion far above'—are marble, after all.

This last is a matter which, of course, the poet has never denied. The recognition that the men and maidens are frozen, fixed, arrested, has, as we have already seen, run through the second, third, and fourth stanzas as an ironic undercurrent. The central paradox of the poem, thus, comes to conclusion in the phrase, 'Cold Pastoral.' The word 'pastoral' suggests warmth, spontaneity, the natural and the informal as well as the idyllic, the simple, and the informally charming. What the urn tells is a 'flowery tale,' a 'leaf-fring'd legend,' but the 'sylvan historian' works in terms of marble. The urn itself is cold, and the life beyond life which it expresses is life which has been formed, arranged. The urn itself is a 'silent form,' and it speaks, not by means of statement, but by 'teasing us out of thought.' It is as enigmatic as eternity is, for, like eternity, its history is beyond time, outside time, and for this very reason bewilders our time-ridden minds: it teases us.

The marble men and maidens of the urn will not age as flesh-and-blood men and women will: 'When old age shall this generation waste.' (The word 'generation,' by the way, is very rich. It means on one level 'that which is generated'—that which springs from human loins—Adam's breed; and yet, so intimately is death wedded to men, the word 'generation' itself has become, as here, a measure of time.) The marble men and women lie outside time. The urn which they adorn will remain. The 'Sylvan historian' will recite its history to other generations.

What will it say to them? Presumably, what it says to the poet now: that 'formed experience,' imaginative insight, embodies the basic and fundamental perception of man and nature. The urn is beautiful, and yet its beauty is based—what else is the poem concerned with?—on an imaginative perception of essentials. Such a vision is beautiful but it is also true. The sylvan historian presents us with beautiful histories, but they are true histories, and it is a good historian.

Moreover, the 'truth' which the sylvan historian gives is the only kind of truth which we are likely to get on this earth, and, furthermore, it is the only kind that we *have* to have. The names, dates, and special circumstances, the wealth of data—these the sylvan historian quietly ignores. But we shall never get all the facts anyway—there is no end to the accumulation of facts. Moreover, mere accumulations of facts—a point our own generation is only beginning to realize—are meaningless. The sylvan historian does better than that: it takes a few details and so orders them that we have not only beauty but insight into essential truth. Its 'history,' in short, is a history without footnotes. It has the validity of myth—not myth as a pretty but irrelevant make-belief, an idle fancy, but myth as a valid perception into reality.

So much for the 'meaning' of the last lines of the 'Ode.' It is an interpretation which differs little from past interpretations. It is put forward here with no pretension to novelty. What is important is the fact that it can be derived from the context of the 'Ode' itself.

And now, what of the objection that the final lines break the tone of the poem with a display of misplaced sententiousness? One can summarize the answer already implied thus: throughout the poem the poet has stressed the paradox of the speaking urn. First, the urn itself can tell a story, can give a history. Then, the various figures depicted upon the urn play music or speak or sing. If we have been alive to these items, we shall not, perhaps, be too much surprised to have the urn speak once more, not in the sense in which it tells a story—a metaphor which is rather easy to accept—but, to have it speak on a higher level, to have it make a commentary on its own nature. If the urn has been properly dramatized, if we have followed the development of the metaphors, if we have been alive to the paradoxes which work throughout the poem, perhaps then, we shall be prepared for the enigmatic, final paradox which the 'silent form' utters. But in that case, we shall not feel that the generalization, unqualified and to be taken literally, is meant to march out of its context to compete with the scientific and philosophical generalizations which dominate our world.

'Beauty is truth, truth beauty' has precisely the same status, and the same justification as Shakespeare's 'Ripeness is all.' It is a speech 'in character' and supported by a dramatic context.

To conclude thus may seem to weight the principle of dramatic propriety with more than it can bear. This would not be fair to the complexity of the problem of truth in art nor fair to Keats's little parable. Granted; and yet the principle of dramatic propriety may take us further than would first appear. Respect for it may at least insure our dealing with the problem of truth at the level on which it is really relevant to literature. If we can see that the assertions made in a poem are to be taken as part of an organic context, if we can resist the temptation to deal with them in isolation, then we may be willing to go on to deal with the world-view, or 'philosophy,' or 'truth' of the *poem as a whole* in terms of its dramatic wholeness: that is, we shall not neglect the maturity of attitude, the dramatic tension, the emotional *and* intellectual coherence in favor of some statement of theme abstracted from it by paraphrase. Perhaps, best of all, we might learn to distrust our ability to represent any poem adequately by paraphrase. Such a distrust is healthy. Keats's sylvan historian, who is not above 'teasing' us, exhibits such a distrust, and perhaps the point of what the sylvan historian 'says' is to confirm us in our distrust.

La Belle Dame Sans Merci

It would be difficult in any reading of Keats' ballad not to be enthralled by the haunting power of its rhythm, by its delicate intermingling of the fragile and the grotesque, the tender and the weird, and by the perfect economy with which these effects are achieved. Snared by the sensuous workings of the poem, one is greatly tempted to evaluate it entirely as a poem whose function is not the expression of human values, but whose end is attained when it fulfills its own stylistic requirements. Nevertheless, out of the dim sense of mystery and incompleteness that its artistry arouses there rise not only richly suggestive overtones, but also dark hints of a meaning that might be available to us could we penetrate its mystery. The imagination, for example, seizes upon the sedge that has withered from the lake and upon the absence of the birds' song, and elaborates the pictorial connotations of these stark images into all barren and desolate autumnal scenes that ever were. And yet, one senses an insufficiency in these affective and image-making energies of the poem, for the overtones also drive the mind to ask questions of conceptual intent. What, one wonders, is the larger meaning couched within the absence of song? why a knight-at-arms and an elfin grot? and what are the significances of the cold hill side and the pale warriors?

Nor are these probings of the mind without justification, since the poem contains within itself the power of compelling us to such questions. For Keats' symbolism is almost always dynamic. His poetry does not lie inert, waiting, like the poetry of Blake and some of the early work of Yeats, to yield itself up to a symbolic reading. Such poetry as theirs assumes that the world is symbolic, and therefore that if the poet selects

From *The Finer Tone: Keat's Major Poems* (John Hopkins Press, 1953), pp. 65–83. Reprinted by permission of the publisher and the author.

images of symbolic import and orders them into an artistic intertexture that corresponds to the meaningful relationships in the cosmos, he has created a symbolic poem, let the reader read it as he will. However, we have seen that Keats' world is not symbolic; it is his vision of the world that is symbolic, and a greeting of the spirit is required to transmute image into symbol. Since 'every mental pursuit takes its reality and worth from the ardour of the pursuer—being in itself a nothing,' Keats must entice a pursuit of his images by the reader, whose ardor will transform them into symbols, 'ethereal things.'

In the ballad, therefore, Keats not only dramatized a myth, but also dramatized the fact that the narrative and its component images are symbolic. The first three stanzas are introductory in that they are addressed by an anonymous someone to the knight-at-arms, whose answer will then constitute the narrative body of the poem. These three stanzas consequently serve to set the story of the knight's adventures in an additional narrative framework, a dialogue between the knight and the stranger, with whom the reader tends to identify himself; and thus the reader is drawn more intimately into the knight's experiences, for he feels himself to be present as the knight speaks in his own person. But even more important, in the introductory stanzas images and human values are gradually blended stereoscopically until at length the reader's mode of poetic vision has been adjusted to see the symbolized value as the third-dimensional projection of the image.

The first two stanzas have identical patterns: the first half of each addresses a question to the knight-at-arms about his spiritual condition; and the second half comments on the natural setting. The similarity of the gaunt, pale appearance of the solitary knight to the desolation and decay of nature is clearly implied, but the absence of any explicit relationship leaves the connection vague and therefore fluid enough so that nature and the knight may later be welded into an organic, instead of a synthetic, union—a method reminiscent of the first stanza of the 'Ode on a Grecian Urn.' The second half of each of these stanzas is built around a coordination of two natural images (sedge and birds, the squirrel's granary and the harvest); and it is noticeable that the first pair are the natural images themselves, while the second are the materials of nature as shaped and molded by creatures for themselves. The progress is toward a closer integration of nature and man: the granary and the harvest are what creatures make of nature for their own use. Corresponding to these pairs of images are two pairs of adjectives in the halves describing the knight, the first pair exactly paralleling the natural images:

alone, no birds sing; palely loitering, the sedge has withered. All these balanced details, equally distributed to nature and the knight, now coalesce in the third stanza.

This stanza takes its structure from that of the second halves of the first two stanzas, for its pattern, too, depends upon the coordination of two natural images, lily and rose, and each image dominates half of the stanza, just as each image in the first two stanzas governs a single line. In other words, the structure of the third stanza is precisely that of the second halves of the first two, expanded to the length of a full stanza. The subject matter of the third stanza, however, is not the appearance of nature, but the spiritual condition of the knight-at-arms, which has been the theme of the first halves of the first two stanzas. By this absorption of the knight into the structural pattern of the natural imagery, the movement from a suggested but unstated relationship of man and nature in stanza one to an implied interrelationship in stanza two has now been completed. In the third stanza the two terms are organically integrated, and human values and natural images have been molded into interchangeable expressions: the lily and the rose are present in the knight's countenance, and his withering is theirs. This structural drama of their coalescence now compels a symbolic reading of the poem, and we cannot well avoid questioning the human relevance of the garlands, the elfin grot, and the cold hill side. If, to use Coleridge's definition, a symbol 'partakes of the reality which it renders intelligible,' the work of the first three stanzas is to make the symbols a living part of that reality.

II

The first three stanzas, which make dramatic the subsequent narrating and excite a symbolic reading, introduce nine precisely balanced stanzas containing the main narrative (4–12). The progress of the knight in the first four (4–7) comes to a climax in the central one (8) when he is taken into the elfin grot, and in the last four (9–12) he withdraws from the grot. The withdrawal brings the poem back to the scene with which it began, the completion of the circular movement being marked by the fact that the last stanza echoes the first.

Whatever the specific source may have been, the narrative clearly belongs to a folk legend best known in the form of the mediaeval ballad 'Thomas Rymer.' In the version available to Keats in Robert Jamieson's *Popular Ballads*, 1806 (the variant in Scott's *Minstrelsy* differs in a few important details), Thomas encounters a beautiful lady whom he thinks to be the Queen of Heaven, but who identifies herself as 'the queen of fair Elfland.' She takes him upon her milk-white steed, for he must serve her for seven years; and for forty days and nights they ride through blood while Thomas sees neither sun nor moon. Forbidden to touch the fruit of this strange country lest he suffer the plagues of hell, Thomas eats the loaf and drinks the claret that the elf-queen has brought. At length they rest before a hill, and the elf-queen, placing his head on her knee, shows him three wonders—the roads to wickedness, to righteousness, and to fair Elfland. It is the last of these that they are to follow, and for seven years 'True Thomas on earth was never seen.' The relations of this narrative to a story of a knight-at-arms carried by a fairy's child to an elfin grot are too obvious to underscore. Apparently the myth of a journey to a mysterious otherworld that is neither heaven nor hell nor earth, and of capture there by the fairy magic of love for one who seems to be 'Queen of Heaven,' constituted a pattern that evoked from Keats a body of speculation ripe for expression and helped give these speculations an artistic shape.

Keats did not simply recast this folk legend into another artistic form but molded it into an expression of his deepest and most vivid conceptions. The legend was not merely an esthetic design that he felt he could bring closer to his idea of literary perfection; to him it was also a meaningful narrative in which he recognized his own journeys heavenward. Since, then, the substance of the folk ballad constitutes mainly the raw materials of Keats' creation, his modifications of the legend and his additions to it are the more obvious clues to his motives. It is noticeable that nearly all the larger narrative elements of the first four stanzas of Keats' central narrative (4–7) are present in the folk ballad also: the meeting with a fairy lady of great beauty, the implication of the lady's desire for Thomas, their sharing the pacing steed, and the knight's eating of the magic food. To these Keats has added three major details that do not appear in the folk ballad, even by implication: the knight weaves for the fairy's child a garland, bracelets, and a girdle of flowers; the lady sings 'A faery's song'; and at length 'in language strange she said—/ "I love thee true." '

What Keats has woven into the narrative, it appears, is another version of the pleasure thermometer, a series of increasing intensities that absorb the self into essence: nature, song, and love. We have already seen the important role of the pleasure thermometer in the 'Ode on a Grecian Urn,' and we shall have occasion to see how functional it is in other poems of Keats. It was 'a regular stepping of the Imagination towards a Truth,' towards that beauty-truth which was his heart's desire, and each aspiration towards it carried him along the route that his heart had marked out. When, for example, Endymion had traveled the 'journey homeward to habitual self' and was buried in his own deadly selfhood,[1] he was prepared for deliverance from 'this rapacious deep' in three stages. First, the riches of nature appeared before him: 'the floral pride / In a long whispering birth enchanted grew / Before his footsteps.'[2] Then music: 'This still alarm, / This sleepy music, forc'd him walk tip-toe.'[3] At length, surrounded by cupids, he observed the love-visitation of Venus and Adonis. And now at last 'some ethereal and high-favouring donor' has presented 'immortal bowers to mortal sense.'[4] By ascending the ladder of intensities, Endymion, too, has been released from the prison house of his mortal self and has attained insight into the mortal-immortal nature of heaven's bourne.

In Keats' ballad these increasing enthrallments of selfhood appear in successive order, each occupying one of three successive stanzas (5, 6, 7); and they lead finally to the heaven's bourne of the elfin grot (8). In folk literature the interiors of hills are often the dwelling places of fairies and elves: Tam Lin dwelled in a green hill, and in the romance of 'Thomas of Erceldoune,' which deals with the same Thomas Rymer, the hero was led 'in at Eldone hill.' Apparently the tradition of elfin grots was especially appropriate to Keats' purpose. Earthly in its form and yet 'elfin' in its nature—within the cold hill side of the physical world and yet being the otherworld mystery within the physical—it corresponds to the oxymoronic realm where life's self is nourished by its proper pith and to which man can ascend by a ladder of intensities. It is the earth spiritually transfigured; its fairyhood is the 'leaven, / That spreading in this dull and clodded earth / Gives it a touch ethereal.'

In calling upon another analogue to Keats' ballad I do not mean to propose that Keats' was directly influenced by it, despite the possibility that he was. Even proof of Keats' indebtedness, could it be found, would be irrelevant to our purpose, for it could not charge his ballad with values not already inherent in it. Nevertheless, it is illuminating to observe what significances the legend of Thomas Rymer held forth to one of Keats' contemporaries, an intimate friend of John Hamilton Reynolds and therefore one who was undoubtedly known to Keats. In the summer of 1818, nearly a year before Keats composed 'La Belle Dame Sans Merci,' John F. M. Dovaston wrote his 'Elfin Bride, a Fairy Ballad,' although it seems not to have appeared in print until 1825.[5] Its source is not the folk ballad but the mediaeval romance 'Thomas of Erceldoune,' which is a more extended version of the same legend.

The argument of the 'Elfin Bride,' Dovaston wrote, is that 'Time has no existence but with motion and matter: with the Deity, "whose centre is everywhere, and circumference nowhere,"—and with "millions of spiritual creatures" . . . Duration is without Time.' Apparently the legend of Thomas has the power of provoking speculations about a condition in which love is forever warm and still to be enjoyed. In Dovaston's ballad Merlin is substituted for Thomas Rymer, his fellow in many mediaeval legends. Merlin meets a 'White Lady' and begs of her that he may see 'that airy country / That wots not of Time nor Place.' They ride away on palfreys to fairyland, where Merlin is treated to a multitude of 'pleasures refin'd.' The passing time seems only a moment, but Merlin is informed that 'to Man in the dull cold world thou has left, / Seven times four Seasons are gone.' When, however, Merlin attempts a physical consummation of his love, the ideal vision is shattered, and he finds himself once again in the world of time and place, which now seems to him insipid and decayed although the memory of the fairy music still rings in his ear:

> He gazed all around the dull heathy ground,
> Neither tree nor bush was there,
> But wide wide wide all on every side
> Spread the heath dry brown and bare.

Returning once again to fairyland, Merlin remains for seven more years until at last a longing grows in him for the mortal and mutable world: he thought

> on the vales and green mountains of Wales
> And his friends so long forgot.

> For blithe are the vales and green mountains of Wales
> And it's blithe to sojourn there.

The wish is sufficient to free him from the land without time and place.

> Then suddenly there small shrilly and clear
> The Fairy-folk ceas'd their singing,
> And the silvery swells of pipes and bells
> No longer around him were ringing.

> And the Fairyland gay all melted away
> In a misty vapour curl'd;
> And his opening eyes beheld with surprize
> The light of this long-left world.

Driven back to earth by his human desires, Merlin awakens to find that his life in fairyland has been a vision, that but a moment has passed, and that he is still in the summer bower where he was when his dream began. Although Dovaston, unlike Keats, drew from his narrative the conclusion that man should be content with his mortal lot, it is obvious that he also found in the legend of Thomas Rymer a myth of a spaceless, timeless realm of pleasure from which man withdraws when the mortal world beckons him and from which he is cast out when he attempts to realize physically the ideal pleasures. In all this one cannot avoid hearing echoes of the 'Ode on a Grecian Urn.'

With Dovaston's ballad in mind we can see even more clearly the meaningfulness of the narrative pattern into which Keats wove the increasing intensities that mark the journey to the elfin grot. Now, dreams often perform in Keats' system of thought the function of the imagination. It is, for example, in dream visions that Endymion is united with Cynthia and hence gains insight into the beauty-truth of heaven's bourne. 'The Imagination,' Keats wrote, 'may be compared to Adam's dream—he awoke and found it truth.'[6] 'Real are the dreams of Gods,'[7] for to them beauty is truth, not merely a foreshadowing of it, as the visions of the human imagination are; but for the man who lives a life of sensations, dreams may at least be prefigurative visions of the beauty-truth reality to come. Therefore, ideally, having ascended the pleasure thermometer, the knight should perceive an immortality of passion, especially since his vision-making imagination is aided by fairy magic.

But the tug of the mutable world is too strong for mere mortals because 'in the world / We jostle'[8] and, as Dovaston wrote, we are drawn away by thoughts of 'the vales and green mountains of Wales / And . . . friends so long forgot.' Even in the heart of his prefigurative visions of heaven's bourne earthly man recalls that human passions leave a heart high-sorrowful and cloyed; his spirit clings to the vision until 'the stings / Of human neighbourhood envenom all.'[9] Merlin found that the desire to consummate physically his love for the 'White Lady' cast him upon 'the heath dry brown and bare,' the cold hill side from which one sees only withered sedge and hears no song of birds. And yet, this is a fate that must befall all mortal aspirations, for so long as man is earth-bound his life is made up of

> the war, the deeds,
> The disappointment, the anxiety,
> Imagination's struggles, far and nigh,
> All human.[10]

Mortal life must necessarily be an incessant struggle against these ills, which are ineradicable; living is the very act of being militant against the dimensional restrictions of the world. And thus all mortals who engage in 'Imagination's struggles' are knights-at-arms. But man cannot gain his quest in this world. No knight-at-arms can remain in the elfin grot because, since he is mortal, he cannot wholly yield himself up to this extra-human realm and gain visionary insight into its nature. He will be impelled to make the visionary physical or will long for 'his friends so long forgot.' This is precisely the realization that came to Keats when he wrote of his visit to Burns' country:

> Scanty the hour and few the steps beyond the bourn of care,
> Beyond the sweet and bitter world,—beyond it unaware!
> Scanty the hour and few the steps, because a longer stay
> Would bar return, and make a man forget his mortal way:
> O horrible! to lose the sight of well remember'd face,
> Of Brother's eyes, of Sister's brow. . . .
> No, no, that horror cannot be, for at the cable's length
> Man feels the gentle anchor pull and gladdens in its strength.[11]

It is man's bond with mankind that prevents him from lingering beyond the bourne of care. There is nothing in Keats' ballad even suggesting the frequent interpretation that the fairy's child is responsible for the knight's expulsion from the elfin grot; only his own inherent attribute of being mortal causes his magic withdrawal, as only the call of Merlin's human and physical impulses caused 'the Fairyland gay' to melt in a misty vapor. The vision of the mortal-immortal can only entice mortal man towards heaven's bourne; it cannot aid him in his aspirations or preserve his vision, which must inevitably be shattered. By this fair enchantment mortal man can only be 'tortured with renewed life.'[12]

It is in this sense that la belle dame is sans merci, without tenderness; this is a description of what provokes man's aspirations, rather than an evaluation of it. Like the lady of the tradition of courtly love, she is the ideal whom the lover must pursue but whom he can never possess; and hence he is doomed to suffer her 'unkindness,' which is her nature although not her fault. Only the inherent meanness of man's dreams, then, draws him back from heaven's bourne, for, instead of being visionary penetrations into that final essence which is beauty-truth, they are only of mutable things. Aspire though he will, the stings of human neighborhood envenom all.

Instead of dreaming of the 'ardent listlessness' which is heaven, the knight finds that death-pale kings, princes, and warriors intrude into his dream, mortal man being the necessary symbol of transitoriness and decay. What man calls living is truly the act of dying, since it is an incessant progress towards the grave; it is what Pope described as 'that long disease, my life.' Only after death, when man can exist in heaven's bourne, does he truly live; and therefore all earthly men are death-pale. Being mortal, and therefore death-pale, is also the condition of being cut off from that realm of pure being where life's self is nourished by its own pith. As death-pale man lives his existence of decay he can only yearn for that region from which his spirit comes, from which it has been divorced, but in which is the vital principle which will hereafter feed his spirit with 'renewed life.' Thus the lips of all mortal men are starved for lack of their spirit's own pith, for lack of the germ of spirit that is to be sucked from 'mould ethereal.'[13]

Yet, instead of aspiring to this spiritual food of heaven, as the knight does, mortal man has circumscribed himself by the physical world, and though death-pale and spiritually starved, fears the attraction of heaven's bourne. The impulse in that direction, Keats wrote in *Endymion,* leaves one 'too happy to be glad,' 'More happy than betides mortality.'[14] 'It is a flaw / In happiness to see beyond our bourn.'[15] Therefore, fearful of the aspiration that agonizes and spoils the apparent splendor of the material world, mortality, despite its own sufferings, warns the knight that 'La Belle Dame sans Merci / Hath thee in thrall!' How strange it is, Keats once mused,

> that man on earth should roam,
> And lead a life of woe, but not forsake
> His rugged path; nor dare he view alone
> His future doom which is but to awake.[16]

It is significant that the warning comes from those who seek to battle the world's ills (warriors) and from men of power (kings and princes). 'I would call the top and head of those who have a proper self.' Keats wrote, 'Men of Power';[17] that is, men who cannot ascend the pleasure thermometer and lose their selves in essence because they are self-contained.

The knight's inherent weakness in being unable to exclude from his visions the self-contained and world-bound mortality dissipates the ideal into which he has entered momentarily, just as the need for the world of men and the desire to materialize the ideal destroy the fairyland for Merlin. The elfin grot once again becomes the cold hill side which is the physical, mutable world, where the knight has been all the while, but which, by means of his visionary insight, took on the magic splendor of the elfin grot, the mystery within the mutable. The vision had momentarily transfigured a real thing into an 'ethereal' thing. Exactly so, it was the poet's vision that transformed the marble embroidery on the Grecian urn into the unchanging vitality of a realm without space, time, and identity; and the shattering of that vision once again froze the immortality of passion into cold, motionless marble. With the dissipation of the vision in the ballad and with the consequent return to the cold physical world, the ladder of intensities which the knight had ascended to reach the ethereal world now crumbles beneath him: love has gone, 'the sedge has wither'd from the lake,' and 'no birds sing.' Love, song, and nature fade and disappear as the knight's capacity for the passionate intensity for fellowship with essence becomes enervate and he returns to normal human weakness.

Now that the knight has been awakened from his dream by the stings of human neighborhood, he is as pale, death-pale, as the kings, princes, and warriors, for he now shares their mortality. Being mortal, his very existence is a progress towards death, and death therefore is in his nature, although in the elfin grot existence, being without time, is without death. Indeed, Keats originally wrote, 'I see *death's* lilly on thy brow . . . And on thy cheeks *death's* fading rose.' By withdrawing from the elfin grot, the knight has also become a Man of Power; the withdrawal is the act of reassuming his own self-containing identity, and thus he is 'alone,' being his own isolated self. His aloneness is the opposite of a fellowship with essence which absorbs the proper self, that self which is cut off from its selfless origin in heaven. At heaven's bourne there can be no aloneness because there are no individual selves, no proper identities; there it is irrelevant to ask, 'Who are these coming to the sacrifice?' Earthly life, then, is a spiritual solitude overcast with the pallor of death, and a denial of the 'honey wild, and manna dew,' the heaven-sent food which is life's proper pith; all mortal living is a movement towards the sacrificial altar. 'Living,' therefore, must be a biding of one's time, a meaningless exhausting of one's mortal lease, since man is only a temporary resident in this world. The elfin grot being truly his home ethereal, mortal man, in the solitude of his self, can only 'sojourn here, . . . palely loitering' on the cold hill side of the world. And the unfinished, hovering quality of the metrics of each stanzaic close ('And no birds sing,' 'On the cold hill's side') perfectly reinforces the aimless solitude with which Keats is investing mortal life.

III

We have already noticed the organization of the poem into two discourses—the questions of the stranger in the first three stanzas, and the knight's reply in the following nine. But within this pattern, another, more intricate and significant, is at work. In this inner configuration the poem falls into four equal groups of three stanzas each, the first of which is the symbol-making address of the stranger. The next six stanzas, the narrative core of the poem, tell of the direct relations of the knight and the fairy lady; of these the first three constitute one unit, and the last three another, the grouping and distinctness being marked by the two opening patterns: 'I met,' 'I made,' 'I set'; and 'She found,' 'She took,' 'And there she lulled me.' The final unit of three stanzas in the poem is a kind of epilogue telling of the aftermath of the encounter with the fairy's child and thus answers the stranger's questions in the three introductory stanzas and brings the poem round full circle so that the final stanza may be an approximate repetition of the first. This last unit is also bound together, nearly as the second three stanzas are: 'I saw,' 'I saw,' 'And this is why I sojourn here.'

But with these balances and intricacies Keats is not merely carving his narrative into fascinating arabesques. His artistry is almost always functional to his meaning and is seldom an end in itself. In stanza four it is noticeable that the only actor is the knight. In the next stanza the knight controls the action of the first two lines, and the lady that of the second two. In stanza six he truly governs only the first line, and it seems significant that Keats altered the action of the folk ballad, where it is the lady who takes Thomas upon her horse. Apparently there is a special intent in giving the action to the knight in the first line so that he may remain an actor throughout these three stanzas, but with diminishing control over the action. Clearly the lady governs the action in the last two lines of stanza six and, in a broader sense, the action of the second line also, for the stanza states that the knight's seeing nothing else is the consequence of the lady's singing.

There is, then, a progressive shrinkage of the 'I' as a power and a corresponding dominance of the 'she,' until in stanza seven, where the height of the pleasure thermometer is reached, the lady alone controls the entire action, and the knight passively yields to her. The consequence of ascending the pleasure thermometer, it will be recalled, is that one enters into the essences of progressive intensities, which are 'Richer entanglements, enthralments far / More self-destroying.' And proportionately as the knight ascends from nature to song to love, his active self is being absorbed into the ideal, which increasingly exercises control over his self. It is in this sense of empathic enthrallment that the knight is cautioned, 'La Belle Dame sans Merci / Hath thee in *thrall!*' Once he has wilfully entered into sensuous essence and set up the lady as an ideal ('I set her on my pacing steed'), he has abandoned his selfhood; even the apparently wilfull act of looking at the fairy's child is the passive consequence of being so absorbed into the essence of song that he can perceive only ideality: 'And nothing else saw all day long.' Since those who have 'a proper self' are 'Men of Power,' the retreat of the 'I' and the emergence of the 'she' as the sources of activity are the grammatical dramatization of the destruction of that power as the knight enters into greater and greater enthrallments.

At the tip-top of the humanly attainable scale is the 'orbed drop / Of light, and that is love'; 'Nor with aught else can our souls interknit / So wingedly.' Consequently, in stanza seven, in which the lady expresses her love, she is the only power, and the knight is completely enthralled by essence, ready now to enter into the heaven's bourne of the elfin grot. Moreover, the interknitting of the soul with essence through love so elevates the soul that it may partake of the spiritual stuff of which it is itself made, and hence 'Life's self is nourish'd by its proper pith, / And we are nurtured like a pelican brood.' In other words, by the knight's entrance into essence through love the ideal nourishes him with the source of his own spiritual mystery—with 'roots of relish sweet, / And honey wild, and manna dew.'

The structural pattern of the main narrative stanzas (4–12) is, then, as precisely balanced as that of the 'Ode on a Grecian Urn.' In the ode the first two stanzas trace the ascent to a perception of the frieze as a timeless, spaceless, selfless realm of endless vitality; the last two, the descent from this realm, bring the poem back to the condition from which it started. And the central stanza both depicts the oxymoronic nature of this area and introduces the chemicals for its destruction. Correspondingly, the first four stanzas (4–7) of the main narrative in the ballad lead towards the oxymoronic elfin grot; the last four (9–12), away from it. And the central stanza (8) both admits the knight into the elfin grot and motivates the dissolution of the vision, for in this stanza the knight takes it upon himself to shut the 'wild wild eyes' of the mystery. In the ode, the heaven's bourne of the frieze is dispelled by a force within the poet himself, the unavoidable recollection of the mortal world; in the ballad, a force within the mortal knight—not an act of the fairy's child—causes him to shut out the wild mystery of the ideal. The tug of mortality converts the timeless and spaceless, but vital, frieze into a physical activity in the ever-recurring journey from the town-world to the altar-heaven; the tug of mortality converts the inward mystery of the elfin grot into its outward and merely physical form, the cold hill side.

With the dissolution of heaven's bourne and of the knight's complete assimilation into essence in stanza seven, the grammatical controls in the poem retrieve his selfhood until once again he is wholly self-contained. The 'stings of human neighbourhood' have envenomed all; and thus when 'thoughts of self came on,' he travels 'The journey homeward to habitual self.' Therefore the empathic order of stanzas four to seven is inverted. In stanza eight the lady governs the action of the first two lines, and the knight that of the last two, for it is the interfering power of his own mortal identity that shuts out the mystery. In the next stanza the lady controls only the action of the first line, and the knight that of the last three. And now at last the knight has fully emerged from the enthrallment, and his self is dominant in the remaining three stanzas. The empathic involvement and withdrawal that were enacted in the 'Ode on a Grecian Urn' by dramatic gesture and verbal moods are here enacted by overt dramatic action and by the gradual transfer of grammatical control from one actor to the other.

One of the remarkable features of the ballad is the intricate interlacing of the meaningfully balanced patterns we have been examining. In one sense the first three stanzas are introductory to the following narrative. Within this main narrative (4–12) the action is perfectly pivoted on the central stanza (8), the narrative, the symbols, and the grammatical controls symmetrically rising to and falling away from this central point. And in yet another sense, the first three stanzas (1–3) and the last three (10–12) are prologue and epilogue, the central six (4–9) being perfectly balanced by the distribution of the opening patterns, 'I' and 'she.' Since we have seen a similar meaningful balance in the 'Ode on a Grecian Urn,' we might well suspect that Keats is far from being merely an associative poet whose only control over structure is the subjective pattern that his feelings spontaneously dictated to him. Quite to the contrary, Keats conceived of a poem as a perfectly ordered cosmos, an experience not only completed but also self-contained by reason of its circularity. And this perfect circularity—because of which he delighted in what he called the 'rondeau'—not only is a control over the work of art as a poetic microcosm but also is itself a meaning functional to the poem. That this sense of the complete and organically meaningful architecture of a work of art was deep in Keats' poetic conceptions is clear from the second of his three axioms of poetry. The touches of beauty in poetry, he wrote,

> should never be half way thereby making the reader breathless instead of content: the rise, the progress, the setting of imagery should like the Sun come natural to him—shine over him and set soberly although in magnificence leaving him in the Luxury of twilight.[18]

IV

What emerges from this analysis is that 'La Belle Dame Sans Merci' has grown out of the same body of conceptions, beliefs, and aspirations that motivate the 'Ode on a Grecian Urn,' and that it is shaped by the same mode of poetic perception. The major difference between the ode and the ballad is that the latter fails to attain the high consolation of the last stanza of the ode; but otherwise the ballad is the projection into myth of what was experienced in the ode as symbol. The increase in psychic distance gained by translating the drama within the consciousness of the poet into objective correlatives allows the poet to stretch out into the chronological span of a narrative a drama that he could express in the ode only as the evolving inward recognition of symbolic values. But the same sense of great harmonic control appears in both poems in their meaningfully pivoted structure and in the interweaving of patterns. And both are variant artistic intertextures of the three coexistent themes that dominate Keats' deepest meditations and profoundest system of values: the oxymoronic heaven's bourne towards which his spirit yearned; the pleasure thermometer which he conceived of as the spiritual path to that goal; and the self-annihilation that he understood to be the condition necessary for the journey. In this sense the ballad differs from the ode essentially in enacting this triune drama in a realm of space and time; and hence the self-conscious identity of the poet becomes the knight, the coexistent symbols of the thermometer are spread out into a context of time, and the journey heavenward is a passage through a spatial world.

Yet, because the ballad lacks the resolution of the ode, the differences are immense. In his discovery that art prefigures an attainable heaven where beauty will be truth, Keats spoke to man an Everlasting Yea; 'La Belle Dame Sans Merci' is his Center of Indifference.

NOTES

1. *Endymion*, II. 276.
2. *Ibid.*, 345–47.
3. *Ibid.*, 357–58.
4. *Ibid.*, 437–38.
5. *Poems, Legendary, Incidental, and Humorous*, Shrewsbury, 1825.
6. Letter to Bailey, November 22, 1817.
7. 'Lamia,' I. 127.
8. 'To J. H. Reynolds, Esq.,' 71–72.
9. *Endymion*, I. 621–22.
10. *Ibid.*, II. 153–56.
11. 'Lines Written in the Highlands after a Visit to Burns's Country,' 29–40.
12. *Endymion*, I. 919.
13. Letter to Reynolds, February 19, 1818.
14. *Endymion*, IV. 819, 859.
15. 'To J. H. Reynolds, Esq.,' 82–83.
16. 'On Death.'
17. Letter to Bailey, November 22, 1817.
18. Letter to Taylor, February 27, 1818.

RICHARD H. FOGLE

A Note on Ode to a Nightingale

Douglas Bush remarks of Keats's poetry in general, 'From first to last Keats's important poems are related to, or grow directly out of . . . inner conflicts,' and of the *Odes* he says

> At first sight Keats's theme in the *Ode to a Nightingale* and the *Ode on a Grecian Urn* . . . is the belief that whereas the momentary experience of beauty is fleeting, the ideal embodiment of that moment in art, in song, or in marble, is an imperishable source of joy. If that were all, these odes should be hymns of triumph, and they are not. It is the very acme of melancholy that the joy he celebrates is joy in beauty that must die.[1]

This comment is valuable, but misleading in emphasis. There are indeed conflicts in Keats's poetry, but in the odes cited by Professor Bush these conflicts are reconciled. The *Odes* do not express 'the very acme of melancholy' any more than they express the very acme of joy. They express an exquisite awareness of the existence of joy and melancholy, pleasure and pain, and art and life. They express a feeling that these are inseparable, although not identical, and they express acceptance of this inseparability of the elements of human experience. In the *Ode to a Nightingale* Keats portrays a state of intense aesthetic and imaginative feeling, too poignant for long duration, which arises with the song of a bird and vanishes when the song is done. The poet records his emotion and its passing without comment.

The impossibility of maintaining this mood of exaltation is the condition of its existence, for it is relative, and describable only by comparing

From *Modern Language Quarterly*, VIII (1947), pp. 81–4. Reprinted by permission of *Modern Language Quarterly*, The University of Washington, and Edward G. Cox, managing editor.

it with more commonplace states of mind. No mood, furthermore, is simple and unalloyed by other feelings. Keats begins,

> My heart aches, and a drowsy numbness pains
> My sense, as though of hemlock I had drunk. . . .

This is not from grief, or envy of the nightingale, but from

> . . . being too happy in thine happiness.

As in the *Ode on Melancholy*[2] he declares that intense pleasure is almost indistinguishable from numbing pain.

The *Nightingale* moves as a whole with the same steady advance and withdrawal as does the *Grecian Urn*. Stanzas II and III, however, represent as it were a false start, after the mood has been established in I. The 'draught of vintage' by whose magic power Keats would escape 'the weariness, the fever, and the fret' of life is rejected. If the last five lines of stanza III are drawn from Keats's own suffering, that suffering is here sublimated.

> Where Beauty cannot keep her lustrous eyes,
> Or new Love pine at them beyond tomorrow

has a serenity and ironic undertone not to be found in the poet's relations with Fanny Brawne.

The true beginning comes in stanza IV. Keats flies to the nightingale—

> Not charioted by Bacchus and his pards,
> But on the viewless wings of Poesy.

The poem reaches its full intensity in this stanza and the three following. This outpouring of imaginative exaltation contrasts with the melancholy of the low-pitched stanza III, by itself unremarkable but functioning as an integral part of the poetic whole. As in the *Eve of St. Agnes* Keats uses life at its most unpromising as a point of departure. Only by being aware of sorrow can the poet devote himself wholeheartedly to joy, conscious the while that his respite will be brief. The soft and heavy texture of the imagery in IV and V reflects a spontaneous luxuriance of feeling and perception, a self-abandonment which is merely another aspect of his previous depression.

Stanza VI commences

> Darkling I listen; and, for many a time
> I have been half in love with easeful Death, . . .

The vivid sensuousness of the two preceding stanzas has been leading toward this. Death itself may offer the fullest sense of life:

> Now more than ever seems it *rich* to die.

If the *Nightingale* is a lament for the brevity of life and joy, as Professor Bush has said, these are sentiments difficult to explain; but if the poem is simply an imaginative reflection of the complexity and intensity of human experience, Death may quite reasonably be viewed as its culmination.[3]

The spell is deepest in stanza VII, of which M. R. Ridley has said that it 'would, I suppose, by common consent be taken along with "Kubla Khan," as offering us the distilled sorceries of Romanticism.'[4] In these lines the apparent contrast between the immortality of the Bird and the fugitive temporality of its hearers is strongly insisted upon:[5]

> No hungry generations tread thee down;
> The voice I hear this passing night was heard
> In ancient days by emperor and clown:
> Perhaps the self-same song that found a path
> Through the sad heart of Ruth, when, sick for home
> She stood in tears amid the alien corn. . . .

Yet this opposition is not real. The 'sad heart of Ruth' is as enduring as the nightingale, and after the same fashion. The temporal Ruth died long ago, the eternal Ruth lives on in poetry. Nor can one separate the temporal from the eternal, for it is by virtue of her grief, her exposure to accidental circumstance long since passed away, that she remains alive. So with the 'magic casements' which follow, but with a difference. Paradoxically, these are immortal because they have long since vanished, or alternatively because they never in cold fact existed. This paradox is the essence of their charm and their reality; viewed faintly down long vistas of time, or created consciously by imagination from diverse materials seized from the actual world, they have a unique being of their own. They exist as fully as the stubbornest, most intractable actuality, but they arise from actuality and cannot live apart from it. In this stanza the notions of temporality and timelessness do not conflict, but are brought together in harmonious relationship.

It is not mere accident that Keats breaks off here, at the peak of imaginative intensity, on the word 'forlorn,' which has its feet in two worlds. For the value of the imaginative experience depends upon its transience; it is only one mode, albeit the highest, among many. With consummate irony and psychological truth 'forlorn' breaks in like the tolling of a bell to signal the end of the poet's emotional exaltation. The 'faery lands' were 'forlorn' because remote and strange; the word itself is enchanted. The second 'forlorn' is homely and familiar, with a half-humorous ruefulness. It dwells upon the common earth, to which the poet now returns.[6]

The final stanza fills out the perfect rondure of the poem in a slow withdrawal, symbolized by the retreat of the bird itself so that objective description and subjective emotion are fused. The fading-away is slow and regular,

> Past the near meadows, over the still stream,
> Up the hill-side; and now 'tis buried deep
> In the next valley-glades . . .

and in the last two verses the process of withdrawal, now solely within the poet, comes to a smooth and quiet end:

> Was it a vision or a waking dream?
> Fled is that music:—Do I wake or sleep?

Keats does not moralize after the event, nor utter lyric cries of pain, as he might be expected to if he were writing, for example, about the sadness of mutability. He has been writing about a full and rich experience, and having described that experience he stops.

NOTES

1. *Mythology and the Romantic Tradition in English Poetry* (Cambridge, Mass., 1937), pp. 82, 107.
2.   Ay, in the very temple of Delight
        Veil'd Melancholy has her sovran shrine . . . (ll. 25–26).
  In the *Ode on Melancholy* Keats emphasizes the close relationship between different modes of experience even more thoroughly than in the *Nightingale*:

Make not your rosary of yew-berries
Nor let the beetle, nor the death-moth be
Your mournful Psyche, nor the downy owl
A partner in your sorrow's mysteries;
For shade to shade will come too drowsily,
And drown the wakeful anguish of the soul (ll. 5–10).

Melancholy in its simple state is invisible; it is beheld only by him 'whose strenuous tongue / Can burst Joy's grape against his palate fine.'

3. Cf. *Why Did I Laugh,* with its conclusion,

Verse, Fame, and Beauty are intense indeed,
But Death intenser—Death is Life's high meed.

4. *Keats's Craftsmanship* (Oxford, 1933), p. 227.

5. One must agree here with Amy Lowell that to object that the nightingale is obviously not immortal (see Robert Bridges, Introduction, *Poems of John Keats,* ed. G. Thorn Drury [London and New York, n.d.], I, lxiv) is to miss the point, although her manners in an argument are enough to provoke a saint (*John Keats* [Boston and New York, 1925], II, 252). She has certainly provoked H. W. Garrod (*Keats* [Oxford, 1926], pp. 113–14), whose saintliness, at least as regards Miss Lowell, is extremely well disguised.

6. Cf. Cleanth Brooks, *Modern Poetry and the Tradition* (Chapel Hill, N. C., 1939), p. 31.

Galaxy Books FOR THE DISCRIMINATING READER